International
Programming
for Microsoft
Windows®

David A. Schmitt

PUBLISHED BY
Microsoft Press
A Division of Microsoft Corporation
One Microsoft Way
Redmond, Washington 98052-6399

Copyright © 2000 by David A. Schmitt

Library of Congress Cataloging-in-Publication Data
Schmitt, David A.
    International Programming for Microsoft Windows / David A. Schmitt.
        p.   cm.
    Includes bibliographical references and index.
    ISBN 1-57231-956-9
    1. Computer programming.   2. Multilingual computing.   3. Microsoft Visual C++.
    4. Microsoft Windows (Computer file)   I. Title.
    QA76.6 .S387 1999
    005.26'9--dc21   99-043753

Printed and bound in the United States of America.

1 2 3 4 5 6 7 8 9   QMQM   5 4 3 2 1 0

Distributed in Canada by Penguin Books Canada Limited.

A CIP catalogue record for this book is available from the British Library.

Microsoft Press books are available through booksellers and distributors worldwide. For
further information about international editions, contact your local Microsoft Corporation
office or contact Microsoft Press International directly at fax (425) 936-7329. Visit our Web
site at mspress.microsoft.com.

ActiveX, Microsoft, Microsoft Press, MSDN, MS-DOS, Visual Basic, Visual C++, Win32,
Windows, and Windows NT are either registered trademarks or trademarks of Microsoft
Corporation in the United States and/or other countries. Other product and company names
mentioned herein may be the trademarks of their respective owners.

The example companies, organizations, products, people, and events depicted herein are
fictitious. No association with any real company, organization, product, person, or event is
intended or should be inferred.

Acquisitions Editor: Ben Ryan
Project Editor: Kathleen Atkins
Technical Editor: Julie Xiao

To my mother-in-law, Grace, who must have inspired the phrase "living gracefully." Thanks is too small a word for the large measure of joy you've brought to my life.

Thanks,

Dave

Table of Contents

Preface

At the start of my programming career more than twenty-five years ago, most American software designers were blissfully ignorant of computer usage outside the United States. There was almost no market for packaged software products because the typical program was developed in house by the company using it. Although the largest firms were multinational, their various, far-flung divisions usually took care of their own software development, often by tediously adapting software originally written by Americans for Americans.

Over the years, I gradually became aware that programmers outside the United States were encountering serious problems as they tried to adapt American-designed software for use in their own countries. For example, at a UNIX conference in Copenhagen I heard European programmers bitterly complain about the American biases built into that operating system. Among their complaints was the pervasive use of non-European characters throughout UNIX and the C language. I learned that in some countries, important C programming characters such as the pound sign (#) and square brackets ([]) don't even appear on the most popular keyboards!

Complaints about what I call "chauvinistic programming" swelled during the 1980s as personal computers appeared on desktops throughout the world and as a vigorous software product industry emerged. I've heard dozens of stories about how a clever programmer cobbled up a kludge in order to get some essential software product working in his or her local environment.

For instance, back in 1984 a friend in Stockholm showed me a little MS-DOS TSR (terminate and stay resident) program he had written to make Lotus 1-2-3 properly display the various accented Scandinavian characters. Lotus was so busy with its exploding American market that they couldn't take the time to change 1-2-3 internally for European character support. Accented characters such as Ä could be entered from the Swedish keyboard, but they showed up on the screen as gobbledygook. My friend solved the problem by having his resident program periodically scan the video memory and convert the special characters to the correct form. Although the solution worked, it was somewhat disturbing to see solid garbage on the screen dissolving into recognizable Swedish as you typed.

Whenever a non-American related one of these stories, the point was usually quite simple: *Programmers should consider international applications in the fundamental software design stage, not as an afterthought.*

This is particularly important now that personal computers are being used by ordinary people who have neither the time nor the background to deal with esoteric computerese. These users want the computer to be a simple tool that is easy to understand and operate. They aren't getting paid to read large manuals and figure ways to overcome the limitations imposed by inadequate hardware and software. They demand that their interface with the computer be conducted in their native language. Ultimately, they will buy and use software only if it feels natural to them.

The more I understood this situation, the more confused I became. After all, like most U.S. programmers, I speak only English. Sure, my four years of high school Latin enable me to figure out the origin of many English words, to find my way around the Milan subway system, and even to make some sense out of Italian or Spanish newspaper headlines. But it appeared that I would have to become fluent in several languages in order to design international software. And while I might be able to learn one or two European languages, others such as Japanese, Chinese, and Arabic looked like formidable barriers.

These depressing thoughts led me to undertake the research which resulted in this book. The first glimmer of hope came when my company's Japanese agent assured me that American programmers don't need to understand Japanese in order to write software that can cope with that country's language and customs. Checking around with other friends and acquaintances throughout the world, I found that they generally agreed: *By following the proper design and coding rules, any programmer can write multilingual software.*

This was really good news! But what are those rules? To discover them, I poked around in the available literature and attended an excellent seminar on Asian dual-byte character sets sponsored by IBM's World Trade division. Through these activities, I discovered that much work has been done in this area. However, the results are scattered throughout documents such as the ANSI C and C++ standards and manuals produced by IBM, Microsoft, and other computer and operating system vendors.

This book is my attempt to pull these diverse sources together and present a methodical approach to international programming for the Microsoft Visual C++ programmer. I decided to concentrate on Visual C++ for several reasons. First, it's the development environment I use and teach most frequently. Second, it's the most popular tool for producing industrial strength Microsoft Windows applications. And finally, I believe that Windows, C++, MFC, and ATL represent the state of the art in international programming.

Acknowledgments

Every technical book is a team effort, but none more so than one which covers a broad topic such as international programming. I was fortunate to work with an excellent team at Microsoft Press, beginning with Ben Ryan, who encouraged me to tackle this daunting topic, and Kathleen Atkins, who applied gentle pressure and positive feedback throughout the 18 months it took me to get the job done.

Julie Xiao went beyond the call of duty. She dug out the "true facts" to correct my technical errors and misconceptions, fleshed out topics where my treatment was too light, and verified each of the sample programs. Naturally, these programs were bug free when I delivered them, but Julie still found some errors. Many thanks, Julie.

Michelle Goodman, Jennifer Harris, and Kathleen Atkins (wearing another hat) ensured that the words formed sentences, that the sentences formed paragraphs, and that they all made sense. Patricia Masserman proofread them all. As with the sample programs, my prose was "perfect" when I delivered it, but somehow the team made it better. Many thanks to you, also.

Of the many people who gave this book its look and feel, Gina Cassill, Michael Kloepfer, and Joel Panchot are most responsible for its interior. If you're standing in a bookstore right now and you grabbed this one off the shelf (because of its eye-catching cover), and you like the figures and overall layout, you're appreciating their work. I know I do.

I also want to thank the people outside Microsoft Press who gave their advice and assistance. Carter Shanklin's courtesy enabled me to get the project started. Avery Bishop and Lori Brownell of Microsoft's Globalization Team willingly answered my questions about Windows 2000, Uniscribe, and other international programming topics. P. J. Plauger, Angelika Langer, and David Smallberg shared their deep knowledge of standard C and C++.

Special thanks to many of my students who encouraged me and contributed interesting anecdotes and useful advice from their diverse ethnic backgrounds. One of the nicest aspects of teaching COM and other subjects for DevelopMentor is that I get to meet so many interesting people.

Finally, after all the words I wrote in this book and others, I've found none to express my gratitude and love for my wife, Karen. I only hope that actions say what words cannot.

David A. Schmitt
January, 2000
Saint Louis, Missouri

Introduction

Nicolas Chauvin was a French soldier known for his excessive devotion and loyalty to Napoleon during the early years of the nineteenth century. His name is the root of the English word *chauvinism,* meaning blind patriotism or partiality. Unfortunately, we've recently warped this fine word so that many believe it characterizes only certain male attitudes toward females. Chauvinism, however, is the perfect way to describe software development practices that make it difficult to adapt programs for use in other countries.

Most of us must plead guilty to some level of chauvinistic software design techniques. We embed prompters and other message text deep in our code so that translation becomes a major programming effort. Our screen and report layouts don't allow translators to rearrange fields or change their lengths to accommodate other languages and cultures. We often use algorithms for sorting, scanning, and generating text that rely upon a specific character set (usually ASCII or EBCDIC) or a specific format, and these algorithms fail when a "foreign character set" or "foreign formats" are introduced.

Software product companies now recognize the need for more cosmopolitan design techniques because of the potential for sales in other countries to people who can't or won't stray very far from their native tongue. Also, multinational corporations are realizing that they can minimize programming costs by developing common software for their divisions and subsidiaries. In both situations, we're encountering a new type of user quite different from the highly trained and specialized personnel who traditionally have worked with computers.

For many years, English was a kind of universal language, a *lingua franca* or an *Esperanto,* among computer programmers, operators, and users. Most people who had day-to-day contact with computers weren't too upset when error messages, manuals, and control panel markings weren't in their native language. They usually had enough education to cope with English, and many of them were fluent in it. If they didn't have that skill, they gradually became proficient as they wrestled with English-oriented computer manuals and programming languages. They were technical types, like us.

The personal computer has caused this situation to change dramatically. Today's typical PC users want to work mainly in their own languages. For typical PC users, the PC isn't an object of veneration as it has been for us technical types. Rather, it's merely a piece of office equipment like a copier or a calculator. They see it as a tool, a means to an end, and they won't waste time with difficult tools. They demand that computers have standard human interfaces like the ones they've come to expect in cars, telephones, and other everyday instruments. They don't want to read a lengthy manual in order to use a program, and they don't want to communicate with the computer in a foreign language.

I've often heard programmers express disdain for this new breed of non-technical computer users. "After all," we geeks say, "the computer isn't a toy; it's a sophisticated piece of equipment, and you have to pay your dues in order to understand it. These users should at least learn how to resolve IRQ problems!" But how many of us understand the inner workings of our cars, televisions, microwave ovens, and camcorders? Do we have much patience when it comes to reading the owner's manual? Would we be happy if all of the instructions and markings were printed in Japanese?

So any software developer who continues to cater only to the technical computer user is ignoring the mainstream of our business. Clearly, the needs of the new user community require that programmers learn more cosmopolitan software design techniques. Even if the resulting programs are larger, slower, and more expensive to develop, modern computer applications demand international solutions, and rapid hardware evolution will compensate for the cost of internationalization.

This book shows how you can become a proficient international programmer by using design techniques that will enable your programs for use in other countries. You'll find that these techniques aren't much of a burden because modern operating systems and programming languages do a lot of the work for you.

Chapters 1 and 2 describe the issues you'll encounter when designing international software. This section of the book takes a broad look at the major language and cultural groups to show how their differences impinge upon your programming activities.

Chapter 3 then traces the history of character sets to show how this evolution has influenced international communication in general and computer programming in particular. Chapter 4 explains how these character set issues affect standard C and C++ programs.

Chapters 5 and 6 explore the standard "locale" feature for C and C++, and Chapter 7 describes the related Microsoft Visual C++ extensions that can simplify international programming.

Chapters 9 and 10 examine the rich set of National Language Support (NLS) features that Microsoft has provided in the Win32 operating system environment. These features go well beyond standard C and C++ by supporting advanced multilingual applications with a graphical user interface. Because the Win32 application programming interface (API) uses a C language interface, C and C++ programmers can call Win32 functions directly.

Chapter 11 concludes by presenting a set of guidelines for developing international software. With these in mind, you should be able to make the proper trade-offs between program complexity and geographic scope.

Chapter 1

The Basic Issues

The challenge before us is to design software that can be easily adapted for use in other countries. To face this challenge, we programmers must first gain a general understanding of the cultural differences that have an effect on software design. This chapter and the next two describe the most important of these differences.

I must make a disclaimer at this point. Although I've traveled outside the United States many times (primarily in Europe and Japan), I'm neither a linguist nor a cultural expert. Sure, I can decipher European road maps[1] and find my way around the Tokyo subway system. I've also become pretty adept at handling foreign currency and don't get cheated too much when haggling with a street vendor. I've never missed a meal (although I probably should) because there's usually something on the menu that I understand. (Besides, every place I've visited has had a McDonald's nearby.)

In other words, my knowledge of non-U.S. locales is about the same as any other well-traveled U.S. businessperson. So how can I presume to write this book? Well, I've seen many examples of both good and bad international software, and I firmly believe that you don't need to be multicultural, multilingual, or a "Renaissance dude" to enable your software for global usage. You must understand the "rules of internationalization," however, and the technology that supports them. Then by diligently following the rules, you will produce generalized programs that other software experts can adapt to specific languages and cultures.

---

1. I must thank the good brothers at Saint Mary's High School who forced me to study Latin for four years. Since many European languages are based on this "dead language," I've found it amazingly easy to decipher maps, road signs, and newspaper headlines. Of course, occasionally I get the wrong meaning, such as that time I drove out of the Frankfurt Airport parking garage via the entrance ramp.

LOCALE-DEPENDENT SOFTWARE

At the risk of stating the obvious, I'll begin by observing that any program with a nontrivial human interface is likely to be locale dependent. Humans usually communicate through words, which are written or spoken, and pictures, which are either drawn or portrayed by some form of body language. This interface works best if it's instinctively familiar to both parties in the conversation—that is, if both people share the same language and culture. For example, the offensive hand gesture known as "flipping the bird" in the United States is done in a completely different way in Italy. The first time I drove in Italy, I thought the Italian drivers were just giving me a friendly wave.

The situation is no different when a human and a computer communicate. The computer would probably be most efficient if you could converse with it in simple binary, but you're most comfortable if the computer uses words and pictures that you can readily understand. Fortunately, the computer has no vote in this matter. It's up to the programmer to instruct the machine to use appropriate human communication techniques.

In most cases, the human-computer dialog is conducted in the human's written language and with the help of some relatively simple pictures such as icons, mathematical charts, or musical scores. These pictures tend to be locale independent, except for words that might be embedded within them. Often the embedded words need no translation because they're part of an international jargon associated with the picture. For instance, musical scores use certain Italian words that are recognized by musicians throughout the world. Similarly, our international community of computer specialists uses a subset of English for Basic, C, C++, Java, Fortran, Pascal, Cobol, RPG, and other programming languages. As I mentioned earlier, this is why many of us mistakenly assume that computer users are also familiar with English.

Some computer applications employ more complex forms of communication such as voice recognition and synthesis or expressive graphics of the "Max Headroom" variety. This book won't describe these forms of communication because relatively few computer users and programmers are currently exposed to them. Furthermore, complex aural and visual communication techniques are still more theory than practice, and the technology is quite expensive. Fortunately, these forms of communication are extremely country dependent, and so the scientists and engineers evolving this branch of computing are already thinking of international solutions. For example, imagine how shortsighted it would be for a car manufacturer to incorporate a computerized verbal warning system that could express itself only in Swedish.

This book concentrates on the more prevalent written forms of human-computer communication, which are implemented by means of keyboards, display screens, and printers. This book also focuses on desktop computers rather than minicomputers or mainframes because most major new human interface work is being done on the various personal computer platforms.

Furthermore, this book examines cosmopolitan software examples that are based on the Microsoft Win32 operating system model and the C++ programming language because they have the most complete set of international programming features that I've found.

Before leaving this topic, I must point out that some software can be chauvinistic even though it has little or no human interface. For example, consider a program that's invoked through a simple command line to sort a file in alphabetical order. This program must cope with the fact that different countries use different alphabets. It can't simply sort characters by their numeric codes, since that usually works only with the English alphabet. This and other subtle locale dependencies are covered in more detail when I describe character sets.

Adaptation Methods

Preparing software for use in a particular country is a two-step process. First the designer must enable the program for international usage. Then someone—probably not the original designer—must adapt the program to each country in which it will be used. In some ways, this enabling and adapting process is similar to the two-step process used in the international book publishing business. The original author writes the book in his or her native language, and then other writers translate it into various languages, depending on where the publisher decides to sell the book.

All of the techniques and guidelines presented in this book are concerned with the enabling step, since that's our primary concern as software designers. We need to understand the adaptation step, however, because it can become a major cost item, especially if we choose the wrong enabling technique.

For example, you can enable a program by isolating all of the prompters and messages and putting them into header files that are compiled with the source files. In this case, the adaptation step requires that someone edit or replace the header files, compile all of the program source, and link the object files to produce a new executable file. This work is best done by another programmer who can handle the inevitable compiler error messages and can do at least a small amount of regression testing to ensure that the new executable works correctly.

Suppose instead that you enable the program by placing prompters and messages into a data file processed during the program's initialization phase. In that case, a nonprogrammer can supply the appropriate data file for his or her country and can easily verify that the program operates correctly with that data. Generally, this second technique makes the adaptation step cheaper and less prone to introducing program errors.

I've found that there's one simple but important question you must ask before choosing a particular enabling technique: *Who will be adapting this software for use in other countries?* The possibilities are

- The original development team
- Another development team
- A professional translation group
- The end user
- The local software distributor

No single answer is the only correct one because teams, projects, products, and markets have so many differences. Furthermore, the adaptation step can be spread out among several organizations, and this often causes the enabling technique to change as the program evolves. Early adaptations for the most important markets are handled by highly skilled people, possibly other programmers, in order to work out the kinks in the enabling technology. Then the later adaptations are handled by less skilled (and less expensive) translators.

For instance, I once worked on a project in which the programming team included a person fluent in German. We used message files to enable the software for international use and then tested this technique by actually doing the German adaptation from the original English. Our major European distributor later adapted the program for the French and Italian markets, while some clever users did the work for Spanish, Flemish, Swedish, and several other languages. In the second version of the software, we gathered all of these adaptations into a library and changed the installation procedure so that the end user could simply choose the appropriate language.

Let's consider the merits of these adaptation methods. Then I'll explain which enabling techniques are appropriate for them.

Adaptation by the Original Development Team

In some ways, the original development team is ideally suited to handle the adaptation of a software package to other languages. They have the knowledge and the tools to build the program from its source code and can deal with language differences at that level, which usually results in the smallest and fastest program. For example, if you plan to recompile for each country, you can embed prompters and messages in the source code as literals.

On the other hand, I doubt that any single development team can handle a broad range of adaptations because most programmers aren't multilingual. Therefore, when we're modifying source code for a different country, we must work with a translator—someone who understands the target country's language and can also communicate with us. This approach usually isn't desirable because it ties up two expensive resources: programmers and translators. Furthermore, the programmers are likely to find the adaptation chore boring, which can lead to sloppiness and bugs. It's even worse when only one or two members of the development team are needed for the adaptation chore. Would you like to be stuck working with a translator while your teammates move on to the next exciting project?

A translator also might find it frustrating to work with a software developer, or so I've been told by several friends who've served as translators. They often found themselves in the position of critics, pointing out where the software design was inadequate to support the target country. Programmers often get their hackles up when a nonprogrammer presumes to criticize their designs.

Overall, my experiences suggest that we programmers shouldn't get deeply involved in the adaptation process. Instead, we should concentrate on providing the enabling technology that will allow nonprogrammers to adapt our software to other languages without changing the source code.

Adaptation by Another Development Team

Some organizations have programming teams that specialize in adapting software written by other teams. Often the second team contains programmers skilled in other languages, so they also serve as translators and might even be called the "translation team." I don't recommend this approach because it can lead to two thorny problems:

- Because they're programmers, the translation team inevitably wants to change the source code because they believe it hasn't been properly enabled for use in other countries (and it probably hasn't). This can cause serious maintenance problems as the two teams squabble over responsibility for bugs.

- If the translation team is prevented from changing the source code, they're forced to engage in an inefficient dialog with the original team to accomplish the adaptation. Not only does this drive up costs by engaging two expensive software development teams, but it frustrates the translation team, who really want to write programs instead of requirements.

In addition to these problems, you'll find that it's very difficult to hire and retain multilingual programmers to staff a group that does nothing but adapt software designed by others. These people want to write original programs, and because they're in demand they can easily find an employer who'll satisfy that craving.

Adaptation by a Professional Translation Group

A better approach is to use a team of professional translators who aren't also frustrated software developers. This has the benefit of drawing sharp lines of responsibility. The programming team provides the enabling technology and the translation team reports all failures and deficiencies in this technology as program bugs. Ideally, the translators never see the program source code but work only with databases that contain the country dependent information.

Only the largest or most prolific organizations can afford to maintain a permanent group of professional translators, so this activity is often outsourced to one or more companies that specialize in adapting software for international use. If you plan to use outside translators, be sure to invite them in for a skull session with the programmers early in the project. That way, the experienced translators can let the developers know what enabling techniques are appropriate for the target markets. Some translation firms even offer formal training courses for programmers involved in the development of international software.

Adaptation by the End User

Nobody understands a program's target environment better than the user. For example, an Italian accountant could probably give excellent advice about adapting a spreadsheet program for use in his country. On the other hand, he probably wouldn't be of much help in adapting a factory automation system.

Because users generally know best about a program's target environment, it's tempting to place the entire adaptation burden in their hands. Why not just give them some kind of message file in English and let them translate it? I've actually seen this work quite well on the project I described earlier.

Serious obstacles to using this approach, however, exist in most cases. First, what do we do about documentation? For complicated software, someone has to write a comprehensive adaptation manual in each target language. This could be more expensive than doing the actual adaptations. Second, what about standards? I suspect that there's an advantage to having a spreadsheet program such as Microsoft Excel or Lotus 1-2-3 appear the same to all of its Italian users. Third, what about your market appearance? If each user has to do a tedious adaptation of your software, it won't sell as well as a product that's already set up for the local language.

For these reasons, it's impractical to foist the entire adaptation burden onto the user. This doesn't mean that this person shouldn't be involved at all. It's quite reasonable to present the user with a list of available country adaptations during program installation or initialization. This allows some flexibility without forcing the user to actually do the translations.

Adaptation by the Local Software Distributor

For many software products, the local distributor is the best adapter. Software distributors usually have ready access to translators because they're often responsible for converting the developer's original documentation into the local language. Also, distributors might benefit from economy of scale because they carry dozens of products needing adaptation, while a typical small software developer might have only one or two such products.

A distributor who translates and augments your documentation and also adapts your software is, in effect, operating as your publisher. I've seen many instances of this kind of firm taking over all manufacturing, shipping, and advertising of adapted products in a certain region. Unless you allow such a company to "private-label" your adapted software, you wind up losing control of the overall appearance and content of your product in that market. This isn't necessarily bad; it's just something you should realize before going down this path. A high-quality distributor who can adapt your software and documentation is a powerful ally for a small software house.

The same can be said of far-flung divisions of a multinational corporation. If you're part of a centralized software development team, you can employ enabling techniques that'll allow the adaptation to be done in those divisions.

When employees of a remote division become involved in software adaptation, you often derive two benefits. First, you usually get adaptations that are better and cheaper than what you'd get from a central organization. Second, you get the managers and users associated with the remote division to accept centrally developed software. Veterans of corporate computing battles are well aware that a centralized software development organization will fail if it can't get the corporate users to endorse its activities.

Enabling Methods

Many ways to enable software for international use exist, but whether a particular approach is appropriate depends on who's to be doing the adaptation. For instance, if you want the user to do the adaptation, you'd probably avoid an enabling technique that requires recompilation and relinking. Most users wouldn't have the programming tools and skills needed to work with the program source code.

Here's a list of the popular enabling techniques, identified according to the software level at which the adaptation is done:

Source Level

At this level, you adapt the program by changing source or header files, recompiling, and relinking the program. This technique requires access to most of the programmer's tools, including an editor, compiler, linker, librarian, and debugger.

Object Level

At this level, you select an appropriate combination of object files and relink the program. This approach assumes that the programmer has provided object files for the various countries, probably by working with translators while the program was being designed. The person doing the adaptation then simply picks the appropriate object files for the target country. The only programming tool required is a linker. Since adaptation doesn't touch the source code, debugging or regression testing usually isn't necessary after linking.

Resource Level

Some systems (for example, Microsoft Windows, OS/2, and Macintosh) support the concept of a *resource database* containing information about an application's user interface features, such as messages, prompters, menus, and dialog boxes. The programmer defines the database items and accesses them through their keys at the appropriate points during execution. Usually the programmer also creates a native version of the resource database that serves as a model for the translators.

The translators then create additional databases for use in the target countries. This is a quasi-programming task that can be accomplished by a translator who's comfortable using word processors, text editors, and graphical editors. Because resource editing doesn't change any executable code, this activity doesn't typically introduce new bugs, although the product must be subjected to regression testing to ensure that all resource items have been properly translated.

Resources are usually attached (that is, bound) to the executable program file, so the final adaptation step requires the use of a "resource binder" tool. This produces an executable tailored for a specific target country, which greatly simplifies installation but makes support and maintenance more complicated. As an alternative, you can delay the binding step until installation time, assuming that you're allowed to ship the resource binder with the product.

To avoid binding resources on a per-country basis, Windows NT supports multilingual resources. The translator produces a single database supporting many environments and binds it to the executable program file, and the program then selects the appropriate resources at run time.

An even better approach is to produce a resource dynamic-link library (DLL) for each country and then select the appropriate DLL at installation or run time. This enables translators to work independently and on different schedules without the need to merge their work into one multilingual resource file.

Installation Level

Most software products have an installation procedure that unpacks the program from its distribution media and prepares it for operation on the user's computer. If the product supports several countries, you can ask the user to select one during this installation step. Then only the appropriate country-dependent information is copied from the distribution media to the user's machine.

This technique can be implemented in many ways. For instance, you could include several resource files in the product, together with a resource binder that's automatically invoked during the installation procedure after the user specifies the country. Alternatively, you could select the appropriate resource DLL, as described earlier.

If you aren't using resources, you could include country dependent object modules and perform an *ad hoc* linking step during installation, assuming that you have access to a redistributable linker. This approach isn't recommended because of the strong possibility that address changes and other linking anomalies could uncover program bugs that would completely confuse the user. Furthermore, linking a large program can take hours, which wouldn't be desirable during installation. Finally, by distributing object modules you expose many of your program's design details, thereby facilitating reverse engineering and software piracy.

Execution Level

Some operating systems, such as MS-DOS, Windows, and OS/2, allow their application programs to determine which country the user selected. In other words, a Windows user can specify his or her country through the Control Panel, and then all application programs running on that system can configure themselves accordingly.

Automatic adaptation is the most sophisticated approach to international software, and it's becoming increasingly popular because it appears so natural to the user. To change from French to German, the user need only inform the operating system, and these sophisticated applications follow along.

Some applications use a less sophisticated form of execution-level adaptation that's similar to the installation-level technique. The first time the program runs, it asks the user which country is preferred, and then it loads the appropriate country-dependent information into memory. Because it's generally not acceptable to engage the user in this dialog each time the application is invoked, the initial setup information is usually saved in a configuration file. Then the program uses the setup dialog only if the configuration file is missing. This type of application usually contains a menu command that allows the user to change the configuration.

The underlying technology for run-time adaptation is usually based on country-dependent resource files, DLLs, or multilingual resource databases as described previously.

Beginning with Chapter 5, the book looks at the programming facilities provided by C++, Win32, and MFC/ATL for implementing these various enabling techniques. The key design decisions, however, should be made before you begin programming. That is, you must consider who'll be adapting the program and choose an appropriate enabling technique. Then as the programming proceeds, you must keep this decision clearly in view so that you don't use programming techniques that hinder your chosen adaptation method.

TERMINOLOGY

So far I've been using *enable* and *adapt* to describe the two steps of international software development. I prefer these terms because they're short and precise, but other terminology is also popular. Enabling is often called *internationalizing* or *globalizing,* and adapting is called *nationalizing, localizing,* or *translating.* Also, *internationalization* and *localization* are used by those who prefer nouns to gerunds, but these words are so cumbersome that some authors abbreviate them as I18N and L10N[2].

A computing system that supports international software is said to have National Language Support (NLS) features. Enabled software, which can be adapted, is said to be *internationalized, globalized,* or the more cumbersome *NLS-enabled.* When it has been adapted, it's said to have been *nationalized, localized,* or *translated.*

The terms *localizing, localized,* and *localization* come from the use of *locale* instead of *country* when referring to a translation target. As we'll see later, you might have to do several translations for one country, such as Canadian English and Canadian French. In this situation, the word *country* isn't sufficiently precise. For that reason, the key to Win32's NLS features is the locale identifier, and the ANSI standards define a locale feature for international programming.

Confused? Just remember that our task as international programmers is to *enable* software so that translators can *adapt* it for use in different *locales.*

---

2. Stumped? Count the underlined letters in INTERNATIONALIZATION and LOCALIZATION.

Chapter 2

Language Differences

We're all more or less aware of language differences, but in order to develop international software we must understand how these differences impinge upon computer programs. Since relatively few programmers are currently working with interactive video and with voice recognition and response, I'll limit this chapter to an examination of the written language issues that affect nearly all of us.

Every written language has three attributes of importance to software developers:

■ Direction, such as whether one reads from left to right by row or from top to bottom by column of a page

■ Symbology, including character sets, code pages, and related topics

■ Usage, including collation,[1] data ranges, punctuation, and other formatting topics

---

1. In this book, *collation* refers to the process of ordering text items according to certain rules, which vary from one culture to another. For example, arranging words in alphabetical order is a collation process for which we need rules giving each letter's *collation value*. An English speaker might assign the letters from A to Z collation values of 1 through 26, while the lowercase letters a to z would have values from 27 through 52. A French speaker would use different collation values in order to place accented characters such as Á in the proper position. If you were producing a telephone directory, phonetic collation might be preferred to alphabetic, so that "McAdams" would appear before "MacNeal."

By understanding these attributes, you can design international software without being able to read, write, or speak the languages of the target locales. Of course, you'll ultimately have to find someone with the skill to translate your program's user interface from your native language, but you don't need this skill yourself in order to develop the program.

This chapter gives some general information about each of the three language attributes that affect software design. I strongly recommend that you dig a little deeper in the bibliography at the end of this book for further details. You'll find that the study of locale differences is worthwhile not only to improve your programming skill but also to broaden your understanding of this fascinating world.

DIRECTION

Written languages are typically page oriented, and users of these languages arrange elementary symbols (characters) into rows and columns on the page. The human eye then traverses these rows and columns in a way that varies from one language to another.

Most written languages in contemporary use are scanned by row from left to right and top to bottom. This means that your eye starts at the upper left corner of the page and moves across each row from left to right, proceeding row by row to the lower right corner of the page. European languages and their derivatives use left-to-right scanning, as do modern forms of Japanese, Korean, Chinese, and other Asian languages. Computer hardware, operating systems, and programming languages tend to favor left-to-right scanning, and so this is the "natural order" for most programmers.

Arabic and Hebrew are scanned by row from right to left and top to bottom, except for numbers and foreign words, which are presented from left to right. These bidirectional, or BIDI, languages are "unnatural" in most computer environments and can cause numerous software design problems. For instance, when you scan an input string to detect a parenthetical phrase, you normally look for a left parenthesis to begin the phrase and a right parenthesis to end it. With a bidirectional language, you must look for the right parenthesis first. Parsing numbers is also a problem because the parser sees the low-order digit first, whereas the high-order digit appears first in a left-to-right language.

Traditional written forms of Chinese and Japanese are scanned from top to bottom and right to left. That is, ideographs (which I'll talk more about shortly) are arranged in columns, with the first column on the right side of the page.

Although this presentation style isn't often used in Asian computing, many newspapers and books still employ it. It can therefore become an issue in Asian word processing and publishing software.

For many years, international programmers found it difficult to support more than one direction in the same program. Thus we often chose to ignore the Arabic, Hebrew, and traditional Asian markets or to handle them with special versions. Graphical systems such as Microsoft Windows have simplified this task by providing sophisticated keyboard and screen drivers that disguise many of the directional differences. Bidirectional scanning within the program remains a challenge, however.

SYMBOLOGY

Each written language is expressed as sequences of symbols—that is, as arrangements of characters in words, sentences, paragraphs, and so on. The complete collection of symbols needed by a specific language is called a *symbol set*. For instance, American English requires a set of about 100 symbols: 26 uppercase letters, 26 lowercase letters, 10 digits, and about two dozen punctuation characters. Many European languages use symbol sets similar to American English, except that they also have accented forms of some letters, and they require a few different punctuation symbols (such as those that denote monetary values).

When two people from different locales want to communicate in writing, each must understand the other's symbols. That is, they must have a common *symbol repertoire,* which is simply the union of the appropriate symbol sets. When you travel outside the United States, you often encounter people with symbol repertoires covering three or four languages. For example, it's not unusual in European airports to see a person carrying an Italian newspaper, a French magazine, and an American novel.

Programmers usually speak about *character sets* rather than symbol sets. The primary distinction is that a symbol set simply lists the required symbols, but a character set assigns a specific number (called a *character code* or a *code point*) to each symbol. In some cases, a character set contains only the symbols for a specific locale, but usually it's the union of several symbol sets and therefore represents an encoding of a symbol repertoire.[2] For example, most Windows applications use the ANSI character set, which contains the symbols needed for English, Spanish, and many other European languages.

---

2. Some character sets are imperfect unions of several symbol sets. For instance, the original IBM PC set, called IBM code page 437, had some but not all of the accented characters needed for certain European languages.

A character set is often called a *code page*. These two terms have essentially the same meaning, except that the former usually refers to a collection of symbols that has been approved as an international standard, while a code page is usually a manufacturer's standard. In other words, the International Organization for Standardization (ISO), the American National Standards Institute (ANSI), the European Manufacturers Association (ECMA), the Japanese Industry Standard (JIS), or other groups usually approve character set standards, while IBM usually sanctions code pages.

Programmers also speak of a *typeface* or a *font*. Although there are some subtle technical differences between these two terms, they both refer to a set of rules for actually drawing the symbols in a character set. A font contains all the characters available in a particular style and weight for a particular design; a typeface contains the design itself. For example, here's an American English sentence encoded into the ISO-8859-1 character set (equivalent to Microsoft Windows code page 1252) rendered in several fonts using different typefaces:

Times Roman, 14 point, proportional spacing

The quick brown fox jumped over the lazy dog.

Courier New, 14 point, fixed spacing

The quick brown fox jumped over the lazy dog.

Lucida Handwriting, 14 point, proportional spacing

The quick brown fox jumped over the lazy dog.

Tahoma, 18 point, proportional spacing

The quick brown fox jumped over the lazy dog.

Although these examples look very different, they all use the same character set, which implies that the program sees exactly the same number sequence for the sentence regardless of how it's displayed.

American Symbology

The most common character sets in the United States are based on ASCII or EBCDIC, which are acronyms for *American Standard Code for Information Interchange* and *Extended Binary Coded Decimal Interchange Code,* respectively.

ASCII is a 7-bit code that originated in the telecommunication industry and is now controlled by ISO. It's the most popular computer character set, being employed on nearly all personal computers, workstations, and non-IBM minicomputers. The original American version, now called USASCII, has been extended far beyond its original 128 characters and is the basis for the 16-bit Unicode character set employed by Microsoft Windows NT.

EBCDIC is an 8-bit code invented by IBM for use on its mainframes and minicomputers, and it remains primarily an IBM character set. It's considerably different from ASCII and presents special programming challenges because the alphabetic characters don't occupy a contiguous range of code values.

European Symbology

American programmers are usually surprised to learn that we don't live in an ASCII/EBCDIC world. These character sets were originally invented for use by English speakers, and they don't contain enough symbols to express most other languages. In fact, I've been told that only three written languages can use unaugmented ASCII: English, Hawaiian, and Swahili. The latter two employ the English alphabet only because they had no written forms until their users were visited by English and American missionaries.

Except for these special cases, every country requires some non-English characters in its written language. Furthermore, when you consider symbols, even the United States and other English-speaking countries have character set differences. For instance, Americans have little use for the pound sterling symbol (£), while the typical U.K. computer user seldom needs the dollar sign ($).

Given that each country requires more than the 128 characters in the ASCII set, we need to ask a fundamental question: How many bits does it take to represent the necessary characters? For countries in Europe, North America, South America, and Australia/Oceania, the answer is "approximately one byte, or 8 bits." So each of these countries can use a *single-byte character set,* or SBCS. In most cases, the bidirectional languages are also in the SBCS category.

For multilingual work, however, the required symbol repertoire usually contains more than 256 characters. For instance, an SBCS won't suffice if you're working with documents containing combinations of French, Russian, and Hebrew.

Asian Symbology

Japanese, Korean, and Chinese need at least two bytes to express each of their characters, which are actually *ideographs,* or stylized pictures representing ideas. For this reason, each of these countries uses a *double-byte character set,* or DBCS. Each language that requires a DBCS also uses a unique set of one-byte phonetic characters together with the Latin alphabet and other symbols from the ASCII character set. So a DBCS language actually uses both single-byte and double-byte characters and is more properly called a *multibyte character set* (MBCS).

Note that we said Japanese, Korean, and Chinese require at least two bytes per ideograph. These languages—especially Japanese and Chinese—are constantly being enriched with new ideographs, which are similar to words in Western languages. More than 80,000 ideographs are used in Chinese literature, and so a complete representation of their language would require three or more bytes per ideograph. However, each DBCS country has defined a commercial subset of its vast symbol repertoire, in which each symbol can be expressed in two bytes.

Arabic and Hebrew Symbology

Although Arabic and Hebrew are SBCS languages, they present a special challenge to programmers. Because they're script languages traditionally written with a pen, a character can take on a different shape depending on where it appears in a word. This is similar to the use of capital letters at the beginning of European and American words. Many Arabic characters, however, have four variations for when the character appears at the beginning, middle, or end of a word and for when it appears by itself.

To further complicate matters, an individual Arabic symbol can be composed from several characters, one of which is the root symbol, while the others are nuances called *diacritical marks* or *accents*. While many European languages also employ diacritical marks, the popular European character sets contain accented characters that can be expressed with a single byte. This isn't as practical in the Arabic world, which uses more diacritical marks.

USAGE

The term *usage* refers to the spelling, punctuation, collation, and other idiomatic rules in a country. Some European countries use a comma instead of a period for the decimal point and a period instead of a comma to group thousands. Also, date formats, currency symbols, and credit-balance notations vary widely. Each country typically has its own collation rules, and these rules for alphabetic and phonetic sorting might even be different from one country to another. For instance, in Sweden the characters **A, Ø,** and **Đ** usually have the same collation value, the number assigned to a character or phrase in order to determine its position relative to other characters or phrases.

When running under an internationally aware operating system, programs can automatically adjust to these differences by consulting "country information tables" for the usage rules that are currently in force. Microsoft Windows provides an extensive repertoire of international settings that the user can select through the Control Panel.

The final area of usage differences is text length. The length of a prompter or other message will often vary quite a bit from one language to another. For example, here is a simple horizontal menu bar displayed in three different languages:

- English form: TITLE: <u>H</u>orizontal <u>V</u>ertical <u>B</u>oth <u>N</u>one

- German form: TITEL: <u>H</u>orizontal <u>V</u>ertikal <u>B</u>eide <u>O</u>hne

- French form: TITRE: <u>H</u>orizontale <u>V</u>erticale <u>T</u>out <u>A</u>ucune

International programs must automatically adjust screen displays and reports to allow for these size differences. Also, the program must be prepared to receive different inputs, depending on the language.

In the preceding example, the user can select each of the four menu items in two ways. One method is to type the letter that's underlined in the menu item you want. In general, you can't force all languages to use the same letters, as this simple example demonstrates. Another method is to highlight the desired menu item using the cursor keys and then press the Enter key. The program must examine the cursor position to determine which word is being selected, and this position inevitably varies with the language. Of course, you could take care of these variations by scanning the menu line for word separators (usually blanks or tabs) to discover which word contains the cursor. But what if the menu choices are rearranged in some language because that culture prefers to list the choices in an order different from what's customary in your culture? Both selection techniques are language dependent, and these variations are shown in the following tables:

Table 2-1. Menu Selection Using Character Position

Item	*English*	*German*	*French*
Horizontal	7	7	7
Vertical	18	18	19
Both	27	27	29
None	32	33	34

Table 2-2. **Menu Selection Using Command Character**

Item	English	German	French
Horizontal	H	H	H
Vertical	V	V	V
Both	B	B	T
None	N	O	A

Clearly, if you want the program to support many languages, these tables can become very complicated. You would certainly not want this complexity to spread throughout your code, and so you would probably concentrate the menu processing in a single routine that returns a language-independent code indicating which of the four items was selected. This is one reason why graphical user interface systems such as Microsoft Windows have become so popular, supplanting the older character-mode display systems in which application programs were much more tightly coupled to the screen layout.

SUMMARY

In order to enable your software for international use, you must understand that language and cultural differences impinge upon your program designs in three ways: direction, symbology, and usage. Then you should develop a general understanding of these characteristics for the locales that you're likely to encounter. This is a rich area for further study, and several of the books described in the bibliography go into much more detail.

Chapter 3

Character Sets

Each written language uses a specific set of symbols. For example, American English requires about 100 relatively simple symbols, including the uppercase and lowercase letters A through Z, the digits 0 through 9, and a few others used for punctuation and number formatting. On the opposite end of the spectrum, Japanese requires a symbol set containing thousands of complex pictorials known as ideographs. Other languages fall between these two extremes.

You can think of a symbol set as the "atoms" of a written language—the lowest level of detail. By arranging these atoms into larger structures (linguistic molecules, crystals, and DNA chains) according to the syntactic and semantic rules of the language, we can record and preserve our thoughts and words. Not too shabby, considering that it all started with burnt sticks scratching on cave walls.

This chapter describes the techniques that have evolved to enable computers to manipulate the many symbol sets used throughout the world. The key concept here is the character set, which is simply an encoding of one or more symbol sets into numbers that can be manipulated by computer hardware and software.

THE EVOLUTION OF CHARACTER SETS

Writing is a mysterious process in which the human mind rapidly associates thoughts and ideas with symbols that represent the sounds made when we speak. By recording those symbols in the proper sequence on a medium such as paper, we enable others to understand our ideas without speaking directly to them.

An ideal recording medium captures symbols efficiently without impeding the mind's flow. Also, such a medium should be light and durable so that written communications can be easily carried over long distances and preserved for future reference.

For many centuries paper and ink offered the best combination of efficiency, mass, and durability. Real history and historical fiction abound with tales of heroic men and women who endured great hazards to deliver vital documents. For nearly its first century, the U.S. Post Office moved important mail on horseback, with brave riders traveling lonely and dangerous frontier trails. This method reached its zenith in the fabled Pony Express, which lasted less than 10 years before giving way to the telegraph and railroads.

Although paper documents remain important in today's world, the computer has become the most powerful way to capture, store, reproduce, and transmit the symbol sequences representing our thoughts. The transition away from paper documents began during the 1970s when it became acceptable to use fax machines in banking, real estate, and legal transactions, thereby avoiding the delay of hand-carried documents. This trend continues today as more and more written communication is being conducted with e-mail.

Of course, under the covers the typical computer operates in a world that has no symbols, only numbers. Therefore, to make the computer an efficient tool for human writing and communication, early designers had to devise encoding schemes that assigned numbers to our symbols. These schemes came to be known as character sets.

From the 1950s to the late 1970s, the most popular character sets were ASCII and EBCDIC because they were well suited to the dominant computing environment of that era, in which *dumb terminals* were connected to mainframe and minicomputer hosts. The terminals were "dumb" in the sense that they did not contain storage and were not user programmable. However, they did possess enough intelligence to convert between human-readable symbols and computer-friendly character sets through their keyboards and built-in character generators.

The late 1980s saw the rise of intelligent workstations with graphical user interfaces (GUIs) such as Microsoft Windows. These GUI systems include substantial storage and computing capability, nowadays providing more power than large host computers (mainframes) in the dumb terminal era.

Because modern workstations employ *all points addressable* (APA) graphics—the mode in which all pixels can be individually manipulated—the software has complete control over the symbols and pictures displayed, overcoming the dumb terminal's dependency on a limited set of hardware-based character generators. Furthermore, combining detachable and programmable keyboards with a variety of pointing devices has made it fairly easy to adapt intelligent workstations to the input requirements of each language.

As the United States and a few other countries evolved from using dumb terminals to using intelligent workstations, the rest of the world was just entering the computer age. Suppliers of this technology soon became aware that the growing international market demanded localized computing hardware and software—that is, the new breed of computer users insisted on working in their own symbol sets.

Clearly the older coding schemes, with their U.S. bias, wouldn't suffice, but fortunately, growth in the international data processing market coincided with the emergence of inexpensive graphical workstations. This happy coincidence led to a variety of new encodings, the most popular of which are the ANSI and Unicode character sets, which use 8 bits and 16 bits per character, respectively.

If you're a programmer interested in international applications, you must be familiar with the "big four" character sets: EBCDIC, ASCII, ANSI, and Unicode. Even though the first two are becoming obsolete, you will encounter them in older programs (called *legacy systems*), which are still used today and are often the basis for more modern designs. Let's examine each of these four character sets more closely, as well as the related topic of *code pages*.

THE EBCDIC CHARACTER SET

EBCDIC is the acronym for Extended Binary Coded Decimal Interchange Code. This 8-bit character set was defined in the early 1960s for use on the IBM 360 computer family, and it lives on in IBM's successors to the 360 mainframe, such as the 3090, and in their midrange offering, the AS/400.

Table 3-1, which is from the IBM RPG/400 Reference, shows the most common form of EBCDIC, although several variations have been defined to include the symbols required for languages not covered by the original definition.[1] To determine the hexadecimal code for a particular character, use the column heading as the high 4 bits. For instance, the letter A is encoded as 0xC1. Note that the lower 64 codes are assigned to control functions instead of displayable characters. Table 3-2 explains the abbreviations used for the control functions.

EBCDIC has its roots in the Hollerith coding system for punched cards, used in the tabulating machines that formed the backbone of IBM's business for the first half of the twentieth century. Because of that heritage, EBCDIC contains unusual gaps in the code sequence and an unusual arrangement of character groups when compared to ASCII-based systems. For instance, the code for letter J isn't the code for letter A plus 10 as in other popular character sets, but the code for letter A plus 16. Furthermore, if you simply compare character codes, lowercase letters collate before uppercase ones, and numbers collate after letters.

Of course, it's not a good idea to write programs that rely on particular character sequences, but most C, C++, and Basic programs use ASCII or its derivatives, and many of them incorporate algorithms that are incompatible with EBCDIC. Specifically, these algorithms assume that uppercase and lowercase letters are encoded into two 26-symbol groups using consecutive codes, that numbers collate before letters, and that uppercase letters collate before lowercase ones.

Because EBCDIC is so radically different from ASCII, it's extremely difficult to move the vast repertoire of C, C++, and Basic programs and libraries to EBCDIC environments. That is why the IBM mainframe and midrange programming community has remained somewhat isolated from the intelligent workstation evolution that began, ironically, with the IBM PC, which is an ASCII system.

---

1. While searching the Internet for information on EBCDIC, I came across this quote in a jargon dictionary maintained by the University of Vaasa, Finland (*http://t2r.uwasa.fi/jargon/ebcdic.html*):

   "EBCDIC: An alleged character set used on IBM dinosaurs. It exists in at least six mutually incompatible versions, all featuring such delights as noncontiguous letter sequences and the absence of several ASCII punctuation characters fairly important for modern computing languages (exactly which characters are absent varies according to which version of EBCDIC you're looking at). IBM adapted EBCDIC from punched card code in the early 1960s and promulgated it as a customer control tactic, spurning the already established ASCII standard. Today, IBM claims to be an open systems company, but IBM's own description of the EBCDIC variants and how to convert between them is still internally classified top-secret, burn-before-reading. Hackers blanch at the very name of EBCDIC and consider it a manifestation of purest evil."

   These folks in Finland don't seem to like EBCDIC very much. They are not alone.

Table 3-1. **EBCDIC Character Set**

	00	10	20	30	40	50	60	70	80	90	A0	B0	C0	D0	E0	F0
0	nul	dle	ds		SP	&	-						{	}	\	0
1	soh	dc1	sos				/		a	j	~		A	J		1
2	stx	dc2	fs	syn					b	k	s		B	K	S	2
3	etx	tm							c	l	t		C	L	T	3
4	pf	res	byp	pn					d	m	u		D	M	U	4
5	ht	nl	lf	rs					e	n	v		E	N	V	5
6	lc	bs	etb	uc					f	o	w		F	O	W	6
7	del	il	esc	eot					g	p	x		G	P	X	7
8	eg	can							h	q	y		H	Q	Y	8
9	rlf	em						`	i	r	z		I	R	Z	9
A	smm	cc	sm		¢	!	¦	:								
B	vt	cu1	cu2	cu3	.	$	,	#								
C	ff	ifs		dc4	<	*	%	@								
D	cr	igs	enq	nak	(	)	_	'								
E	so	irs	ack		+	;	>	=								
F	si	ius	bel	sub	|	¬	?	"								

Table 3-2. **EBCDIC Control Codes**

Code	Name	Description	Code	Name	Description
00	nul	Null character	20	ds	Digit select
01	soh	Start of heading	21	sos	Start of significance
02	stx	Start of text	22	fs	Field separator
03	etx	End of text	23		
04	pf	Punch off	24	byp	Bypass
05	ht	Horizontal tab	25	lf	Line feed
06	lc	Lowercase	26	etb	End transmission block
07	del	Delete	27	esc	Escape
08	eg	End of guarded area	28		

(continued)

Table 3-2. *continued*

Code	Name	Description	Code	Name	Description
09	rlf	Reverse line feed	29		
0A	smm	Start manual message	2A	sm	Set mode
0B	vt	Vertical tab	2B	cu2	Customer use 2
0C	ff	Form feed	2C		
0D	cr	Carriage return	2D	enq	Enquiry
0E	so	Shift out	2E	ack	Acknowledge
0F	si	Shift in	2F	bel	Bell
10	dle	Data link escape	30		
11	dc1	Device control 1	31		
12	dc2	Device control 2	32	syn	Synchronous idle
13	tm	Tape mark	33		
14	res	Restore	34	pn	Punch on
15	nl	New line	35	rs	Reader stop
16	bs	Backspace	36	uc	Uppercase
17	il	Idle	37	eot	End of transmission
18	can	Cancel	38		
19	em	End of medium	39		
1A	cc	Cursor control	3A		
1B	cu1	Customer use 1	3B	cu3	Customer use 3
1C	ifs	Interchange file separator	3C	dc4	Device control 4
1D	igs	Interchange group separator	3D	nak	Negative acknowledge
1E	irs	Interchange record separator	3E		
1F	ius	Interchange unit separator	3F	sub	Substitute

At the risk of offending programmers of IBM mainframes and midrange computers, I'll seldom mention EBCDIC throughout the rest of the book, simply because it isn't a significant factor on most Win32 client/server systems.

Clearly, if you access IBM mainframe hosts from a Win32 platform, there must be some conversion between EBCDIC and the preferred Win32 character sets, ANSI and Unicode. However, this is usually hidden by host access services such as Open Database Connectivity (ODBC) drivers.

THE ASCII CHARACTER SET

ASCII is the acronym for American Standard Code for Information Interchange. It's a 7-bit character set designed during the 1950s for electromechanical teleprinters such as the Teletype Models 33 and 35. Teleprinters began evolving in the 1890s, replacing the key/clicker units that telegraphers used to transmit and receive written messages by Morse Code. ASCII made its way into the data processing world during the late 1960s when early minicomputers used low-cost teleprinters, especially the Teletype Model 33, as their terminals.

By the time teleprinters became popular as computer terminals, the telegraphy and teleprinter industry had evolved from Morse Code through the 5-bit Baudot Code to the 7-bit format that ultimately became the ASCII character set. This evolution resulted from the demand to transmit complex messages faster and more accurately.

Morse Code

Samuel Morse invented the telegraph in 1837, pioneering the bitwise representation of human communication symbols. Some might argue that this technique was employed by earlier signaling devices such as mirrors, lanterns,[2] semaphores, and smoke signals. Nonetheless, Morse was the first to send messages electrically without relying on line-of-sight transmission by encoding a variable number of bits for each character and transmitting these bits with a rudimentary form of pulse width modulation—in other words, dots and dashes.

To keep things as simple as possible, Morse encoded only the 26 uppercase English letters and the 10 digits. Punctuation was supplied by spelling out words, such as using *STOP* to end a sentence. Later variations added a few punctuation characters. Table 3-3 shows today's International Morse Code.

---

2. The American revolution, which resulted in the formation of the United States, began with a simple message transmitted by lamp from a church steeple. The encoding scheme was, "One (light) if by land, two if by sea."

Table 3-3. **Morse Code**

Symbol	Code	Symbol	Code	Symbol	Code	Symbol	Code
A	• –	M	– –	Y	– • – –	/	– • • – •
B	– • • •	N	– •	Z	– – • •	,	– – • • – –
C	– • – •	O	– – –	1	• – – – –	.	• – • – • –
D	– • •	P	• – – •	2	• • – – –	?	• • – – • •
E	•	Q	– – • –	3	• • • – –	:	– – – • • •
F	• • – •	R	• – •	4	• • • • –	'	• – – – – •
G	– – •	S	• • •	5	• • • • •	–	– • • • • –
H	• • • •	T	–	6	– • • • •	( )	– • – – • –
I	• •	U	• • –	7	– – • • •	"	• – • • – •
J	• – – –	V	• • • –	8	– – – • •		
K	– • –	W	• – –	9	– – – – •		
L	• – • •	X	– • • –	0	– – – – –		

    If you think of a dot as a 0 bit and a dash as 1 bit, you can map Morse Code into variable-length bit strings or even coerce them into bytes. This is often done when computers handle Morse Code messages, as in telegraphy training software. Nonetheless, this code is properly expressed as dots and dashes because it's usually transmitted by pulse width modulation under the following rules:

- A dash is three times as wide as a dot.

- Each bit in a character is separated by the width of a dot.

- Each character is separated by the width of a dash.

- Each word is separated by the width of seven dots.

- A character consisting of eight dots tells the receiver to ignore the preceding word.

    Notice that Morse chose an encoding scheme in which the most common letters in the English language have the shortest code sequences and can therefore be transmitted quickly. This makes Morse Code fairly efficient for transmission over low bandwidth or noisy channels. For that reason, it's still used throughout the world, especially for emergency communications.

To deal with language differences, Morse Code telegraphers use a complicated scheme of phonetic spelling combined with lots of heuristic techniques. If you care to learn more about this subject, search the Internet for *Morse Code* and *American Radio Relay League*. Also, because the Federal Communications Commission still requires amateur radio operators (also called *hams*) to learn Morse Code, you can obtain a good deal of relevant information from the U.S. Government Printing Office.

Baudot Code

In 1874 Emile Baudot[3] invented an electromechanical teleprinter that employed a more sophisticated character set than Morse Code. He used 5 bits to represent the 26 uppercase letters and 4 special characters: space, carriage return, line feed, and null. The remaining 2 code points were assigned to locking shifts, thereby opening another space of 30 codes that Baudot used for digits and punctuation. Since the four special characters were common to both modes, Baudot's scheme encoded a total of 58 characters, consisting of 26 letters, 26 figures (digits and punctuation), 4 special characters, and 2 locking shifts.

Because it relies on locking shifts, Baudot Code isn't stateless. In order to properly interpret a particular 5-bit code, you need to know whether the character stream is currently in the *letter mode* or the *figure mode*—that is, whether or not the teleprinter is shifted. This is similar to using the Shift Lock key on a typewriter.

Baudot Code was modified slightly and then standardized in 1932 by the International Telegraph and Telephone Consultation Committee (CCITT) as CCITT Code 2, also known as International Telegraphic Alphabet Number 2 (ITA2).[4] Since only 55 of the available 58 codes were needed for English, the standard generously allowed the other three to be assigned for local usage. Table 3-4 shows American Baudot Code, a variant of ITA2 with the following differences:

- In ITA2, the bell character is shifted 0x1A and the apostrophe is shifted 0x14.

- In ITA2, shifted 0x11 is the plus sign (+) instead of the double quote (").

---

3. The term *baud* as in "9600 baud modem" is a tribute to Baudot, who is generally considered to be the father of character encoding techniques used in computers and communication devices.

4. Although ITA2 is different, many people refer to it as Baudot Code because Baudot's original encoding is no longer used.

Table 3-4. **American Baudot Code**

	Letter	Figure		Letter	Figure
00	null	null	11	E	3
01	T	5	11	Z	"
02	cr	cr	12	D	$
03	O	9	13	B	?
04	space	space	14	S	bell
05	H	#	15	Y	6
06	N	,	16	F	!
07	M	.	17	X	/
08	lf	lf	18	A	–
09	L	)	19	W	2
0A	R	4	1A	J	'
0B	G	&	1B	Figure shift	Figure shift
0C	I	8	1C	U	7
0D	P	0	1D	Q	1
0E	C	:	1E	K	(
0F	V	;	1F	Letter shift	Letter shift

The three shaded characters are usually replaced for other languages, thereby producing other ITA2 variants. The two codes, 0x1B and 0x1F, are used to shift into the figure mode and the letter mode, respectively.

You might wonder why the code assignments seem so arbitrary. Why don't the letters have sequential numbers? The most plausible explanation I've heard is that Baudot chose an encoding scheme that enabled his teleprinter to operate rapidly with minimum wear and tear.

Also, if you conduct a little research into Baudot Code and its derivatives, you will probably find an encoding that looks completely different from Table 3-4. For instance, the code for the letter D is often shown as 0x09 instead of 0x12 because of some confusion about bit ordering. Since both Baudot and ITA2 specified the code in terms of bits rather than decimal, octal, or hexadecimal numbers, each character has two representations, as shown here for the letter D:

Bit	*0*	*1*	*2*	*3*	*4*
D =	0	1	0	0	1

Bit	*4*	*3*	*2*	*1*	*0*
D =	1	0	0	1	0

Table 3-4 uses the second representation, with bit 0 on the right, which is most familiar to Win32 programmers.

ASCII

Baudot Code is still used today in the form of ITA2, which was updated as recently as 1988. However, its limited character repertoire and awkward use of shift states, combined with advances in electromechanical technology, led U.S. teleprinter companies to invent a richer 7-bit code in the 1950s that evolved into ASCII.

This improved code provided for 94 printing characters, including all symbols needed for normal messages in American English. In addition, 32 were reserved for communication control functions, and the remaining two of the 128 available codes were assigned as the space and delete characters. Since many people consider space and delete part of the printable character group, we programmers usually say that ASCII contains 96 graphic characters and 32 control characters. Interestingly, the control group was defined with two locking shifts for possible expansion using Baudot's technique, as well as a nonlocking shift known as the escape character.

Because this 7-bit character set was designed by companies concerned with reliable communication over noisy lines, an ASCII data stream was usually transmitted with a parity bit for each character. When computer programmers began to use ASCII for text processing and storage, they had several choices for dealing with the parity bit: preserve it, reset it, set it, or use it for tagging certain characters. Well-behaved programs simply preserved the parity bit, treating ASCII as an 8-bit code. The other techniques, particularly storing tags in the parity bit, led to many conversion problems as ASCII evolved into a true 8-bit code.

ISO-646

In 1967 the International Organization for Standardization (ISO) adopted ASCII as ISO-646, which was subsequently updated in 1983 and 1991. This standard preserves the U.S. encoding (renamed as USASCII) and defines a method for assigning up to 12 of the 96 display characters for local use. This has led to more than a dozen standard variants covering most of the Western European languages.

Table 3-5 shows USASCII with the 12 replaceable characters in boldface type. To find the hexadecimal value for a particular character, use the column number as the high-order digit. For instance, the letter Q is 0x51. Note that this variant is officially designated as ISO-646-US. Table 3-6 shows the German (or Deutsch) variant, designated as ISO-646-DE. Table 3-7 explains the control codes, which range from 0x00 through 0x1F and are common to all ISO-646 variants.

Table 3-5. **ISO-646-US Character Set (USASCII)**

	00	10	20	30	40	50	60	70
0	nul	dle	space	0	@	P	`	p
1	soh	dc1	!	1	A	Q	a	q
2	stx	dc2	"	2	B	R	b	r
3	etx	dc3	#	3	C	S	c	s
4	eot	dc4	$	4	D	T	d	t
5	enq	nak	%	5	E	U	e	u
6	ack	syn	&	6	F	V	f	v
7	bel	etb	'	7	G	W	g	w
8	bs	can	(	8	H	X	h	x
9	ht	em	)	9	I	Y	I	y
A	lf	sub	*	:	J	Z	j	z
B	vt	esc	+	;	K	[	k	{
C	ff	is4	,	<	L	\	l		
D	cr	is3	-	=	M	]	m	}
E	ls1	is2	.	>	N	^	n	~
F	ls0	is1	/	?	O	_	o	del

Table 3-6. **ISO-646-DE Character Set (German)**

	00	10	20	30	40	50	60	70
0	nul	dle	space	0	§	P	`	p
1	soh	dc1	!	1	A	Q	a	q
2	stx	dc2	'	2	B	R	b	r
3	etx	dc3	#	3	C	S	c	s
4	eot	dc4	$	4	D	T	d	t
5	enq	nak	%	5	E	U	e	u
6	ack	syn	&	6	F	V	f	v
7	bel	etb	'	7	G	W	g	w
8	bs	can	(	8	H	X	h	x
9	ht	em	)	9	I	Y	I	y

	00	*10*	*20*	*30*	*40*	*50*	*60*	*70*
A	lf	sub	*	:	J	Z	j	z
B	vt	esc	+	;	K	Ä	k	ä
C	ff	fs	,	<	L	Ö	l	ö
D	cr	gs	–	=	M	Ü	m	ü
E	so	rs	.	>	N	^	n	ß
F	si	us	/	?	O	_	o	del

Table 3-7. ISO-646 (ASCII) Control Codes

Code	*Name*	*Description*	*Code*	*Name*	*Description*
00	nul	Null character	**10**	dle	Data link escape
01	soh	Start of heading	**11**	dc1	Device control #1
02	stx	Start of text	**12**	dc2	Device control #2
03	etx	End of text	**13**	dc3	Device control #3
04	eot	End of transmission	**14**	dc4	Device control #4
05	enq	Enquiry (Who are you?)	**15**	nak	Negative acknowledge
06	ack	Acknowledge	**16**	syn	Synchronous idle
07	bel	Bell	**17**	etb	End of transmission block
08	bs	Backspace	**18**	can	Cancel
09	ht	Horizontal tab	**19**	em	End of medium
0A	lf	Line feed	**1A**	sub	Substitute
0B	vt	Vertical tab	**1B**	esc	Escape
0C	ff	Form feed	**1C**	fs	File separator
0D	cr	Carriage return	**1D**	gs	Group separator
0E	so	Shift out (locking shift 1)	**1E**	rs	Record separator
0F	si	Shift in (locking shift 0)	**1F**	us	Unit separator

Although the ISO-646 variants provide easy access to the most common local symbols needed for simple text processing in one language, the 12-character repertoire is inadequate for more complex work involving obscure local symbols or multiple languages. Also, since the 12 replaceable codes include USASCII characters—such as { and }—that are important in C and other programming languages, it's difficult to produce readable programs using local characters in text strings. You can either understand the program or the text strings, but not both.[5]

To deal with this limitation ISO-646, like Baudot Code, defines locking shifts that can switch to a second character set. Typically this feature is used to switch only the 12 replaceable characters, leaving the core ASCII set available in either shift state. For instance, suppose you design a messaging system that needs to support both American and German users. You can employ ISO-646-US and ISO-646-DE, using the shift character to switch between the two.

However, the shifting approach is more suitable for serial transmission than data processing. The typical transmission program simply moves characters without interpreting them. A data processing program usually needs to randomly access characters in memory and interpret them for purposes such as sorting. This is difficult when the meaning of a code differs depending on whether or not a locking shift code occurred earlier in the text string.[6]

For languages that use accented forms of English letters, ISO-646 specifies another technique to overcome the limitation of 12 local characters. In those cases, you can combine a letter and a punctuation mark, such as an apostrophe, to produce a single accented character on the display or printer. However, this technique is rarely used because it turns ASCII into a multibyte character set (MBCS) in which some symbols require more than one byte. This is actually another manifestation of the problem with shifted strings mentioned earlier. Many programmers have found that MBCS programs are difficult to write, test, and maintain because the meaning of any random byte in a text string depends on other bytes in the string.

These problems have caused the ISO-646 variants and the shifting and accenting schemes to fall out of favor, and today ISO-646 is generally treated as a synonym for "good old U.S. ASCII."

---

5. The C standard approved by ISO does, in fact, extend the language to support the use of ISO-646 variants, but the extension, based on three-character sequences called *trigraphs,* is somewhat cumbersome to use. Chapter 5 will cover this further.

6. Clever programmers use the parity bit to distinguish shifted and unshifted characters, transforming ISO-646 into an 8-bit code with exactly one byte per character. When employing this technique, the shift characters are removed from an input string and regenerated when the string is later sent to an output device.

ISO-2022

As the limitations of the 7-bit ISO-646 code became apparent, communication and computing organizations began to covet the eighth bit. After all, data transmission and processing systems had evolved to more sophisticated error detection methods, and so the per-character parity bit was seldom needed. Many hardware and software vendors therefore began to expand ASCII into a 256-character code, and these efforts eventually led to the ISO-2022 standard developed in 1986.

ISO-2022 has three purposes. First, it specifies how to expand ISO-646 into an 8-bit character set. Second, it generalizes the concept of shift states for both 7-bit and 8-bit sets. Third, it establishes a method for vendors to register their particular 2022-compliant character sets as ISO standards.

The second goal highlights the ongoing bad news of character set evolution: Even 256 characters aren't sufficient for some languages and for many multilingual scenarios! In other words, after moving to an 8-bit character set, we still have to deal with multibyte characters and shifted character streams. Bummer! It was clear even in 1986 that the next evolutionary step would have to introduce *wide characters* containing more than 8 bits.

Although the inadequacy of 8-bit character sets for international data processing became apparent soon after ISO-2022 was published, the standard remains extremely important because modern data processing systems that use wide characters internally often return to an ISO-2022 character set for data transmission. Shifted character sets may require less bandwidth and aren't especially difficult to handle in the I/O sections of a program where the data is processed serially instead of randomly.

So even if you plan to use a wide character set such as Unicode within your software, you should be familiar with ISO-2022 and the popular 8-bit encodings that conform to its rules. This isn't difficult because, like most ISO character standards, ISO-2022 is derived from 7-bit ASCII, which contains a control group and a graphical group consisting of 32 characters and 96 characters, respectively.

The standard preserves this group concept by dividing the 8-bit character set into four areas: control left (CL), graphical left (GL), control right (CR), and graphical right (GR), as shown in Table 3-8. These areas support two control groups, designated C0 and C1, and four graphical groups, designated G0, G1, G2, and G3. The largest compliant character set can therefore have a repertoire of 64 control characters and 384 graphical characters.[7]

---

7. Actually, an ISO-2022 graphical group that will be used in the GL area contains 94 characters because code 0x20 must be a space and code 0x7F must be the delete character.

In an ISO-2022-compliant 8-bit character set, control groups C0 and C1 are mapped into CL and CR, respectively. The shift and escape characters must be in the C0 group using the encoding shown in Table 3-8. Additional control codes are specified in a related standard, ISO-6429, with the C0 group essentially conforming to ISO-646, good old ASCII. Some ISO-2022 character sets map this standard C0 group into both CL and CR.

Table 3-8. ISO-2022 Character Groups

	00	10	20	30	40	50	60	70	80	90	A0	B0	C0	D0	E0	F0
0			space													
1																
2																
3																
4	**C**				**C**				**C**						**C**	
5	**L**				**L**				**R**						**R**	
6																
7																
8																
9																
A																
B		esc														
C																
D																
E	so															
F	si							del								

An ISO-2022 character set must use locking shift techniques to map the four graphical groups G0 through G3 into GL and GR. The standard defines three codes in CL for this purpose: SO (code 0x0E), SI (code 0x0F), and ESC (code 0x1B). The first two are single-character locking shifts, while the ESC code requires two characters. Since G0 can only be mapped into GL, the standard requires seven locking shifts, as Table 3-9 shows.

Table 3-9. **ISO-2022 Locking Shift Sequences**

Name	*Codes*	*Characters*	*Description*
LS0	**0x0F**	**SI**	G0 to GL
LS1	**0x0E**	**SO**	G1 to GL
LS2	**0x1B, 0x6E**	**ESC n**	G2 to GL
LS3	**0x1B, 0x6F**	**ESC o**	G3 to GL
LS1R	**0x1B, 0x7E**	**ESC ~**	G1 to GR
LS2R	**0x1B, 0x7D**	**ESC }**	G2 to GR
LS3R	**0x1B, 0x7C**	**ESC |**	G3 to GR

ISO-2022 and related standards such as ISO-6429 and ISO-2375 define many other character set features, including nonlocking shifts in C1 and various control functions[8] as code sequences beginning with ESC. Some of these control functions are called *announcers* and enable the sending system to tell the receiver about the character set being used.

When dealing with an ISO-2022 character stream that can contain locking shifts, you must know the current shift state. Rather than require every transmission to begin with a known sequence of locking shifts or an announcer sequence, the standard specifies a default group mapping, as follows:

- C0 is mapped into CL.

- G0 is mapped into GL.

- C1 (or C0 if C1 isn't defined) is mapped into CR.

- G1 (or G0 if G1 isn't defined) is mapped into GR.

Therefore, without using any shift sequences, an ISO-2022 set can make 192 graphical characters readily available. This type of character set is often called *extended ASCII* because it extends traditional 7-bit ASCII into an 8-bit encoding that contains an additional 96 graphical characters.

---

8. A control function is an action that influences data recording, processing, transmitting, or interpreting and that has a coded representation with one or more bit combinations.

I've probably told you more about the complicated ISO-2022 standard than you want to know, so now I'll move on to a specific instance of ISO-2022 encoding, the Windows ANSI set, also known as ISO-8859-1. But first let's visit an important character set topic: code pages.

CODE PAGES

Most PC programmers, myself included, detest shifted character sets of the ISO-2022 variety. Although these sets solve many international data transmission problems, their extensive use of shift states makes text processing programs complicated to write and maintain. In an ideal world, I would use a single-byte character set (SBCS) with no shift states and only a few control codes such as the null terminator, newline, tab, and form feed.

Indeed, while the ISO mulled over ISO-2022 and other global standards, U.S. developers of the IBM PC did what came naturally: They concentrated on extensions that preserved the single-byte nature of ASCII, while adding another 128 characters and dropping unneeded control codes. In other words, they grabbed that eighth bit and used it to double the size of the ASCII character set.

This was more pragmatic than the ISO-2022 approach and perhaps a little shortsighted, but since the ISO didn't possess nuclear weapons, they couldn't deter the PC juggernaut. So, for almost 10 years PC programmers sailed under the IBM flag, inflicting the dreaded code page scourge on international customers. Ultimately, however, rapprochement occurred in the form of the ANSI character set used in Windows and standardized as ISO-8859.

In IBM's parlance, a code page is nothing more than a character set containing 256 *code points*—single-byte indices into the code page. The character set can use EBCDIC encoding, ASCII encoding, or some other scheme. However, workstations using the IBM PC architecture usually employ code pages derived from ASCII. Therefore, code points in the range 0x20 to 0x7F are assigned to the ASCII graphic characters, and additional graphic characters occupy the range 0x80 to 0xFF.

As the PC grew in popularity during the early 1980s, IBM and other vendors defined a plethora of these extended ASCII sets, identifying each with a unique number. Eventually the non-Asian versions of MS-DOS included a repertoire of the code pages needed for many languages throughout Europe, North America, and South America. (See Table 3-10.) These became known as *OEM code pages* because they were supplied by the original equipment manufacturer as part of the hardware and software package. If an application program required other character sets, its setup procedure would install the necessary code page tables.

Table 3-10. **MS-DOS Code Pages**

Page	Description
437	United States
850	Multilingual (Latin 1)
852	Slavic (Latin 2)
860	Portuguese
863	Canadian French
865	Nordic

Code page 437, abbreviated CP437, is particularly important because it's common to all PCs and was the default for many programs written during the PC's early years. Furthermore, it served as the base from which the other ASCII code pages were derived. As shown in Table 3-11, CP437 provides USASCII in the lower 128 code points and a motley collection of other characters in the upper 128 code points.[9] Since code pages are oriented towards display instead of transmission, CP437 overloads the ASCII control codes in the range 0x00 to 0x1F with a set of dingbat characters. Of course, these dingbats must be used carefully in programs that manipulate strings containing ASCII control characters such as newlines and tabs.

When users in other countries found CP437 lacking, somebody (usually IBM) made the necessary changes and registered a new code page. By convention, each new page retained its ability to faithfully represent American English by preserving USASCII characters in the lower 128 code points. This worked fine for programs that had to deal with only one language or with the local language plus American English. But as European trade barriers fell and we entered the age of the global economy, many software packages had to handle several languages at once, and the need to frequently switch code pages became an enormous programming obstacle.

---

9. The code point identified as *nbsp* is a nonbreaking space. Word processors use it within a group of words that should be treated as a unit.

Table 3-11. Code Page 437

	00	10	20	30	40	50	60	70	80	90	A0	B0	C0	D0	E0	F0
0	nul	►	space	0	@	P	`	p	Ç	É	á	▓	└	╨	α	≡
1	☺	◄	!	1	A	Q	a	q	ü	æ	í	▓	┴	┬	β	±
2	☻	↕	"	2	B	R	b	r	é	Æ	ó	▓	┬	┬	Γ	≥
3	♥	‼	#	3	C	S	c	s	â	ô	ú	│	├	╨	π	≤
4	♦	¶	$	4	D	T	d	t	ä	ö	ñ	┤	─	└	Σ	⌠
5	♣	§	%	5	E	U	e	u	à	ò	Ñ	╡	┼	╒	σ	⌡
6	♠	▬	&	6	F	V	f	v	å	û	ª	╢	╞	╓	µ	÷
7	•	↨	'	7	G	W	g	w	ç	ù	º	╖	╟	╫	τ	≈
8	◘	↑	(	8	H	X	h	x	ê	ÿ	¿	╕	╚	╪	Φ	°
9	○	↓	)	9	I	Y	i	y	ë	Ö	⌐	╣	╔	┘	Θ	∙
A	◙	→	*	:	J	Z	j	z	è	Ü	¬	║	╩	┌	Ω	·
B	♂	←	+	;	K	[	k	{	ï	¢	½	╗	╦	█	δ	√
C	♀	∟	,	<	L	\	l			î	£	¼	╝	╠	▄	∞	ⁿ
D	♪	↔	-	=	M	]	m	}	ì	¥	¡	╜	═	█	ø	²
E	♫	▲	.	>	N	^	n	~	Ä	₧	«	╛	╬	▐	ε	■
F	☼	▼	/	?	O	_	o	⌂	Å	ƒ	»	┐	┴	▀	∩	nbsp

In response to this growing problem, IBM defined CP850 to handle a large set of European, North American, and South American languages without needing to switch pages. Table 3-12 shows this "universal, single-byte code page"; the shaded characters indicate the changes from CP437, which was the earlier "universal" page. So, five years after the PC emerged as the standard base for building intelligent workstations, programmers finally had a single-byte character set that could accommodate a large number of users. Even though it wasn't truly universal, CP850 was attractive enough that many organizations expended a great deal of effort to convert their programs from CP437 and other local code pages.

Despite CP850's acceptance in the Western Hemisphere, Asian PC users had problems with it simply because no SBCS could handle the thousands of symbols that their languages require. IBM, Microsoft, and other vendors addressed this problem by defining extended code pages such as CP932 (Japanese), CP949 (Korean), CP936 (Simplified Chinese), and CP950 (Traditional Chinese).

Table 3-12. Code Page 850

	00	10	20	30	40	50	60	70	80	90	A0	B0	C0	D0	E0	F0
0	nul	►	space	0	@	P	`	p	Ç	É	á	▓	└	ð	Ó	≡
1	☺	◄	!	1	A	Q	a	q	ü	æ	í	▒	┴	Đ	ß	±
2	☻	↕	"	2	B	R	b	r	é	Æ	ó	▓	┬	Ê	Ô	═
3	♥	‼	#	3	C	S	c	s	â	ô	ú	│	├	Ë	Ò	¾
4	♦	¶	$	4	D	T	d	t	ä	ö	ñ	┤	─	È	õ	¶
5	♣	§	%	5	E	U	e	u	à	ò	Ñ	Á	┼	ı	Õ	§
6	♠	▬	&	6	F	V	f	v	å	û	ª	Â	ã	Í	µ	÷
7	•	↨	'	7	G	W	g	w	ç	ù	º	À	Ã	Î	þ	¸
8	◘	↑	(	8	H	X	h	x	ê	ÿ	¿	©	╚	Ï	Þ	°
9	○	↓	)	9	I	Y	i	y	ë	Ö	®	╣	╔	┘	Ú	¨
A	◙	→	*	:	J	Z	j	z	è	Ü	¬	║	╩	┌	Û	·
B	♂	←	+	;	K	[	k	{	ï	ø	½	╗	╦	█	Ù	¹
C	♀	∟	,	<	L	\	l	|	î	£	¼	╝	╠	▄	ý	³
D	♪	↔	-	=	M	]	m	}	ì	Ø	¡	¢	=	¦	Ý	²
E	♫	▲	.	>	N	^	n	~	Ä	×	«	¥	╬	Ì	¯	■
F	☼	▼	/	?	O	_	o	⌂	Å	ƒ	»	¬	¤	■	´	nbsp

An Asian code page actually contains a base page and a number of extension pages, thus providing many more than 256 code points. The base page is usually derived from CP437 or CP850 and contains nonlocking shift characters in many of the code points above 127. Within a text stream, each shift character is followed by a second byte referring to a code point in the extension page associated with the shift code.[10]

---

10. IBM calls this a double-byte character set (DBCS) even though some characters require only a single byte. The C and C++ standards more properly call this an MBCS. As this chapter will explain later, Unicode is truly a DBCS because each character requires exactly two bytes (except for surrogates and combining characters). However, since IBM usurped the term DBCS, most people refer to Unicode as a wide character set (WCS). Confusing, huh?

Nadine Kano's book (See Bibliography) contains an extensive appendix showing the various Asian code pages, so I won't repeat all that information here. Table 3-13 shows an example of a DBCS base page: the Japanese CP932, in which the codes from 0x81 to 0x9F and from 0xE0 to 0xFC are used as nonlocking shift characters. The codes from 0xA0 to 0xDF are single-byte Katakana symbols used for phonetic spelling of non-Japanese words.[11] By using the shift codes, you can access up to 64 extension pages for a total of approximately 16,000 symbols. Since CP932 assigns about 10,000 of the available codes to the Japanese Industrial Standard symbol set, it's sometimes called *shift-JIS* or *JISCII*.

Table 3-13. Code Page 932

	00	10	20	30	40	50	60	70	80	90	A0	B0	C0	D0	E0	F0
0	nul	►	space	0	@	P	`	p					ー	タ	ミ	
1	☺	◄	!	1	A	Q	a	q		**S**	°	ア	チ	ム		**S**
2	⬤	↕	"	2	B	R	b	r		**h**	「	イ	ツ	メ		**h**
3	♥	‼	#	3	C	S	c	s		**i**	」	ウ	テ	モ		**i**
4	♦	¶	$	4	D	T	d	t		**f**	、	エ	ト	ヤ		**f**
5	♣	§	%	5	E	U	e	u		**t**	·	オ	ナ	ユ		**t**
6	♠	▬	&	6	F	V	f	v		**t**	ヲ	カ	ニ	ヨ		
7	•	↨	'	7	G	W	g	w			ァ	キ	ヌ	ラ		
8	◘	↑	(	8	H	X	h	x			イ	ク	ネ	リ		**C**
9	○	↓	)	9	I	Y	i	y		**C**	ゥ	ケ	ノ	ル		**C**
A	◎	→	*	:	J	Z	j	z		**o**	エ	コ	ハ	レ		**o**
B	♂	←	+	;	K	[	k	{		**d**	オ	サ	ヒ	ロ		**d**
C	♀	∟	,	<	L	\	l	|		**e**	ャ	シ	フ	ワ		**e**
D	♪	↔	-	=	M	]	m	}			ュ	ス	ヘ	ン		**s**
E	♫	▲	.	>	N	^	n	~		**s**	ョ	セ	ホ	゛		
F	☼	▼	/	?	O	_	o	Δ			ッ	ソ	マ	゜		

11. Don't be discouraged by the seemingly endless number of complex symbols used in Japanese and other Asian languages. You don't need to speak, read, or write these languages in order to work productively on software for Asian users. Obviously, the user interface design must be guided by someone familiar with the language and culture, but you as the programmer primarily need to understand and focus on the encoding and manipulation rules for Asian symbol sets.

THE ANSI CHARACTER SET

PC code pages were introduced in the early 1980s long before the emergence of Microsoft Windows, IBM OS/2 Presentation Manager, and other graphical user interfaces.[12] During that period, the typical PC had a monochrome display operating as a "glass teletype" that communicated with MS-DOS or another command-line operating system.

All Characters Addressable Mode

Despite the command-line orientation of popular PC operating systems, the PC display hardware and firmware did support an *all characters addressable* (ACA) mode. Typically the ACA mode enabled the program to treat the screen as a character array of 80 columns and 25 rows. Pioneering applications such as Lotus 1-2-3 employed this architecture to break out of the command-line environment, using the entire screen in a visually appealing manner.

As the PC became popular with less technical users, they expressed their intense dislike of the command-line interface because of its arcane abbreviations and inconsistent syntax. Many software vendors met this market need by introducing screen-oriented or form-based products.

Screen-oriented applications relied on the fact that the PC code pages included a set of line-segment characters to facilitate the drawing of rectangular frames around windows and data entry fields. You can see these characters scattered around the upper code points of CP437 and CP850 in Table 3-11 and Table 3-12, respectively. Note that the latter sacrifices some of the line segments to provide more European symbols. In Japanese CP932 (Table 3-13), all line drawing characters were moved to extension pages to provide single-byte access to the Katakana symbols.

Since MS-DOS provided little operating system support for ACA operations, application programmers handled low-level screen details by writing directly into the video memory. Later, several software vendors attempted to generalize this approach with MS-DOS extension libraries such as Curses, TopView, and WindowBoss, but no ACA windowing system achieved significant traction before Microsoft Windows and IBM OS/2 Presentation Manager supplanted them with APA mode.

---

12. I know, I know! The Apple Macintosh was a popular GUI way back in the mid-1980s. Unfortunately, this pioneer of graphical workstations, like many other trailblazers, wound up lying along the trail with arrows in its back. Interestingly, Apple shot most of the arrows at itself.

All Points Addressable Mode

Toward the end of the decade, many PCs shipped with color monitors capable of all points addressable (APA) graphics at a reasonably high resolution. In APA mode, the software controls individual pixels on the screen instead of character cells as in ACA mode. This fine-grained control enables the software to present much more attractive forms and drawings.

Inexpensive APA video hardware opened the door for graphical applications such as computer-aided design (CAD) to run on the ubiquitous PC, whereas these programs had previously been restricted to more costly workstations. The initial versions of graphical PC applications used the APA capability directly as memory-mapped video or indirectly through various graphical libraries, but this trend abated as Windows began to dominate the market.

Although the first two versions of Windows were introduced during the mid-1980s, it remained an expensive and unwieldy APA graphics solution until version 3 appeared in 1990. At that point a fortunate coincidence occurred: Windows got better, and PC hardware got cheaper.

Windows version 3 corrected many performance and user interface problems that had plagued earlier releases, and it introduced an attractive three-dimensional look. This was possible because the typical PC in 1990 included a relatively fast 286 or 386 processor, several megabytes of memory, and an APA video adaptor supporting 640 by 480 points with 256 colors each. All this was bundled into a package that cost less than $3000, often with a few popular applications thrown in.

Code Page 1252

Like most earlier PC programs, Windows version 3 used extended ASCII character sets defined as code pages. However, the line drawing characters in CP437 were no longer needed because an APA application could draw lines, boxes, and even curved figures on a point-by-point basis. Microsoft therefore replaced CP850 with an "even more universal" set called CP1252, which Table 3-14 shows. This page omits the line drawing characters, adds a few more punctuation and symbol characters, shuffles the accented letters into different code points, and leaves the eight shaded code points unassigned.

Table 3-14. Code Page 1252

	00	10	20	30	40	50	60	70	80	90	A0	B0	C0	D0	E0	F0
0	nul	▶	space	0	@	P	`	p			nbsp	°	À	Ð	à	ð
1	☺	◀	!	1	A	Q	a	q		'	¡	±	Á	Ñ	á	ñ
2	☻	↕	"	2	B	R	b	r	,	'	¢	²	Â	Ò	â	ò
3	♥	‼	#	3	C	S	c	s	ƒ	"	£	³	Ã	Ó	ã	ó
4	♦	¶	$	4	D	T	d	t	„	"	¤	´	Ä	Ô	ä	ô
5	♣	§	%	5	E	U	e	u	…	•	¥	µ	Å	Õ	å	õ
6	♠	▬	&	6	F	V	f	v	†	–	¦	¶	Æ	Ö	æ	ö
7	•	↨	'	7	G	W	g	w	‡	—	§	·	Ç	×	ç	÷
8	◘	↑	(	8	H	X	h	x	ˆ	˜	¨	¸	È	Ø	è	ø
9	○	↓	)	9	I	Y	i	y	‰	™	©	¹	É	Ù	é	ù
A	◎	→	*	:	J	Z	j	z	Š	š	ª	º	Ê	Ú	ê	ú
B	♂	←	+	;	K	[	k	{	‹	›	«	»	Ë	Û	ë	û
C	♀	∟	,	<	L	\	l	|	Œ	œ	¬	¼	Ì	Ü	ì	ü
D	♪	↔	-	=	M	]	m	}				½	Í	Ý	í	ý
E	♫	▲	.	>	N	^	n	~			®	¾	Î	Þ	î	þ
F	☼	▼	/	?	O	_	o	del		Ÿ	¯	¿	Ï	ß	ï	ÿ

ISO-8859-1

When CP1252 was being defined, the PC community had become aware of ISO's efforts to standardize ASCII-derived character sets. CP1252 therefore followed ISO-2022 guidelines by moving all important extension characters from the CR area. (See Table 3-8.) The GR area was then encoded exactly as ISO-8859-1, the Latin 1 alphabet[13] for Western European languages.

Now for a character set to be truly compliant with ISO-2022, CL and CR can't contain any graphical characters because those areas are reserved for transmission and device controls. However, PC code page designers generally use almost all of the 256 code points for display characters in order to provide the maximum number of symbols in an SBCS.

---

13. The name Latin 1 indicates that the character set contains the symbols used by a group of languages derived from Latin. This was, of course, the official language of the Roman Empire, which served as an ad hoc standards organization several years before ISO was formed.

To partially reconcile these different goals, ISO-based code pages such as CP1252 relegate seldom-used punctuation and dingbat characters to CL and CR. Even so, you must avoid sending a Windows character stream to a device that expects ISO encoding, since any CL/CR codes embedded in the stream for display purposes might have undesirable effects. In other words, it can be a serious programming mistake to blindly assume that CP1252 is identical to ISO-8859-1.

Because CP1252 became the U.S. standard, it's often called the ANSI code page. Despite this name, the character set handles not only American English but also the same Western European languages as CP850 and ISO-8859-1. Table 3-15 lists the other ISO-based code pages that cover the parts of Europe and the Middle East not handled by CP1252.

Table 3-15. Windows Code Pages

Page	ISO	Description
1250	8859-2	Latin 2 (Central Europe)
1251	8859-5	Cyrillic (Slavic)
1252	8859-1	Latin 1 (ANSI)
1253	8859-7	Greek
1254	8859-9	Latin 5 (Turkish)
1255	8859-8	Hebrew
1256	8859-6	Arabic
1257	8859-4	Scandinavia and Baltic Rim

The Limits of SBCS

After all this evolution from text-based to GUI systems and all the attempts to support multiple languages with the so-called universal code pages, we programmers wound up facing the unavoidable fact: Pure single-byte encoding can't support even the European countries and is woefully inadequate for other parts of the world. Furthermore, programmers worldwide had expressed their dislike for shifting, code page switching, and MBCS techniques. Many software projects encountered a geometric rise in development expenses when they ventured away from general-purpose SBCS pages such as CP850 and CP1252.

Clearly the next step in character set evolution would have to dramatically increase the number of code points while preserving the simplicity of these SBCS techniques. ISO took this step when it produced "the last character set standard," called ISO-10646, which is the basis of the preferred Win32 character set known as Unicode.

THE UNICODE CHARACTER SET

The plethora of standards based on ISO-646 (ASCII) and ISO-2022 (extended ASCII) did a thorough job of defining and exploring the domain of byte-oriented character sets with and without shift states (i.e., MBCS and SBCS). During the early 1990s, ISO turned its attention to wide character sets, in which symbols are encoded into numbers using more than 8 bits,[14] with each character having the same number of bits.

At the same time, Microsoft and other industry leaders began looking for a solution to the problems caused by code page switching and shifted code pages. Since they were searching for a truly universal code page, they formed a committee called the Unicode Consortium.

Fortunately, the ISO and Unicode efforts merged almost as soon as they became aware of each other in 1991. As a result, the ISO-10646 wide character standard and the universal wide character code page, called Unicode, are closely related and often thought of as identical. You can find a complete description of Unicode in *The Unicode Standard* published by Addison-Wesley. I'll cover the important programming aspects here.

The Unicode Character Spectrum

As with the other popular ISO and code page character sets, Unicode is an extended form of ASCII. Earlier we examined how the ISO standards and the various MS-DOS and Windows code pages extended ASCII from 7 bits to 8 bits, providing up to 128 additional SBCS code points. Unicode extends ASCII to 16 bits, giving us a spectrum of 65,536 code points. The standard documentation identifies each code point with the notation U+*nnnn*, in which *nnnn* is a hexadecimal number ranging from 0000 through FFFF.

The first 128 Unicode points (U+0000 through U+007F) match ISO-646, and the first 256 points (U+0000 through U+00FF) match ISO-8859-1. Therefore, if the high 9 bits of a Unicode character are zero, you can safely treat the low 7 bits as plain old ASCII. Likewise, if the high byte is zero, you can safely treat the low byte as an ANSI character. This implies that you can convert ASCII or ANSI characters to Unicode by the simple insertion of zeros. For example, the null-terminated string "Hello" is encoded as shown in Table 3-16.

---

14. ISO prefers the term *octet* to *byte,* although most writers prefer the latter. ISO adopted their terminology because *octet* means precisely 8 bits, whereas *byte* (to some people) means the smallest addressable item, which could theoretically be an amount other than 8 bits. Practically speaking, it's doubtful that any computer designer could convince the rest of the industry that a byte is any amount other than 8 bits.

Table 3-16. **"Hello" in ASCII and Unicode**

Symbol	ASCII	Unicode
H	48	0048
e	65	0065
l	6C	006C
l	6C	006C
o	6F	006F
nul	00	0000

The standard preserves the ISO-646 and ISO-8859-1 code point assignments because they are firmly entrenched in existing software and cover a large number of languages. Other symbol sets are assigned values in the Unicode spectrum according to the allocation scheme shown in Table 3-17.

Version 2.0 of The Unicode Standard assigns code points to 38,885 characters, leaving ample room for future needs. In addition, the standard specifies a technique for extending the repertoire, with an additional 1 million (actually 0x100000 or 1,048,576) symbols using *surrogate pairs*. (I'll talk more about the surrogate pair in the section titled "Extending Unicode.") Although this technique is similar to the use of nonlocking shifts in earlier standards, it eliminates most of the context problems associated with shifted character sets, as I'll explain later.

Table 3-17. **Unicode Allocation Scheme**

Start	End	Name	Description
U+0000	U+1FFF	General scripts	Symbol sets for languages with small alphabets, such as Latin, Cyrillic, and Greek
U+2000	U+2FFF	Symbols	Punctuation, dingbats, mathematical operators, and other specialized symbols
U+3000	U+33FF	CJK phonetics and symbols	Punctuation, phonetics, and special symbols for Chinese, Japanese, and Korean (CJK)
U+4E00	U+9FFF	CJK ideographs	The unified CJK ideograph set (also called Unified Han), currently containing 20,902 symbols

Start	End	Name	Description
U+AC00	U+D7A3	Hangul syllables	Korean syllabic compositions, containing 11,172 symbols
U+D800	U+DFFF	Surrogates	Used to extend Unicode with an additional 1 million symbols by juxtaposing a high and low surrogate
U+E000	U+F8FF	Private use	Employed by software providers and end users for special symbols and controls
U+F900	U+FFFF	Compatibility area and special codes	Encodings needed for compatibility with prior usage, plus special Unicode controls

Serializing Unicode Characters

If you had your thinking cap on while examining the Unicode values for "Hello" in Table 3-16, you probably wondered what happens when a Unicode string is serialized into a byte stream for transmission or storage. Since each Unicode character contains 2 bytes, we can serialize the string "Hello" in two ways:

Low byte first (little endian[15])

48 00 65 00 6C 00 6C 00 6F 00 00 00

High byte first (big endian)

00 48 00 65 00 6C 00 6C 00 6F 00 00

Which is correct? The standard clearly states that the default byte ordering is big endian unless you use little endian. In other words, "It depends...."

Actually, the Unicode Consortium and ISO wisely chose to ignore the debate over which is the "correct" byte order since both are widely used. Recognizing that most data transfer occurs between similar systems, they suggested that programmers do whatever comes naturally. So when your Microsoft Windows NT workstation talks to a Windows NT server, you don't need to worry about Unicode byte order because both systems are little endian.

---

15. Little endian means that the low-order byte is stored first in a text stream, and big endian, high-order byte first.

However, if your Windows NT workstation chats with a Unix server that is big endian, one system must do some byte swapping to process Unicode characters. (If both systems swap bytes, you're right back where you started.) In that case, *The Unicode Standard* offers the following two alternatives:

- When dissimilar systems exchange Unicode streams without using some higher-level protocol, the characters should be transferred using big endian ordering.[16] The standard calls this the *canonical byte order*. However, reliance on canonical byte order is discouraged in favor of the second technique, which is safer.

- Each Unicode stream should begin with the code U+FEFF, which the standard defines as the *byte order mark*, or the *zero-width nonbreaking space*. The code U+FFFE, which is the swapped version of U+FEFF, is permanently reserved as an unassigned code point. Therefore, if the receiver sees U+FFFE as the first code, it will know that the bytes must be swapped.

You can see the second method in action by generating a Unicode text file with the Windows NT Notepad, as shown in Figure 3-1. For this example, I used the MS Mincho font and the Windows NT Character Map utility (shown in Figure 3-2), and I selected the Save As Unicode option (shown in Figure 3-3). Then I opened the file with the Microsoft Visual C++ 6 editor to produce the hexadecimal view shown in Figure 3-4. The Visual C++ 6 editor automatically switches to the hexadecimal view when it sees that the first two bytes aren't normal ASCII characters used in C and C++ programming. If the editor were enabled for Unicode, it presumably would open a text view just as the one in Figure 3-1.

The preceding explanation leads to three rules for transferring pure Unicode text:

1. If all programs involved in Unicode data transfer use the same byte order, no special action is needed. This is the case when a program uses a file to store private Unicode text or when two Intel-based Windows NT systems exchange Unicode text.

---

16. Since Microsoft's systems are usually little endian, I assume they lost the byte order battle in the standards committee.

2.   If you want to publish a plain text file so that a variety of systems can read it, Unicode provides a clever technique for marking byte order that detects when the text stream requires byte swapping— simply begin the file with the character U+FEFF.

3.   For more complex storage and transmission situations, a higher-level protocol is usually employed because Unicode text is interspersed with other types of data. Of course, each embedded Unicode string can begin with U+FEFF to cause byte swapping when necessary; otherwise, the need for swapping can be determined from other information in the data set.

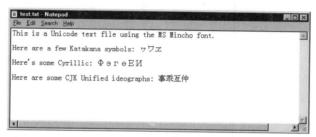

Figure 3-1. *Unicode text in Notepad.*

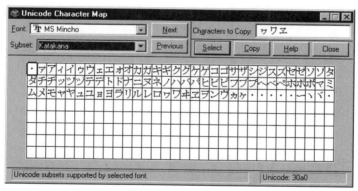

Figure 3-2. *Unicode character map utility.*

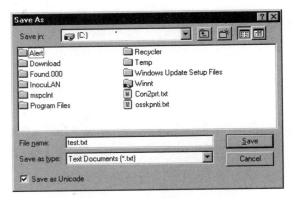

Figure 3-3. *Saving a Unicode text file.*

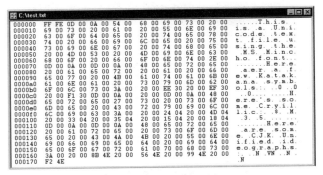

Figure 3-4. *Unicode file in hexadecimal.*

Unicode Transformation Formats

Despite its clever technique for handling byte-ordering issues, Unicode might not be the most efficient way to store and transmit text, especially in the Americas and many parts of Europe. Since programs serving these locations can often get by with 256 or even 128 characters, much of the Unicode spectrum is unused. In other words, the high byte of most characters is zero. Even in countries that require double-byte encoding, such as Japan, many documents contain a large number of characters from the 7-bit and 8-bit sets.

Programmers who are interested in minimizing storage consumption and maximizing transmission throughput often convert between Unicode and MBCS. This conversion occurs at the "edges" of the program, just before text is written or sent and just after text is read or received. Thus the programmer has the convenience of using Unicode internally and the efficiency of MBCS for storage and transmission.

The question, though, is which character set to use for compressing Unicode because the typical MBCS does not contain code points for all Unicode characters. The Unicode Consortium recognized this problem and defined two multibyte encodings that can handle all Unicode characters. This type of encoding is called a Unicode Transformation Format (UTF), and the two standard variations are UTF-7 and UTF-8.

UTF-7 is intended for use with legacy systems that store and transmit 7-bit values. These systems originated in the ASCII days and include important Internet protocols such as Multipurpose Internet Mail Extensions (MIME). Since UTF-7 employs 7-bit encoding, it isn't really a Unicode compression format; indeed, UTF-7 usually requires more bytes than the equivalent Unicode representation, even for text that is primarily ASCII.

On the other hand, UTF-8 is a compression format for text that contains ASCII and other characters below U+0800. This part of the Unicode spectrum accounts for most of the symbols used by American, European, and Mid-Eastern languages. UTF-8 isn't a good choice if the text has a preponderance of characters above U+07FF because it expands these code points to 3 bytes. UTF-8 is particularly popular on Unix systems and was, in fact, originally defined by a Unix standards group called X/Open.

The algorithms for converting between Unicode and UTF-7 or UTF-8 are well documented in *The Unicode Standard*, so I won't repeat that information here. Windows NT 4 and Windows 2000 include these algorithms in the API functions named *WideCharToMultiByte* and *MultiByteToWideChar*, which we'll explore in Chapter 8.

Extending Unicode

It probably seems strange that Unicode has an extension mechanism. After all, doesn't it include all the symbol sets needed throughout the world? Well, the folks who defined Unicode and ISO-10646 had experienced the pain of developing software that had to use clunky techniques such as locking shifts and switched code pages. They therefore decided to invent an extension technique that is gentle on programmers.

Unicode allocates the codes from U+D800 through U+DBFF as a set of *high surrogates* and the codes from U+DC00 through U+DFFF as a set of *low surrogates*. The term "surrogate" means that these codes aren't normal 16-bit displayable Unicode characters but are substitutes or stand-ins, just like surrogate mothers. An extension character consists of a high surrogate followed by a low surrogate, with the surrogate pair treated as an atomic unit. Since each surrogate range contains 1024 code points, the standard allows for 1,048,576 extension characters.

A high or low surrogate can never appear by itself, and the high surrogate must always precede the low one with no intervening codes. This means that a program can detect an extension character by simple inspection for a high or low surrogate, and then it has to move forward or backward by only one step to retrieve the other surrogate half. This reduces the context window to three Unicode values and is considerably easier than locking shift states, in which the context can extend over many code values.

At this point, neither ISO nor the Unicode Consortium has assigned any characters to this extension space. Nonetheless, archaeologists and antiquarians now have a way to computerize the symbol sets of the Egyptians and other ancient terran civilizations. Furthermore, it's nice to know that Unicode can handle the symbol sets of alien civilizations we might discover as we, in the words of Star Trek's Captain Picard, "boldly go where no one has gone before."

SUMMARY

The people forming a particular cultural group communicate by means of a symbol set. When two people from different cultures want to communicate, each must understand the other's symbol set, or they must share a common repertoire of symbols.

The past 150 years saw the invention of digital devices such as the telegraph, teleprinter, and computer, all of which enabled people to communicate efficiently across long distances. These devices required that human language symbols be converted to numeric form, which led to the development of character sets. In other words, a character set is a numeric mapping of one or more symbol sets.

Character sets evolved from small collections of a few dozen symbols (such as Morse Code and Baudot Code), to sets containing a hundred or more symbols (such as ASCII and extended ASCII), to Unicode and its thousands of symbols.

Two factors caused this evolution: the spread of digital communication throughout the world and the increase in international trade. The former compelled character set designers to deal with languages requiring thousands of symbols, such as Chinese, Japanese, and Korean. The latter required designers to define composite character sets that handled more than one symbol set simultaneously.

As with most lengthy technological evolutions, many stages were imperfect because of the limitations of contemporary technology. Thus, Morse Code had a limited symbol repertoire using variable bit encoding to accommodate the human hand that operated the telegraph key. Although computers extended the earlier encodings of Morse and Baudot, they were forced to use imperfect 7-bit and 8-bit character sets for many years because memory, processor cycles, and bandwidth were too expensive. Dramatic improvements in computer price/performance ratios have finally made wide character sets such as Unicode feasible.

Is Unicode the final code page, the Holy Grail of character set standards? Time will tell, but at this point it's clear that Unicode is rapidly gaining acceptance among operating system designers, software toolmakers, and application programmers. It's the native character set of Windows NT, which is arguably becoming the standard workstation and server operating system. It fits comfortably with C, C++, Java, and other popular programming languages. As pure SBCS/MBCS systems such as Windows 3.x and hybrids such as Windows 95 and Windows 98 fade, application programmers will be free to develop pure Unicode software. Undoubtedly its use will spread, and it will be with us for many years.

But just in case 16-bit characters are too limiting, ISO-10646 treats Unicode as a subset of a larger 32-bit character set.

Chapter 4

Character Sets in Standard C and C++

Because C and UNIX originated in Bell Telephone Laboratories (my employer during the 1970s), they were slow to reflect the demands of countries other than the United States. As part of the AT&T-regulated monopoly, Bell Labs had little contact with products and markets outside North America at that time. As a result, we remained blissfully ignorant of linguistic and cultural differences, which made our favorite programming language and operating system difficult to use in other countries.[1]

Of course, C and UNIX did have some presence in Europe because AT&T routinely licensed them to universities for education and research purposes,

---

1. During this same period, ITT and other telephone software developers were cooperating to design an international telephone programming language called CHILL (for Consultative Committee on International Telephone and Telegraphy (CCITT) High Level Language). Although some within Bell Labs were aware of this effort and urged the adoption of CHILL, Bell Labs project managers successfully resisted because they had already invested heavily in C and C++. Later there was similar pressure to consider the use of ADA, another language developed with international usage in mind, but once again the momentum of C and C++ was unstoppable.

and they became immensely popular in academic circles. The resulting open discussions led some Europeans to think about internationalizing these useful American tools, and these ideas eventually found their way into the ANSI and, subsequently, the ISO committees considering C, C++, and UNIX standards.

By the time AT&T was deregulated in 1984 and had begun promoting UNIX as a commercial operating system, C had become quite popular outside Bell Labs because it provided an efficient way to program desktop systems. As the personal computer became ubiquitous, C programmers throughout the world created ad hoc solutions for the language's chauvinism.

Most of these solutions appeared in the form of library functions, since the compilers themselves were firmly controlled by U.S. companies such as Microsoft, Borland, and Lattice. Often a solution itself was chauvinistic and thus useful only within a particular locale or on a particular hardware platform. For instance, the Japanese publishers of Lattice C enhanced the library to work with the JIS (Japanese Industry Standard) character set as required by the Japanese software market. With a little extra effort, these additions could have been generalized to work with other double-byte character set (DBCS) locales.

This market-driven evolution presented a challenge to the ISO committee when they began considering international features. The committee received many suggestions from language experts and academics throughout the world, but their ability to accept this useful input was tempered by the current needs and limitations of commercial compiler vendors and programmers.

Perhaps if the committee had been given free reign, they would have moved the C language toward a more general solution, such as Unicode. Instead, they had to devise language and library standards that would allow future migration to a wide character set while retaining compatibility with existing single-byte character set (SBCS) and multibyte character set (MBCS) environments. This was a difficult compromise and an example of how frustrating it can be to participate in a standardization effort.

Nonetheless, the C and C++ standards now have pretty good support for international character sets through orthogonal families of keywords, functions, and classes. However, because these language and library features do not hide character width issues, converting from one environment to another, such as SBCS to WCS, is somewhat messy and requires extensive use of conditional compilation (such as *#ifdef* statements). Microsoft Visual C++ augments the standard language and library so that you can easily write code that will work with any character width.

INTERNATIONALIZING C AND C++

Since C and C++ were invented by U.S. programmers, these languages use American English keywords such as *for*, *if*, and *while*. This leads to a fundamental question regarding internationalization: Should the keywords be localized so that each programmer writes C and C++ in his or her native language? This same question applies to the function names and other symbols in the standard library: Should they be translated for different programming locales?

Furthermore, C and C++ operator and punctuation characters are derivatives of ASCII, the 7-bit code that was popular during the 1960s when C originated. Although ASCII was standardized in ISO-646, the base portion of that standard doesn't include all the symbols routinely used in C and C++. That is, programmers need some of the American English characters from ISO-646-US that are often replaced in other locales. How can other locales deal with the American English characters required by C and C++?

Another character set issue arises when a programmer wants to embed quoted text that contains non-ASCII characters: Should the programming language permit this, or should the programmer be required to write the actual numeric codes for the non-ASCII characters? What is the syntax for these literals using SBCS, MBCS, and WCS coding techniques?

And finally the ANSI and ISO committees had to deal with character sign extension: Should the traditional signed character type be changed to unsigned in order to work with extended ASCII?

Before improving the standard library to handle a broader range of character sets at run time, the ANSI and ISO committees had to wrestle with these fundamental compile-time questions. Fortunately, they made reasonable choices that enabled both languages to grow in popularity throughout the world, and now C and C++ programmers handle most of the "heavy lifting" in software.

Localized Keywords? Just Say "No!"

The standards committees concluded that keywords should not be localized for many sound reasons, of which I have three favorites. First, localizing keywords would require major changes or additions to existing compilers and related tools, expensive work that the compiler vendors were reluctant to undertake. Second, software development, testing, and distribution would become extremely complicated in multinational projects that intermingle source code from several locales. Third, localized versions of C and C++ might isolate programmers and stifle the free exchange of ideas and algorithms that made C and C++ so popular and useful.

These and other arguments outweighed the arguments of supporters of localized keywords, who made a questionable case for programming and political convenience. Supposedly, programmers and politicians would support the language more if it were localized, especially in countries concerned about "polluting" their native language with Americanisms.

Fortunately, the standards committees operate like medical practitioners, whose primary rule is, "First, do no harm." Translated into programming terms, the rule is, "First, break no existing code." Thus the committees correctly concluded that C and C++ were too firmly entrenched in programming communities worldwide to introduce a major disruption with localized keywords. They extended this decision to the standard library, which was derived from versions that had existed for many years in Unix, MS-DOS, and other popular operating systems developed in the United States.

So, for better or worse, C and C++ programmers must know enough American English to deal with the keywords and library symbols. Comments can, of course, be written in any language.[2]

Localized Punctuation? Just Say "Trigraphs!"

Despite the decision to leave C and C++ keywords in American English, the liberal use of USASCII for C and C++ punctuation was a major sore point with programmers in other countries. Since their keyboards often didn't contain characters such as [and], programmers outside the United States had to either acquire a USASCII keyboard or resort to awkward and error-prone typing techniques.

The standards committees might have solved this problem by finding a suitable set of characters common to all keyboards. However, this proved to be impossible because the ISO-646 base set didn't fill the punctuation needs of C and C++, and the committees didn't have the clout to define a "programmer's keyboard" with the required additional characters. Also, the guiding principle ("First, break no code!") mandated that the punctuation solution must be backward compatible with existing source code.

After much discussion, the committees adopted a scheme for representing each troublesome punctuation symbol with a sequence of three ISO-646 characters (called a *trigraph*), as shown in Table 4-1. Thus any programmer whose keyboard contained the ISO-646 base set could type C and C++ source code by using trigraphs for the missing American English characters.

Table 4-1. **C and C++ Trigraphs**

Punctuation	*Trigraph*	*Punctuation*	*Trigraph*
#	??=	|	??!
[	??(	^	??'
]	??)	\	??/
{	??<	~	??-
}	??>		

2. I suppose you could use *#define* statements to localize most of the keywords. Pascal programmers forced to work in C sometimes use this technique to replace left and right braces with *begin* and *end*, respectively.

Each trigraph is converted to the appropriate punctuation character early in the compilation process. The double question mark (??) was chosen because it's unlikely to occur frequently in normal text. Where this combination does occur, you can use the backslash character (\) or the trigraph for the backslash character (??/) to suppress the conversion. For example, suppose you want to create this embedded text string:

```
"(What do you want??)"
```

Normally trigraph conversion converts this string to

```
"(What do you want]"
```

To suppress the conversion, place a backslash or its trigraph in front of the second question mark in the following ways:

```
"(What do you want?\?)"
"(What do you want???/?)"
```

Although trigraphs solve the keyboard problem, they haven't gained much favor among programmers, probably because they are just as cumbersome as other techniques, such as using the Alt and numeric keys to enter the actual character codes. Nonetheless, trigraphs are implemented in every standard C and C++ compiler, so you must be wary of unintended conversions when using text literals that resemble trigraphs.[3]

The Mysterious ISO646.h Header File

To supplement the compiler's trigraph feature, the C committee defined a header file named ISO646.h containing pseudo-keywords for various operators, as shown in Table 4-2. Later the C++ committee added these symbols to the language as real keywords, eliminating the need for the header file.

Apparently both committees believed that programmers would use the keywords instead of the actual operators to insulate their code from source character set (SCS) differences. So in an environment where the SCS isn't ISO-646 (ASCII), the C header file or C++ compiler can be changed to employ the proper trigraphs or local character codes, or both. For instance, these two statements are equivalent:

```
if((a != b) || (c == d)) x = 3;
if((a not_eq b) or (c == d)) x = 3;
```

Perhaps this seemed like a good idea at the time, but I don't know of any C programmer who actually uses the header file, and I haven't met any C++

---

3. Trigraph conversion occurs only at compile time and has no effect on the text that is generated and manipulated at run time.

Table 4-2. **Keywords Defined in ISO646.h**

Keyword	Operator	Keyword	Operator
and	&&	not_eq	!=
and_eq	&=	or	||
bitand	&	or_eq	|=
bitor	|	xor	^
compl	~	xor_eq	^=
not	!		

programmer who knows that the symbols defined in the header file are valid C++ keywords. C++ authority P. J. Plauger had this to say about ISO646.h: "I can imagine only the rarest of circumstances under which you might wish to include this header anyway." [4]

Extended ASCII? Just Say "Code Pages!"

Programmers throughout the world often want to enter text literals containing characters specific to their locales. For instance, a program that works with British and Japanese currency amounts might include the following *printf* statements:

```
British:   printf("The price is £%d.\n", i);
Japanese:  printf("The price is ¥%d.\n", i);
```

The currency symbols for British pounds (£) and Japanese yen (¥) are not in the USASCII character set, but they are in CP850 as code points 156 (0x9C) and 190 (0xBE), respectively. Since the language allows any 8-bit code to be placed in a character literal using an escape sequence, these statements can be written with hexadecimal escapes as:

```
British:   printf("The price is \x9c%d.\n", i);
Japanese:  printf("The price is \xbe%d.\n", i);
```

In other words, if you know that the execution environment supports a richer character set than the compilation environment, you can use hexadecimal escape sequences to insert non-ASCII characters into literals. Although this approach is cumbersome, international programmers have used it for years.

When the standards committees began to examine this issue, the text editors used by many programmers, especially on the PC, had evolved to the

---

4. Plauger, page 36.

point where they readily supported extended ASCII code pages. In addition, the typical commercial compiler was now tightly coupled with an editor to facilitate source-level debugging, so programmers routinely placed extended ASCII in text literals. The committees simply had to ratify this common practice.

The committees did this by specifying that compilers must distinguish between the *source character set* (SCS) and the *execution character set* (ECS). The former is the code page used by the text editor and compiler, while the latter is the page used by the run-time system. The standard doesn't require that they be the same, although programming is easiest if the SCS is identical to or a subset of the ECS.

For instance, an ASCII editor and compiler can produce programs for use with any ASCII-based code page, such as CP437 or CP850, although the programmer will have to use escape sequences for extended characters such as the currency symbols in the previous examples. To avoid the need for escape sequences in text literals, some editors use CP850 or another "universal character set." However, if the SCS is CP850 and the ECS is CP437, the programmer can readily enter text literals that can't be faithfully displayed because CP850 isn't a subset of CP437.

When the C standard emerged in the late 1980s, CP850 represented the state of the art in international character sets. Therefore, IBM, Microsoft, and other major players urged its adoption as the "multilingual ASCII character set" for C (and later C++) programming. As a result, many compiler vendors used CP850 as a springboard to international programming.

Visual C++ and most other Microsoft Windows development environments now use CP850's successor, the ANSI character set, which is practically the same as CP1252 and ISO-8859-1. Perhaps at some point Microsoft will offer a Unicode editor for the convenience of programmers who regularly work with wide characters.

Wide Characters? Give 'em L!

Considering that C and C++ originated in the single-byte (actually 7-bit) ASCII world, you would expect major language changes to support wide character sets such as Unicode. The standards committees (especially C++) could have done more in this area. For instance, they could have added some operators to convert between wide and narrow characters. Also, it would be nice to have a variation of the *sizeof* operator that returns the number of characters instead of the number of bytes.

After examining these and other possible improvements, the committees decided to place most wide character support in the standard library instead of making major changes to the C and C++ languages. This decision was based on the fact that compiler changes are hard, while library changes are relatively easy.

However, one language change was unavoidable because programmers needed a convenient way to create text literals using wide characters. Although a programmer can produce wide text by concatenating hexadecimal values to create arrays of unsigned short integers, this was viewed as awkward and error prone. Therefore, the committees introduced the *L* modifier for text literals. Here are some examples:

```
unsigned short WideChar = L'a';            // 'a' as a wide character
unsigned short WideText[] = L"abc\x03a9";  // "abcΩ" as a wide string
```

When you use the *L* prefix, the literal text still comes from the source character set, which is usually a single-byte ASCII derivative. To convert the literal text to wide characters, the compiler merely inserts a 0 byte next to each source character. If you want to include characters with code points greater than 255, you must use an escape sequence with the Unicode value as shown earlier to produce the correct 16-bit value. In the previous example, the Greek omega (Ω) has the Unicode value 0x03a9.

At some point, not too far off, I hope, editors and compilers will become smart enough to let us enter Unicode directly into wide character literals. Of course, if you are engaging in safe international programming, your source code shouldn't contain any text literals. All text strings should be stored in a separate database where they can be localized by a translator who will probably be able to manage them with a Unicode editor.

Multibyte Characters? No Problem (Maybe)!

Asian programmers were using C with multibyte character sets for some time before the C standards committee existed. Because the MBCS community generally had to use existing ASCII compilers, they made a crucial compatibility decision: They reserved the null byte for use as a string terminator. In other words, the popular multibyte code pages guarantee that a null byte will never appear within a multibyte character. Because of this decision, programmers can construct properly terminated multibyte text strings using escape sequences or an MBCS editor. Furthermore, as you'll see later, many ASCII string functions in the standard library work correctly with MBCS strings. Given this insight, the committee breathed a sigh of relief and claimed that the standard C compiler would support any MBCS using null terminators.

This doesn't imply that MBCS programming is a slam dunk. In fact, it's messy and error prone because you can't employ the simple indexing and pointer manipulation techniques that work well with SBCS and WCS text, in which each character has the same size. To understand this, let's explore multi-byte programming in more detail.

Recall from earlier chapters that each MBCS uses a variable number of bytes to encode its characters. For instance, in the commercial Japanese character set (CP932) each character requires 1 or 2 bytes, while a full set of traditional Chinese ideographs requires an MBCS with characters up to 3 bytes long.

It's illuminating to compare the C or C++ syntax and byte layout for an MBCS string and its Unicode equivalent. Multibyte text literals use the same syntax as SBCS quoted text, but unless you have a compatible MBCS editor, you must use escape sequences for characters with more than one byte. For instance, here is the string *"abc 唖 def"* using the multibyte and the Unicode syntax with ASCII as the SCS:

```
char sMulti[] = "abc\x88\xA0" "def";      // Multibyte string
wchar_t sWide[] = L"abc\x5516" L"def";     // Unicode string
```

The multibyte form assumes that CP932 will be active when the program executes, so the 唖 ideograph is encoded with 0x88 as the lead byte and 0xA0 as the second byte.[5] The same symbol has the Unicode value 0x5516. In both cases, the trailing *"def"* substring must use concatenation syntax; otherwise, the compiler will attempt to process it as part of the hexadecimal escape sequence. This isn't necessary if the trailing substring doesn't begin with a hexadecimal digit character.

The MBCS string requires 9 bytes, while Unicode uses 16, as shown below with the appropriate hexadecimal value given for each byte. This example illustrates two important differences between MBCS and WCS.

MBCS String *"abc 唖 def"* (CP932)

61	62	63	88	A0	64	65	66	00

Unicode String *"abc 唖 def"*

61	00	62	00	63	00	16	55	64	00	65	00	66	00	00	00

First, Unicode strings that contain a lot of ASCII or extended ASCII characters are considerably larger than their MBCS counterparts, but the difference disappears for strings containing only ideographs. Thus if you are starting a new project that will process mostly Asian ideographs and if you aren't constrained to MBCS by legacy or platform issues, Unicode will simplify the programming with no significant storage or transmission burden.

---

5. See Kano, Appendix G, for CP932 and the Unicode equivalents. The lead byte refers to the byte value that is the first half of a double-byte character; the second byte (also known as the trail byte) refers to the second half of a double-byte character.

Second, MBCS strings must be processed bytewise, so it's dangerous to use integer semantics in your software. For instance, it isn't proper to say that the ideograph ? has the code 0x88A0 in CP932, but you should say that it has the byte sequence (0x88, 0xA0). To see why this is important, consider the statements in Listing 4-1.

```
char sCorrect[] = "\x88\xA0";   // Correct multibyte string
char sWrong[] = "\x88A0";       // Compilation error (Constant is
                                //    too large.)

union                           // Be careful with MBCS byte ordering!
    {
    char bytes[4];
    unsigned short words[2];
    } sTricky;
sTricky.words[1] = 0;           // Terminator is OK for MBCS and WCS.

// Create one-character Unicode string through union.
sTricky.words[0] = 0x5516;      // OK on all processors
sTricky.bytes[0] = 0x16;        // Wrong byte order on some processors
sTricky.bytes[1] = 0x55;
sTricky.bytes[0] = 0x55;        // Wrong byte order on other processors
sTricky.bytes[1] = 0x16;

// Create one-character MBCS string through union.
sTricky.words[0] = 0x88A0;      // Wrong byte order on some processors
sTricky.words[0] = 0xA088;      // Wrong byte order on other processors
sTricky.bytes[0] = 0x88;        // OK on all processors
sTricky.bytes[1] = 0xA0;
```

Listing 4-1. *Byte order problems in MBCS and WCS.*

If you study the code in the previous listing carefully, you'll see why you should never use integer semantics with multibyte characters and you should always use them with Unicode. It's basically an issue of byte ordering. Different processors place bytes in different order. Most Intel processors, for instance, place the low-order byte at the lower address, while most Motorola processors place the high-order byte first. When processing MBCS text one byte at a time, the lead byte must always appear before (at a lower address than) the trailing byte or bytes. On the other hand, Unicode text is processed in 2-byte chunks, and the bytes must be arranged in storage so that the proper code values are formed.

Unsigned Characters? Dealer's Choice!

C and C++ traditionally treat the *char* type as a signed integer ranging from −128 through +127. Since most processors prefer to work with integers, the compiler typically promotes *char* to *int* by extending the sign bit. This works fine with 7-bit characters where the values are always positive or 0, but it presents problems with ASCII derivatives that use code points from 128 through 255. When these upper code points are converted to negative integers, some algorithms get confused, as shown in Listing 4-2.

```
// Check whether the argument is a control character.
bool IsControlChar(char x)
{
    if(x < ' ') return true;
    return false;
}
```

Listing 4-2. *Function with ASCII dependencies.*

IsControlChar should test whether its argument, a signed character, is in the ISO-646 control group consisting of the code points from 0 through 31. Since the space character is at code point 32, just above the control group, the function returns *true* if its argument is below that point.

This is a time-honored ASCII technique, but it fails if a program calls the function with a code point above 127. In most environments, the code point gets converted into an integer with a negative value, which is certainly less than the space character. Therefore, the function reports that all extended ASCII code points look like control characters.

IsControlChar would be more robust if it used an unsigned character argument or more thoroughly tested the signed character. Listing 4-3 shows both techniques.

If you examine your conscience, you'll probably have to confess to writing sloppy, sign-insensitive code at some point in your programming career. Repentance is not enough to correct this sin. You must revisit those algorithms and make amends. What a humbling experience!

```
// Use an unsigned character argument to suppress sign extension.
// Note that callers can still use signed characters.
bool IsControlChar(unsigned char x)
    {
    if(x < ' ') return true;
    return false;
    }

// Do a more thorough test of the signed character.
bool IsControlChar(char x)
    {
    if((x >= 0) && (x <= 31)) return true;
    return false;
    }
```

Listing 4-3. *Improved function for extended ASCII.*

The standards committee faced a difficult choice here. If they mandated that the *char* data type would be treated as an unsigned integer, sign extension problems would be eliminated and existing 7-bit ASCII programs would work with extended ASCII. However, many programmers also use the *char* type as a small integer, especially in embedded systems that employ limited microprocessors that don't promote *char* to *int*. Those programs would probably break if signed characters suddenly became unsigned.

What to do, what to do? In true committee fashion, they decided to punt the issue to the compiler vendors. The standard doesn't specify whether *char* is signed or unsigned. Clearly it must be one or the other, but each vendor can choose the setting that makes the most sense in the target environment.

The standard header file limits.h contains two *#define* statements that define the symbols *CHAR_MIN* and *CHAR_MAX*, which give the minimum and maximum values for a character.[6] You can determine if your development system uses signed characters by checking whether *CHAR_MIN* is less than zero.

Compilers usually provide some kind of option for changing the default setting. Visual C++ defaults to signed characters unless the */J* option is present. If you specify the */J* option, the compiler defines the symbol *_CHAR_UNSIGNED*, which is used in limits.h to set the appropriate character range.

---

6. The limits.h header file is a treasure trove of information about the execution environment. It defines symbols, giving the usable ranges of the various data types. You should use these symbols in all your range checking logic.

INTERNATIONALIZING THE C AND C++ LIBRARIES

Even though the standards committees had long discussions about international character set features in C and C++, the actual compiler changes were quite small. The difficult work was relegated to the libraries, where most text manipulations actually occur. For instance, neither language can perform a simple string copy, so you can't compile this code:

```
char A[] = "xyz";       // Source string
char B[4];              // Destination string buffer
B = A;                  // ERROR: Array assignment is not supported.
```

Since C strings are just character arrays and since the language doesn't allow array assignment, C programmers generally use a library function such as *strcpy*, and C++ programmers often employ a string class with an overloaded assignment operator, resulting in the code shown in Listing 4-4.

```
// C PROGRAMMING
#include <string.h>       // Standard C header file
char A[] = "xyz";         // Source string
char B[4];                // Destination string buffer
strcpy(B, A);             // Copy A to B

// C++ PROGRAMMING
#include <string>          // Standard C++ header file (no .h extension)
using namespace std;       // Standard C++ namespace
string A("xyz");           // Source string object
string B;                  // Destination string object
B = A;                     // String class has overloaded assignment
                           //   operator.
```

Listing 4-4. *Copying Strings in C and C++.*

Of course, both examples will work in C++ because it's a superset of C and includes the standard C library. Notice that standard C++ header files don't have the traditional .h extension, so these two code snippets are including different header files. Also notice that the standard C++ libraries are in the *std* namespace.[7]

---

7. If you want to use C library functions within a C++ program and limit those functions to the *std* namespace, use the traditional header file with a C prefix and no extension. For instance, to include the symbols in string.h with the *std* namespace, use this statement:

```
#include <cstring>
```

Extended ASCII Issues

Since extended ASCII character sets such as CP850 use single-byte encoding, it's reasonable to assume that they are fully compatible with the standard string functions—as long as the library is carefully written to avoid sign extension problems. This assumption is valid except for functions that compare characters or convert between uppercase and lowercase.

Traditional ASCII algorithms assume an American English alphabet with 26 uppercase letters occupying code points 0x41 through 0x5A and 26 lowercase letters occupying 0x61 through 0x7A. Given this definition, it's easy to write collation and case conversion algorithms. To collate two characters in ascending sequence, simply compare the code points and place the lower value first. To convert from uppercase to lowercase, check if the character value is in the range from 0x41 to 0x5A, and if it is, add 0x20. To convert lowercase to uppercase, check if the character value is in the range from 0x61 to 0x7A, and if it is, subtract 0x20.

Now what happens if you are using an ASCII comparison algorithm with CP850, and you want to arrange the sequence AEIOUÄËÖ in the proper order? Since the characters in the ÄËÖ substring have code points above 0x7F, the ASCII sorting algorithm places them after the other characters in the string. However, the European countries that use these extended ASCII characters usually want the string to be sorted as AÄEËIOÖU. Similarly, the *isupper* function will report that Ä isn't an uppercase character even though most Europeans would disagree.

These examples indicate that international programs can't contain built-in assumptions about character encoding. Unfortunately, ASCII algorithms were endemic to traditional library functions such as *strcmp*, *isupper*, *islower*, *toupper*, and *tolower*. Furthermore, this ASCII disease infected many existing programs that used these functions.

Before the C committee began their work, European programmers had invented the *locale database* as a means to eliminate ASCII dependencies from the library. By specifying the current locale, a European programmer could adjust the behavior of text-oriented functions such as *isupper* to work correctly with extended ASCII character sets. The next two chapters show how this approach was improved by the C and C++ committees.

Wide Characters in C

Now let's consider a modification to the C code in the preceding example so that it will handle Unicode characters. First change the *char* data type to *unsigned short*, and then use an *L* modifier on the string literal to produce wide characters. When calling *strcpy*, you'll also have to cast the *A* and *B* arguments into *char* pointers, resulting in the code shown in Listing 4-5.

```
// C PROGRAMMING
#include <string.h>          // Standard C header file
unsigned short A[] = L"xyz";  // Source string
unsigned short B[4];          // Destination string buffer
strcpy((char*)B,(char*)A);    // Copy A to B, using nasty casting.
```

Listing 4-5. *Incorrect casting of wide characters to narrow characters.*

This programming style is definitely *not recommended* because it uses casting to override the compiler's type checking. Nonetheless, many C programmers still code this way to suppress compiler error messages[8]—which, in this case, is a serious mistake.

How does *strcpy* behave if we are dumb enough to use this code? It fails miserably! On an Intel processor, where the low-order byte comes first, the literal *L"xyz"* is stored in the following sequence, with consecutive byte addresses read from left to right:

     x   0   y   0   z   0   0   0

Since *strcpy* looks at each byte as a character and stops at the first null byte, the destination will contain the following sequence, in which *???* indicates the bytes that aren't changed by the *strcpy* function:

     x   0   ???   ???   ???   ???   ???   ???

This isn't a faithful copy of the source and isn't even a valid wide character string of length one because the third and fourth bytes don't necessarily contain a null terminator.

Clearly, *strcpy* and the other string functions in the standard C library can't handle wide characters.[9] Therefore the standards committees defined a parallel set of functions for this purpose. Listing 4-6 shows the wide character version of the preceding C example.

```
// C PROGRAMMING
#include <wchar.h>       // Wide character functions
wchar_t A[] = L"xyz";    // Source string
wchar_t B[4];            // Destination string buffer
wcscpy(B, A);            // Copy A to B.
```

Listing 4-6. *Copying wide character strings in C.*

---

8. Some C++ experts argue that casting should be severely curtailed or even eliminated from the language because it has been a major source of bugs in C programs. Of course, the committees could not excise this feature without breaking a lot of existing C code, so they came up with safer casting operators such as *dynamic_cast* and discouraged (in their original words, deprecated) the traditional style of spoofing the compiler.

9. The *memcpy* function handles Unicode characters correctly, because it simply moves the number of bytes you specify without looking for a null terminator.

The *wchar_t* data type is defined in the C header files as an unsigned short,[10] and the *wcscpy* string function is the wide character version of *strcpy*. In general, every traditional string function beginning with *str* has a wide character counterpart beginning with *wcs*. Notice that the new functions will work no matter which WCS is being used, as long as the string terminator is a *wchar_t* value of 0.

Wide Characters in C++

The C++ *string* class is safer than *strcpy* because the compiler generates all kinds of warnings and errors if you try to force the *string* class to handle wide characters. Sure, a clever programmer can employ casting to fool a *string* object, but it will be a lot harder to do than with *strcpy* and the result will be even worse because the code will probably commit access violations at run time.

So instead of trying to force the *string* class to perform unnatural acts, you need a similar class that knows how to handle wide characters. The standards committees invented just such a beast and called it *wstring*. Listing 4-7 shows a version of the preceding C++ example using the "wide string" class.

```
// C++ PROGRAMMING
#include <string>          // Standard C++ header file (no .h extension)
using namespace std;       // Standard C++ namespace
wstring A(L"xyz");         // Source string object
wstring B;                 // Destination string object
B = A;                     // String class has overloaded assignment
                           //   operator.
```

Listing 4-7. *Copying wide character strings in C++.*

The standard C++ library also provides wide character versions of other text-oriented classes, such as those involved with stream I/O. For instance, *istream* and *ostream* are available in wide character versions named *wistream* and *wostream*.

Multibyte Characters in C

It was relatively easy to upgrade the standard C library for wide characters because the new functions were simply clones of traditional ASCII services (such

---

10. The C and C++ committees should receive the Ugly Symbol Award for forcing us to write names such as *wchar_t* and *size_t* using all lowercase letters and underscores. I prefer a simpler symbol such as *wchar* or a more descriptive one such as *WideChar*. I guess I'm just biased against underscores because they're hard for me to type and they tend to disappear from documents and slides.

as *strcpy*) with the added locale database features. MBCS support was more challenging for several reasons, as described in the following subsections.

How Long Is an MBCS Character?

In an SBCS or WCS environment, each character uses the same number of bytes,[11] making it easy to access strings with simple pointer and index operations, as shown in Listing 4-8.

```
#ifdef _WCS            // You must define _WCS for wide characters.
wchar_t text[100];     // 100 wide characters
wchar_t* p;            // Wide character pointer
#else
char text[100];        // 100 narrow characters
char* p;               // Narrow character pointer
#endif

// Scan string by index.
for(i = 0; text[i]; i++) ProcessCharacter(text[i]);

// Scan string by pointer.
for(p = text; *p; p++) ProcessCharacter(*p);
```

Listing 4-8. *SBCS and WCS string access.*

It's much more difficult to work with MBCS strings because you must inspect each character to determine its length. Furthermore, the inspection algorithm depends on the particular character set or code page in use, which is usually determined by the locale.

The C standards committee recognized this difficulty and introduced the *mblen* function as a partial solution. This function accepts a *char* pointer and returns the number of bytes in that character. Thus, programmers can support MBCS environments by rewriting their text manipulation logic to use *mblen*—which is hardly a trivial undertaking.

The call to the *ProcessCharacter* function in Listing 4-8 illustrates another MBCS problem. Presumably this function is defined to take an argument of the *char* type for SBCS or the *wchar_t* type for WCS. Which data type should it use for MBCS? Clearly, *char* is inadequate and *wchar_t* is inappropriate. The general answer is that MBCS functions must use a pointer for an argument no matter

---

11. The standard allows a WCS to use any number of bytes as long as every character in a string has the same length. It's doubtful that we'll ever see WCS lengths other than 2 and 4.

whether the argument represents a string or a single character. Similarly, the return type for MBCS functions can't be character values but must be pointers.[12]

How Long Is an MBCS String?

Since an MBCS string can contain characters of various lengths, you can't use *strlen* to count the number of characters. When you need to know the length in bytes (in other words, the *physical length*), *strlen* is appropriate. However, when you need to know the number of characters in an MBCS string (the *logical length*), *strlen* is inadequate. To make matters worse, there is no simple algorithm for computing one length given the other.

The C committee couldn't redefine *strlen* to return a character count because it's commonly used in memory allocation logic where the physical length is essential. Unfortunately, the committee chose not to introduce a new function to measure the logical length of an MBCS string. You can write one yourself using *mblen*, but many commercial compilers have extended the standard library to include this and other multibyte services. In Visual C++ the logical length function is named *_mbslen*.

MBCS String Pointers Move Forward by Leaps and Bounds

Moving forward in an SBCS or WCS string is easy, as you saw in Listing 4-8. Moving forward in an MBCS string is more challenging because you must examine each character to determine its size. The pointer or index will then advance from 1 to *n* bytes, depending on the character size. Therefore, an MBCS program must replace all pointer and index incrementing operations with the appropriate call to *mblen* or an equivalent. For instance, Listing 4-9 depicts a simple function that moves forward one character using *mblen* to determine the character length.

```
#include <stdlib.h>
char* NextChar(char* p)
    {
    p += mblen(p, MB_CUR_MAX);
    return p;
    }
```

Listing 4-9. *Function to increment an MBCS pointer.*

Note that *mblen* works correctly only if the pointer is positioned at the start of a character. This is a general requirement when working with MBCS text: Pointers and indices must never land within a multibyte character.

---

12. Many compilers promote *char* arguments and return values to *int*. Some MBCS programmers have relied on this to pass multibyte characters by value, which is not portable and should therefore be avoided. However, you can employ a structure to safely pass multibyte characters by value. The structure should contain a byte array large enough to hold the longest multibyte character.

When checking for a lead byte, *mblen* consults the locale database, which the next chapter will cover. In addition, the standard library initializes an integer named *MB_CUR_MAX* to give the maximum number of bytes per character in the current locale. Another interesting symbol is *MB_LEN_MAX*, the maximum number of bytes per character in any supported locale. If *MB_CUR_MAX* is 1, the current locale uses SBCS encoding. If *MB_LEN_MAX* is 1, the library offers no MBCS support at all.

MBCS String Pointers Move Backward Very Slowly

Moving backward through a multibyte string is especially difficult because you must conduct a nontrivial search for the start of the preceding character. Again, this isn't a problem in the SBCS and WCS environments because of their fixed-length characters.

Only one technique for backward movement works correctly for any MBCS. You must start at the beginning of the string and search forward until you reach the current position, remembering the start of the previous character at each step. Listing 4-10 shows the algorithm.

```
char* PrevChar(char* pCurrent, char* pStart)
   {
   char* pPrev = 0;          // Previous char pointer
   char* p = pStart;         // Scan pointer
   while(p < pCurrent)       // Scan forward
      {
      pPrev = p;                 // Save this char pointer.
      p = NextChar(p);           // Move to next char.
      }
   return pPrev;             // Return pointer to previous char.
   }
```

Listing 4-10. *Function to decrement an MBCS pointer.*

This function is very slow when the current position is toward the end of a long string. Wouldn't it be more efficient to scan backward from the current position looking for a lead byte and then scan forward as above? Listing 4-11 shows some code you might try, using the standard *isleadbyte* function to perform the necessary test for lead bytes.

The function scans backward one byte at a time, hoping to find a lead byte. If no lead byte is found, you have all single-byte characters from the start of the string to the current position, so the function simply decrements the pointer by 1. If a lead byte is found, the function scans forward just as in Listing 4-10.

```
char* PrevChar(char* pCurrent, char* pStart)
  {
  char* pPrev = 0;                    // Previous character
  char* p = pCurrent;                 // Scan pointer
  if(pCurrent == pStart) return 0;    // Cannot move backward
  while(--p >= pStart)                // Scan backward for a lead
                                      //   byte.

      if(isleadbyte(*p)) break;
  if(p < pStart)                      // No lead byte found, all
                                      //   single-byte

      return pCurrent - 1;
  while(p <= pCurrent)                // Lead byte found, now scan
                                      //   forward

      {
      pPrev = p;                      // Save this char pointer.
      p = NextChar(p);                // Move to next char.
      }
  return pPrev;                       // Return pointer to previous
                                      //   char.

  }
```

Listing 4-11. *More efficient yet unsafe MBCS pointer decrement function.*

Listing 4-11 is more efficient than Listing 4-10 if the string contains a pre-ponderance of multibyte characters. Listing 4-11 assumes, however, that a lead byte can occur only at the beginning of a character, which isn't true in the popular MBCS code pages. For instance, examine the byte layout for the Katakana string "ムメモャヤュ" using Japanese CP932:

MBCS String "ムメモャヤュ" (CP932)

Byte	0	1	2	3	4	5	6	7	8	9	10	11	12
Code	83	80	83	81	83	82	83	83	83	84	83	85	00

CP932 reserves the code points from 0x81 through 0x9F and from 0xE0 through 0xFC as lead bytes of the two-byte characters. The trail byte can have any value from 0x40 through 0xFC except 0x7F.

Now suppose your pointer refers to the fourth character (pointing to byte 6) in the string, and you want to move it back to the preceding character. The algorithm in Listing 4-11 backs up to examine byte 5 and sees that it's a valid lead byte for the character 'c' which has the code (0x82, 0x83).[13] Therefore, the function returns a pointer to that position, and you're now in serious trouble

---

13. Multibyte code pages usually treat the single-byte extended ASCII as half-width characters and offer full-width versions using double-byte encoding. When a full-width character is displayed, it occupies the same rectangular area as an ideograph, resulting in a monospaced appearance.

because the pointer is positioned within a multibyte character. Subsequent attempts to process characters using that pointer will yield unpredictable results. For instance, if you call *NextChar* four times, it will advance the pointer to byte 7, byte 9, byte 11, and finally to byte 13, which is beyond the end of the string. This program is headed for an access violation or mutilated memory.

The C Committee Punts

Because time was running short and comprehensive MBCS support would require major work in the library, the C committee decided to punt the issue to the compiler vendors. The committee correctly decided that their limited time would be better spent on the locale issues discussed in the next chapter. As a result, the standard library support for MBCS consists of *mblen* and four conversion functions: *mbtowc*, *mbstowcs*, *wctomb*, and *wcstombs*.

The conversion functions are particularly interesting because they encourage a programming style that solves most of the MBCS problems described earlier. Since it's much easier to work with fixed-length characters, many programmers prefer to convert MBCS text to and from WCS at the program boundaries. In other words, when MBCS text is read from an input device or file, it's immediately converted into wide characters for internal processing. Then the WCS text is converted back to MBCS before being sent to an output device or file.

If the program uses Unicode internally, it will often employ UTF-8 for storing text in files. Although UTF-8 isn't a classical MBCS defined in terms of a code page, it behaves like an MBCS for computational purposes. Furthermore, UTF-8 is cleverly designed to avoid the problem illustrated by Listing 4-11.

Multibyte Characters in C++

The C++ library defines a *string* class containing members similar to the *str* functions in the C library as well as some new text services. Even though it was designed long after MBCS arrived on the scene, this class uses the same SBCS programming techniques as the older *str* functions in order to remain small and fast. Therefore, the class would need a major rewrite in order to handle multibyte characters.

As with the C library, the C++ committee decided that this effort wasn't necessary because programmers can easily convert MBCS text into the WCS equivalent and use the *wstring* class. Since *wstring* is built from the same *basic_string* template used for the *string* class, it doesn't offer any special multibyte conversions. However, these are easily accomplished with *mbstowcs* and the related functions in the C library.

SUMMARY

C and C++ are rooted in the ASCII world of the United States. Nonetheless, the languages are simple and resilient enough that the ANSI and ISO committees didn't have to make major compiler changes to support multibyte and wide character sets. Most of the work affected the standard C and C++ libraries by adding new functions and classes. The most difficult library changes involved the introduction of the locale database described in the next two chapters.

Chapter 5

Locales in Standard C

Cultures differ not only in the symbol sets they use for writing but also in the way they use symbols to represent shared concepts. For instance, although all countries have monetary systems, few nations agree on details such as currency symbols and denominations. Similarly, people generally agree that time is measured by the cycles of the earth and the moon, but the Gregorian calendar used in Europe and North America isn't necessarily employed everywhere else in the world. Because of these differing views, the international programmer must diligently seek out and implement the rules for presenting data to and accepting data from people in the target cultures. Unless you have developed a compelling "can't live without it" application, customers will shy away from your product if it doesn't conform to their idea of "the way things ought to be."

A growing awareness of this situation caused some trepidation in the ANSI C committee during the 1980s. It appeared that the standard for this relatively simple programming language would become hopelessly complicated if it had to deal with international formatting and computational issues beyond the character set features described in Chapter 4.[1]

After much discussion, the committee decided to add the *locale feature* as a reasonable compromise. This feature enables you to access the formatting

---

1. P. J. Plauger describes the committee's quandary in his book, *The Standard C Library,* which also contains a detailed example of one implementation of the locale feature described in this chapter.

and conversion rules for specific cultures. In fact, many of the standard library functions use these rules. The C++ committee later built on the work of the C committee to extend the locale feature into several classes and templates, as I'll show in Chapter 6.

THE *SETLOCALE* FUNCTION

International programming support in standard C uses (conceptually[2]) a global data structure that contains the formatting rules appropriate to the current execution environment. Application programs use this information indirectly when they call standard library functions. Some of the rules are also visible to application programs for cases in which the standard library doesn't perform the required formatting.

The locale data structure is filled with information obtained from a database that contains the rules for several locales[3]. By default, the structure is initialized with the classical C rules so that legacy programs will behave correctly. An internationalized program will usually adjust some or all of these default settings by calling the *setlocale* function. In many cases, *setlocale* is used only near the beginning of the program in *main*, *WinMain*, or *InitInstance*. Some programs might need to use *setlocale* at other places to support multiple locales.

Listing 5-1 is a simple console application that prints the current date using the formatting rules of several locales. After obtaining the current date and time information by calling the *time* and *gmtime* functions, the program calls *setlocale* several times with different country strings as the second argument. After each call, the program displays the return string, which fully describes the selected locale, and it then uses *strftime* and *printf* to format and display the date. Figure 5-1 shows the resulting console output.

```
#include <locale.h>
#include <stdio.h>
#include <time.h>

void main()
    {
    char *pLocale;        // Locale string returned by setlocale
    time_t Time;          // Time as a long integer
    struct tm *pTime;     // Time as a structure
```

Listing 5-1. *Program to demonstrate* setlocale.

---

2. The exact storage technique for the currently selected formatting rules is an implementation detail that's mostly hidden from the C programmer.

3. The implementation of the locale database isn't specified by the C standard and is usually of no importance to the C programmer.

```
unsigned char b[256];    // Buffer for strftime
time(&Time);             // Get the current time.
pTime = gmtime(&Time);


pLocale = setlocale(LC_ALL, "C");         // Use standard C locale.
printf("C locale is \"%s\"\n", pLocale);
strftime(b, sizeof(b), "%#x", pTime);
printf("  Date is \"%s\"\n\n", b);


pLocale = setlocale(LC_ALL, "");  // Use default (native) locale.
printf("Native locale is \"%s\"\n", pLocale);
strftime(b, sizeof(b), "%#x", pTime);
printf("  Date is \"%s\"\n\n", b);


pLocale = setlocale(LC_ALL, "French");  // Use French locale.
printf("French locale is \"%s\"\n", pLocale);
strftime(b, sizeof(b), "%#x", pTime);
printf("  Date is \"%s\"\n\n", b);


pLocale = setlocale(LC_ALL, "German");   // Use German locale.
printf("German locale is \"%s\"\n", pLocale);
strftime(b, sizeof(b), "%#x", pTime);
printf("  Date is \"%s\"\n\n", b);


pLocale = setlocale(LC_ALL, "Swedish"); // Use Swedish locale.
printf("Swedish locale is \"%s\"\n", pLocale);
strftime(b, sizeof(b), "%#x", pTime);
printf("  Date is \"%s\"\n\n", b);


printf("Press ENTER to exit\n");
gets(b);
}
```

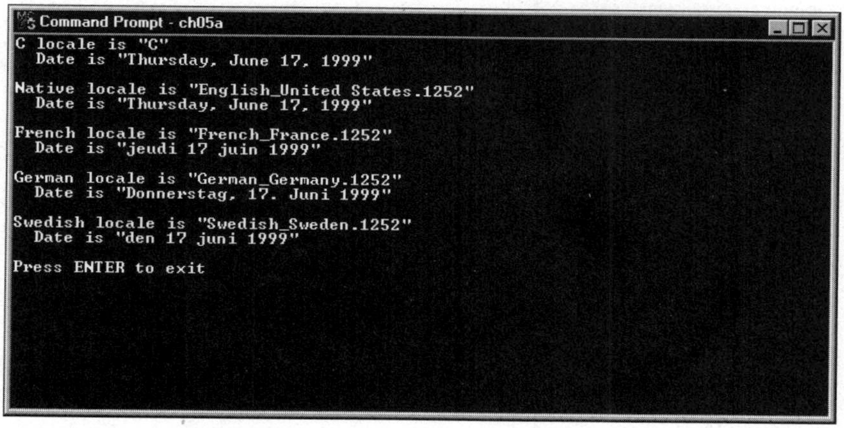

Figure 5-1. *Output of Listing 5-1.*

The *setlocale* function is deceptively simple, having only two arguments (an integer and a string) and returning a string pointer. As usual, the devil is in the details, so let's examine the function in more detail.

Locale Categories

Listing 5-1 uses *LC_ALL* as the first argument in each call to indicate that all categories of formatting information should be changed to the locale specified by the second argument. The locale.h header file defines several other category symbols beginning with *LC_*, as shown in Table 5-1. In other words, each category symbol specifies which functions in the standard library will be affected by the locale change.

Table 5-1. **Locale Categories for *setlocale***

Category	Meaning
LC_ALL	Affects all categories
LC_COLLATE	Affects collation functions
LC_CTYPE	Affects character type functions
LC_MAX	Maximum category code; used for looping
LC_MIN	Minimum category code; used for looping
LC_MONETARY	Affects monetary (currency) functions
LC_NUMERIC	Affects numeric conversion functions
LC_TIME	Affects time and date functions

Since Listing 5-1 formats only date and time values (by calling the *strftime* function), the program can use *LC_TIME* instead of *LC_ALL*. Listing 5-2 illustrates how you can use specific categories to establish a mixed locale. This program uses the native locale for numeric formatting, the French locale for date and time formatting, and the German locale for currency formatting. After establishing the desired locale settings, the program uses *setlocale* in a different way than Listing 5-1 to query for the settings, producing the output shown in Figure 5-2. I'll explain these output strings a little later in the chapter.

```
#include <locale.h>
#include <stdio.h>

void main()
    {
    char *pLocale;

    setlocale(LC_NUMERIC, "");          // Use native numeric locale.
    setlocale(LC_TIME, "French");       // Use French time locale.
    setlocale(LC_MONETARY, "German");   // Use German monetary locale.
```

Listing 5-2. *Setting and querying multiple locales.*

```
        // Query the locale settings by category.
        pLocale = setlocale(LC_NUMERIC, 0);
        printf("\nNumeric locale:\n\"%s\"\n", pLocale);

        pLocale = setlocale(LC_TIME, 0);
        printf("\nTime locale:\n\"%s\"\n", pLocale);

        pLocale = setlocale(LC_MONETARY, 0);
        printf("\nMonetary locale:\n\"%s\"\n", pLocale);

        pLocale = setlocale(LC_ALL, 0);
        printf("\nComplete locale:\n\"%s\"\n\n", pLocale);

        printf("Press ENTER to exit\n");
        }
```

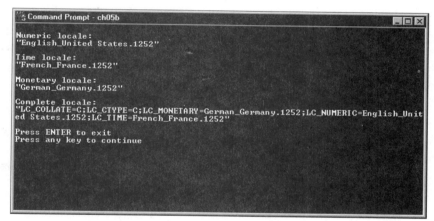

Figure 5-2. *Output of Listing 5-2.*

Language Names

As you saw in Listings 5-1 and 5-2, the second argument to *setlocale* is a string that specifies a locale in terms of its dominant language. Believe it or not, the C standard doesn't define the contents of this string except in these three simple cases:

- If the string pointer is null, the function returns the current locale setting for the specified category. Listing 5-2 uses this querying technique.

- If the string is *C*, the traditional C locale is used. This is essentially an ASCII environment, although many compilers use an extended

ASCII set such as CP850 or CP1252 in this mode. Formatting and conversions use U.S. conventions. The C locale is the default setting for the standard library if you do not call *setlocale* in your program.

■ If the string is empty (that is, "" instead of a null pointer), the native locale is used. A well-implemented version of *setlocale* consults the operating system to determine the proper formatting and conversion rules as well as the character set.

The *C* standards committee left it to each compiler vendor to define locale language strings according to market needs, and as you might expect, this has led to some confusion. As a result, modern compilers usually support several popular schemes. Table 5-2 shows some[4] of the language strings recognized by Microsoft Visual C++. The Standard column contains three-character abbreviations that are widely used in the UNIX and OS/2 world and are, in effect, the nearest thing to a standard in this area. The Alternatives column contains "friendlier" versions of the standard abbreviations.

Table 5-2. **Popular Language Names**

Language	*Sublanguage*	*Standard*	*Alternatives*
Chinese			"chinese"
Chinese	Hong Kong	"chh"	"chinese-hongkong"
Chinese	Simplified	"chs"	"chinese-simplified"
Chinese	Singapore	"chi"	"chinese-singapore"
Chinese	Traditional or Taiwan	"cht"	"chinese-traditional" "chinese-taiwan"
Czech		"csy"	"czech"
Danish		"dan"	"danish"
Dutch		"nld"	"dutch"
Dutch	Belgian	"nlb"	"belgian" "dutch-belgian"
English			"english"
English	Australian	"ena"	"australian" "english-aus"
English	Belize	"enl"	"english-belize"
English	Canadian	"enc"	"canadian" "english-can"
English	Caribbean	"enb"	"english-caribbean"

4. The actual language names supported on your system might be slightly different depending on your version of Visual C++ and your system configuration.

Language	Sublanguage	Standard	Alternatives
English	Irish	"eni"	"english-ire" "irish-english"
English	Jamaican	"enj"	"english-jamaica"
English	New Zealand	"enz"	"english-nz"
English	South African	"ens"	"english-south africa"
English	Trinidad and Tobago	"ent"	"english-trinidad y tobago"
English	United Kingdom	"eng"	"uk" "english-uk"
English	United States	"enu"	"us" "usa" "american" "american english" "american-english" "english-american" "english-us" "english-usa"
Finnish		"fin"	"finnish"
French		"fra"	"french"
French	Belgian	"frb"	"french-belgian"
French	Canadian	"frc"	"french-canadian"
French	Swiss	"frs"	"french-swiss"
German		"deu"	"german"
German	Austrian	"dea"	"german-austrian"
German	Lichtenstein	"dec"	"german-lichtenstein"
German	Luxembourg	"del"	"german-luxembourg"
German	Swiss	"des"	"german-swiss" "swiss"
Greek		"ell"	"greek"
Hungarian		"hun"	"hungarian"
Icelandic		"isl"	"icelandic"
Italian		"ita"	"italian"
Italian	Swiss	"its"	"italian-swiss"
Japanese		"jpn"	"japanese"
Korean		"kor"	"korean"
Norwegian			"norwegian"
Norwegian	Nynorsk	"non"	"norwegian-nynorsk"
Norwegian	Bokmal	"nor"	"norwegian-bokmal"

(continued)

Table 5-2. *continued*

Language	Sublanguage	Standard	Alternatives
Polish		"plk"	"polish"
Portuguese		"ptg"	"portuguese"
Portuguese	Brazilian	"ptb"	"portuguese-brazilian"
Russian		"rus"	"russian"
Slovak		"sky"	"slovak"
Spanish		"esp"	"spanish"
Spanish	Argentina	"ess"	"spanish-argentina"
Spanish	Bolivia	"esb"	"spanish-bolivia"
Spanish	Chile	"esl"	"spanish-chile"
Spanish	Colombia	"eso"	"spanish-colombia"
Spanish	Costa Rica	"esc"	"spanish-costa rica"
Spanish	Dominican Republic	"esd"	"spanish-domincan republic"
Spanish	Ecuador	"esf"	"spanish-ecuador"
Spanish	El Salvador	"ese"	"spanish-el salvador"
Spanish	Guatemala	"esg"	"spanish-guatemala"
Spanish	Honduras	"esh"	"spanish-honduras"
Spanish	Mexican	"esm"	"spanish-mexican"
Spanish	Modern	"esn"	"spanish-modern"
Spanish	Nicaragua	"esi"	"spanish-nicaragua"
Spanish	Panama	"esa"	"spanish-panama"
Spanish	Paraguay	"esz"	"spanish-paraguay"
Spanish	Peru	"esr"	"spanish-peru"
Spanish	Puerto Rico	"esu"	"spanish-puerto rico"
Spanish	Uruguay	"esy"	"spanish-uruguay"
Spanish	Venezuela	"esv"	"spanish-venezuela"
Swedish		"sve"	"swedish"
Swedish	Finnish	"svf"	"swedish-finland"
Swiss		"des"	
Turkish		"trk"	"turkish"

Listing 5-3 is a simple program that enables you to check whether your system recognizes a particular language string. Figure 5-3 shows the console during a typical session with this program. You can also construct a file of language strings, feed it to the program as standard input, and dump the results to a standard output file for later analysis. For example, if test.txt contains language strings on separate lines, you can type the line *ch05c <test.txt >test.out* in a console window to produce a file named test.out:

```c
#include <locale.h>
#include <stdio.h>

void main()
    {
    unsigned char b[256];    // Buffer for user input
    char *pLocale;           // Locale string returned by setlocale

    while(gets(b))           // Loop until no more input strings.
        {
        pLocale = setlocale(LC_ALL, b);
        printf("Input:  \"%s\"\n", b);
        if(pLocale) printf("Output: \"%s\"\n\n", pLocale);
        else printf("Output: ERROR\n\n", b);
        }
    }
```

Listing 5-3. *Program for checking language strings.*

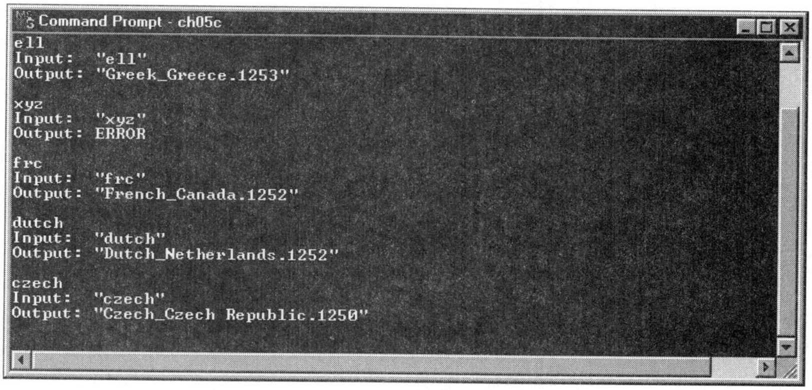

Figure 5-3. *Typical session with Listing 5-3.*

Fully Qualified Locale Names

Notice that *setlocale* returns a pointer to a string. A null pointer indicates failure and means that you supplied an invalid locale category or language string. Otherwise, the pointer returned refers to the fully qualified locale name. As with the country name in the second argument, the C standards committee didn't specify the contents of this returned locale name.

Figures 5-1, 5-2, and 5-3 show how these qualified locale names are formatted by Visual C++. The general format is *language_country.code page*, in which the *language* substring is one of the friendly names from the Alternatives column of Table 5-2, and the *country* substring is similarly obtained from the Alternatives column of Table 5-3. The *code page* substring identifies the character set required for the proper rendering of text in the locale if Unicode isn't used.

Therefore, when *setlocale* was called with the language string *frc* as in Figure 5-3, it returned the string *French_Canada.1252* indicating that the language is French, the country is Canada, and the normal code page is 1252. Similarly, the language string *ell* produced *Greek_Greece.1253* to indicate the Greek language as used in Greece with CP1253.

Table 5-3. Country/Region Strings

Country/Region	Standard	Alternatives
Australia	"aus"	"australia"
Austria	"aut"	"austria"
Belgium	"bel"	"belgium"
Brazil	"bra"	"brazil"
Canada	"can"	"canada"
Czech Republic	"cze"	"czech"
Denmark	"dnk"	"denmark"
Finland	"fin"	"finland"
France	"fra"	"france"
Germany	"deu"	"germany"
Greece	"grc"	"greece"
Hong Kong	"hkg"	"hong kong" "hong-kong"
Hungary	"hun"	"hungary"
Iceland	"isl"	"iceland"
Ireland	"irl"	"ireland"
Italy	"ita"	"italy"
Japan	"jpn"	"japan"
Mexico	"mex"	"mexico"
Netherlands	"nld"	"holland" "netherlands"
New Zealand	"nzl"	"new zealand" "new-zealand" "nz"
Norway	"nor"	"norway"

Country/Region	Standard	Alternatives
People's Republic of China	"chn"	"china" "pr china" "pr-china"
Poland	"pol"	"poland"
Portugal	"prt"	"portugal"
Russia	"rus"	"russia"
Singapore	"sgp"	"singapore"
Slovak Republic	"svk"	"slovak"
South Korea	"kor"	"korea" "south korea" "south-korea"
Spain	"esp"	"spain"
Sweden	"swe"	"sweden"
Switzerland	"che"	"switzerland"
Taiwan	"twn"	"taiwan"
Turkey	"tur"	"turkey"
United Kingdom	"gbr"	"britain" "england" "great britain" "uk" "united kingdom" "united-kingdom"
United States	"usa"	"america" "united states" "united-states" "us"

In Listing 5-2 and Figure 5-2, notice that the final query asks for all categories by specifying *LC_ALL* as the first *setlocale* argument. Since the preceding code established a mixed locale, this final query returns a complex string with a separate substring for each category. The substrings are separated by semicolons, and each qualified locale is preceded by its category and an equal sign (=). Thus the mixed locale established by Listing 5-2 is fully specified by this string, with the substrings shown on separate lines for clarity:

```
"LC_COLLATE=C;
LC_CTYPE=C;
LC_MONETARY=German_Germany.1252;
LC_NUMERIC=English_United States.1252;
LC_TIME=French.France.1252"
```

Fully qualified names provide an easy way to restore previous settings when you need to temporarily change locales while the program is running. Listing 5-4 shows a function named *GetFrenchDate* that switches the *LC_TIME* category to the French style, formats a date, and then restores the previous locale setting.

```c
#include <locale.h>
#include <stdio.h>
#include <stdlib.h>
#include <string.h>
#include <time.h>

int GetFrenchDate(struct tm *pTime, char *pOut, size_t nOut)
    {
    char *pLocale;
    char *pPrevLocale = 0;
    int nChars = 0;
    *pOut = 0;
    pLocale = setlocale(LC_TIME, 0);      // Get current time locale.
    if(pLocale)                           // Make a copy.
        {
        pPrevLocale = (char*)malloc(strlen(pLocale) + 1);
        if(pPrevLocale) strcpy(pPrevLocale, pLocale);
        else return 0;
        }
    if(setlocale(LC_TIME, "french"))      // Switch to French time.
        nChars = strftime(pOut, nOut, "%#x", pTime);
    if(pPrevLocale)                 // Restore the previous locale.
        {
        setlocale(LC_TIME, pPrevLocale);
        free(pPrevLocale);
        }
    return nChars;
    }

void main()
    {
    time_t Time;                          // Time as a long integer
    struct tm *pTime;                     // Time as a structure
    unsigned char b[256];                 // Buffer for output string

    time(&Time);                          // Get the current time.
    pTime = gmtime(&Time);

    strftime(b, sizeof(b), "%#x", pTime); // Show date in
                                          // default format.
```

Listing 5-4. *Temporarily changing the locale.*

```
printf("  Default date is \"%s\"\n\n", b);

GetFrenchDate(pTime, b, sizeof(b));   // Show date in
                                      // French format.
printf("  French date is \"%s\"\n\n", b);
}
```

Notice that you must allocate a buffer to save the qualified locale string, since each invocation of *setlocale* might invalidate the pointer returned by the preceding call. Be careful here, because some implementations of the C standard might work correctly if you forget to copy the qualified string to your own buffer. However, the standard allows *setlocale* to use a static character array for its return string, and this is the typical implementation.

To change more than one category—for instance, *LC_TIME* and *LC_CTYPE*—it's more efficient to query for *LC_ALL* and then use the return string to restore the locale.

Incidentally, Listing 5-4 contains a subtle assumption that can easily exhibit itself as a bug in certain environments. The *GetFrenchDate* function produces a string using CP1252, but this string is printed using whichever code page is active in the *main* function. This can cause some of the French symbols to display incorrectly if the active code page in the *main* function is incompatible with CP1252. It's easy to fall into this kind of trap when you're not using Unicode.

Listing 5-4 illustrates another interesting aspect of the *setlocale* function. Recall that the C standards committee did not specify the exact format for the locale string returned by the function. I built the examples in this chapter with Visual C++, so the locale strings displayed in the screen dumps use Microsoft's conventions. Other compilers might produce different results. Nonetheless, as this program demonstrates, you are rarely interested in the specific content of qualified locale strings. You simply save them away and then pass them back to *setlocale* later.

USING LOCALE SETTINGS THROUGH THE STANDARD C LIBRARY

Table 5-4 shows which functions in the standard C library are affected by the various locale categories[5]. Theoretically, you need only establish the proper locale settings for each category and the library functions will then perform the necessary conversions under the hood. In actual practice, the use of locales isn't completely painless, but the library does a pretty good job of hiding the ugly stuff.

---

5. See Chapter 7 for a similar table showing which Microsoft extensions to the standard C library are affected by the locale settings.

Table 5-4. **Locale-Sensitive Functions in the Standard C Library**

Function	Purpose	Category
atof, atoi, atol	Convert text to numeric value	*LC_NUMERIC*
isalpha, isleadbyte, and so on	Character tests	*LC_CTYPE*
localeconv	Get numeric formatting rules	*LC_MONETARY, LC_NUMERIC*
MB_CUR_MAX	Maximum multibyte character length	*LC_CTYPE*
mblen	Validate and measure a multibyte character	*LC_CTYPE*
mbstowcs, mbtowc, wcstombs, wctomb	Convert between MBCS and WCS	*LC_CTYPE*
fprintf, printf, sprintf, and so on	Formatted output	*LC_NUMERIC*
fscanf, scanf, sscanf, and so on	Collate strings Formatted input	*LC_COLLATE* *LC_NUMERIC*
strcoll, wcscoll, strxfrm, wcsxfrm	Collate strings	*LC_COLLATE*
strftime, wcsftime	Format date and time values into text	*LC_TIME*
strtod, strtol, strtoul, wcstod, wcstol, wcstoul	Convert text to numeric value	*LC_NUMERIC*
tolower, toupper, towlower, towupper	Character case conversion	LC_CTYPE

The function *SortGermanText* in Listing 5-5 applies the German collation rules to two strings and returns a relative position value like the one returned by *strcmp*. After switching the *LC_COLLATE* category to the German locale, the function uses *strxfrm* to transform the two input strings into equivalent strings that can be correctly compared by *strcmp*. This transformation uses a table (initialized by *setlocale*) containing a collation value for each character in the code page associated with the *LC_COLLATE* category.

```
#include <locale.h>
#include <stdio.h>
#include <stdlib.h>
#include <string.h>
```

Listing 5-5. *Using the locale collation setting.*

```
#ifdef _WIN32                           // For WIN32 console functions
#include <windows.h>
#endif

int SortGermanText(unsigned char *a, unsigned char *b)
    {
    char *pLocale;
    char *pPrevLocale = 0;
    int ret = 0;
    pLocale = setlocale(LC_COLLATE, 0); // Get current
                                        // collation locale.
    if(pLocale)                         // Make a copy.
        {
        pPrevLocale = (char*)malloc(strlen(pLocale) + 1);
        if(pPrevLocale) strcpy(pPrevLocale, pLocale);
        else return 0;
        }
    if(setlocale(LC_COLLATE, "german")) // Switch to German
                                        // collation.
        {
        int aSize = strxfrm(0, a, 0);   // Allocate transformation
                                        // buffers.
        int bSize = strxfrm(0, b, 0);
        char *aTest = (char*)malloc(aSize + 1);
        char *bTest = (char*)malloc(bSize + 1);
        // Malloc error checking omitted here
        strxfrm(aTest, a, aSize);       // Transform input strings.
        strxfrm(bTest, b, bSize);
        ret = strcmp(aTest, bTest);     // Compare transformed strings.
        free(aTest);                    // Release transformation
                                        // buffers.
        free(bTest);
        }
    if(pPrevLocale)                     // Restore previous locale.
        {
        setlocale(LC_COLLATE, pPrevLocale);
        free(pPrevLocale);
        }
    return ret;
    }

// Test program
void main()
```

(continued)

Listing 5-5. *continued*

```
{
unsigned char a[1024];
unsigned char b[1024];
char *sPos;
int rPos;

#ifdef _WIN32                        // For proper WIN32 console I/O
SetConsoleCP(1252);
SetConsoleOutputCP(1252);
#endif

while(1)
    {
    if(!gets(a)) break;
    if(!gets(b)) break;
    rPos = SortGermanText(a, b);
    if(rPos == 0) sPos = "equal to";
    else if(rPos < 0) sPos = "below";
    else sPos = "above";
    printf("\"%s\" is %s \"%s\"\n\n", a, sPos, b);
    }
}
```

Figure 5-4 is a console snapshot of an interactive session with the test program in Listing 5-5. This program illustrates a common situation in which the standard locale feature must be augmented with some platform-specific code. Notice the lines that are conditionally compiled with the *_WIN32* symbol. They include the windows.h header file and invoke the Win32 API functions *SetConsoleCP* and *SetConsoleOutputCP* in order to place the console into the proper state for entering and displaying German text. Since the German locale uses CP1252, I supply that code page to both API calls.

This is necessary because Visual C++ initially connects the standard input and output files (*stdin* and *stdout*) to the console using the system default code page, which is CP437 on a typical U.S. PC. Although this doesn't prevent the entry of CP1252 characters by using the Alt key[6] and the numeric keypad, code points higher than 127 won't display properly with CP437. In addition, the console font must be changed to one that's compatible with CP1252. I did this with the Properties dialog box of the console window when producing to avoid cluttering the test program with more Win32 API calls.[7]

---

6. Microsoft's operating systems allow you to enter any 8-bit character by pressing the Alt key while entering the three-digit decimal character code on the numeric keypad.

7. Chapter 8 describes Win32 console operations in more detail.

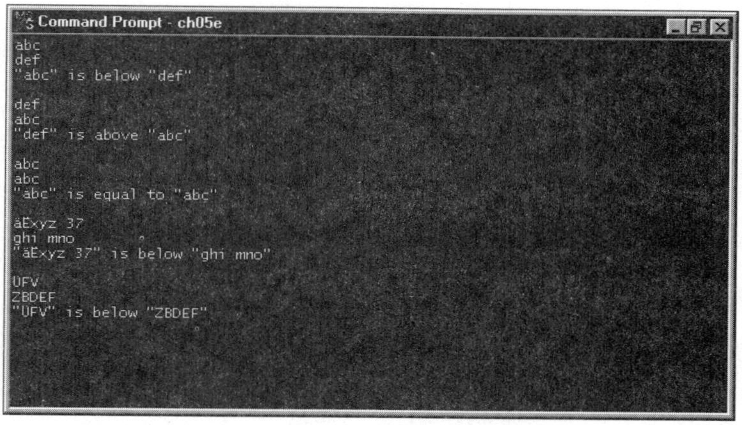

Figure 5-4. *Console session with the program in Listing 5-5.*

In general, the standard locale feature operates on data in memory. It has no knowledge of character set issues that arise during I/O operations. If translation is required between memory and I/O devices or files, you must supply the necessary algorithms, which can vary from one environment to another.

CUSTOM FORMATTING WITH *LCONV*

The locale-sensitive functions in Table 5-4 represent a subset of the text processing work that most commercial programs must do. For instance, the standard library has no locale-sensitive functions that handle currency values and strings, even though many international applications need to work with different types of money.

Although they addressed the date and time formatting issues, the C standards committee chose to avoid a protracted examination of the world's monetary systems. Instead, they added a general set of currency formatting information to the locale database and opened a porthole into the database with the *localeconv* function and the *lconv* structure. The abbreviation *conv*, which stands for *conversion* indicates that the information contained in *lconv* is used for converting between computational values and the corresponding text strings. In practice, most of these conversions are from the internal binary form to the displayable text form.

Listing 5-6 is an annotated version of the *lconv* structure extracted from the locale.h header file. It also includes the prototype of the *localeconv* function, which returns a pointer to the *lconv* structure for the current locale.

```
struct lconv
    {
    // These items are used for numeric formatting.
    // They are affected by the LC_NUMERIC category.
    char *decimal_point;        // Decimal point
    char *thousands_sep;        // Thousands (group) separator
    char *grouping;             // Group widths

    // These items are used for currency formatting.
    // They are affected by the LC_MONETARY category.
    char *int_curr_symbol;     // International currency symbol
    char *currency_symbol;     // Local currency symbol
    char *mon_decimal_point;   // Decimal point
    char *mon_thousands_sep;   // Thousands (group) separator
    char *mon_grouping;        // Group widths
    char *positive_sign;       // Positive sign
    char *negative_sign;       // Negative sign
    char int_frac_digits;      // International fraction size
    char frac_digits;          // Local fraction size
    char p_cs_precedes;        // 1 if symbol precedes positive value
    char p_sep_by_space;       // 1 if space separates positive value
                               // and symbol
    char n_cs_precedes;        // 1 if symbol precedes negative value
    char n_sep_by_space;       // 1 if space separates negative value
                               // and symbol
    char p_sign_posn;          // Sign position for positive value
    char n_sign_posn;          // Sign position for negative value
    };

// Function to obtain lconv structure for the current locale
struct lconv* localeconv(void);
```

Listing 5-6. *The* lconv *structure.*

This structure contains the rules for formatting numeric and monetary values. The standard C library uses this information only in *printf* and *scanf*, which merely consult the numeric decimal point. It would have been nice if the C committee had gone one step further and added numeric and currency formatting functions similar to *strftime*. This omission has forced many international programmers to write their own versions of these functions.[8]

To gain an understanding of *lconv*, let's develop yet another set of numeric and currency formatting functions. But first let's look at a simple utility program that displays the *lconv* structure for a selected locale. This program is handy for checking the locale settings when testing functions such as the ones I'll talk about

---

8. The C++ library corrects most of these deficiencies, but it cannot be used by C programmers.

next. Listing 5-7 is the utility program, and Figure 5-5 shows its output. It simply retrieves a language name from the user, activates that locale, and then dumps the contents of *lconv*.

```c
#include <locale.h>
#include <stdio.h>

#ifdef _WIN32                       // For WIN32 console functions
#include <windows.h>
#endif

void main()
    {
    unsigned char b[256];       // Buffer for user input
    char *pLocale;              //
 Locale string returned by setlocale
    struct lconv *pData;        // Locale data
    int i;                      // Loop counter

    #ifdef _WIN32               // For proper WIN32 console I/O
    SetConsoleCP(1252);
    SetConsoleOutputCP(1252);
    #endif

    while(gets(b))              // Loop till no more input strings
        {
        pLocale = setlocale(LC_ALL, b);
        printf("Input:  \"%s\"\n", b);
        if(!pLocale)
            {
            printf("Output: ERROR\n\n", b);
            continue;
            }
        printf("Locale: \"%s\"\n\n", pLocale);

        pData = localeconv();
        if(!pData) continue;

        printf("%20s = \"%s\"\n", "decimal_point",
            pData->decimal_point);
        printf("%20s = \"%s\"\n", "thousands_sep",
            pData->thousands_sep);

        printf("%20s = ", "grouping");
        for(i = 0; pData->grouping[i]; i++)
```

Listing 5-7. *Program to display* lconv *structure.*

(continued)

Listing 5-7. *continued*

```
        printf("%c%d", (i ? ',' : ' '),
                (int)pData->grouping[i]);
    printf("\n");

    printf("%20s = \"%s\"\n", "int_curr_symbol",
            pData->int_curr_symbol);
    printf("%20s = \"%s\"\n", "currency_symbol",
            pData->currency_symbol);
    printf("%20s = \"%s\"\n", "mon_decimal_point",
            pData->mon_decimal_point);
    printf("%20s = \"%s\"\n", "mon_thousands_sep",
            pData->mon_thousands_sep);

    printf("%20s = ", "mon_grouping");
    for(i = 0; pData->mon_grouping[i]; i++)
        printf("%c%d", (i ? ',' : ' '),
                (int)pData->mon_grouping[i]);
    printf("\n");

    printf("%20s = \"%s\"\n", "positive_sign",
            pData->positive_sign);
    printf("%20s = \"%s\"\n", "negative_sign",
            pData->negative_sign);
    printf("%20s = %d\n", "int_frac_digits",
            (int)pData->int_frac_digits);
    printf("%20s = %d\n", "frac_digits",
            (int)pData->frac_digits);
    printf("%20s = %d\n", "p_cs_precedes",
            (int)pData->p_cs_precedes);
    printf("%20s = %d\n", "p_sep_by_space",
            (int)pData->p_sep_by_space);
    printf("%20s = %d\n", "n_cs_precedes",
            (int)pData->n_cs_precedes);
    printf("%20s = %d\n", "n_sep_by_space",
            (int)pData->n_sep_by_space);
    printf("%20s = %d\n", "p_sign_posn",
            (int)pData->p_sign_posn);
    printf("%20s = %d\n", "n_sign_posn",
            (int)pData->n_sign_posn);
    printf("\n");
    }
}
```

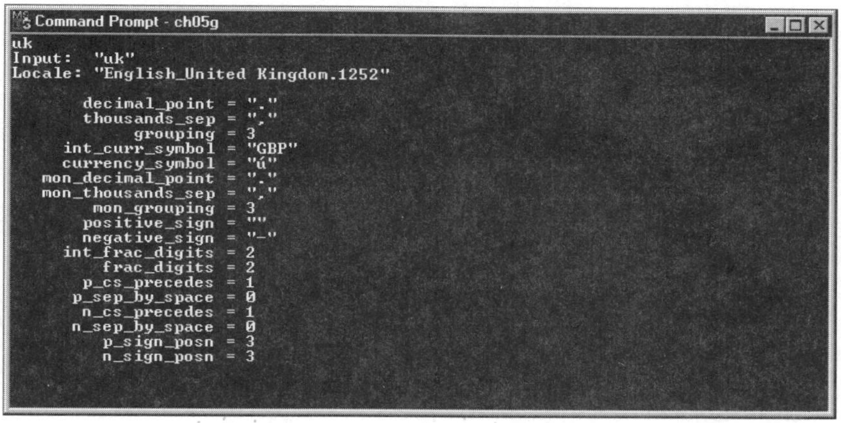

Figure 5-5. *Output of Listing 5-7.*

Now let's develop some functions that work with locale-dependent numeric and currency strings. We now pause for programming...

??☋☋☋?σ?☋☋?ιφ☋?♫☋☾♂♀☼ιφσ☋?☋☋☋☺©™$$$♂♀

That wasn't so difficult, was it? The functions *TextFromInt*, *TextFromReal*, and *TextFromMoney* are shown in Listings 5-8, 5-9, and 5-10, respectively. Each listing also contains a simple test program that is compiled only when building the debugging version. This trio converts numbers into text strings that have the proper punctuation.

```c
#include <limits.h>
#include <locale.h>
#include <stdio.h>
#include <stdlib.h>
#include <string.h>

// Convert an integer to a punctuated text string.
int TextFromInt(char *t, int tsize, long v)
    {
    char b[32];                        // Work buffer
    int i = sizeof(b), j;              // Buffer index and length
    struct lconv *pLoc = localeconv(); // Locale stuff
    char *pGroup = pLoc->grouping;     // Group size(s)
    int nGroup =                       // Default group size is 0.
        (pGroup && (pGroup[0] > 0)
        && (pGroup[0] != CHAR_MAX)) ? pGroup[0] : 0;
```

Listing 5-8. TextFromInt *function.*

(continued)

Listing 5-8. *continued*

```
    int bMinus = 0;                          // Minus flag
    if(v < 0)          {
        bMinus = 1;
        v = -v;
        }
    b[--i] = 0;
    while(1)
        {
        b[--i] = '0' + (char)(v % 10);
        v /= 10;
        if(v == 0) break;
        if(nGroup && (--nGroup == 0))
            {
            b[--i] = pLoc->thousands_sep[0];
            if(!pGroup[0] || (pGroup[0] == CHAR_MAX)) nGroup = 0;
            else if(pGroup[1]) nGroup = *++pGroup;
            else nGroup = *pGroup;
            }
        }
    if(bMinus) b[--i] = '-';
    *t = 0;
    j = strlen(&b[i]);
    if(!t) return j;          // Return actual size if no output buffer.
    if(j >= tsize) return -j;    // Return -size if buffer too small.
    strcpy(t, &b[i]);             // Copy output and return size.
    return j;
    }

#if _DEBUGGING
void main()
    {
    long v;
    char in[256], out[256];
    setlocale(LC_ALL, "");
    while(gets(in))
        {
        v = atol(in);
        TextFromInt(out, sizeof(out), v);
        printf("\"%s\"\n\n", out);
        }
    }
#endif
```

```
#include <limits.h>
#include <locale.h>
#include <stdio.h>
#include <stdlib.h>
#include <string.h>

// Convert a real number to a punctuated text string.
int TextFromReal(char *t, int tsize, double v, unsigned int dec)
    {
    char b[40], c;                      // Work buffer and character
    int i, j;                           // Buffer indices
    struct lconv *pLoc = localeconv();  // Locale stuff
    char *pGroup = pLoc->grouping;      // Group size(s)
    int nGroup =                        // Default group size is 0.
        (pGroup && (pGroup[0] > 0) &&
        (pGroup[0] != CHAR_MAX)) ? pGroup[0] : 0;
    if(dec > 15) dec = 15;              // No more than 15 decimal places
    j = sprintf(b, "%#.*f", dec, v);    // Convert value to text.
    i = sizeof(b) - 1;                  // Move fraction to end of buffer.
    while(j >= 0)
        {
        c = b[i--] = b[j--];
        if(c == pLoc->decimal_point[0]) break;
        }
    while(j >= 0)                       // Punctuate integer portion.
        {
        b[i--] = b[j--];
        if(nGroup && (--nGroup == 0) && (j >= 0) && (b[j] != '-'))
            {
            b[i--] = pLoc->thousands_sep[0];
            if(!pGroup[0] || (pGroup[0] == CHAR_MAX)) nGroup = 0;
            else if(pGroup[1]) nGroup = *++pGroup;
            else nGroup = *pGroup;
            }
        }
    *t = 0;
    j = strlen(&b[i + 1]);
    if(!t) return j;         //Return actual size if no output buffer.
    if(j >= tsize) return -j;   // Return -size if buffer too small.
    strcpy(t, &b[i + 1]);       // Copy output and return size.
    return j;
    }
```

Listing 5-9. TextFromReal *function.*

(continued)

Listing 5-9. *continued*

```
#if _DEBUGGING
void main()
    {
    double v;
    char in[256], out[256], *pEnd;
    setlocale(LC_ALL, "");
    while(gets(in))
        {
        v = strtod(in, &pEnd);
        TextFromReal(out, sizeof(out), v, 4);
        printf("\"%s\"\n\n", out);
        }
    }
#endif
```

```
#include <limits.h>
#include <locale.h>
#include <stdio.h>
#include <stdlib.h>
#include <string.h>

// Local currency format table, per Plauger's
// "The Standard C Library"
static char *FormatTable[2][2][5] =
    {
        {
        {   "(V$)",      "-V$", "V$-", "V-$", "V-$"  },
        {   "($V)",      "-$V", "$V-", "-$V", "$-V"  }
        },
        {
        {   "(V $)",     "-V $", "V $-", "V- $", "V $-"  },
        {   "($ V)",     "-$ V", "$ V-", "-$ V", "$ -V"  }
        }
    };

// Convert a money value to a punctuated text string.
int TextFromMoney(char *t, int tsize, double v, int scale,
                int bIntl)
    {
    char a[128], b[40], c;              // Work buffers
    int i, j;                          // Buffer indices
    char *pValue;                      // Punctuated value
    struct lconv *pLoc = localeconv(); // Locale stuff
```

Listing 5-10. TextFromMoney *function.*

```
char *pGroup = pLoc->mon_grouping;   // Group size(s)
int nGroup =                         // Default group size is 0.
    (pGroup && (pGroup[0] > 0) &&
    (pGroup[0] != CHAR_MAX)) ? pGroup[0] : 0;
int dec =                            // Decimal digits
    bIntl ? pLoc->int_frac_digits : pLoc->frac_digits;
int bMinus =  (v < 0) ? 1 : 0;       // Negative number


char *fmt = bIntl ? "$-V" : 0;       // Get international format
if(!bIntl)                           // or get local format.
    {
    int x, y, z;
    if(bMinus)
        {
        x = (pLoc->n_sep_by_space == 1);
        y = (pLoc->n_cs_precedes == 1);
        if((pLoc->n_sign_posn >= 0) && (pLoc->n_sign_posn <= 4))
            z = pLoc->n_sign_posn;
        else z = 0;
        }
    else
        {
        x = (pLoc->p_sep_by_space == 1);
        y = (pLoc->p_cs_precedes == 1);
        if((pLoc->p_sign_posn >= 0) && (pLoc->p_sign_posn <= 4))
            z = pLoc->p_sign_posn;
        else z = 0;
        }
    fmt = FormatTable[x][y][z];
    }


// Form the decimal value string.
if(bMinus) v = -v;                   // Flip negative value.
if((scale < 0) || (scale > 10))      // Adjust scale factor.
    scale = 0;
for(dec -= scale; dec < 0; dec++, scale--) v /= 10;
j = sprintf(b, "%#.*f", dec, v);     // Convert value to text.
i = sizeof(b) - 1;                   // Move fraction to end of buffer.
while(j >= 0)
    {
    c = b[j--];
    if(c != pLoc->decimal_point[0]) b[i--] = c;
    else
        {
        while(scale--)
```

(continued)

Listing 5-10. *continued*

```
                {
                if(j >= 0) c = b[j--];
                else c = '0';
                b[i--] = c;
                }
            b[i--] = pLoc->mon_decimal_point[0];
            break;
            }
        }
    while(j >= 0)                           // Punctuate integer portion.
        {
        b[i--] = b[j--];
        if(nGroup && (--nGroup == 0) && (j >= 0) && (b[j] != '-'))
            {
            b[i--] = pLoc->mon_thousands_sep[0];
            if(!pGroup[0] || (pGroup[0] == CHAR_MAX)) nGroup = 0;
            else if(pGroup[1]) nGroup = *++pGroup;
            else nGroup = *pGroup;
            }
        }
    if(b[i+1] == pLoc->mon_decimal_point[0]) b[i--] = '0';
    pValue = &b[i+1];

    // Form the currency string.
    for(i = 0; *fmt; i += strlen(&a[i])) switch(c = *fmt++)
        {
        case 'V':                          // Insert value.
        strcpy(&a[i], pValue);
        continue;

        case '-':                              // Insert sign.
        if(bMinus) strcpy(&a[i], pLoc->negative_sign);
        else strcpy(&a[i], pLoc->positive_sign);
        continue;

        case '$':                          // Insert currency symbol.
        if(bIntl) strcpy(&a[i], pLoc->int_curr_symbol);
        else strcpy(&a[i], pLoc->currency_symbol);
        continue;

        case '(':               // Ignore parentheses unless negative.
        case ')':
        if(!bMinus) continue;
        // These cases flow together.
        default:                               // Copy literal text.
        a[i++] = c;
```

```
        a[i] = 0;
        continue;
        }


    *t = 0;
    if(!t) return i;          // Return actual size if no output buffer.
    if(i >= tsize) return -i;  // Return -size if buffer too small.
    strcpy(t, a);             // Copy output and return size.
    return i;
    }
#if _DEBUGGING
void main()
    {
    double v;
    char in[256], out[256], *pEnd;
    setlocale(LC_ALL, "");
    while(gets(in))
        {
        v = strtod(in, &pEnd);
        TextFromMoney(out, sizeof(out), v, 2, 0);
        printf("Local:         \"%s\"\n\n", out);
        TextFromMoney(out, sizeof(out), v, 2, 1);
        printf("International: \"%s\"\n\n", out);
        }
    }
#endif
```

Formatting Integers and Real Numbers

TextFromInt and *TextFromReal* convert integers and real numbers into text and then insert the group separator character in the appropriate spots. This is a little tricky because the *grouping* member of *lconv* can specify several group sizes. For instance, suppose the grouping string is \x03\x02 when *TextFromInt* is formatting the value 123456789. The resulting string will be *12,34,56,789* because the first (rightmost) group will have three digits and the other groups will have two digits each.

Formatting Monetary Values

TextFromMoney is complicated because of the many variables involved in monetary formatting. In addition, my implementation[9] includes a scaling feature that

---

9. I based my implementation on the version P. J. Plauger presented in *The Standard C Library*.

can help reduce the round-off problems that often occur when a program uses floating point numbers to represent money.

When formatting monetary values, you must consider the relative positions of the value itself, the sign, and the currency symbol. Furthermore, some locales require a space between the currency symbol and the rest of the string. Finally, positive and negative values can have different formatting rules.

TextFromMoney is governed by format strings derived from the various members of *lconv*, as shown in Table 5-5. The column labeled SP indicates the state of *p_sep_by_space* or *n_sep_by_space* for positive and negative values, respectively. Similarly, the PRE column indicates the state of *p_cs_precedes* or *n_cs_precedes*. The numbered columns (0 through 4) correspond to values in *_sign_posn* or *n_sign_posn*.[10] Table 5-5 also shows the results of formatting the values 123.45 and −123.45 for each case.

The format strings use the uppercase V, the minus sign (−), the dollar sign ($), and the parentheses [()] as metacharacters. They will be removed or replaced according to the currency value and the contents of *lconv*, as explained in Table 5-6.

Notice that each locale has a local and an international monetary format. *TextFromMoney* accepts an argument called *bIntl* to indicate which type of string to produce. The international monetary format always uses *$-V* as the format string, and its currency symbol and number of decimal places are supplied by *lconv.int_curr_symbol* and *lconv.int_frac_digits*, respectively.

Listing 5-10 also illustrates a scaling technique often employed when using floating point numbers to represent monetary amounts.[11] Floating point computations are prone to rounding errors because rational decimal fractions are often irrational binary fractions. When these errors accumulate, they cause the so-called "penny problems" that keep accountants awake at night.

The easiest solution is to avoid converting between decimal and binary fractions, which implies that monetary values should be represented as integers. For instance, a financial program running in the United States should perform all computations in pennies or even mils (tenths of a penny). Then the text formatting functions perform the necessary scaling by inserting the decimal point in the appropriate place and rounding off any excess digits on the right. Thus a value of 1234567 mils will be presented as $1,234.57 because the rightmost digit (representing 7 mils or $7/10$¢) will be rounded off.

---

10. Don't you just love the naming conventions of the C standards committee? I really hate to type underscores!

11. The C standard suggests only the string format for monetary amounts. It doesn't specify a computational representation. The most popular binary formats are floating point and long integers. Numerous libraries have been designed to manipulate money as packed decimal numbers, super long integers, and exotic composites of integers and fractions.

Table 5-5. Currency Format Strings

SP	PRE	0	1	2	3	4
0	0	"(V$)" 123.45$ (123.45$)	"–V$" 123.45$ –123.45$	"V$–" 123.45$ 123.45$–	"V–$" 123.45$ 123.45–$	"V$–" 123.45$ 123.45$–
0	1	"($V)" $123.45 ($123.45)	"–$V" $123.45 –$123.45	"$V–" $123.45 $123.45–	"–$V" $123.45 –$123.45	"$–V" $123.45 $–123.45
1	0	"(V $)" 123.45 $ (123.45 $)	"–V $" 123.45 $ –123.45 $	"V $–" 123.45 $ 123.45 $–	"V– $" 123.45 $ 123.45– $	"V $–" 123.45 $ 123.45 $–
1	1	"($ V)" $ 123.45 ($ 123.45)	"–$ V" $ 123.45 –$ 123.45	"$ V– $ 123.45 $ 123.45–	"–$ V" $ 123.45 –$ 123.45	"$ –V" $ 123.45 $ –123.45

The *long int* data type isn't adequate in most financial programs because it provides only nine decimal digits, which limits monetary values to $999,999.99 when computing in U.S. mils.[12] However, the *double* data type has a 52-bit mantissa, providing 15 decimal digits, which is adequate for most situations. Also, it isn't necessary to carry monetary values around as mils (or the equivalent in other locales) because the natural rounding that occurs during floating point computations will handle fractional pennies properly.

Therefore, *TextFromMoney* accepts an argument called *scale*, which is simply the power of 10 by which the *value* argument should be divided. If the program is computing in pennies, the scale factor is 2. For traditional computation, in which the value represents dollars and fractional dollars with no concern about rounding errors, the scale factor is 0. When using scaled monetary values, the scale factor should normally be the same as the number of fractional digits specified by *lconv.int_frac_digits* or *lconv.frac_digits*. If they differ, *TextToMoney* (Listing 5-12) makes the necessary adjustments to add or remove digits on the right.

---

12. Visual C++ provides 64-bit integers by using the *_int64* data type, but that isn't part of standard C.

Table 5-6. **Currency Format Codes**

Format Code	Action
V	Replaced with punctuated decimal string. The decimal point is obtained from *lconv.mon_decimal_point*, and the grouping information comes from *lconv.mon_grouping* and *lconv.mon_thousands_sep*. The number of digits to the right of the decimal point is determined by *lconv.int_frac_digits* for international formatting or *lconv.frac_digits* for local formatting.
<;$MI>	Replaced with *lconv.positive_sign* or *lconv.negative_sign* for a positive or a negative value, respectively.
$	Replaced with *lconv.int_curr_symbol* for international formatting and *lconv.currency_symbol* for local formatting.
()	Removed if the value is positive or 0. P. J. Plauger's implementation doesn't do this, but I believe the parentheses should be displayed only for negative values. I've also encountered business programs written in Cobol and RPG that replace the parentheses with blanks for non-negative values, thereby preserving column alignment. Which approach is best? You be the judge!
	All other characters are simply copied to the output string.

Notice that for a non-zero scale factor, the function does not actually perform a division to conduct the scaling because that might introduce fraction errors. Instead, it calls *sprintf* to format the *double* into a fixed point decimal string, and then it adjusts the position of the decimal point. While performing the adjustment, the function replaces the *sprintf* decimal point (obtained from *lconv.decimal_point*) with the symbol specified by *lconv.mon_decimal_point*.

INPUT CONVERSIONS

So far this chapter has concentrated on output conversions in which the program's binary data is converted to text for display to users in their preferred formats. Now let's look at input conversions, in which the program must analyze user-supplied text strings according to the locale rules to produce the appropriate binary representations.

Numeric Input Conversions

Table 5-4 lists the standard library functions affected by the *LC_NUMERIC* category. Functions such as *atof*, *strtod*, and *sscanf* consult the locale settings as they convert text into binary values. However, in the typical library implementation these functions simply check for the decimal point character (more generally known as the *radix point*) from the current locale. They do not handle the group separator.

Of course, most users enter only the minus sign and the radix point to punctuate their numbers, but suppose you want to offer that capability? Listing 5-11 shows two functions named *TextToInt* and *TextToReal* that take a reasonable approach to the conversion of punctuated number strings. They behave much like *strtol* and *strtod* except that group separator characters, as specified by *lconv.thousands_sep*, are ignored. I say this approach is "reasonable" because it allows separators to appear anywhere in the integer portion of the number. A more rigorous approach would enforce the punctuation rule in *lconv.grouping*, but that seems like overkill to me.

```c
#include <locale.h>
#include <ctype.h>
#include <stdio.h>
#include <stdlib.h>

// Convert a punctuated text string to an integer.
int TextToInt(char *t, long *v)
    {
    int i;                                  // String index
    int bMinus = 0;                         // Negative flag
    struct lconv *pLoc = localeconv();      // Locale stuff
    *v = 0;
    for(i = 0; t[i]; i++)                   // Eat white space.
        if(!isspace(t[i])) break;
    if(t[i] == '-')                         // Eat minus sign.
        {
        i++;
        bMinus = 1;
        }
    while(t[i])                             // Convert decimal digits.
        {
        if(isdigit(t[i])) *v = (*v * 10) + (t[i] - '0');
        else if(t[i] != pLoc->thousands_sep[0]) break;
        i++;
        }
    if(bMinus) *v = -*v;                    // Flip if negative.
    return i;                // Return number of characters.
    }

// Convert a punctuated text string to a real number.
int TextToReal(char *t, double *v)
```

Listing 5-11. TextToInt *and* TextToReal *functions.*   *(continued)*

Listing 5-11. *continued*

```
    {
    int i;                              // String index
    char *pEnd;                         // End pointer
    double vLeft=0, vRight=0;           // Left and right components
    int bMinus = 0;                     // Negative flag
    struct lconv *pLoc = localeconv();  // Locale stuff
    for(i = 0; t[i]; i++)               // Eat white space.
        if(!isspace(t[i])) break;
    if(t[i] == '-')                     // Eat minus sign.
        {
        i++;
        bMinus = 1;
        }
    while(t[i])                         // Convert left part (integer).
        {
        if(isdigit(t[i])) vLeft = (vLeft * 10) + (t[i] - '0');
        else if(t[i] != pLoc->thousands_sep[0]) break;
        i++;
        }
    pEnd = &t[i];                       // Convert right part (fraction).
    if(*pEnd == pLoc->decimal_point[0])
        vRight = strtod(pEnd, &pEnd);
    *v = vLeft + vRight;                // Combine two parts.
    if(bMinus) *v = -*v;                // Flip if negative.
    return pEnd - t;                    // Return number of characters.
    }

#if _DEBUGGING
void main()
    {
    int i;
    long vInt;
    double vReal;
    char in[256];
    setlocale(LC_ALL, "");
    while(gets(in))
        {
        i = TextToInt(in, &vInt);
        printf("TextToInt:  %ld  Excess: \"%s\"\n", vInt, &in[i]);
        i = TextToReal(in, &vReal);
        printf("TextToReal: %f  Excess: \"%s\"\n\n", vReal, &in[i]);
        }
    }
#endif
```

Monetary Input Conversions

Parsing an input string that represents a monetary value is a nontrivial procedure because of the many locale-dependent representations for this type of input. Listing 5-12 shows a function named *TextToMoney* that does a pretty good job, using the scaling technique described earlier in conjunction with the *TextFromMoney* function. As with the integer and real number input conversions, *TextToMoney* handles the group separator loosely, allowing it to appear anywhere in the integer part of the input value.

This function also illustrates one of the weird aspects of the standard locale feature. Notice that when parsing an input string, you must try both the positive and the negative format. Because of the format codes described in Tables 5-5 and 5-6, most locales allow the user to enter negative amounts in two formats. For instance, the United States locale uses −*$V* and *($V)* for the negative format. Therefore, you can enter a negative balance of 123 dollars as either −*$123* or *($123),* and *TextToMoney* will produce the correct result.

```c
#include <ctype.h>
#include <limits.h>
#include <locale.h>
#include <stdio.h>
#include <stdlib.h>
#include <string.h>

// Local currency format table, per Plauger's "Standard C Library"
static char *FormatTable[2][2][5] =
    {
        {
            {   "(V$)",      "-V$",   "V$-",  "V-$",   "V$-"   },
            {   "($V)",      "-$V",   "$V-",  "-$V",   "$-V"   }
        },
        {
            {   "(V $)",     "-V $",  "V $-", "V- $",  "V $-"  },
            {   "($ V)",     "-$ V",  "$ V-", "-$ V",  "$ -V"  }
        }
    };

// Helper function for TextToMoney
static int DoTextToMoney(char *t, double *v, int scale,
                         int bIntl, char *fmt)
    {
    char b[64], c, *pEnd;              // Miscellaneous
    int i, j, k;                       // Miscellaneous
    struct lconv *pLoc = localeconv(); // Locale stuff
    char *pCurrSym =                   // Currency symbol
```

Listing 5-12. *TextToMoney function.*

(continued)

Listing 5-12. *continued*

```
      bIntl ? pLoc->int_curr_symbol : pLoc->currency_symbol;
  int bMinus = 0;                       // Negative number
  int bValue = 0;                       // Value seen
  double vLeft = 0, vRight = 0;         // Value accumulators
  *v = 0;                               // Reset output value.
  if(scale < 0) return 0;          // Negative scaling not allowed
  if(scale > 8) return 0;               // Max scale factor is 8.
  for(i = 0; t[i]; i++)                 // Eat white space.
      if(!isspace(t[i])) break;
  while(c = *fmt++) switch(c)           // Process next format field.
      {
      case ' ':                         // White space
      while(isspace(t[i])) i++;
      continue;

      case '-':                         // Sign
      j = strlen(pLoc->positive_sign);
      k = strlen(pLoc->negative_sign);
      if(j && !strncmp(&t[i], pLoc->positive_sign, j)) i += j;
      else if(k && !strncmp(&t[i], pLoc->negative_sign, k))
          {
          i += k;
          bMinus = 1;
          }
      else if(j) return -i;    // Error if required sign is absent
      continue;

      case '$':                         // Currency symbol
      j = strlen(pCurrSym);
      if(j && !strncmp(&t[i], pCurrSym, j)) i += j;
      else if(j) return -i;   // Error if required symbol is absent
      continue;

      case '(':                         // Credit balance start
      if(t[i] == '(')
          {
          i++;
          bMinus = 2;                    // Use 2 for open parenthesis.
          }

      case ')':                         // Credit balance end
      if((bMinus == 2) && (t[i] == ')'))
          {
          i++;
          bMinus = 1;
          }
```

```
            continue;

        case 'V':                          // Value
        // Convert digits left of decimal point.
        k = i;
        while(t[i])
            {
            if(isdigit(t[i])) vLeft = (vLeft * 10) + (t[i] -
'0');
            else if(t[i] != pLoc->mon_thousands_sep[0]) break;
            i++;
            }
        // Scale the value with right digits and/or padding.
        if(t[i] == pLoc->mon_decimal_point[0])
            {
            while(isdigit(t[++i]) && (scale-- > 0))
            vLeft = (vLeft * 10) + (t[i] - '0');
            if(scale > 0) while(scale-- > 0) vLeft *= 10;
            else
                {
                b[0] = pLoc->decimal_point[0];
                for(j = 1; isdigit(t[i]); b[j++] = t[i++]);
                b[j] = 0;
                vRight = strtod(b,&pEnd);
                }
            }
        else while(scale-- > 0) vLeft *= 10;
        *v = vLeft + vRight;               // Combine the two parts.
        if(i > k) bValue = 1;
        continue;

        default:                           // Matching character
        if(t[i] == c) i++;
        continue;
        }

    if(bMinus > 1) return -i;              // Error if missing right
                                           // parenthesis
    if(!bValue) return -i;                 // Error if no value found
    if(bMinus) *v = -*v;
    return i;
    }
// Convert a punctuated text string to a money value.
int TextToMoney(char *t, double *v, int scale, int bIntl)
    {
    int i;                                 // String index
    struct lconv *pLoc = localeconv();     // Locale stuff
```

(continued)

Listing 5-12. *continued*

```
    char *FmtPos = "$-V";                    // Get international formats.
    char *FmtNeg = "$-V";
    if(!bIntl)                               // Or get local formats.
        {
        int x, y, z;
        x = (pLoc->n_sep_by_space == 1);
        y = (pLoc->n_cs_precedes == 1);
        if((pLoc->n_sign_posn >= 0) && (pLoc->n_sign_posn <= 4))
            z = pLoc->n_sign_posn;
        else z = 0;
        FmtNeg = FormatTable[x][y][z];

        x = (pLoc->p_sep_by_space == 1);
        y = (pLoc->p_cs_precedes == 1);
        if((pLoc->p_sign_posn >= 0) && (pLoc->p_sign_posn <= 4))
            z = pLoc->p_sign_posn;
        else z = 0;
        FmtPos = FormatTable[x][y][z];
        }

    // Try positive and negative format.
    i = DoTextToMoney(t, v, scale, bIntl, FmtPos);
    if(i <= 0) i = DoTextToMoney(t, v, scale, bIntl, FmtNeg);
    return i;
    }

#ifdef _DEBUGGING
void UserTest()
    {
    int x, y, z;
    char b[256];
    double v;
    char *FmtPos = "$-V";
    char *FmtNeg = "$-V";
    struct lconv *pLoc;

    setlocale(LC_ALL, "usa");
    pLoc = localeconv();

    // Get negative format.
    x = (pLoc->n_sep_by_space == 1);
    y = (pLoc->n_cs_precedes == 1);
    if((pLoc->n_sign_posn >= 0) && (pLoc->n_sign_posn <= 4))
        z = pLoc->n_sign_posn;
    else z = 0;
FmtNeg = FormatTable[x][y][z];
```

```
             // Get positive format.
      x = (pLoc->p_sep_by_space == 1);
      y = (pLoc->p_cs_precedes == 1);
      if((pLoc->p_sign_posn >= 0) && (pLoc->p_sign_posn <= 4))
          z = pLoc->p_sign_posn;
      else z = 0;
      FmtPos = FormatTable[x][y][z];

      while(1)
          {
          printf("\nEnter monetary amount or press ENTER to quit.\n");
          printf("Use format \"%s\" or \"%s\"\n", FmtPos, FmtNeg);
          if(!gets(b) || !b[0]) break;
          x = TextToMoney(b, &v, pLoc->frac_digits, 0);
          printf("Value: %f  Return: %d\n", v, x);
          }
      }

void main()
    {
    setlocale(LC_ALL, "");
    UserTest();
    }
#endif
```

Date and Time Input Conversions

Although the functions *strftime* and *wcsftime* do a fine job of producing date and time output strings, the C standard defines no functions that work conversely to convert input text into binary date and time structures. Furthermore, the standard doesn't provide any means similar to *localeconv* and *lconv* so that you can write your own input conversions.

This gaping hole in the standard forces you to delve into the guts of your C/C++ development system to determine how it stores and accesses locale information. We'll take a closer look at this process when we examine Visual C++ in Chapter 7.

WIDE CHARACTER SUPPORT

Although I've shown only examples of the C locale feature using narrow characters, the standard also supports wide character sets such as Unicode. The *setlocale* function always takes a narrow string to specify the language, although Visual C++ adds a nonstandard function named *_wsetlocale* that accepts wide characters. Also, the text in *lconv* uses narrow characters. The other standard locale-dependent functions come in both flavors, as Table 5-4 shows. For example, *wcsftime* is the wide character version of *strftime*.

SUMMARY

While the standard C library acknowledges the existence of countries other than the United States, its international support has many holes. Specifically, its ability to parse locale-sensitive input text is quite limited, and it has no monetary conversion functions at all. Also, it contains no facility for easily writing one set of source code that will work for the SBCS, MBCS, and WCS environments.

Nonetheless, we should be thankful that the C committee took the time to approach the problem of internationalization because their work set the stage for the more complete solution developed by the C++ committee, which the next chapter discusses. In addition, the C standard provides a framework so that compiler vendors can add the missing features as reasonable extensions. Chapter 7 shows the Visual C++ form of these extensions.

Chapter 6

Locales in Standard C++

The C++ standard builds on the locale feature defined by the C committee, but as you might expect, C++ handles internationalization with classes instead of functions. Since C++ is upwardly compatible with C, you can continue to use *setlocale* and the other C functions as described in Chapter 5. The C++ approach, however, is more complete and also easier to use once you become familiar with its somewhat bizarre template-based architecture.

LOCALE AND FACET OBJECTS

Recall that C has, in effect, a single global data structure containing the current international settings. The typical C program dealing with multiple locales must therefore repeatedly call *setlocale* to change this structure, and at any instant the shared international data could have settings from several locales, separated according to categories. For instance, the program could be using United States rules for numbers, French rules for currency, and Norwegian rules for dates.

The C++ committee correctly viewed this as a poor programming model with serious bookeeping, performance, and threading problems. So they defined the *locale* class to replace the shared data structure. Each time a C++ program needs to change the current locale rules, it creates a locale object, specifying the new rules in the constructor. The object can then be used directly for international formatting, or it can be attached to locale-sensitive objects such as I/O streams in order to supply the proper formatting rules.

The *locale* class actually generates a lightweight proxy object that typically contains only a pointer or a *handle* (an integer), depending on how the library is implemented. It's easy and efficient to pass locale objects by value, which greatly simplifies their use.

Under the covers, the proxy refers to an internal thread-safe object that holds a set of references to other thread-safe objects that are derived from the *facet* class.[1] Facet objects are usually implemented as singletons that can be shared by numerous locale objects. The typical library implementation creates these facet singletons on demand in order to reduce memory requirements.

THE DINKUM C++ LIBRARY

Dinkumware is a company formed by P.J. Plauger to provide compiler vendors with conformant implementations of the standard C and C++ libraries. Microsoft licensed the Dinkum C++ Library for inclusion in Visual C++ 6, using a version that conforms to the C++ standard as of 1996. Dinkumware subsequently fixed some bugs in the library and updated it in accordance with post-1996 amendments to the standard. While writing this book, I uncovered additional errors, which are now corrected in the latest Dinkum library.

The examples in this book use version 2.34 of the Dinkumware library in place of the one included with Visual C++ 6. Some examples won't work correctly without this update or a later one. The update is available at *www.dinkumware.com* for a modest price. A future version will probably include the updated Dinkumware library or an equivalent implementation of the latest C++ standard.

Each facet provides member functions to perform a related set of locale-sensitive operations. For instance, the C character–oriented functions such as *isalpha* and *iswalpha* are provided by facets *ctype<char>* and *ctype<wchar_t>* for narrow and wide characters, respectively.

---

1. I found it interesting that the *locale* class handles facets using a technique similar to COM aggregation or tearoffs. It also provides life-cycle management via reference counts just as in COM.

Every locale object supports at least a set of facets that handle the C locale categories described in Chapter 5. (See Table 5-1.) Table 6-1 identifies these standard facets and the *locale* class symbols corresponding to the *LC_* category codes used in C. The *locale* class also defines the symbols *all* and *none*. The former is equivalent to *LC_ALL* and is simply the logical OR of all the other category symbols. The latter is 0, and I've yet to find a use for it.

You can't interchange C and C++ category symbols. The former are only for use with *setlocale*, while the latter can only be used with the C++ classes. The *LC_* symbols are numeric codes and can't be ORed together. On the other hand, the *locale* category codes are bit flags that can be, and often are, when a developer constructs a mixed locale, as you'll see later.

Table 6-1. C++ Locale Categories and Facets

C Category	*C++ Category*	*Facets*
LC_COLLATE	*locale::collate*	*collate<char>* *collate<wchar_t>*
LC_CTYPE	*locale::ctype*	*ctype<char>, ctype<wchar_t>* *codecvt<char, char, mbstate_t>* *codecvt<wchar_t, char, mbstate_t>*
LC_MONETARY	*locale::monetary*	*moneypunct<char>* *moneypunct<wchar_t>* *moneypunct<char, true>* *moneypunct<wchar_t, true>* *money_get<char>* *money_get<wchar_t>* *money_put<char>* *money_put<wchar_t>*
LC_NUMERIC	*locale::numeric*	*numpunct<char>,* *numpunct<wchar_t>* *num_get<char>* *num_get<wchar_t>* *num_put<char>* *num_put<wchar_t>*
LC_TIME	*locale::time*	*time_get<char>* *time_get<wchar_t>* *time_put<char>* *time_put<wchar_t>*
	locale::messages	*messages<char>* *messages<wchar_t>*

Notice that *facet* derivatives are declared as template classes in order to provide common source code for SBCS, MBCS, and WCS programming. The C++ locale feature uses templates extensively. That fact, together with terse names and sparse comments (at least in the Dinkumware implementation), makes the feature extremely difficult to understand were you simply to browse the header files and the library source code. Once you get used to the template syntax, however, you'll find C++ locale support fairly easy to use and quite a bit more powerful than the C techniques described in Chapter 5. To illustrate this ease of use, Listing 6-1 is a C++ version of the C *setlocale* demonstration program shown earlier in Listing 5-1.

```cpp
#include <iostream>        // Stream I/O classes
#include <locale>          // Locale classes
using namespace std;       // Must use standard namespace
void main()
{
time_t Time = time(0);                  // Get the current time.
tm* pTime = gmtime(&Time);

try
    {
    locale locC = locale::classic();  // Classic C locale
    cout.imbue(locC);
    cout << "C locale is \"" << locC.name() << "\"\n";
    cout << "Date is \"";
    _USE(locC, time_put<char>).put(cout, cout, ' ',
                              pTime, 'x', '#');
    cout << "\"\n\n";

    locale locNative("");             // Native locale
    cout.imbue(locNative);
    cout << "Native locale is \"" << locNative.name() << "\"\n";
    cout << "Date is \"";
    _USE(locNative, time_put<char>).put(cout, cout, ' ',
                              pTime, 'x', '#');
    cout << "\"\n\n";

    locale locFrench("french");       // French locale
    cout.imbue(locFrench);
    cout << "French locale is \"" << locFrench.name() << "\"\n";
    cout << "Date is \"";
    _USE(locFrench, time_put<char>).put(cout, cout, ' ',
                              pTime, 'x', '#');
    cout << "\"\n\n";

    locale locGerman("german");       // German locale
    cout.imbue(locGerman);
    cout << "German locale is \"" << locGerman.name() << "\"\n";
    cout << "Date is \"";
    _USE(locGerman, time_put<char>).put(cout, cout, ' ',
                              pTime, 'x', '#');
    cout << "\"\n\n";
```

Listing 6-1. *Sample use of* locale *object.*

```
        locale locXYZ("xyz");           // This should throw exception.
        }
catch(runtime_error e)
        {
        cout << "\nRuntime error: " << e.what() << endl;
        }
catch(bad_cast e)
        {
        cout << "\nBad cast error: " << e.what() << endl;
        }
catch(...)
        {
        cout << "\nUnidentified exception\n";
        }
}
```

Rather than repeatedly calling *setlocale*, the C++ program creates separate locale objects, passing each one the appropriate language name from Table 5-2. Then the program uses the *time_put<char>* facet for each locale object to produce a formatted date and time string from a *tm* structure. Let's look at one of these sequences in more detail:

```
locale locFrench("french");
cout.imbue(locFrench);
cout << "French locale is \"" << locFrench.name() << "\"\n";
cout << "Date is \"";
_USE(locFrench, time_put<char>).put(sbi, cout, ' ', pTime, 'x', '#');
cout << "\"\n\n";
```

Line 1 constructs a French locale object by passing the language name *"french"* just as you do with *setlocale*.[2] I'll show you several other forms of the constructor later in this chapter. Line 2 attaches the new locale to *cout*, the console output stream. This ensures that formatting operations on that stream will use the correct code page. You'll get a closer look at the stream and locale connection later in this chapter. Lines 3, 4, and 6 send some boilerplate text to the stream. Line 5 calls the *put* member function of the *time_put<char>* facet[3] to generate a date string, which is sent to *cout*.

---

2. The C++ committee didn't define a standard set of language names, but the popular names are identical to those listed in Table 5-2. As in C, you can also use *"C"* for the classic C locale and *""* for the default, or native, locale.

3. This function is one that changed after Visual C++ 6 was released. The Visual C++ 6 version doesn't accept a fill character as the third argument, as the standard now requires.

The details of this call are hidden within a macro named _USE[4] because many C++ compilers (including Visual C++ 6) can't handle the standard syntax for *use_facet*, which is defined as the following template:

```
template <class Facet> const Facet& use_facet(const locale&);
```

Notice that the template parameter *Facet* isn't one of the function arguments. So, the C++ standard requires that you access the *time_put* facet for the French locale with an unusual call:

```
use_facet<time_put<char>>(locFrench).put(sbi, cout, ' ',
                                          pTime, 'x', '#');
```

This statement says, in effect, "Call the version of *use_facet* that knows how to access the *time_put<char>* facet, specifying the locale object named *locFrench*. Then use the result of that call to invoke the *put* member function that produces a time string." Some compilers as of mid-1999 didn't yet handle this style of template function call because it was a relatively recent addition to the C++ syntax. As a workaround, the current libraries typically define *use_facet* as follows:[5]

```
template <class Facet>
const Facet& use_facet(const locale&, const Facet*, bool bCreate);
```

The second argument is a dummy pointer that enables the compiler to construct the proper form of the function. The third argument, when *true*, indicates that a facet object should be created if one doesn't already exist for the specified locale. If this argument is false and the facet doesn't already exist, *use_facet* throws a *bad_case* exception. So, the sample program would have to use the following call in order to compile with Visual C++ 6:

```
use_facet(locFrench, (time_put<char>*)0, true).put(sbi,
    cout, ' ', pTime, 'x', '#');
```

Clearly, this workaround looks very different from the standard version, and so it's good programming practice to hide the difference behind a macro. When the compiler supports the correct syntax, a simple redefinition of the macro will update existing application code. Visual C++ 6 provides two macros for this purpose, _USE and _USEFAC, which are defined as follows:

```
#define _USE(loc, fac) use_facet(loc, (fac*)0, true)
#define _USEFAC(loc, fac) use_facet(loc, (fac*)0, false)
```

---

4. Plauger defined the _USE macro in his reference implementation of the Standard Template Library, which is employed by Visual C++ Version 6.

5. This is the Plauger definition employed by many popular compilers, including Visual C++. The third argument provides some control over the dynamic creation of facet objects.

The only difference between these macros is that *_USE* requests that the facet be created if it doesn't exist, while *_USEFAC* throws an exception in that case. So the syntax *_USE(locFrench ,time_put<char>)* requests that the *time_put* facet be retrieved from the *locFrench* locale object, with facet creation occuring if necessary.

Now refer back to Listing 6-1. Unfortunately, the standard C++ library doesn't overload the I/O shift operators for the *time_put* facet, so you must call the facet's *put* function directly, passing the output stream object, the time structure, the format code, and the format modifier. The actual call is

```
put(cout, cout, ' ', pTime, 'x', '#');
```

The output stream *cout* is passed twice because the function requires an iterator[6] as the first argument and a stream as the second. You can use *cout* in place of the iterator because the compiler knows how to construct an *ostreambuf_iterator* object from an *ostream* object. The third argument is a fill character to use in the event that the output field requires padding. The fourth argument, *pTime*, points to a *tm* structure, and the final two arguments are combined into the *"%#x"* format specification string for the internal call to *strftime*.[7] Later in this chapter, I'll show how to write a custom inserter so that the shift operator can be used instead of a direct call to the *put* function.

Notice that you should create locale objects and access their facets within a try block because the *locale* constructor and the *use_facet* function both throw exceptions to indicate failure. The constructor throws a *runtime_error* exception if it doesn't recognize the language name, while *use_facet* throws a *bad_cast* exception if the facet doesn't exist or can't be created.[8]

CLASSIC AND GLOBAL LOCALES

The C++ standard defines a static function, *locale::classic*, to access the traditional C locale settings, also called the *classic locale*. You can use this locale directly or clone it as in Listing 6-1. It provides the same settings as when you call *setlocale* with *LC_ALL* as the category and C as the language.

---

6. An iterator is essentially a smart pointer to some type of data collection, and so an output stream iterator provides a means to access an output stream using iterator syntax and semantics. This abstraction is a fundamental concept in the Standard Template Library, which is now part of the C++ standard.

7. Under the covers, many of the C++ facet functions use *setlocale*, *strftime*, and other C library functions, as described in Chapter 5.

8. Since *use_facet* throws a *bad_cast* exception, the library designers obviously considered it to be a form of casting in which a locale can be converted to a facet. This is reminiscent of COM's *QueryInterface* function.

121

The standard also provides a *global locale* that gives the C++ programmer a convenient way to change the C locale. This is handy when your program uses both the C and the C++ library. For instance, here's how you can temporarily adjust the C locale to match a C++ locale that uses French rules:

```
// Create French locale and adjust C settings.
locale locFrench("french");
locale locSave = locale::global(locFrench);
// Use locale-sensitive C function.
char a[]= "abc", b[] = "def";
int x = strcoll(a, b);
// Restore C settings.
locale::global(locSave);
```

Internally, the *global* function calls *locFrench.name* to extract the qualified locale name, which is then passed as the language name to *setlocale* with *LC_ALL* as the category. The fully qualified language name returned by *setlocale* is used to create a locale object for return to the caller of *locale::global*. If you save that information as above, you can restore the C locale to its previous state.

The C++ standard guarantees that the global locale will have the classic settings when your program starts—that is, when your *main* function is called. Also, if you use the default constructor to create a new locale object, the object will be initialized with the current global locale settings. Throughout the C++ library, the global locale is used as the default whenever you don't specify another one.

USING MULTIPLE LOCALES

When working with multiple locales in C, you must repeatedly call *setlocale* to adjust the capabilities of the single locale data structure. Furthermore, since this data is shared by all parts of the program, you must ensure that a function that changes a setting restores the previous state when it returns. I showed this technique in Listing 5-4 by having the *GetFrenchDate* function temporarily change the *LC_TIME* category to use French formatting rules.

The C++ approach is considerably different because the standards committee wanted to avoid the use of changeable shared data. Instead, they made it easy and efficient to manipulate multiple locale objects.

As I mentioned earlier, a locale object simply holds a reference to an internal object that maintains a collection of facet pointers. The collection can be populated when the locale object is constructed, or facets can be dynamically attached as the application program invokes *use_facet*. The facet objects themselves can be statically allocated during library initialization or dynamically created as needed. Regardless of the approach the library uses internally, the facet repertoire of a locale object is immutable. That is, the facets associated with it are specified when the locale object is created and can't change thereafter.[9]

In the typical library implementation, a facet object can be attached to multiple locale objects. To avoid messy ownership issues, each facet object controls its own lifetime by means of reference counters. The actual plumbing that accomplishes this feat is pretty complicated, but you don't need to know the details unless you want to design custom facet classes or extend the standard facets. The key points to remember are

- It's inexpensive to create locale objects.

- It's efficient to pass locale objects by value because they are quite small, usually just 32 bits.

Given these characteristics, the preferred approach to multilocale programming is to create a locale object having the desired facets for a particular context and to discard it when that context is no longer valid. In practice, this means that you'll frequently create locale objects on the stack, whereas in C you must frequently call *setlocale*. To illustrate this, Listing 6-2 is a C++ version of the C program shown earlier in Listing 5-4. This sample program also illustrates some of the other minutiae involved in the C++ locale feature.

```
#include <iostream>
#include <locale>
#include <strstream>
using namespace std;

int GetFrenchDate(struct tm *pTime, char *pOut, size_t nOut)
{
try
    {
    ostrstream s(pOut, nOut-1);   // Wrap pointer in a stream.
    locale locFrench("french");   // Create French locale
                                  // and use it.
    s.imbue(locFrench);           // Attach locale to stream.
    _USE(locFrench, time_put<char>).put(s, s, ' ', pTime,
                                  'x', '#');
    s.put(0);                     // Append null terminator.
```

Listing 6-2. *Using multiple locales in C++.*   *(continued)*

---

9. This is similar to one of the fundamental rules of COM, which states that an object's interface repertoire must remain constant for the life of the object.

Listing 6-2. *continued*

```
    if(s.fail()) throw 0;        // Check for stream problems.
    return strlen(pOut);         // Return character count.
    }
catch(...)
    {
    *pOut = 0;                    // Return empty string on error.
    return 0;
    }
}

void main()
{
time_t Time = time(0);           // Get the current time.
tm* pTime = gmtime(&Time);
char b[256];                     // Output buffer

cout << "Classic date is \"";    // Show date in classic format.
// The following statement could throw an exception,
// but it's unlikely.
_USE(locale::classic(), time_put<char>).put(cout, cout, ' ',
                                    pTime, 'x', '#');
cout << "\"\n\n";

GetFrenchDate(pTime, b, sizeof(b)); // Show date in French format.
cout << "French date is " << b << "\n\n";
}
```

First look at the *main* function, in which the program displays the date in the traditional C format. As described earlier, the program uses the classic locale for this purpose by means of the following statement:

```
_USE(locale::classic(), time_put <char>).put(cout,cout, ' ',
                                    pTime, 'x', '#');
```

Next look at the *GetFrenchDate* function. It accepts a character array pointer and length. How do you pass this information to the *time_put* facet? The *put* function requires a character iterator, which is essentially a smart pointer to a character array. You can easily create one of these critters as a temporary *ostrstream* wrapper around the caller's character array pointer. The facet's *put* function then uses the iterator's *put* function to place characters in the array and check for overflow. Notice that I decreased the array size by 1 when constructing the *ostrstream* object in order to reserve space for the null terminator. After the facet function returned, I appended the terminator by calling the stream's *put* function. Don't forget to do this because (as I learned the hard way) some facet functions don't generate null-terminated strings.

USING MIXED LOCALES

So far, I've created locale objects in which all facets use the same language context. Now let's see how to create an object that has facets from several different contexts. First, remember that a locale object's facets must be specified at construction time and can't change thereafter. This means that you must specify the locale mixture when invoking the constructor. To see how to do this, let's look at the *locale* class declaration. Listing 6-3 is a simplified version that shows the public interface without the exception specifiers.

```
class locale
    {
    public:
    // Type and constant definitions for this class
    class facet;                // Base class for facets
    class id;                   // General identifier class
    typedef int category;       // Category type definition
    static const category       // Category codes
        none    = 0,
        collate = 0x010,        // Like LC_COLLATE
        ctype   = 0x020,        // Like LC_CTYPE
        monetary = 0x040,       // Like LC_MONETARY
        numeric = 0x080,        // Like LC_NUMERIC
        time    = 0x100,        // Like LC_TIME
        messages = 0x200,       // No C equivalent
        all = collate | ctype | monetary | numeric | time
              | messages;

    // Constructors
    locale();
    locale(const locale& other);
    explicit locale(const char* name, category cat = all);
    locale(const locale& other, const char* name,
           category cat = all);
    template <class Facet> locale(const locale& other,
            Facet* fac);
    template <class Facet> locale(const locale& other,
            const locale& one);
    locale(const locale& other, const locale& one, category cat);

    // Destructor
    ~locale();

    // Assignment operator
    const locale& operator = (const locale& other);
```

Listing 6-3. *Simplified declaration of* locale *class.*   *(continued)*

Listing 6-3. *continued*

```
// Get locale name string.
basic_string <char> name() const;

// Equality test operations
bool operator == (const locale& other) const;
bool operator != (const locale& other) const;

// Parentheses operator
template <class charT, class Traits, class Allocator>
    bool operator()
        (const basic_string<charT, Traits, Allocator>& s1,
         const basic_string<charT, Traits, Allocator>& s2)const;

// Static locale objects:
static locale global(const locale&);
static const locale& classic();
};
```

The following list describes the seven constructors for the *locale* class in more detail.

- ■ *locale();*   Constructs a locale object having the same facets as the global locale, which always corresponds to the locale established by the most recent call to *setlocale*. This is the default constructor.

- ■ *locale(const locale& other);*   Constructs a locale object having the same facets as the *other* locale object. This is the copy constructor.

- ■ *explicit locale(const char*name, category cat = all);*   Constructs a locale object having the same facets as the global locale object, except that the facets for the categories in *cat* are obtained from the language specified by *name*. This is not a conversion constructor, and so it is marked as *explicit* to prevent the compiler from performing implicit conversions.

- ■ *locale(const locale& other, const char* name, category cat);*   Constructs a locale object having the same facets as the *other* locale object, except that the facets for the categories in *cat* are obtained from the language specified by *name*.

- ■ *template <class Facet> locale(const locale& other, Facet* fac);*   Constructs a locale object having the same facets as the *other* locale object except for the facet *fac*.

- **template <class Facet> locale(const locale& other, const locale& one);**   Constructs a locale object having the same facets as the *other* locale object except for the facet specified by the template parameter, which is copied from the locale object specified by *one*. Visual C++ 6 and other compilers don't support this syntax, which uses a relatively new C++ language feature that doesn't require the template parameter to appear in the constructor's argument list. You can achieve the same result by using the preceding constructor.

- **locale(const locale& other, const locale& one, category cat);**   Constructs a locale object having the same facets as the *other* locale object except for the facets specified by *cat*, which are copied from the locale object specified by *one*. Listing 6-4 shows how to use these constructors to create mixed locale objects, that is, locales containing facets for different languages.

```cpp
#include <iostream>
#include <locale>
#include <strstream>
using namespace std;

#include <conio.h>
static void pause()
{
cout << "Press ENTER to continue" << endl;
getch();
cout << endl;
}

static void ShowName(ostream& out, const string& s)
{
const char* pName = s.c_str();
while(*pName)
    {
    out << *pName;
    if(*pName++ == ';') out << endl;
    }
}

void main()
{
time_t Time = time(0);                  // Get the current time.
tm* pTime = gmtime(&Time);
```

Listing 6-4. *Working with mixed locales.*   *(continued)*

Listing 6-4. *continued*

```
cout.setf(ios_base::showbase);        // Force currency symbols.

// Create United States locale.
locale loc1("English_United States");
cout.imbue(loc1);
cout << "Locale loc1(\"English_United States\")\n";
ShowName(cout, loc1.name());
cout << "\n\nDate: \"";
_USE(loc1, time_put<char>).put(cout, cout, ' ', pTime, 'x', '#');
cout << "\"\nNumber 12345.6789: \"";
_USE(loc1, num_put<char>).put(cout, cout, '*', 12345.6789);
cout << "\"\nMoney 12345.6789: \"";
_USE(loc1, money_put<char>).put(cout, false, cout, '*',
12345.6789);
cout << "\"\n\n";
pause();

// Use French time facets.
locale loc2(loc1, "French_France", locale::time);
cout.imbue(loc2);
cout << "\nLocale loc2(loc1, \"French_France\", locale::time)\n";
ShowName(cout, loc2.name());
cout << "\nDate: \"";
_USE(loc2, time_put<char>).put(cout, cout, ' ', pTime, 'x', '#');
cout << "\"\nNumber 12345.6789: \"";
_USE(loc2, num_put<char>).put(cout, cout, '*', 12345.6789);
cout << "\"\nMoney 12345.6789: \"";
_USE(loc2, money_put<char>).put(cout, false, cout, '*',
12345.6789);
cout << "\"\n\n";
pause();

// Use German money facets.
locale loc3(loc2, "German_Germany", locale::monetary);
cout.imbue(loc3);
cout <<
    "\nLocale loc3(loc2, \"German_Germany\", locale::monetary)\n";
ShowName(cout, loc3.name());
cout << "\nDate: \"";
_USE(loc3, time_put<char>).put(cout, cout, ' ', pTime, 'x', '#');
cout << "\"\nNumber 12345.6789: \"";
_USE(loc3, num_put<char>).put(cout, cout, '*', 12345.6789);
cout << "\"\nMoney 12345.6789: \"";
_USE(loc3, money_put<char>).put(cout, true, cout, '*',
12345.6789);
cout << "\"\n\n";
pause();
}
```

In this case, I want a locale that uses French rules for formatting dates, German rules for money, and United States rules for all other cases. In order to achieve this combination, the program has to create three locale objects as follows:

```
locale loc1("English_United States");
locale loc2(loc1, "French_France", locale::time);
locale loc3(loc2, "German_Germany", locale::monetary);
```

The first object, *loc1*, is a "pure" locale using United States rules. It then serves as the basis for *loc2*, which replaces the time facet with French rules. The third object, *loc3*, uses *loc2* as its base and replaces the money facet with German rules.

Figure 6-1 shows the output of this program running on a Windows 2000 system. Notice that all facets appear to use CP1252, the ANSI code page, which contains the necessary English, French, and German characters. Nonetheless, the French date string is garbled, displaying as *lundi 30 ao√t 1999* when it should be *lundi 30 août 1999* to properly represent August 30, 1999. Indeed, you may have noticed that all preceding examples in this chapter exhibit the same behavior.

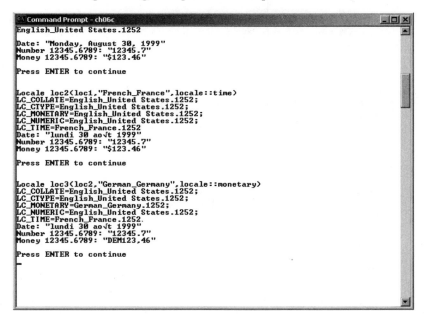

Figure 6-1. *Output of Listing 6-4.*

This problem arose because the console window was using CP437 while the locale objects were using CP1252. That is, my computer is configured for convenient use in the United States, where CP437 is the traditional PC character encoding, also called the OEM code page. As with *setlocale* in the standard C library, the typical implementation of the *locale* class in standard C++ makes no attempt to change the operating system's code page configuration. The code pages associated with a locale object determine only how characters are generated and manipulated in memory, not how they appear on the screen.

As you saw in Chapter 5 when I described *setlocale* (see Listing 5-5), the application program must specifically adjust the system settings to be compatible with the locale settings. Listing 5-5 solved the problem by adjusting the console output code page with the Win32 function *SetConsoleOutputCP*. Here's another technique that doesn't require the use of the Win32 API:

```
locale loc1("English_United States.OCP");
locale loc2(loc1, "French_France", locale::time);
locale loc3(loc2, "German_Germany", locale::monetary);
```

In Microsoft's implementation of the standard C and C++ libraries, you can use the symbol *OCP* to represent the OEM code page, which is the page that the operating system employs by default for console programs. Introducing this change into Listing 6-4 causes the French date to display properly, as shown in Figure 6-2.

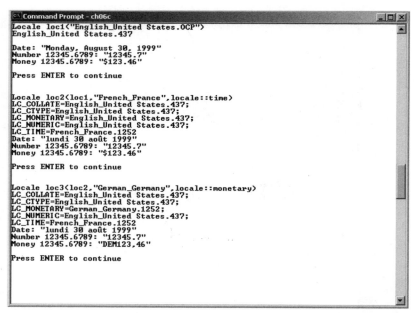

Figure 6-2. *Using the OEM code page.*

Notice, however, that the program continues to report that the French and German facets are using CP1252. This is misleading because they're actually using the OEM page, which is CP437 on my system. What's going on here? Well, the Microsoft Visual C++ 6 implementation of *setlocale*, which is used internally by the *locale* class, tracks only two code pages, one for the *LC_COLLATE* category and one for *LC_CTYPE* and all other categories. Thus the *numeric, time, monetary,* and *message* facets all use the code page established for the *ctype* facet, which is CP437 in this example.

It's possible that a C++ development system from another vendor or a future version from Microsoft will switch code pages dynamically within the locale facets. So the sample program needs another adjustment in order to ensure that all facets use the OEM page. Here's one possibility, which produces the output shown in Figure 6-3:

```
locale loc1("English_United States.OCP");
locale loc2(loc1, "French_France.OCP", locale::time);
locale loc3(loc2, "German_Germany.OCP", locale::monetary);
```

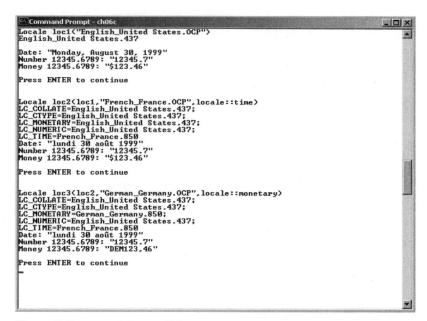

Figure 6-3. *Using OCP on all facets.*

Oops, that didn't solve the problem. Although the French date still displays correctly, the French and German facets now report that they're using CP850, which is the usual OEM page in Europe. In other words, the OCP specification requests the OEM page for the specified locale,[10] not the OEM page being used on the current system.

---

10. Microsoft's Win32 locale database specifies the preferred OEM (console) code page for each locale. It also specifies the preferred ANSI (Windows) code page, which you can access by using the ACP suffix on a language string.

In order to make all facets use the same code page, either you must specify the page number explicitly at design time, or the program must extract and propagate the page number from the *ctype* facet at run time. Here's an example of the first technique:

```
// U.S. English using CP437
locale loc1("English_United States.437");

// Add French time rules with CP437.
locale loc2(loc1, "French_France.437", locale::time);

// Add German monetary rules with CP437.
locale loc3(loc2, "German_Germany.437", locale::monetary);
```

The second technique is more general because it determines the appropriate code page at run time. Here's an illustration of that approach using the *string* class. It produces the output shown in Figure 6-4.

```
locale loc1("English_United States.OCP");
string name = loc1.name();
string cp = ".OCP";
int x = name.find_last_of('.');
if(x >= 0) cp = name.substr(x, name.length() - x);
name = "French_France" + cp;
locale loc2(loc1, name.c_str(), locale::time);
name = "German_Germany" + cp;
locale loc3(loc2, name.c_str(), locale::monetary);
```

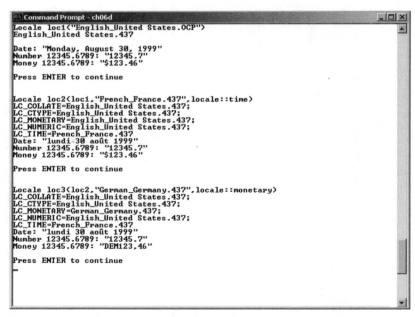

Figure 6-4. *Setting all facets to proper OEM page.*

After creating *loc1* to use United States rules with the OEM code page, the program extracts the code page substring from that locale. The substring is then appended to the language name for each subsequent locale so that they all use the OEM code page associated with *loc1*.

Listing 6-5 shows the final result of the changes necessary to make Listing 6-4 display the proper symbols and be relatively safe from possible future changes in the locale and facet classes. Essentially, Listing 6-5 coerces all facets to work with the OEM code page instead of the page they would naturally prefer.

```cpp
#include <iostream>
#include <locale>
#include <strstream>
using namespace std;

#include <conio.h>
static void pause()
{
cout << "Press ENTER to continue" << endl;
getch();
cout << endl;
}

static void ShowName(ostream& out, const string& s)
{
const char* pName = s.c_str();
while(*pName)
    {
    out << *pName;
    if(*pName++ == ';') out << endl;
    }
}

void main() // Check global names when using mixed mode.
{
time_t Time = time(0);              // Get the current time.
tm* pTime = gmtime(&Time);

cout.setf(ios_base::showbase);      // Force currency symbols.

// Create United States locale.
locale loc1("English_United States.OCP");
```

Listing 6-5. *Final version of mixed locale example.*   *(continued)*

Listing 6-5. *continued*

```
cout.imbue(loc1);
cout << "Locale loc1(\"English_United States.OCP\")\n";
ShowName(cout, loc1.name());
cout << "\n\nDate: \"";
_USE(loc1, time_put<char>).put(cout, cout, ' ', pTime, 'x', '#');
cout << "\"\nNumber 12345.6789: \"";
_USE(loc1, num_put<char>).put(cout, cout, '*', 12345.6789);
cout << "\"\nMoney 12345.6789: \"";
_USE(loc1, money_put<char>).put(cout, false, cout, '*',
12345.6789);
cout << "\"\n\n";
pause();

// Get ambient OEM code page.
string name = loc1.name();
string cp = ".OCP";
int x = name.find_last_of('.');
if(x >= 0) cp = name.substr(x, name.length() - x);

// Use French time facets.
name = "French_France" + cp;
locale loc2(loc1, name.c_str(), locale::time);
cout.imbue(loc2);
cout << "\nLocale loc2(loc1, \"" << name << "\", locale::time)\n";
ShowName(cout, loc2.name());
cout << "\nDate: \"";
_USE(loc2, time_put<char>).put(cout, cout, ' ', pTime, 'x', '#');
cout << "\"\nNumber 12345.6789: \"";
_USE(loc2, num_put<char>).put(cout, cout, '*', 12345.6789);
cout << "\"\nMoney 12345.6789: \"";
_USE(loc2, money_put<char>).put(cout, false, cout, '*',
12345.6789);
cout << "\"\n\n";
pause();

// Use German money facets.
name = "German_Germany" + cp;
locale loc3(loc2, name.c_str(), locale::monetary);
cout.imbue(loc3);
cout <<
    "\nLocale loc3(loc2, \"" << name << "\", locale::monetary)\n";
```

```
ShowName(cout, loc3.name());
cout << "\nDate: \"";
_USE(loc3, time_put<char>).put(cout, cout, ' ', pTime, 'x', '#');
cout << "\"\nNumber 12345.6789: \"";
_USE(loc3, num_put<char>).put(cout, cout, '*', 12345.6789);
cout << "\"\nMoney 12345.6789: \"";
_USE(loc3, money_put<char>).put(cout, true, cout, '*',
12345.6789);
cout << "\"\n\n";
pause();
}
```

Even though the program now seems OK, you must be very careful when coercing a locale to use an "unnatural" code page. This example works only because CP437 is compatible with CP850 and CP1252 (the "natural" European pages) to the extent that it contains the symbols needed for French dates and German money. CP437 can't correctly display all Western European characters, however, so it would be better to switch the console to CP850 or CP1252, as shown in Chapter 5. In Listing 6-5 you can accomplish this by using ACP instead of OCP when constructing the first locale. ACP requests the ANSI code page, which is the one registered for use by Windows applications running on the system. Usually it will provide better multilanguage coverage than the OEM page. Of course, Unicode is the best approach because it eliminates these code page issues.

USING LOCALES WITH STREAMS

The examples in this chapter send their text strings to the console output stream, an object named *cout* that's defined in the standard C++ library. Programs can send data to *cout* and other streams in three ways: by using overloaded shift operators, by directly calling stream functions such as *put* and *write*, and by passing the stream to other functions such as *time_put<char>::put*.

Some of these operations perform locale-sensitive formatting and conversions, and so the stream object needs access to a locale object. The standards committee could have mandated that all streams use the global locale, but that would lead to the same awkward programming as when you're dealing with the single shared locale in C. In fact, the global locale *is* the C locale.

Fortunately, the committee took a more flexible approach by defining an *imbue* function[11] that attaches a locale object to a stream. That's why all the examples in this chapter call *cout.imbue* after creating a new locale object. Notice that the *GetFrenchDate* function in Listing 6-2 also uses *imbue* with the *ostrstream* object, which is an output stream wrapped around a character array. If you don't imbue a stream with a specific locale, it uses the global locale.

Streams utilize their imbued locales primarily when processing overloaded shift operators. These operators usually do some type of data conversion and text formatting, such as transforming integers and floating point values into punctuated character strings. This works in both directions. That is, input streams also have overloaded shift operators that parse incoming text and convert it into binary representations such as integers and floating point numbers.

Locale facets also employ the imbued locales when they operate on the streams that are supplied as facet function arguments. For that reason, streams provide the *getloc* function to obtain the currently imbued locale. This function is declared in both *ios_base* and *basic_streambuf*, which are the fundamental base classes for the stream subsystem.

Using Facets in Custom Inserters

Although the standards committee defined locale-sensitive output stream inserters for the simple numeric types, they didn't define inserters for data representing dates, times, and monetary amounts. This leads to the somewhat awkward programming style exhibited in the preceding examples, in which facet function calls must be intermixed with stream shifting operations.

I suspect the committee omitted these inserters to avoid wrangling over the "correct" way to represent the data. As you are no doubt aware, the C++ world abounds with different techniques for representing time and money data. Nonetheless, once you've chosen a data representation, it's pretty easy to write custom inserters that hide the facet function calls behind the left shift operator. Usually, you must package the data in a class that hides its exact structure, provides conversions to other representations used in your system, and carries the additional formatting information needed by the locale facets. Let's examine this technique for the time and money facets.

Designing a time facet inserter

Listing 6-6 shows the *tmFmt* class, which I designed as a wrapper around a *tm* structure that carries date and time information. I chose the *tm* data type because it's popular among C and C++ programmers and is used by the time facet.

---

11. The word *imbue* means *to tinge or dye deeply* and is synonymous with *permeate* and *infuse*. The more pragmatic among us would probably have chosen *attach,* which has long been the popular term to describe object associations such as the stream and locale connection. But some stream classes already had an *attach* function to manage the connection between the stream and the underlying C file.

```
class tmFmt
{
public:
// Constructors
tmFmt(const tm& t, const char *fmt = "%c") :
    m_Time(t), m_Format(fmt) {}
tmFmt(time_t t = time(0), const char* fmt = "%c") :
    m_Time(*localtime(&t)), m_Format(fmt) {};

// Accessors
const tm& Time() const
    { return m_Time; }
const string& Format() const
    { return m_Format; }

// Mutators
tm& Time()
    { return m_Time; }
string& Format()
    { return m_Format; }

// Cast operators
operator tm*()
    { return &m_Time; }
operator tm&()
    { return m_Time; }
operator tm() const
    { return m_Time; }

// Pseudo-manipulator
const tmFmt& SetFormat(char* fmt)
    {
    m_Format = fmt;
    return *this;
    }

// Internal stuff
private:
tm m_Time;
string m_Format;
};
```

Listing 6-6. *The* tmFmt *class.*

The class offers two constructors. One copies a *tm* structure into the *m_Time* member. The other converts a *time_t* item into the *tm* form and places the result in *m_Time*. It also serves as the default constructor because it accesses the current system time if you don't supply a *time_t* value. You could easily add more constructors to convert other popular time representations such as the Win32 *SYSTEMTIME* and *FILETIME* structures.

The second argument of each constructor is a formatting string which defaults to *"%c"* in order to supply the default date and time string for the current locale. This string uses the codes defined for the *strftime* function, which the *time_put* facet calls internally.

The class includes accessors, mutators, and cast operators for its private data items, so you can write statements like these:

```
tm tt;                        // Creates tm structure
tmFmt f(tt);                  // Creates corresponding tmFmt object
f.Format() = "%A";            // Changes the format string
tt = f.Time();                // Extracts m_Time via accessor
tt = f;                       // Extracts m_Time via implicit cast
char *s = asctime(f);         // Works directly with m_Time
s = asctime(&(tm)f);          // Works with copy of m_Time
s = asctime(&(tm&)f);         // Works directly with m_Time
```

SetFormat is a special property access function that can be used to change the format string on the fly in conjunction with the left shift operator, as I'll show later. Since this function is somewhat similar to a stream manipulator, I call it a *pseudo-manipulator*.

Listing 6-7 shows some additional classes derived from *tmFmt* for programming convenience when you want to temporarily change the output format during a stream insertion. These derivations have constructors that supply different format strings to the underlying *tmFmt* object. Each constructor takes a *tm* item as its only argument, but since *tmFmt* can implicitly cast itself to the *tm* type, the derived class constructor can effectively copy a *tmFmt* object and replace its format string with a simple cast operation.

```
class tmFmtDate : public tmFmt
{
public:
tmFmtDate(const tm& t) : tmFmt(t, "%x") {}
};

class tmFmtDateLong : public tmFmt
{
public:
tmFmtDateLong(const tm& t) : tmFmt(t, "%#x") {}
};
```

Listing 6-7. *Derivations from* tmFmt.

```
class tmFmtDateMilitary : public tmFmt
{
public:
tmFmtDateMilitary(const tm& t) : tmFmt(t, "%d %b %Y") {}
};

class tmFmtTime : public tmFmt
{
public:
tmFmtTime(const tm& t) : tmFmt(t, "%X") {}
};
```

Listing 6-8 shows the overloaded left shift operator that serves as the output stream inserter for the *tmFmt* class. I must confess that I cloned this code from one of the standard inserters in order to get it right, since template-based inserters are somewhat arcane.[12] The basic goal is to call *time_put::put* for the character type specified by template parameters *CharType* and *CharTraits*. The two type definitions *Iterator* and *Facet* simplify the syntax of the call. The *sentry* object named *OK* initializes the stream for extraction and guards it in a multithreaded environment. The *if* statement casts the sentry to a *bool* value in order to check whether the stream is in a safe state for extraction. The remaining statements ensure that problems in the facet or stream will be properly reported by means of the stream status flags, with exceptions propagated as necessary.

```
template <class CharType, class CharTraits>
inline basic_ostream<CharType, CharTraits>& operator <<
    (basic_ostream<CharType, CharTraits>& Stream, const tmFmt& Time)
{
typedef ostreambuf_iterator<CharType, CharTraits> Iterator;
typedef time_put<CharType, Iterator> Facet;
ios_base::iostate state = ios_base::goodbit;
const typename
    basic_ostream<CharType, CharTraits>::sentry OK(Stream);
if(OK)
    {
    try
        {
        if(_USE(Stream.getloc(), Facet).put
            (
            Iterator(Stream.rdbuf()),
```

Listing 6-8. *Stream inserter for* tmFmt *class.*   *(continued)*

---

12. Plauger described a similar approach to facet inserters and extractors in his column for
    C++ User's Journal.

Listing 6-8. *continued*

```
            Stream,
            Stream.fill(),
            &Time.Time(),
            &*Time.Format().begin(),
            &*Time.Format().end()
            ).failed()) state |= ios_base::badbit;
        }
    catch(...)
        {
        Stream.setstate(ios_base::badbit, true);
        }
    }
Stream.setstate(state);
return(Stream);
}
```

Now we can test the *tmFmt* class and its inserter. Listing 6-9 is a simple test program showing various date and time formatting operations in several locales. Figure 6-5 shows the console output from the test program.

```
void main()
{
tmFmt t;

cout << "Classic formats:\n";
cout << "Default is " << t << endl;
cout << "tmFmtDate is " << tmFmtDate(t) << endl;
cout << "tmFmtTime is " << tmFmtTime(t) << endl;
cout << "tmFmtDateLong is " << tmFmtDateLong(t) << endl;
cout << "tmFmtDateMilitary is " << tmFmtDateMilitary(t) << endl;
cout << "tmFmt(t, \"%A\") is " << tmFmt(t, "%A") << endl;

locale locNative(".OCP");
cout.imbue(locNative);

cout << "\nNative formats:\n";
cout << "Default is " << t << endl;
cout << "tmFmtDate is " << tmFmtDate(t) << endl;
cout << "tmFmtTime is " << tmFmtTime(t) << endl;
cout << "tmFmtDateLong is " << tmFmtDateLong(t) << endl;
cout << "tmFmtDateMilitary is " << tmFmtDateMilitary(t) << endl;
cout << "tmFmt(t, \"%A\") is " << tmFmt(t, "%A") << endl;
```

Listing 6-9. *Examples of* tmFmt *inserter.*

```
locale locFrench("French_France.OCP");
cout.imbue(locFrench);

cout << "\nFrench formats:\n";
cout << "Default is " << t << endl;
cout << "tmFmtDate is " << tmFmtDate(t) << endl;
cout << "tmFmtTime is " << tmFmtTime(t) << endl;
cout << "tmFmtDateLong is " << tmFmtDateLong(t) << endl;
cout << "tmFmtDateMilitary is " << tmFmtDateMilitary(t) << endl;
cout << "tmFmt(t, \"%A\") is " << tmFmt(t, "%A") << endl;

locale locSwedish("Swedish_Sweden.OCP");
cout.imbue(locSwedish);

cout << "\nSwedish formats:\n";
cout << "Default is " << t << endl;
cout << "tmFmtDate is " << tmFmtDate(t) << endl;
cout << "tmFmtTime is " << tmFmtTime(t) << endl;
cout << "tmFmtDateLong is " << tmFmtDateLong(t) << endl;
cout << "tmFmtDateMilitary is " << tmFmtDateMilitary(t) << endl;
cout << "tmFmt(t, \"%A\") is " << tmFmt(t, "%A") << endl;

cout << "\nSetFormat(\"%A\") is " << t.SetFormat("%A") << endl;
cout << "New default is " << t << endl;

pause();
}
```

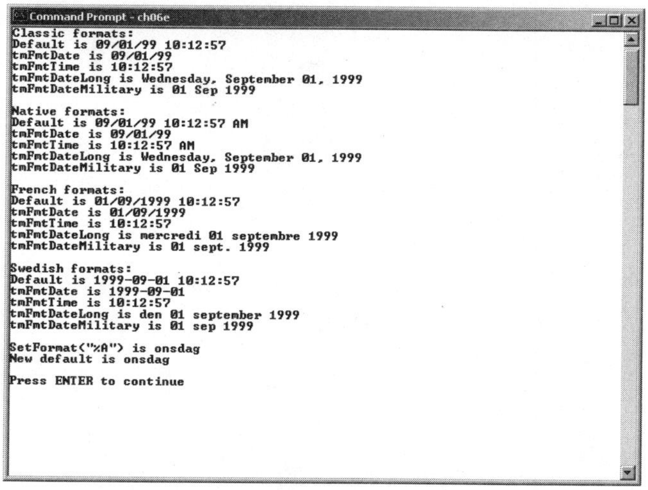

Figure 6-5. *Output of* tmFmt *test program.*

Now let's examine five statements that use the *tmFmt* object called *t*:

```
cout << "Default is " << t << endl;
cout << "tmFmtDate is " << tmFmtDate(t) << endl;
cout << "tmFmtDate is " << (tmFmtDate)t << endl;
cout << "tmFmt(t, \"%A\" is " << tmFmt(t, "%A") << endl;
cout << "\nSetFormat(\"%A\") is " << t.SetFormat("%A") << endl;
```

Line 1 formats the embedded *tm* data using the default string *"%c"*, which produces a date and time representation appropriate for the imbued locale. Line 2 constructs a temporary *tmFmtDate* object, initializes it with the *tm* data from *t*, produces a date string using *"%x"* as the format, and then discards the temporary object. Line 3 has the same effect as line 2, but it uses casting syntax instead of constructor syntax. I prefer the constructor syntax because it looks better and is more flexible, as line 4 illustrates. The first four lines don't change the original *tmFmt* object, but lines 2 through 4 incur the cost of constructing a temporary object and copying a *tm* structure. Line 5 avoids this cost by calling *t.SetFormat*, but that function changes the *tmFmt* object, which might not be desirable. You can call *SetFormat* as part of the stream operation because it returns a reference to its *tmFmt* object.

Designing a money facet inserter

The monetary facet uses real numbers to represent money, employing the technique I described in Chapter 5. That is, the real number expresses the amount in the smallest currency units, such as pennies for the United States or yen for Japan. This approach simplifies computation errors caused by the binary representation of decimal fractions. When the monetary facet converts between this internal representation and the human-readable text form, it inserts the proper punctuation to represent the appropriate number of decimal places.

Listing 6-10 shows the *Money* class, which holds the information needed by the monetary facet inserter. The money amount is supplied to the constructor and stored in the member *m_Value*, which is a *long double* hiding behind the type named *money_t*. I chose this data type because that's what the monetary facet uses, but you could easily change to some other form, such as *double*, *long*, or Microsoft's *_int64*.

```
// Money represented as a real number
typedef long double money_t;

class Money
{
public:
Money(money_t v, bool bIntl = false, bool bSymbol = true) :
    m_Value(v), m_bIntl(bIntl), m_bSymbol(bSymbol) {}
```

Listing 6-10. *The* Money *class.*

```
// Accessors
money_t Value() const
    { return m_Value; }
bool bIntl() const
    { return m_bIntl; }
bool bSymbol() const
    { return m_bSymbol; }

// Mutators
money_t& Value()
    { return m_Value; }
bool& bIntl()
    { return m_bIntl; }
bool& bSymbol()
    { return m_bSymbol; }

// Cast operators
operator money_t() const
    { return m_Value; }

// Pseudo-manipulators
Money& SetIntl(bool bIntl = true)
    {
    m_bIntl = bIntl;
    return *this;
    }

Money& SetSymbol(bool bSymbol = true)
    {
    m_bSymbol = bSymbol;
    return *this;
    }

// Internal stuff
private:
money_t m_Value;
bool m_bIntl;
bool m_bSymbol;
};
```

Two Boolean variables represent what I consider to be the most important monetary formatting options: *m_bIntl* is true for international format, false for domestic format; *m_bSymbol* is false to prevent the currency symbol from appearing in the output text. Both of these variables are constructor arguments with default values of false for *m_bIntl* and true for *m_bSymbol*.

Money also contains the appropriate accessors, mutators, casts, and pseudo-manipulators that I described earlier for the *tmFmt* class.

Listing 6-11 shows the inserter for the *Money* class. It's similar to the one I described earlier for *tmFmt*. Notice that the *showbase* flag in the stream object is temporarily changed to reflect the state of *m_bSymbol*. The facet *put* function uses this flag to enable or suppress the currency symbol. Since the *showbase* flag is used by other inserters, it shouldn't be permanently changed within the *Money* inserter. Also, notice that this approach decouples *Money* objects from the stream's *showbase* and *noshowbase* manipulators. In other words, the currency symbol depends only on the state of *m_bSymbol* in the *Money* object, not on the ambient stream settings. I consider this to be a useful feature, but some might consider it a flaw.

```cpp
template<class CharType, class CharTraits>
inline basic_ostream<CharType, CharTraits>& operator <<
    (basic_ostream<CharType, CharTraits>& Stream, Money& money)
{
typedef ostreambuf_iterator<CharType, CharTraits> Iterator;
typedef money_put<CharType, Iterator> Facet;
ios_base::iostate state = ios_base::goodbit;
ios_base::fmtflags flags = Stream.setf
    (
    money.bSymbol() ? ios_base::showbase : 0,
    ios_base::showbase
    );
const typename
    basic_ostream<CharType, CharTraits>::sentry OK(Stream);
if(OK)
    {
    try
        {
        if(_USE(Stream.getloc(), Facet).put
            (
            Iterator(Stream.rdbuf()),
            money.bIntl(),
            Stream,
            Stream.fill(),
            money.Value()
            ).failed()) state |= ios_base::badbit;
        }
    catch(...)
        {
        Stream.setstate(ios_base::badbit, true);
        }
    }
Stream.setf(flags, ios_base::showbase);
Stream.setstate(state);
return(Stream);
}
```

Listing 6-11. *Inserter for* Money *class.*

The monetary facet also has the ability to take a text string representing a decimal number and punctuate it to represent a currency amount. Therefore I designed a class named *MoneyText* as well as the corresponding inserter function, shown in Listings 6-12 and 6-13. They're nearly identical to their *Money* counterparts, except that the money value is carried as a string instead of as a real number. Also, *MoneyText* is a template to allow for different character types.

```cpp
template<class CharType>
class MoneyText
{
public:
MoneyText(const CharType* t, bool bIntl = false,
          bool bSymbol = true) :
          m_sText(t), m_bIntl(bIntl), m_bSymbol(bSymbol) {}
MoneyText(const basic_string<CharType>& t, bool bIntl = false,
          bool bSymbol = true) :
          m_sText(t), m_bIntl(bInto), m_bSymbol(bSymbol) {}

// Accessors
const basic_string<CharType>& Text() const
    { return m_sText; }
bool bIntl() const
    { return m_bIntl; }
bool bSymbol() const
    { return m_bSymbol; }

// Mutators
basic_string<CharType>& Text()
    { return m_sText; }
bool& bIntl()
    { return m_bIntl; }
bool& bSymbol()
    { return m_bSymbol; }

// Cast operators
operator const char*() const
    { return m_sText.c_str(); }
operator const basic_string<CharType>&() const
    { return m_sText; }

// Pseudo-manipulators
MoneyText<CharType>& SetIntl(bool bIntl = true)
    {
    m_bIntl = bIntl;
    return *this;
    }
```

Listing 6-12. *The* MoneyText *class.*   *(continued)*

Listing 6-12. *continued*

```
MoneyText<CharType>& SetSymbol(bool bSymbol = true)
    {
    m_bSymbol = bSymbol;
    return *this;
    }

private:
basic_string<CharType> m_sText;
bool m_bIntl;
bool m_bSymbol;
};
```

```
template<class CharType, class CharTraits>
inline basic_ostream<CharType, CharTraits>& operator <<
    (basic_ostream<CharType, CharTraits>& Stream,
    MoneyText<CharType>& money)
{
typedef ostreambuf_iterator<CharType, CharTraits> Iterator;
typedef money_put<CharType, Iterator> Facet;
ios_base::iostate state = ios_base::goodbit;
ios_base::fmtflags flags = Stream.setf
    (
    money.bSymbol() ? ios_base::showbase : 0, ios_base::showbase
    );
const typename basic_ostream
    <CharType, CharTraits>::sentry OK(Stream);
if(OK)
    {
    try
        {
        if(_USE(Stream.getloc(), Facet).put
            (
            Iterator(Stream.rdbuf()),
            money.bIntl(),
            Stream,
            Stream.fill(),
            money.Text()
            ).failed()) state |= ios_base::badbit;
        }
    catch(...)
        {
        Stream.setstate(ios_base::badbit, true);
        }
```

Listing 6-13. *Inserter for the* MoneyText *class.*

```
    }
Stream.setf(flags, ios_base::showbase);
Stream.setstate(state);
return(Stream);
}
```

Listing 6-14 shows a test program for the two money classes and their inserters, and Figure 6-6 is the output when you run the program on Windows 2000. Notice that the monetary facet rounds up the fractional part when the amount is expressed as a real number, but it truncates the fraction when the money is expressed as a text string. In other words, the facet assumes that the string was produced by some means that performed the rounding, so it can just ignore everything to the right of the decimal point.

```
void main()
{
money_t dPos = 1234.5678;
money_t dNeg = -1234.5678;
char* sPos = "1234.5678";
Money mReal(dPos);
MoneyText<char> mText(sPos);

cout << "Classic formats:\n";
cout << "Money(" << dPos << ") is " << mReal << endl;
cout << "Money(" << dNeg << ") is " << Money(dNeg) << endl;
cout << "Money(" << dNeg << ",true) is " << Money(dNeg, true)
    << endl;
cout << "MoneyText(\"" << sPos << "\") is " << mText << endl;
cout << "Guarded field is " << setw(20) << setfill('*')
    << mReal << endl;

locale locNative(".OCP");
cout.imbue(locNative);

cout << "\nNative formats:\n";
cout << "Money(" << dPos << ") is " << mReal << endl;
cout << "Money(" << dNeg << ") is " << Money(dNeg) << endl;
cout << "Money(" << dNeg << ", true) is "
    << Money(dNeg, true) << endl;
cout << "MoneyText(\"" << sPos << "\") is " << mText << endl;
cout << "Guarded field is " << setw(20) << setfill('*')
    << mReal << endl;

locale locFrench("French_France.OCP");
cout.imbue(locFrench);
```

Listing 6-14. *Examples of* Money *and* MoneyText *inserters.*   *(continued)*

Listing 6-14. *continued*

```
cout << "\nFrench formats:\n";
cout << "Money(" << dPos << ") is " << mReal << endl;
cout << "Money(" << dNeg << ") is " << Money(dNeg) << endl;
cout << "Money(" << dNeg << ", true) is "
    << Money(dNeg, true) << endl;
cout << "MoneyText(\"" << sPos << "\") is " << mText << endl;
cout << "Guarded field is " << setw(20) << setfill('*')
    << mReal << endl;

locale locSwedish("Swedish_Sweden.OCP");
cout.imbue(locSwedish);

cout << "\nSwedish formats:\n";
cout << "Money(" << dPos << ") is " << mReal << endl;
cout << "Money(" << dNeg << ") is " << Money(dNeg) << endl;
cout << "Money(" << dNeg << ", true) is "
    << Money(dNeg, true) << endl;
cout << "MoneyText(\"" << sPos << "\") is " << mText << endl;
cout << "Guarded field is " << setw(20) << setfill('*')
    << mReal << endl;

cout << "\nSetIntl is " << mReal.SetIntl() << endl;
cout << "Money(" << dPos << ") is " << mReal << endl;
cout << "Money(" << dPos << ", false, false) is "
    << Money(dPos, false, false) << endl;
}
```

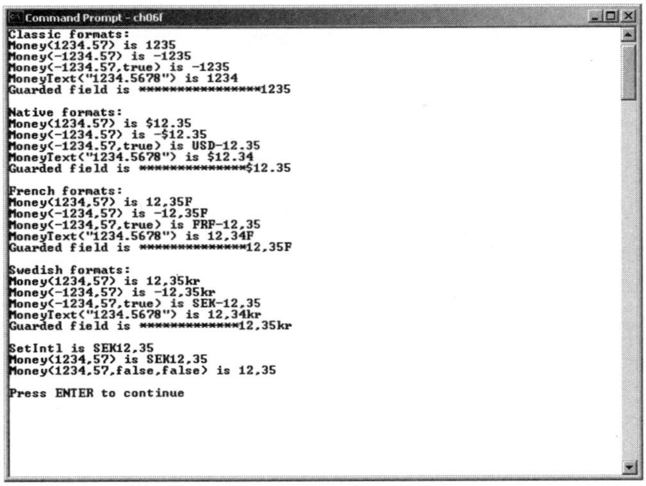

Figure 6-6. *Output of* Money *inserter test program.*

Using Facets in Custom Extractors

As with inserters, there are no standard extractors for date, time, and monetary data. This isn't a major deficiency because modern programs typically obtain this type of input data from dialog boxes instead of command lines. The dialog form usually provides separate fields with labels prompting the user to enter the month, day, year, hour, minute, second, and money amount as simple numbers. Indeed, many Windows or Web applications present a pop-up calendar or a clock to further simplify data entry.

These techniques obviate the need for the user to enter and the program to parse punctuated strings representing complicated data types. Nonetheless, it's relatively easy to design custom extractors that perform locale-sensitive parsing of date, time, and money strings.

Designing a time facet extractor

In order to parse a date or time string, you must know which of several possible formats it uses or you must try parsing with all applicable formats to see which one succeeds. The typical implementation (Dinkumware) of the *time_get* facet employs the former approach. Time strings must be presented in the form *hh:mm:ss,* where *hh, mm,* and *ss* are decimal integers representing the hour, minute, and second of a 24-hour clock. While this format is almost universally recognized, I was surprised to find it hard-coded within the Dinkumware (and Visual C++) *time_get* facet rather than governed by the locale database.

Even more surprising is the format required for a date string: *month day year.* The *month* field must be the long or short month name in the specified locale, such as *September* or *Sep.* This style is definitely not universal and shouldn't be hard-coded in the *time_get* facet. Some locales require these three items in a different order, and I suspect that most users would prefer to type dates in a short form, such as *mm/dd/yy.* Because of these considerations, the following extractor recognizes the short date format as well as the long format supported by *time_get.* The extractor uses the facet's *dateorder* setting to parse the short date properly.

Listing 6-15 shows the changes to the *tmFmt* class in order to support the extractor shown in Listing 6-16.

```
class tmFmt
{
public:
// Constructors
tmFmt(const tm& t, const char *fmt = "%c") :
    m_Time(t), m_Format(fmt), m_xFormat(tmFmt::xTime) {}
tmFmt(time_t t = time(0), const char* fmt = "%c") :
    m_Time(*localtime(&t)), m_Format(fmt),
          m_xFormat(tmFmt::xTime) {};

// Extraction format codes
enum
    {
    xDate          = 0x0001,   // Extract short date.
    xTime          = 0x0002,   // Extract short time.
    xDateLong      = 0x0004,   // Extract long date.
    };

// Accessors
const tm& Time() const
    { return m_Time; }
const string& Format() const
    { return m_Format; }
int xFormat() const
    { return m_xFormat; }

// Mutators
tm& Time()
    { return m_Time; }
string& Format()
    { return m_Format; }
int& xFormat()
    { return m_xFormat; }

// Cast operators
operator tm*()
    { return &m_Time; }
operator tm&()
    { return m_Time; }
operator tm() const
    { return m_Time; }

// Pseudo-manipulator for insertion
const tmFmt& SetFormat(char* fmt)
    {
    m_Format = fmt;
    return *this;
    }
```

Listing 6-15. *Extractor additions to* tmFmt *class.*

```
// Pseudo-manipulator for extraction
tmFmt& SetFormat(int fmt)
    {
    m_xFormat = fmt;
    return *this;
    }

// Internal stuff
private:
tm m_Time;
string m_Format;
int m_xFormat;
};
```

```
template<class CharType, class CharTraits> inline
basic_istream<CharType, CharTraits>& operator >>
    (basic_istream<CharType, CharTraits>& Stream, tmFmt& Time)
{
typedef istreambuf_iterator<CharType, CharTraits> Iterator;
typedef time_get<CharType, Iterator> Facet;
ios_base::iostate state = ios_base::goodbit;
const typename basic_istream
    <CharType, CharTraits>::sentry OK(Stream);
if(OK)
    {
    try
        {
        const Facet& facet = _USE(Stream.getloc(), Facet);
        time_base::dateorder order = facet.date_order();
        switch(Time.xFormat())
            {
            case tmFmt::xDateLong:
            facet.get_date
                (
                Iterator(Stream.rdbuf()),
                Iterator(0),
                Stream,
                state,
                &Time.Time()
                );
            break;

            case tmFmt::xDate:
            unsigned short a, b, c;
            CharType sep1, sep2;
```

Listing 6-16. *Extractor for* tmFmt *class.*

(continued)

Listing 6-16. *continued*

```
                Stream >> a;
                Stream.get(sep1);
                Stream >> b;
                Stream.get(sep2);
                Stream >> c;
                if(order == time_base::dmy)
                    {
                    Time.Time().tm_mday = a;
                    Time.Time().tm_mon = b - 1;
                    Time.Time().tm_year = c;
                    }
                else if(order == time_base::ymd)
                    {
                    Time.Time().tm_mday = c;
                    Time.Time().tm_mon = b - 1;
                    Time.Time().tm_year = a;
                    }
                else    // mdy
                    {
                    Time.Time().tm_mday = b;
                    Time.Time().tm_mon = a - 1;
                    Time.Time().tm_year = c;
                    }
                if(Time.Time().tm_year >= 1900)
                    Time.Time().tm_year -= 1900;
                break;

                case tmFmt::xTime:
                facet.get_time
                    (
                    Iterator(Stream.rdbuf()),
                    Iterator(0),
                    Stream,
                    state,
                    &Time.Time()
                    );
                }
            }
        catch (...)
            {
            Stream.setstate(ios_base::badbit, true);
            }
        }
    Stream.setstate(state);
    return(Stream);
    }
```

The code *m_xFormat* tells the extractor which format to expect, using the following enumerated symbols:

xDateLong	Use date parsing built into the *time_get::get_date* function.
xTime	Use time parsing built into the *time_get::get_time* function.
xDate	Parse the date as *a/b/c* where *a, b,* and *c* are decimal numbers representing the year, month, and day in the order specified by the *time_get::dateorder* function. The slash separator character is hard-coded, although you can usually obtain it from the locale database by writing some platform-sensitive code. Because of my sloppy implementation in Listing 6-16, any non-numeric string can be used as a separator.

The revised *tmFmt* class provides a second version of *SetFormat* that serves as a pseudo-manipulator, allowing you to set the flags from within a stream input statement. You should use this manipulator only once in each stream input statement because the compiler might not execute the calls in left-to-right order, which would lead to parsing errors. Listing 6-17 illustrates this restriction and also shows some other sample uses of the *tmFmt* extractor.

```
void main()
{
char b[200];
locale locNative(".OCP");
cout.imbue(locNative);
cin.imbue(locNative);

cout << "\nEnter time (example " << tmFmtTime(t) << ")\n";
while(!cin.eof())
    {
    cin >> t.SetFormat(tmFmt::xTime);
    if(cin.good()) break;
    cin.clear();
    cin >> b;
    cout << "Error! Residual input is \"" << b << "\"\n";
    }
cout << "You entered " << tmFmtTime(t) << endl;

cout << "\nEnter date (example " << tmFmtDate(t) << ")\n";
while(!cin.eof())
    {
    cin >> t.SetFormat(tmFmt::xDate);
    if(cin.good()) break;
    cin.clear();
    cin >> b;
```

Listing 6-17. *Examples of* tmFmt *extractor.* *(continued)*

Listing 6-17. *continued*

```
        cout << "Error! Residual input is \"" << b << "\"\n";
        }
cout << "You entered " << tmFmtDate(t) << endl;

cout << "\nEnter date and time (example " << tmFmtDate(t) << " "
    << tmFmtTime(t) << ")\n";
while(!cin.eof())
    {
    cin >> t.SetFormat(tmFmt::xDate) >> ws;
    cin >> t.SetFormat(tmFmt::xTime);
    if(cin.good()) break;
    cin.clear();
    cin >> b;
    cout << "Error! Residual input is \"" << b << "\"\n";
    }
cout << "You entered " << tmFmtDate(t) << " "
    << tmFmtTime(t) << endl;
}
```

Designing a money facet extractor

The extractor for the *Money* class (see Listing 6-18) is simpler than the date and time extractor because monetary strings have only two options. First, the extractor needs to know whether to check for the domestic or international monetary format. This information is provided by *m_bIntl* in the *Money* class. Second, the extractor must know whether it should expect a currency symbol. The *money_get* facet uses the *showbase* option in the stream object for this purpose. Listing 6-19 shows how to use the *Money* extractor.

```
template <class CharType, class CharTraits> inline
basic_istream <CharType, CharTraits>& operator >>
    (basic_istream <CharType, CharTraits>& Stream, Money& money)
{
typedef istreambuf_iterator <CharType, CharTraits> Iterator;
typedef money_get <CharType, Iterator> Facet;
ios_base::iostate state = ios_base::goodbit;
ios_base::fmtflags flags = Stream.setf
    (
    money.bSymbol() ? ios_base::showbase : 0,
    ios_base::showbase
    );
const typename
    basic_istream <CharType, CharTraits>::sentry OK(Stream);
if(OK)
    {
```

Listing 6-18. *Extractor for* Money *class.*

```
        try
            {
            long double value;
            _USE(Stream.getloc(), Facet).get
                (
                Iterator(Stream.rdbuf()),
                Iterator(0),
                money.bIntl(),
                Stream,
                state,
                value
                );
            if((state & ios_base::failbit) == 0)
                money.Value() = value;
            }
        catch (...)
            {
            Stream.setstate(ios_base::badbit, true);
            }
        }
Stream.setf(flags, ios_base::showbase);
Stream.setstate(state);
return(Stream);
}
```

```
void main()
{
char b[200];
locale locNative(".OCP");
cout.imbue(locNative);
cin.imbue(locNative);

mReal.SetSymbol(true);

cout << "\nEnter money amount in domestic format with symbol\n";
cout << "For example, " << Money(1234.5678, false, true) << endl;
while(!cin.eof())
    {
    cin >> mReal.SetIntl(false);
    if(cin.good()) break;
```

Listing 6-19. *Examples of* Money *extractor.*   *(continued)*

Listing 6-19. *continued*

```
        cin.clear();
        cin >> b;
        cout << "Error! Residual input is \"" << b << "\"\n";
        }cout << "You entered " << mReal << endl;

    cout << "\nEnter money amount in international format "
        << "with symbol...\n";
    cout << "For example, " << Money(1234.5678, true, true) << endl;
    while(!cin.eof())
        {
        cin >> mReal.SetIntl(true);
        if(cin.good()) break;
        cin.clear();
        cin >> b;
        cout << "Error! Residual input is \"" << b << "\"\n";
        }
    cout << "You entered " << mReal << endl;

    mReal.SetSymbol(false);

    cout << "\nEnter money amount in domestic format "
        << "without symbol...\n";
    cout << "For example, " << Money(1234.5678, false, false) << endl;
    while(!cin.eof())
        {
        cin >> mReal.SetIntl(false);
        if(cin.good()) break;
        cin.clear();
        cin >> b;
        cout << "Error! Residual input is \"" << b << "\"\n";
        }
    cout << "You entered " << mReal << endl;

    cout << "\nEnter money amount in international format "
        << "without symbol...\n";
    cout << "For example, " << Money(1234.5678, true, false) << endl;
    while(!cin.eof())
        {
        cin >> mReal.SetIntl(true);
        if(cin.good()) break;
        cin.clear();
        cin >> b;
        cout << "Error! Residual input is \"" << b << "\"\n";
        }
    cout << "\nYou entered " << mReal << endl;
    }
```

SUMMARY

C++ replaces the *setlocale* function with the *locale* class and a set of facets that encapsulate the many locale-sensitive operations required by an international program. Locale objects have a lightweight design, so they can be created and destroyed frequently. This eliminates many of the problems caused by the single shared locale structure in C.

The standard facet repertoire provides all of the features available through functions in the standard C library, plus improved handling of dates, times, and monetary amounts. Other parts of the C++ library, such as the stream classes, employ the standard locale objects and facets in order to support international programming.

Chapter 7

Visual C++ Extensions

Microsoft Visual C++ includes C and C++ compilers and libraries that comply with the current language standards. In addition, Visual C++ provides extensions and augmentations that facilitate programming in the various Microsoft environments. This chapter describes the extensions that are particularly important for international programming with the Microsoft Win32 API.

THE TCHAR.H HEADER FILE

Although standard C and C++ support character sets of the SBCS, MBCS, and WCS varieties, the standard makes little attempt to hide the differences. So if an international programmer wants to use a standard compiler and library to produce common source code for different character widths, the software will have to include many conditional compilation sequences, as shown in Listing 7-1.

```
#ifdef _UNICODE                      // Use WCS if _UNICODE is defined.
wchar_t text[100];                   // 100 wide characters
wchar_t* p;                          // Wide character pointer
void ProcessCharacter(wchar_t);      // Character processing function
#else                                // Use SBCS if _UNICODE is undefined.
```

Listing 7-1. *SBCS/WCS string access.*   *(continued)*

Listing 7-1. *continued*

```
char text[100];            // 100 narrow characters
char* p;                   // Narrow character pointer
void ProcessCharacter(char);  // Character processing function
#endif

// Scan string by index.
for(int i = 0; text[i]; i++) ProcessCharacter(text[i]);

// Scan string by pointer.
for(p = text; *p; p++) ProcessCharacter(*p);
```

Here the programmer must define the symbol *_UNICODE* before compiling for a wide-character environment; otherwise, the source code uses SBCS techniques.[1]

Because the differences between an SBCS and a WCS algorithm often boil down to simply choosing the *char* or *wchar_t* data type, it's easy to write a simple macro that obviates the need for explicit conditional compilation. Listing 7-2 illustrates this technique, which is the basis for Microsoft's tchar.h header file.

```
// Define TCHAR data type for WCS or SBCS.
#ifdef _UNICODE            // WCS definitions
typedef wchar_t TCHAR;
#else                      // SBCS definitions
typedef char TCHAR;
#endif

void ProcessCharacter(TCHAR);
TCHAR text[100];           // 100 characters
TCHAR* p;                  // Character pointer

// Scan string by index.
for(i = 0; text[i]; i++) ProcessCharacter(text[i]);

// Scan string by pointer.
for(p = text; *p; p++) ProcessCharacter(*p);
```

Listing 7-2. *SBCS/WCS programming with macros.*

---

1. As mentioned in Chapter 5, Listing 7-1 is unsuitable for the MBCS environment unless you redefine *ProcessCharacter* to accept a character pointer or a union that includes the largest possible multibyte character sequence. Since the most popular multibyte sets require a maximum of 2 bytes per character, a 16-bit integer is an acceptable union.

The tchar.h header file was introduced with the Win32 Software Development Kit (SDK) and later absorbed into the Visual C++ package.[2] Its primary purpose is to minimize the need for conditional compilation when producing common source code for the SBCS, MBCS, and WCS environments. While tchar.h doesn't solve all of the character set problems left behind by the C and C++ standards committees, it goes a long way. For that reason it's widely used by Win32 programmers and is fully supported by the Visual C++ MFC and ATL wizards.

For example, a skeleton program produced by the MFC Application Wizard uses tchar.h to make a single source code base that will work correctly for the SBCS, MBCS, and WCS environments. By default, the wizard (at least in Visual C++ 6) uses the ANSI character set in an MBCS environment. This might seem like a strange choice, but the MBCS support in tchar.h eliminates most of the sign extension problems you might encounter when using the standard SBCS library with ANSI code points higher than 0x7F. If you're working strictly with United States characters, you can remove the *_MBCS* symbol and build a pure SBCS version, which is slightly smaller and faster. Similarly, you need only replace *_MBCS* with *_UNICODE* and rebuild the program to get a pure WCS (Unicode) version.

Regardless of the symbol combination you choose, your program will remain relatively independent of character set issues as long as you continue to use the tchar.h symbols instead of those from the standard C library. Of course, you must also use unbiased (character-neutral) programming techniques, as described in Chapters 4 through 6. The tchar.h data types are a great help in that regard.

The bottom line is that tchar.h makes it easy to develop common source code for the ANSI and Unicode character sets. It also greatly simplifies MBCS programming, although you must still wrestle with character length and sign issues in your own algorithms. Let's examine tchar.h in more detail.

Conditional Compilation Symbols

To make tchar.h work its magic, you must first specify the type of character set you'll be using. You do this using two preprocessor symbols, *_UNICODE* and *_MBCS*, as shown in Table 7-1. Note that both symbols begin with a single underscore.

---

2. The Visual C++ version of tchar.h is more advanced than the one shipped with the Win32 SDK. Visual C++ now contains much of the Win32 SDK, so programmers rarely need to install the SDK package separately. But if you do install the SDK, make sure that the Visual C++ version of tchar.h is the one that gets included when you compile.

IS IT _*UNICODE* OR *UNICODE*?

Although tchar.h uses the symbol *_UNICODE* to specify the WCS mode, many other Visual C++ header files use the symbol *UNICODE* without the leading underscore. Some of these files include preprocessor sequences to ensure that both symbols have the same state, either defined or undefined, but other headers omit this safeguard. The best approach is to explicitly define both symbols when you want to compile for the Unicode environment.

Table 7-1. **Character Set Specification for tchar.h**

_UNICODE	_MBCS	Character Set
Undefined	Undefined	SBCS
Undefined	Defined	MBCS (and SBCS)
Defined	Undefined	WCS (Unicode)
Defined	Defined	Invalid. Defaults to Unicode, but might cause other problems.

Leaving both symbols undefined produces pure SBCS code, which is the classic C and C++ environment. While this is a highly efficient approach, it's the proper choice only if you don't need to support a broad range of languages.

Defining *_MBCS* is less efficient but necessary if you must support multibyte code pages, such as those used in China, Japan, and Korea. As I mentioned earlier, this setting also helps prevent sign extension problems when you're using an extended ASCII character set. But even though tchar.h offers much help in the MBCS environment, it can't hide all of the messy algorithms needed to process variable-length characters.

The best blend of efficiency and generality occurs when you define *_UNICODE* and use wide character programming techniques. Many programmers prefer this technique even when processing MBCS data sets, because it's fairly easy to convert between MBCS and WCS at the program boundaries.

Visual C++ programmers can adjust these symbols in several ways. It's critically important that all compilation units (source modules) are processed with the same settings. Failure to do this will lead to chaos when the program runs. In MFC applications, you can define the appropriate symbols at the very beginning of stdafx.h because that's the first file included in every source module. Another approach is to use the Project Settings and Build Configurations dialog boxes to adjust the symbols, as shown in Figure 7-1 through Figure 7-4.

Figure 7-1 shows the default settings produced by the Visual C++ 6 Application Wizard when you request a simple "Hello, world" console program. You can see the default settings by clicking the C/C++ tab on the Project Settings dialog. Notice that the wizard defines the _MBCS symbol to enable MBCS programming, as I mentioned earlier. If you're working strictly within the United States, you can remove this definition to get slightly more efficient code.

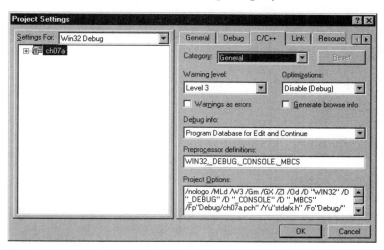

Figure 7-1. *Visual C++ Project Settings for MBCS.*

Unfortunately, most of the Visual C++ 6 wizards don't create a configuration for building Unicode debug and release versions of the program. Figure 7-2 through Figure 7-4 show how you can create these configurations manually. First choose Configurations from the Build menu to open the Configurations dialog shown in Figure 7-2.

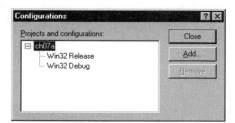

Figure 7-2. *Visual C++ Build Configurations dialog.*

Click the Add button to open the Add Project Configuration dialog in Figure 7-3. Change the word in the Configuration text box to "Unicode Debug" in order to create a new configuration named Win32 Unicode Debug based on the Win32 Debug configuration supplied by the Application Wizard. Dismiss the Add Project Configuration dialog box, and then click the Add button again in the Configurations dialog in order to create the Win32 Unicode Release configuration based on Win32 Release. Dismiss both dialogs.

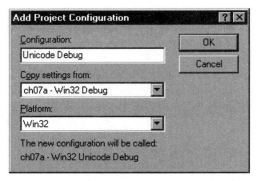

Figure 7-3. *Adding a new configuration.*

Choose Settings from the Project menu to make the changes shown in Figure 7-4 for each of the new Unicode configurations. These changes are made in the Preprocessor Definitions text box on the C/C++ page and consist of removing the *_MBCS* definition, and adding *_UNICODE* and *UNICODE*.

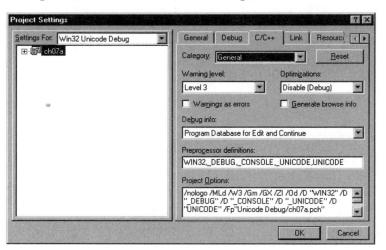

Figure 7-4. *Visual C++ project settings for Unicode.*

Data Types and Macros

The *_UNICODE* and *_MBCS* symbols cause tchar.h to define several data types and macros as shown in Table 7-2. These definitions have important implications if you want to write code that minimizes character set dependencies.

Table 7-2. Data Types and Macros in tchar.h

Name	Meaning	SBCS	MBCS	WCS
_TCHAR	Character	char	char	wchar_t
_TSCHAR	Signed character	signed char	signed char	wchar_t
_TUCHAR	Unsigned character	unsigned char	unsigned char	wchar_t
_TXCHAR	Unsigned character	char	unsigned char	wchar_t
_TINT	Integer	int	unsigned int	wint_t
_TEOF	End of file value	EOF	EOF	WEOF
_T(*x*)	Text literal macro	*x*	*x*	L##*x*
_TEXT(*x*)	Same as _T(*x*)	*x*	*x*	L##*x*
TCHAR	Same as _TCHAR	char	char	wchar_t

Here are some general rules:

- Use *_TCHAR* (or its synonym, *TCHAR*[3]) wherever you would normally use *char* or *wchar_t*.

- Use *_TINT* when converting between one of the *_TCHAR* types and an integer type. This will produce unsigned integers for use in MBCS and extended ASCII situations.

- Use *_TEOF* to check for an end-of-file condition when calling the standard I/O functions.

- Enclose every text literal within the *_T* or *_TEXT* macro, which are synonymous.

---

3. For typing convenience, tchar.h defines some of the frequently used symbols, such as *TCHAR*, without a leading underscore. Strictly speaking, this violates the C standard, which says that nonstandard symbols defined by a compiler vendor should begin with an underscore. This rule is supposed to help programmers avoid collisions with compiler-specific names, but in situations like *TCHAR*, many programmers prefer to risk collisions rather than type the cumbersome underscore.

Multimode Functions

Programs using tchar.h don't call the standard C library functions by their usual names. For instance, Listing 7-3 shows several ways to read a character from a file. Without tchar.h, you must call the standard library function *fgetc* or *fgetwc* for narrow or wide characters, respectively. With tchar.h, you use *_fgettc*, a macro that calls the appropriate standard function based on the *_UNICODE* setting.[4]

```
// Without tchar.h
#ifdef _UNICODE                             // Compiled for WCS
wchar_t c = L'A';                           // Character literal
wchar_t msg[] = L"Message 12\n";            // String literal
wchar_t *p = msg;                           // String pointer
wint_t x = fgetwc(stdin);                   // Testing for end of file
if(x == WEOF) { /* do something */ }
#else                                       // Compiled for SBCS or
                                            // MBCS
char c = 'A';                               // Character literal
char msg[] = "Message 12\n";                // String literal
char *p = msg;                              // String pointer
int x = fgetc(stdin);                       // Testing for end of file
if(x == EOF) { /* do something */ }
#endif


// With tchar.h
TCHAR c = _T('A');                          // Character literal
TCHAR msg[] = _T("Message 12\n");           // String literal
TCHAR *p = msg;                             // String pointer
TINT x = _fgettc(stdin);                    // Testing for end of file
if(x == _TEOF) { /* do something */ }
```

Listing 7-3. *Using tchar.h data types.*

Most of tchar.h consists of these multimode wrapper functions, which are listed in Table 7-3. Many of them are merely *#define* symbols selected by *#ifdef* tests of the options listed in Table 7-1. Using this approach is effective for the SBCS and WCS cases, but it can cause warning messages when compiling for MBCS because of conversions between signed and unsigned characters. To eliminate the warnings and provide better type checking and conversions, tchar.h now contains inline versions of many MBCS wrappers.

---

4. Because the *_fgettc* function calls *fgetc* for the MBCS environment as well as for SBCS, you have to test for a lead byte and make additional calls to acquire all the bytes of a character.

If your program contains many separate compilation units, you can define the preprocessor symbol *_NO_INLINING* to replace the inline functions with versions linked from a Visual C++ library. This practice will reduce memory consumption, but performance will also be reduced because of the extra overhead needed to penetrate the wrappers.

Dealing with Unfriendly Names

The standard C library uses traditional function names dating back to the early days of UNIX, when C compilers and linkers limited these names to a maximum of seven characters and ignored case differences. This led to the cryptic symbols that are still favored by many UNIX programmers even though earlier C limitations were removed years ago.

In contrast, Microsoft usually defines its own library functions with longer names using mixed case and few underscores, such as *GetWindowText* in the Windows API. Many programmers find these symbols easier to remember and the extra keystrokes only a minor impediment. Nonetheless, when Microsoft programmers created tchar.h, they reverted to short names so that the multimode functions would closely resemble those in the standard library. Thus we have to struggle with confusing names like *_tcsnccat* and *_tcsncat*. These functions both perform string concatenation, but the former uses a character length while the latter uses a byte length. Accidentally adding or omitting a *c* produces a bug that can be very difficult to find.

To avoid this type of problem, I prefer the longer and more descriptive names as used in the Win32 API. So I've augmented tchar.h with my own tcharx.h header file, whose symbols are shown in the left column of Table 7-3. Although my symbols are considerably longer than the ones in tchar.h, they should feel quite natural to programmers who work with Windows, MFC, and ATL. I find them easier to type because they don't contain underscores and easier to remember because they contain complete words instead of abbreviations. In addition, tcharx.h uses inline functions instead of preprocessor symbols where possible, which results in more thorough type checking. Furthermore, in a C++ environment tcharx.h employs function overloading to shorten some of the symbols.

If you think tcharx.h will make your international programming chores easier, you can obtain the file from the companion CD-ROM for this book.

Table 7-3. Alternatives for Standard and Microsoft C Functions in tchar.h and tcharx.h

tcharx.h	Description	tchar.h	SBCS	MBCS	WCS
	Get a character from a stream (macro).	_gettc	getc	getc	getwc
	Get a character from the standard input stream (macro).	_gettchar	getchar	getchar	getwchar
	Put a character to a stream (macro).	_puttc	putc	putc	putwc
	Put a character to the standard output stream (macro).	_puttchar	putchar	putchar	putwchar
tCharIsAlpha	Test if a character is alphabetic.	_istalpha	isalpha	_ismbcalpha	iswalpha
tCharIsAlphaNumeric	Test if a character is alphabetic or numeric.	_istalnum	isalnum	_ismbcalnum	iswalnum
tCharIsAscii	Test if a character is ASCII.	_istascii	isascii	isascii	iswascii
tCharIsControl	Test if a character is in a control group.	_istcntrl	iscntrl	iscntrl	iswcntrl
tCharIsDigit	Test if a character is a decimal digit.	_istdigit	isdigit	_ismbcdigit	iswdigit
tCharIsGraphic	Test if a character is a displayable graphic other than a space.	_istgraph	isgraph	_ismbcgraph	iswgraph
tCharIsHexDigit	Test if a character is a hexadecimal digit.	_istxdigit	isxdigit	isxdigit	iswxdigit
tCharIsLead	Check if an unsigned value is the lead byte of a multibyte character.	_istlead	(0)	_ismbblead	(0)
tCharIsLead[Signed]	Check if a signed value is the lead byte of a multibyte character. Although isleadbyte is the standard function, it's not as robust as Microsoft's _ismbblead because the latter uses an unsigned integer argument, thereby avoiding the sign extension problems of the former.	_istleadbyte	(0)	isleadbyte	(0)
tCharIsLowerCase	Test if a character is lowercase.	_istlower	islower	_ismbclower	iswlower
tCharIsMultiByte	Check if an unsigned integer represents a valid multibyte character.	_istlegal	(1)	_ismbclegal	(1)

(continued)

Table 7-3. *continued*

tcharx.b	Description	tchar.b	SBCS	MBCS	WCS
tCharIsPrintable	Test if a character is a displayable graphic including a space.	_istprint	isprint	_ismbcprint	iswprint
tCharIsPunctuation	Test if a character is a displayable graphic other than a space or an alphanumeric.	_istpunct	ispunct	_ismbcpunct	iswpunct
tCharIsSpace	Test if a character is white space, including not only the space character but also tabs, newlines, and so on.	_istspace	isspace	_ismbcspace	iswspace
tCharIsUpperCase	Test if a character is uppercase.	_istupper	isupper	_ismbcupper	iswupper
tCharToLowerCase	Convert a character to lowercase if possible.	_totlower	tolower	_mbctolower	towlower
tCharToUpperCase	Convert a character to uppercase if possible.	_totupper	toupper	_mbctoupper	towupper
tDirChangeCurrent	Change the current working directory.	_tchdir	_chdir	_chdir	_wchdir
tDirFindFirst	Find the first matching file in a directory.	_tfindfirst	_findfirst	_findfirst	_wfindfirst
tDirFindFirst[I64]	Find the first matching file in a directory, using 64-bit file positions.	_tfindfirsti64	_findfirsti64	_findfirsti64	_wfindfirsti64
tDirFindNext	Find the next matching file in a directory.	_tfindnext	_findnext	_findnext	_wfindnext
tDirFindNext[I64]	Find the next matching file in a directory, using 64-bit file positions.	_tfindnexti64	_findnexti64	_findnexti64	_wfindnexti64
tDirGetCurrent	Get the current directory for the default drive.	_tgetcwd	_getcwd	_getcwd	_wgetcwd
tDirGetCurrent[ForDrive]	Get the current directory for the specified drive.	_tgetdcwd	_getdcwd	_getdcwd	_wgetdcwd
tDirMake	Make a new directory.	_tmkdir	_mkdir	_mkdir	_wmkdir
tDirRemove	Remove a directory.	_trmdir	_rmdir	_rmdir	_wrmdir
tEnvGet	Get environment variable.	_tgetenv	getenv	getenv	_wgetenv
tEnvPut	Put environment string.	_tputenv	_putenv	_putenv	_wputenv
tEnvSearch	Search environment path for a specific file.	_tsearchenv	_searchenv	_searchenv	_wsearchenv
tFileCreate	Create a file.	_tcreat	_creat	_creat	_wcreat
tFileGetAccessFlags	Get the access permission flags for a file.	_taccess	_access	_access	_waccess

(continued)

Table 7-3. *continued*

tcbarx.b	Description	tcbar.b	SBCS	MBCS	WCS
tFileGetFullPath	Get the full (absolute) path for a file.	_tfullpath	_fullpath	_fullpath	_wfullpath
tFileGetStatus	Get file status.	_tstat	_stat	_stat	_wstat
tFileGetStatusI[64]	Get file status, using 64-bit size and position information.	_tstati64	_stati64	_stati64	_wstati64
tFileGetTempName	Get a unique temporary file name for use in the current directory.	_ttmpnam	tmpnam	tmpnam	_wtmpnam
tFileGetTempName[Ex]	Get a unique temporary file name for use in the specified directory.	_ttempnam	_tempnam	_tempnam	_wtempnam
tFileMakeTempName	Make a unique temporary file name using the specified template.	_tmktemp	_mktemp	_mktemp	_wmktemp
tFileOpen	Open a file.	_topen	_open	_open	_wopen
tFileOpenShared	Open a file in a sharing mode.	_tsopen	_open	_open	_wsopen
tFileRemove	Remove a file.	_tremove	remove	remove	_wremove
tFileRename	Rename a file.	_trename	rename	rename	_wrename
tFileSetAccessFlags	Change the access permission flags for a file.	_tchmod	_chmod	_chmod	_wchmod
tFileSetUpdateTime	Set the update time of a file.	_tutime	_utime	_utime	_wutime
tFileUnlink	Unlink (remove) a file.	_tunlink	_unlink	_unlink	_wunlink
tMain	Main function for a console application.	_tmain	main	main	wmain
tSetLocale	Set or query the current locale.	_tsetlocale	setlocale	setlocale	_wsetlocale
tStreamAttachFile	Attach a file handle to a stream.	_tfdopen	_fdopen	_fdopen	_wfdopen
tStreamGetChar	Get a character from a stream.	_fgettc	fgetc	fgetc	fgetwc
tStreamGetChar[Std]	Get a character from the standard input stream.	_fgettchar	_fgetchar	_fgetchar	_fgetwchar
tStreamGetFmt	Get formatted data from a stream.	_ftscanf	fscanf	fscanf	fwscanf

(continued)

Table 7-3. *continued*

tcharx.h	*Description*	*tchar.h*	*SBCS*	*MBCS*	*WCS*
tStreamGetFmtStd	Get formatted data from the standard input stream.	_tscanf	scanf	scanf	wscanf
tStreamGetString	Get a string from a stream.	_fgetts	fgets	fgets	fgetws
tStreamGetString[Std]	Get a string from the standard input stream.	_getts	gets	gets	_getws
tStreamOpen	Open a stream.	_tfopen	fopen	fopen	_wfopen
tStreamOpen[Shared]	Open a stream in shared mode.	_tfsopen	_fsopen	_fsopen	_wfsopen
tStreamOpenPipe	Open a stream based on a pipe.	_tpopen	_popen	_popen	_wpopen
tStreamPrintError	Print an error message on the standard error stream.	_tperror	perror	perror	_wperror
tStreamPutChar	Put a character to a stream.	_fputtc	fputc	fputc	fputwc
tStreamPutChar[Std]	Put a character to the standard output stream.	_fputtchar	_fputchar	_fputchar	_fputwchar
tStreamPutFmt	Put formatted data to an output stream	_ftprintf	fprintf	fprintf	fwprintf
tStreamPutFmt[List]	Put formatted data to an output stream using an argument list.	_vftprintf	vfprintf	vfprintf	vfwprintf
tStreamPutFmt[Std]	Put formatted data to the standard output stream.	_tprintf	printf	printf	wprintf
tStreamPutFmt[StdList]	Put formatted data to the standard output stream using an argument list.	_vtprintf	vprintf	vprintf	vwprintf
tStreamPutString	Put a string to a stream.	_fputts	fputs	fputs	fputws
tStreamPutString[Std]	Put a string to the standard output stream.	_putts	puts	puts	_putws
tStreamReopen	Reopen a stream.	_tfreopen	freopen	freopen	_wfreopen
tStreamUngetChar	Push a character back to an input stream.	_ungettc	ungetc	ungetc	ungetwc
tStringAppend	Append one string to another.	_tcscat	strcat	strcat	wcscat
tStringAppend[Chars]	Append one string to another, limited by a character count.	_tcsnccat	strncat	_mbsncat	wcsncat

(continued)

Table 7-3. *continued*

tcbarx.b	Description	tcbar.b	SBCS	MBCS	WCS
tStringAppendBytes	Append one string to another, limited by a byte count.	_tcsncat	strncat	_mbsnbcat	wcsncat
tStringCollate	Collate two strings.	_tcscoll	strcoll	_mbscoll	wcscoll
tStringCollate[Chars]	Collate two strings, limited by a character count.	_tcsnccoll	_strncoll	_mbsncoll	_wcsncoll
tStringCollate[Chars]NoCase	Collate two strings using case-insensitive comparison, limited by a character count.	_tcsncicoll	_strnicoll	_mbsnicoll	_wcsnicoll
tStringCollateBytes	Collate two strings, limited by a byte count.	_tcsncoll	_strncoll	_mbsnbcoll	_wcsncoll
tStringCollateBytesNoCase	Collate two strings using case-insensitive comparison, limited by a byte count.	_tcsnicoll	_strnicoll	_mbsnbicoll	_wcsnicoll
tStringCollateNoCase	Collate two strings using case-insensitive comparison.	_tcsicoll	_stricoll	_mbsicoll	_wcsicoll
tStringCompare	Compare two strings.	_tcscmp	strcmp	_mbscmp	wcscmp
tStringCompare[Chars]	Compare two strings, limited by a character count.	_tcsnccmp	strncmp	_mbsncmp	wcsncmp
tStringCompare[Chars]NoCase	Compare two strings without regard to case, limited by a character count.	_tcsncicmp	_strnicmp	_mbsnicmp	_wcsnicmp
tStringCompareBytes	Compare two strings, limited by a byte count.	_tcsncmp	strncmp	_mbsnbcmp	wcsncmp
tStringCompareBytesNoCase	Compare two strings without regard to case, limited by a byte count.	_tcsnicmp	_strnicmp	_mbsnbicmp	_wcsnicmp
tStringCompareNoCase	Compare two strings without regard to case.	_tcsicmp	_stricmp	_mbsicmp	_wcsicmp
tStringCopy	Copy a string.	_tcscpy	strcpy	strcpy	wcscpy
tStringCopy[Chars]	Copy a string, limited by a character count.	_tcsnccpy	strncpy	_mbsncpy	wcsncpy
tStringCopyBytes	Copy a string, limited by a byte count.	_tcsncpy	strncpy	_mbsnbcpy	wcsncpy
tStringDuplicate	Duplicate a string.	_tcsdup	_strdup	_strdup	_wcsdup

(continued)

Table 7-3. *continued*

tcbarx.h	Description	*tcbar.h*	SBCS	MBCS	WCS
tStringFindBreak	Find the next break character.	_tcspbrk	strpbrk	_mbspbrk	wcspbrk
tStringFindChar	Find a character.	_tcschr	strchr	_mbschr	wcschr
tStringFindCharReverse	Find a character, starting at the end of the string.	_tcsrchr	strrchr	_mbsrchr	wcsrchr
tStringFindCharSpan	Get the length of the initial substring whose characters are in the specified group.	_tcscspn	strcspn	_mbscspn	wcscspn
tStringFindString	Find the first occurrence of a substring.	_tcsstr	strstr	_mbsstr	wcsstr
tStringFindToken	Find the next token.	_tcstok	strtok	_mbstok	wcstok
tStringFromI64	Convert a 64-bit signed integer to a decimal number string.	_i64tot	_i64toa	_i64toa	_i64tow
tStringFromInt	Convert a signed integer to a decimal number string.	_itot	_itoa	_itoa	_itow
tStringFromLong	Convert a signed long integer to a decimal number string.	_ltot	_ltoa	_ltoa	_ltow
tStringFromTime	Convert a tm structure to a standard date/time string.	_tasctime	asctime	asctime	_wasctime
tStringFromTime_t	Convert a time_t value to a date/time string adjusted to the local time zone.	_tctime	ctime	ctime	_wctime
tStringFromTime[Fmt]	Convert a tm structure to a formatted date/time string.	_tcsftime	strftime	strftime	wcsftime
tStringFromUnsigned64	Convert an unsigned 64-bit integer to a decimal number string.	_ui64tot	_ui64toa	_ui64toa	_ui64tow
tStringFromUnsignedLong	Convert an unsigned long integer to a decimal number string.	_ultot	_ultoa	_ultoa	_ultow
tStringGetByteCount	Get the byte count of the first N characters in a string.	_tcsnbcnt	_strncnt	_mbsnbcnt	_wcsncnt

(continued)

Table 7-3. *continued*

tcharx.h	Description	tchar.h	SBCS	MBCS	WCS
tStringGetCharCount	Get the character count of the first N bytes in a string.	_tcsnccnt	_strnccnt	_mbsnccnt	_wcsncnt
tStringGetFmt	Get data from a formatted string.	_stscanf	sscanf	sscanf	swscanf
tStringGetNextChar	Get the next character from a string.	_tcsnextc	_strnextc	_mbsnextc	_wcsnextc
tStringGetSpan	Get the number of characters at the beginning of a string that are in the specified set.	_tcsspn	strspn	_mbsspn	wcsspn
tStringGetSpanPtr	Get a pointer to the first character in a string that isn't in the specified set.	_tcsspnp	_strspnp	_mbsspnp	_wcsspnp
tStringLength	Get the number of characters in a string, not including the null terminator. Note that _mbslen uses the current code page. Call _mbstrlen to use the code page for the current locale.	_tcslen	strlen	_mbslen	wcslen
tStringMakePath	Make a path string from its components.	_tmakepath	_makepath	_makepath	_wmakepath
tStringNext	Move a string pointer to the next character.	_tcsinc	_strinc	_mbsinc	_wcsinc
tStringPrev	Move a string pointer to the previous character.	_tcsdec	_strdec	_mbsdec	_wcsdec
tStringPutFmt	Generate a string from a format specifier.	_stprintf	sprintf	sprintf	swprintf
tStringPutFmt[Chars]	Generate a string from a format specification, limited to the specified number of characters.	_sntprintf	_snprintf	_snprintf	_snwprintf
tStringPutFmt[List]	Put formatted data into a string using an argument list.	_vstprintf	vsprintf	vsprintf	vswprintf
tStringPutFmt[ListChars]	Put formatted data into a string using an argument list, limited by a character count.	_vsntprintf	_vsnprintf	_vsnprintf	_vsnwprintf
tStringReverse	Reverse the characters in a string.	_tcsrev	_strrev	_mbsrev	_wcsrev
tStringSet	Set all characters of a string to the specified character.	_tcsset	_strset	_mbsset	_wcsset

(continued)

Table 7-3. *continued*

tcbarx.h	Description	tchar.h	SBCS	MBCS	WCS
tStringSet[Chars]	Set the first N characters of a string to the specified character.	_tcsncset	_strnset	_mbsnbset	_wcsnset
tStringSetBytes	Set the first N bytes of a string to the specified character, blank padding the residual bytes of the last multibyte character.				
tStringSkipChars	Skip the specified number of characters.	_tcsninc	_strninc	_mbsninc	_wcsninc
tStringSplitPath	Split a path string into its components.	_tsplitpath	_splitpath	_splitpath	_wsplitpath
tStringToDouble	Convert a string to a double precision real number.	_tcstod	strtod	strtod	wcstod
tStringToI64	Convert a string to a signed 64-bit integer.	_ttoi64	_atoi64	_atoi64	_wtoi64
tStringToInt	Convert a string to a signed integer.	_ttoi	atoi	atoi	_wtoi
tStringToLong	Convert a decimal number string to a signed long integer.	_ttol	atol	atol	_wtol
tStringToLong[Based]	Convert a string to a signed long integer, using the specified number base.	_tcstol	strtol	strtol	wcstol
tStringToLowerCase	Convert a string to lowercase.	_tcslwr	_strlwr	_mbslwr	_wcslwr
tStringToUnsignedLong	Convert a decimal number string to an unsigned long integer.	_tcstoul	strtoul	strtoul	wcstoul
tStringToUpperCase	Convert a string to uppercase.	_tcsupr	_strupr	_mbsupr	_wcsupr
tStringTransform	Transform a string into collation codes for the LC_COLLATE locale.	_tcsxfrm	strxfrm	strxfrm	wcsxfrm
tSysCommand	Execute a system command.	_tsystem	system	system	_wsystem
tSysExecL	Execute a command, using explicit arguments.	_texecl	_execl	_execl	_uexecl
tSysExecLE	Execute a command, using explicit arguments and environment variables.	_texecle	_execle	_execle	_uexecle

(continued)

Table 7-3. *continued*

tcbarx.b	Description	tcbar.b	SBCS	MBCS	WCS
tSysExecLP	Execute a command from the PATH, using explicit arguments.	_texeclp	_execlp	_execlp	_uexeclp
tSysExecLPE	Execute a command from the PATH, using explicit arguments and environment variables.	_texeclpe	_execlpe	_execlpe	_uexeclpe
tSysExecV	Execute a command, using an argument vector.	_texecv	_execv	_execv	_uexecv
tSysExecVE	Execute a command, using argument and environment vectors.	_texecve	_execve	_execve	_uexecve
tSysExecVP	Execute a command on the PATH, using an argument vector.	_texecvp	_execvp	_execvp	_uexecvp
tSysExecVPE	Execute a command on the PATH, using argument and environment vectors.	_texecvpe	_execvpe	_execvpe	_uexecvpe
tSysGetDate	Get the system date string.	_tstrdate	_strdate	_strdate	_ustrdate
tSysGetTime	Get the system time string.	_tstrtime	_strtime	_strtime	_ustrtime
tSysSpawnL	Spawn a process, using explicit arguments.	_tspawnl	_spawnl	_spawnl	_uspawnl
tSysSpawnLE	Spwan a process, using explicit arguments and environment variables.	_tspawnle	_spawnle	_spawnle	_uspawnle
tSysSpawnLP	Spawn a process from the PATH, using explicit arguments.	_tspawnlp	_spawnlp	_spawnlp	_uspawnlp
tSysSpawnLPE	Spawn a process from the PATH, using explicit arguments and environment variables.	_tspawnlpe	_spawnlpe	_spawnlpe	_uspawnlpe
tSysSpawnV	Spawn a process, using an argument vector.	_tspawnv	_spawnv	_spawnv	_uspawnv
tSysSpawnVE	Spawn a process, using argument and environment vectors.	_tspawnve	_spawnve	_spawnve	_uspawnve
tSysSpawnVP	Spawn a process on the PATH, using an argument vector.	_tspawnvp	_spawnvp	_spawnvp	_uspawnvp
tSysSpawnVPE	Spawn a process on the PATH, using argument and environment vectors.	_tspawnvpe	_spawnvpe	_spawnvpe	_uspawnvpe
tWinMain	Main function for a Windows application.	_tWinMain	WinMain	WinMain	uWinMain

Extended MBCS Support

As I explained in Chapter 5, the standard C library offers only minimal support for MBCS programming. While it's true that many standard functions were redesigned to work correctly in an MBCS environment, others have problems with sign-extension or with the distinction between the physical (byte) and logical (character) length of MBCS strings. For a variety of techno-political reasons, the standards committee decided not to define MBCS versions of these problematic functions. Instead, they added a few specific functions, such as *isleadbyte* and *mblen,* to deal with the messy issues of multibyte characters.[5]

Recognizing the importance of MBCS in Asian markets, Microsoft[6] long ago extended the standard C library with MBCS functions that duplicate many of the services available to SBCS and WCS programmers. In Table 7-3, these extensions appear as italic entries in the MBCS column, whereas the entries in the SBCS and WCS columns are not italic. For instance, *isalpha* and *iswalpha* are the standard SBCS and WCS functions that test for an alphabetic character. The Microsoft library adds *_ismbcalpha* to perform this test on an MBCS character packed into an unsigned integer. Then tchar.h wraps the *_istalpha* macro around these three functions, and tcharx.h does the same thing with an inline function named *tCharIsAlpha.*

In addition to providing MBCS versions of standard C functions, Microsoft added functions to simplify the character length issues that arise when you try to use the same source code for SBCS, MBCS, and WCS. For instance, *_tcsinc* advances a string pointer to the next character by calling *_strinc, _mbsinc,* or *_wcsinc* as appropriate. These functions aren't defined in the standard library, but just about every MBCS programmer needs them or something similar.

For example, Listing 7-4 is a simple function that uses the standard library and the Microsoft extensions to find the next alphabetical character in a string. This code works correctly regardless of the character set because it uses *_tcsnextc* to get the next character, *_istalpha* to test it, and *_tcsinc* to advance the string pointer. Referring to Table 7-3, notice that *_tcsnextc* and *_tcsinc* have no standard implementation, so Microsoft supplied the SBCS and WCS versions as well as MBCS in order to facilitate common source code.

---

5. The C++ committee addressed MBCS issues more thoroughly, and their work required some changes in the underlying C standard. This work appeared as Amendment 1, which includes additional MBCS support in the area of stream I/O.

6. Microsoft wasn't alone. Other C compiler vendors made similar MBCS extensions to their implementations of the standard library. Unfortunately, since the C standards committee dropped the ball on this issue, the use of these extensions tends to lock you into a particular vendor.

```
TCHAR* FindNextAlpha(TCHAR* p)
{
_TINT c;
while(c = _tcsnextc(p))          // Get next character until null.
    {
    if(_istalpha(c)) return p;   // Return pointer to alpha char.
    p = _tcsinc(p);              // Else advance the pointer.
    }
return 0;                        // Return null if no alpha char found.
}
```

Listing 7-4. *Using tchar.h to find the next alphabetical character.*

The Microsoft library also provides MBCS versions of many nonstandard functions that were added over the years for competitive reasons and for customer convenience. Some of these are traditional UNIX services, such as unbuffered file operations (*open*, *close*, *read*, *write*, and so on), that were omitted from the standard library. Others are useful extensions, such as *_strrev*, which reverses the characters of a string, and *_strdup*, which duplicates a string. In Table 7-3, these Microsoft-specific functions are italicized in the *tchar.h* column as well as in the SBCS, MBCS, and WCS columns.

Putting tchar.h to Work

Listing 7-5 shows how to use tchar.h and tcharx.h in a typical text-processing program, which counts the number of times each word occurs in a text file. This is a console program written in C++ but using only the standard C library services.

```
#include "tcharx.h"

// This class holds one word and its usage counter.

class Word
{
friend class WordTree;
private:
Word* pLeft;        // Left branch
Word* pRight;       // Right branch
TCHAR* pText;       // Word
int nUsed;          // Usage count

public:
Word(TCHAR* s) : pLeft(0), pRight(0), nUsed(1),
                 pText(tStringDuplicate(s)) {}
```

Listing 7-5. *Using tchar.h and tcharx.h in a word count program.*

```
~Word()
    {
    if(pText) free(pText);
    delete pLeft;
    delete pRight;
    }
void Increment()
    { nUsed++; }
int GetCount() const
    { return nUsed; }
TCHAR* GetText() const
    { return pText; }
int Compare(const TCHAR* s) const
    { return tStringCollate(s, pText); }
void InsertYourself(Word* array[], int& i)
    {
    array[i++] = this;
    if(pLeft) pLeft->InsertYourself(array, i);
    if(pRight) pRight->InsertYourself(array, i);
    }
};

// This class holds a collection of words in a tree organized so
// that the leftmost word is the lowest in alphabetical order.

class WordTree
{
private:
Word* pRoot;           // Root of the tree
int nWords;            // Word count
Word** pWordArray;     // Array of words for frequency report

Word* DoAddWord(Word* pBase, TCHAR* s);
void DoPrintByWord(FILE* pOut, Word* pWord);
int NextWord(TCHAR*& pNext, TCHAR* pWord, int size);

public:
WordTree() : pRoot(0), nWords(0), pWordArray(0) {}
~WordTree() { Reset(); }

void AddWord(TCHAR* s);
void PrintByFrequency(FILE* pFile = stdout);
void PrintByWord(FILE* pFile = stdout);
void Reset();
int Scan(FILE* pFile = stdin, bool bReset = true);
};
```

(continued)

Listing 7-5. *continued*

```
// Reset the tree, deleting all words and buffers.

void WordTree::Reset()
{
delete pWordArray;
delete pRoot;
pWordArray = 0;
pRoot = 0;
nWords = 0;
}

// Scan the input file, placing all words into the tree.

int WordTree::Scan(FILE* pFile, bool bReset)
{
TCHAR b[2000], word[100];
if(bReset) Reset();
while(tStreamGetString(b, tSizeOf(b)-1, pFile))
    {
    tStringToLowerCase(b);         // No case distinction in dictionary
    TCHAR* p = b;
    while(NextWord(p, word, tSizeOf(word)-1)) AddWord(word);
    }
return nWords;
}

// Get the next word from the input file.

int WordTree::NextWord(TCHAR*& pNext, TCHAR* pWord, int size)
{
TCHAR* pStart = pNext;                       // Save word start.
for(int nChars = 0; nChars < size; pNext = tStringNext(pNext))
    {
    TINT c = tStringGetNextChar(pNext);
    if(c == 0) break;                        // End of string
    if(nChars == 0)                          // Check if first character.
        {
        if(!tCharIsGraphic(c)) continue;     // Must be graphic
                                             // Nonspace
        if(tCharIsDigit(c)) continue;        // Cannot be digit
        if(tCharIsPunctuation(c)) continue;  // Cannot be punctuation
        pStart = pNext;                      // Update word start.
        }
    else                                     // Check for end of word.
{
```

```
            if(!tCharIsGraphic(c)) break;       // Not graphic,
                                                // possibly space
            if(tCharIsPunctuation(c)) break;    // Punctuation
            }
        nChars++;                               // Count logical
                                                // characters.

        }
    if(nChars)
        {
        int nTCHAR = pNext - pStart;            // Number of TCHARs
        memcpy(pWord, pStart, nTCHAR * tCharSize); // Copy word
                                                // from string.
        pWord[nTCHAR] = 0;                      // Append terminator.
        }
    return nChars;                              // Return logical char count.
    }


// Add a word, or count it if it is already in the tree, using a
// private recursive function. Beware of stack overflow if the
// words are presented in order.

void WordTree::AddWord(TCHAR* s)
{
pRoot = DoAddWord(pRoot, s);
}


Word* WordTree::DoAddWord(Word* pRoot, TCHAR* s)
{
if(pRoot == 0)                      // Adding a new word
    {
    nWords++;
    return new Word(s);
    }
int position = pRoot->Compare(s);
if(position == 0)
    pRoot->Increment();
else if(position < 0)
    pRoot->pLeft = DoAddWord(pRoot->pLeft, s);
else
    pRoot->pRight = DoAddWord(pRoot->pRight, s);
return pRoot;
}
// Print the words in alphabetical order, using a private
// recursive function.

void WordTree::PrintByWord(FILE* pOut)
{
```

(continued)

Listing 7-5. *continued*

```
tStreamPutFmt
    (
    pOut,
    TEXT("Collated list of %d unique words...\n"),
    nWords
    );
DoPrintByWord(pOut, pRoot);
tStreamPutFmt(TEXT("\n\n"));
}

void WordTree::DoPrintByWord(FILE* pOut, Word* pWord)
{
if(!pWord) return;
DoPrintByWord(pOut, pWord->pLeft);
tStreamPutFmt(pOut, TEXT("%4d %s\n"), pWord->GetCount(),
            pWord->pText);
DoPrintByWord(pOut, pWord->pRight);
}

// Print the words in frequency order, using a sorted array
// of pointers to the Word objects.

static int CompareFrequency(const void* a, const void* b)
{
Word** ppa = (Word**)(a);
Word** ppb = (Word**)(b);
return (*ppb)->GetCount() - (*ppa)->GetCount();
}

void WordTree::PrintByFrequency(FILE* pOut)
{
delete pWordArray;
tStreamPutFmt
    (
    pOut,
    TEXT("Frequency list of %d unique words...\n"),
    nWords
    );
if(!nWords) return;
pWordArray = new Word*[nWords];
int index = 0;
pRoot->InsertYourself(pWordArray, index);
qsort(pWordArray, nWords, sizeof(Word*), CompareFrequency);
for(int i = 0; i < nWords; i++) tStreamPutFmt
    (
    pOut,
```

```
    TEXT("%4d %s\n"),
    pWordArray[i]-> GetCount(),
    pWordArray[i]-> pText
    );
tStreamPutFmt(TEXT("\n\n"));
}


// Main program for console environment; uses STDIN and STDOUT

void tMain()
{
WordTree tree;
tree.Scan();
tree.PrintByWord();
tree.PrintByFrequency();
#if _DEBUG
getchar();          // Debugging pause
#endif
}
// Create ANSI text file, switch to binary in
// Unicode mode & see what happens.
```

The two classes, *Word* and *WordTree*, keep track of the words coming in from the text file. The latter is a tree collection whose data items are instances of the former. The collection object also provides a linear array of *Word* pointers for cases in which the words must be sorted into a different order than in the tree.

The *Word* class holds a pointer to a word string, plus an integer to count the number of occurrences. In addition, it has pointers to two other *Word* objects, designated by the left and right branches. The left branch is either null or points to a *Word* object that collates before the current one. Similarly, the right branch is either null or points to a *Word* object that collates after the current one.

As each new word is broken out of the input text, it's saved in a *Word* object, which is then inserted into the tree according to its collation position. For instance, suppose the input text is, "The quick brown fox jumped over the lazy yellow dog." The tree is then organized as shown in Figure 7-5, and *WordTree.pRoot* points to the first *Word* object ("The"), which is at the top of the tree.

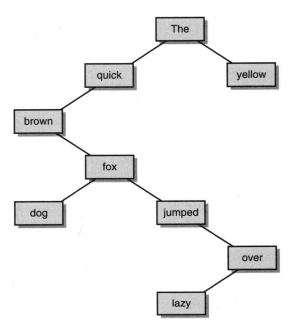

Figure 7-5. *Sample word tree.*

Notice that the program makes no attempt to balance the tree in order to minimize its depth. This feature (or nonfeature) of the program is a major flaw if the words arrive in nearly sorted or reverse sorted order, because either the left or right branch would then contain most of the words. Not only would this make tree operations quite slow, but it could also lead to stack overflows in recursive functions such as *Word.InsertYourself.* I avoided balanced tree techniques in order to keep this example simple.

Creating the word tree

The *tMain* function shows how to use *WordTree* by simply creating an instance and calling *WordTree.Scan*. This function accepts a stream pointer (a FILE*) and a flag indicating whether the tree should be reset. If this flag is false, the words from the file will be added to those already accumulated.

WordTree.Scan reads the text lines from the file one at a time. For each line, it repeatedly calls *WordTree.NextWord* and *WordTree.AddWord*. When all lines have been processed, *Scan* returns a count of the unique words it found. *AddWord* delegates to a helper named *DoAddWord*, which simply walks down the tree recursively. At each step, *DoAddWord* checks the left and right branches against the new word to see which path to follow. This check uses *tStringCollate* to perform a locale-sensitive comparison. When the path reaches a null branch pointer, the new word is inserted.

NextWord is a more complicated function, implementing a parsing technique that works for a broad range of locales. A word begins with any graphic character except a space, a digit, or a punctuation character, and it ends on a space, a punctuation character, or a nongraphic character. This function is somewhat biased toward Western languages, for which the concept of a *word* is more important than for the Asian ideographic languages.[7] Nonetheless the bias isn't really a problem because the program has no practical use in a locale where the word concept doesn't apply.

Notice the somewhat convoluted technique that *NextWord* uses to copy characters from the input string to the word buffer. The word is a substring of the input string and doesn't have a null terminator, so I couldn't use *tStringCopy* (or *_tcscpy*) because it requires the source string to be properly terminated. Since the loop develops a logical character count in *nChars*, I considered using *tStringCopyChars* (or *_tcsnccpy*) with *nChars* as the size limit, but this function doesn't append a null terminator to the destination. For the SBCS and WCS cases, I could append the terminator with this statement:

```
pWord[nChars] = 0;
```

But in the MBCS case, this statement might fail because the number of logical characters doesn't usually translate directly into a string index. For example, if an MBCS string has a physical length of 7 bytes (not counting the null) and contains two double-byte characters, its logical length is five characters.

So the copy algorithm must compute the physical length of the word string, which is the difference between *pNext* and *pStart*. This is actually the number of *TCHARs* in the string and is a suitable index for appending the null terminator. As long as I had to compute that value, I simply used *memcpy* to extract the word from the input string rather than incurring the overhead of *tStringCopyChars* or *tStringCopyBytes*. Since *memcpy* expects a byte count, I multiplied the number of *TCHARs* by the size of a single *TCHAR*, which is provided by *tCharSize* or *sizeof(TCHAR)*.

You might also be wondering why I chose to read complete text lines in the *Scan* function rather than use *tStreamGetChar* (or *_fgettc*). I've found that MBCS programming is a lot easier when you can be assured that all bytes of each character are in memory when you need them. This is because neither the C standard committee nor Microsoft provides a version of *fgetc* that fetches the next multibyte character from an input stream. As you can see from Table 7-3,

---

7. I've been told by Asian friends that a single ideographic symbol, which represents a thought or idea, can become a word, phrase, sentence, or even a paragraph when translated to a European or American language.

the SBCS and MBCS character stream input functions are identical. Both of them are *fgetc*. Since they supply characters 1 byte at a time, you must call *tCharIsLead* (or *_istlead*) after each call to see if additional calls are needed to get the rest of the character.

On the other hand, Microsoft provides the handy *_tcsnextc* function (which I call *tStringGetNextChar*) to get the next character from a string. In an MBCS program, if the next character requires multiple bytes, *_tcsnextc* packs them into an unsigned integer. So if you must support MBCS, it's more convenient to work with complete strings in memory than to obtain them piecemeal from an input stream.

Printing the word tree alphabetically

WordTree::PrintByWord prints the words in ascending lexical (alphabetical) order by walking through the tree in a way similar to *AddWord*. If you study the helper function *DoPrintByWord* carefully, you'll see that it calls itself recursively to print the left branch. Then it prints the current word and calls itself recursively again to print the right branch. Since the left and right branches are handled by a recursive call, the words appear in sorted order. Mirabile dictu! Ain't recursion grand?

Printing the word tree by frequency

WordTree::PrintByFrequency prints the words in descending frequency order so that the most popular word appears first. To do this, the function constructs an array of *Word* pointers and uses the standard *qsort* function to sort it based on the counter values. This is all pretty easy except for the use of *Word::InsertYourself*, which is a recursive function that helps build the array or *Word* pointers. Notice that this function accepts a reference to the array index so that the nested calls can increment the index.

MBCS on the Outside, Unicode on the Inside

Now let's try an experiment in which we'll build the Unicode version of Listing 7-5 and feed an SBCS/MBCS text file[8] to it. I used Notepad to make a file named input.txt containing the nonsense paragraph shown in Figure 7-6, and then I used the Visual C++ 6 editor in binary mode to display the ANSI character codes in Figure 7-7. As you can see, the input file contains no Unicode characters.

---

8. Remember that the standard C library makes no distinction between SBCS and MBCS text files. It treats both types as byte-oriented files processed with the same functions. It's up to the application programmer to detect the lead byte of a multibyte character and take the appropriate action.

Input.txt - Notepad
File Edit Search Help
The quick brown fox jumped over the lazy dog
and landed in a puddle of brown mud.
A frog in the puddle jumped up and landed on a
brown log, which rolled over and squashed him.

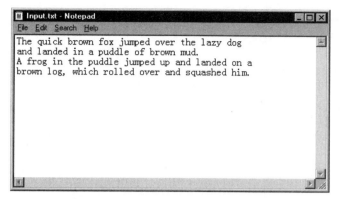

Figure 7-6. *Sample MBCS text file.*

Input.txt
000000 54 68 65 20 71 75 69 63 6B 20 62 72 6F 77 6E 20 The quick brown
000010 66 6F 78 20 6A 75 6D 70 65 64 20 6F 76 65 72 20 fox jumped over
000020 74 68 65 20 6C 61 7A 79 20 64 6F 67 0D 0A 61 6E the lazy dog..an
000030 64 20 6C 61 6E 64 65 64 20 69 6E 20 61 20 70 75 d landed in a pu
000040 64 64 6C 65 20 6F 66 20 62 72 6F 77 6E 20 6D 75 ddle of brown mu
000050 64 2E 0D 0A 41 20 66 72 6F 67 20 69 6E 20 74 68 d...A frog in th
000060 65 20 70 75 64 64 6C 65 20 6A 75 6D 70 65 64 20 e puddle jumped
000070 75 70 20 61 6E 64 20 6C 61 6E 64 65 64 20 6F 6E up and landed on
000080 20 61 0D 0A 62 72 6F 77 6E 20 6C 6F 67 2C 20 77 a..brown log, w
000090 68 69 63 68 20 72 6F 6C 6C 65 64 20 6F 76 65 72 hich rolled over
0000a0 20 61 6E 64 20 73 71 75 61 73 68 65 64 20 68 69 and squashed hi
0000b0 6D 2E 0D 0A m...

Figure 7-7. *Character codes in sample MBCS text file.*

Next I fed the input file to the word count program by executing the following command in an MS-DOS window:

```
ch07b <input.txt >output.txt
```

This produced the file named output.txt, which is shown as text in Figure 7-8 and as hexadecimal character codes in Figure 7-9.

Notice that the output, like the input, contains no Unicode characters. How is it possible for the Unicode version of the word count program to read and write an SBCS/MBCS text file with no special effort on our part?

The answer lies in Amendment 1 of the C standard, which defines the wide stream feature that I briefly described in Chapter 4. This feature enables the library to automatically convert between external SBCS/MBCS text and the corresponding WCS representation that an application program uses internally. Microsoft actually implemented wide streams before Amendment 1, and, fortunately, their version conforms nicely to the standard.

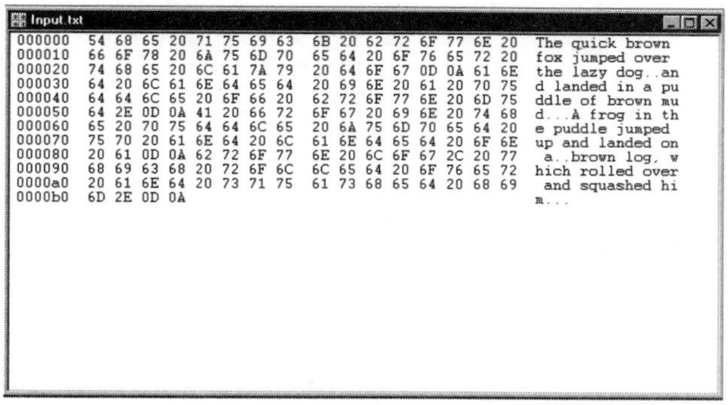

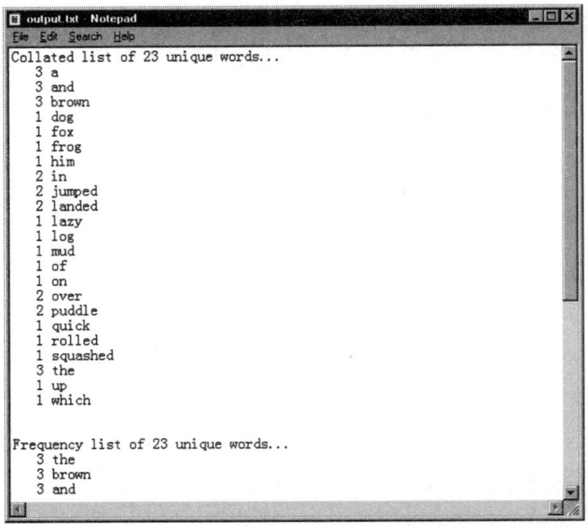

Figure 7-8. *Output of Unicode word counter with SBCS/MBCS input.*

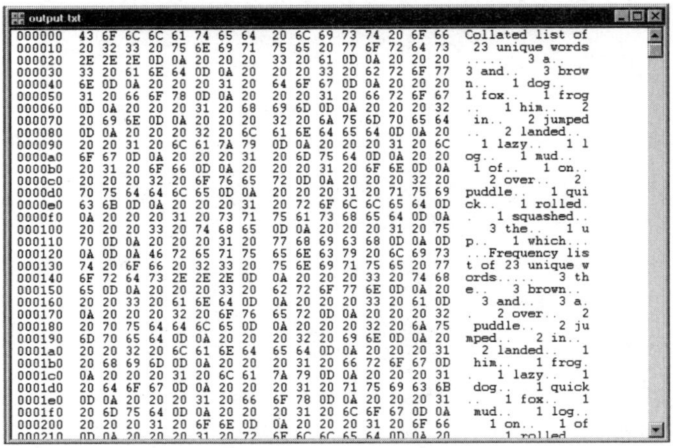

Figure 7-9. *Character codes in output file.*

The word count program reads text from the standard input stream and writes it to the standard output stream, both of which default to the text mode. When the Unicode version calls *tStreamGetString*, the tcharx.h and tchar.h macros route it to *fgetws*. Since the input stream is in text mode, *fgetws* assumes that the file contains MBCS characters rather than Unicode. Therefore, the function converts each character to Unicode using the code page established for the *LC_CTYPE* category.[9] Similarly, when the program calls *fwprintf* through *tStreamPutFmt*, the library converts Unicode to MBCS characters in the appropriate code page.

The program can now use simpler algorithms because all characters have the same size. These simplifications occur in the *Scan* and *NextWord* functions, as shown in Listing 7-6. Although the improvements aren't dramatic in this example, it's easy to find situations for which this technique makes a major difference in the coding effort.

```
// Scan the input file, placing all words into the tree.

int WordTree::Scan(FILE* pIn, bool bReset)
{
TCHAR word[100];
if(bReset) Reset();
while(NextWord(pIn, word, tSizeOf(word)-1)) AddWord(word);
return nWords;
}


// Get the next word from the input file.

int WordTree::NextWord(FILE* pIn,TCHAR* pWord, int size)
{
for(int nChars = 0; nChars < size;)
    {
    TINT c = tStreamGetChar(pIn);
    if(c == TEOF) break;              // End of file
    if(nChars == 0)                   // Check if first character.
        {
        if(!tCharIsGraphic(c)) continue;   // Must be graphic,
                                           // Nonspace
        if(tCharIsDigit(c)) continue;      // Cannot be digit
        if(tCharIsPunctuation(c)) continue;// Cannot be
                                           // punctuation
        }
    else                              // Check for end of word.
        {
        if(!tCharIsGraphic(c)) break;// Not graphic, possibly space
        if(tCharIsPunctuation(c)) break;   // Punctuation
        }
```

Listing 7-6. *Unicode version of* Scan *and* NextWord.   *(continued)*

---

9. See Chapter 5 for an explanation of *LC_CTYPE* and the other locale categories.

Listing 7-6. *continued*

```
    pWord[nChars++] = c;                    // Save character.
    }
pWord[nChars] = 0;                          // Append terminator.
return nChars;                              // Return logical char count.
}
```

If you decide to use MBCS on the outside and Unicode on the inside, you should never build your program with the *_MBCS* symbol defined because the fixed-width algorithms will undoubtedly fail when you try to use them with multibyte text. Of course, since the SBCS environment uses fixed-width characters, you can build an SBCS version by leaving both *_MBCS* and *_UNICODE* undefined. You rarely need to use that strategy, however, because the Unicode version works correctly in an SBCS environment. Specifically, it works correctly with Windows 95 and Windows 98 because it doesn't require Unicode support in the operating system.

As I mentioned previously in Chapter 4, few applications can actually use the library's ability to automatically convert MBCS streams to and from Unicode. In many cases, you're working with a stream that contains structured mixtures of text and binary data (also called *records*). In that case, you must access the stream in binary mode, which deactivates the automatic conversion feature, which means, then, that you have to tediously perform the conversions on the text portions of each record.

For projects in which you have the luxury of defining a new file structure rather than working with a legacy format, you should consider storing text fields in Unicode. If most of the fields are binary, the use of wide characters won't significantly inflate the file size but will greatly simplify your programming chores. If the bulk of each record consists of text, however, and the characters are predominately European and American (single byte), you'll probably want to use an MBCS encoding in the file. Later in this chapter, I'll show how to handle this situation using the standard C++ library.

WHAT ABOUT THE STANDARD C++ LIBRARY?

In order to provide robust support for international programming in the MS-DOS and Windows environments, Microsoft made many extensions to the standard C library. As we've seen, these extensions converge in the tchar.h header file, which all C (and most C++) programmers using Visual Studio should understand thoroughly. MBCS programmers should be particularly interested in tchar.h because it does such a good job hiding many MBCS problems.

In contrast, Microsoft has (at least through Visual C++ 6) made no significant international extensions to the standard C++ library. I discern several reasons for this hands-off approach.

First, the C++ standard emerged after Microsoft had made a major commitment to Unicode in Win32. Given good operating system support, Unicode is the most efficient way to avoid problems with signed and multibyte characters. As a consequence, the C++ standard includes many features that facilitate the programming technique of "MBCS on the outside and Unicode on the inside," and so Microsoft was able to avoid extending the C++ library with a lot of MBCS helper classes and functions.

Second, since much of the standard C++ library uses templates, application programmers can easily produce the C++ equivalent of tchar.h, as I'll show in the section "Using TCHAR in C++ Template" later in this chapter. In other words, it's not difficult to write source code that will compile and run correctly for the different character set environments.

Third, rather than adding major functionality by fussing with the standard classes, Microsoft produces separate class libraries, thereby keeping the standard library pure. For instance, the MFC and ATL class libraries deal with Windows and COM programming tasks, which aren't covered by the standard. Through Visual C++ 6, these libraries used the standard classes sparingly and actually implemented some services that subsequently became standard, such as collections and strings.[10] Now that the standard library has matured, future releases of the Microsoft libraries will undoubtedly rely on it more heavily.

Putting the Standard C++ Library to Work

Listing 7-7 is a version of the word count program that uses the standard C++ classes instead of C library functions. Let's examine the differences.

```
#include "tchar.h"
#include <iomanip>
#include <iostream>
#include <locale>
#include <string>
using namespace std;


// Define types and names based on TCHAR.
// NOTE: This stuff is normally in tcharx.h or <tcharx>.
```

Listing 7-7. *Word count program using C++ library.*   *(continued)*

---

10. Alas, the MFC collection and string classes aren't compatible with those defined by the C++ standards committee. This doesn't imply that one is better or worse than the other, so if you're an MFC programmer using *CString*, don't waste a lot of time rewriting your program to use the standard string class.

Listing 7-7. *continued*

```
#define TEXT _TEXT
#define TINT _TINT
#define tMain _tmain
typedef basic_filebuf<TCHAR> tfilebuf;
typedef basic_fstream<TCHAR> tfstream;
typedef basic_ifstream<TCHAR> tifstream;
typedef basic_ios<TCHAR> tios;
typedef basic_iostream<TCHAR> tiostream;
typedef basic_istream<TCHAR> tistream;
typedef basic_istringstream<TCHAR> tistringstream;
typedef basic_ofstream<TCHAR> tofstream;
typedef basic_ostream<TCHAR> tostream;
typedef basic_ostringstream<TCHAR> tostringstream;
typedef basic_streambuf<TCHAR> tstreambuf;
typedef basic_string<TCHAR> tstring;
typedef basic_stringbuf<TCHAR> tstringbuf;
typedef basic_stringstream<TCHAR> tstringstream;
#ifdef _UNICODE
#define tStdIn wcin
#define tStdOut wcout
#else
#define tStdIn cin
#define tStdOut cout
#endif

// This class holds one word and its usage counter.

class Word
{
friend class WordTree;
private:
Word* pLeft;           // Left branch
Word* pRight;          // Right branch
tstring sText;         // Word
int nUsed;             // Usage count

public:
Word(const tstring& s) : pLeft(0), pRight(0), nUsed(1), sText(s)
{}
~Word()
    {
    delete pLeft;
    delete pRight;
    }
void Increment()
    { nUsed++; }
```

```
int GetCount() const
    { return nUsed; }
const tstring& GetText() const
    { return sText; }
int Compare(const tstring& s) const
    {
    #if 1                          // Use C++ collation method.
    locale loc;
    return _USE(loc, collate<TCHAR>).compare
        (
        s.c_str(),
        s.c_str()+ s.size(),
        sText.c_str(),
        sText.c_str()+ sText.size()
        );
    #else                        // Use C collation method.
    return tStringCollate(s.c_str(), sText.c_str());
    #endif
    }
void InsertYourself(Word* array[], int& i)
    {
    array[i++] = this;
    if(pLeft) pLeft->InsertYourself(array, i);
    if(pRight) pRight->InsertYourself(array, i);
    }
};

// This class holds a collection of words in a tree organized so
// that the leftmost word is the lowest in alphabetical order.

class WordTree
{
private:
Word* pRoot;           // Root of the tree
int nWords;            // Word count
Word** pWordArray;     // Array of words for frequency report

Word* DoAddWord(Word* pBase, const tstring& s);
void DoPrintByWord(tostream& fOut, Word* pWord);
int NextWord(tistream& fIn, tstring& sWord);

public:
WordTree() : pRoot(0), nWords(0), pWordArray(0) {}
~WordTree() { Reset(); }

void AddWord(const tstring& s);
void PrintByFrequency(tostream& fOut = tStdOut);
```

(continued)

Listing 7-7. *continued*

```
void PrintByWord(tostream& fOut = tStdOut);
void Reset();
int Scan(tistream& fIn = tStdIn, bool bReset = true);
};

// Reset the tree, deleting all words and buffers.

void WordTree::Reset()
{
delete pWordArray;
delete pRoot;
pWordArray = 0;
pRoot = 0;
nWords = 0;
}


// Scan the input file, placing all words into the tree.

int WordTree::Scan(tistream& fIn, bool bReset)
{
tstring word;
if(bReset) Reset();
while(NextWord(fIn, word)) AddWord(word);
return nWords;
}
// Get the next word from the input file.

int WordTree::NextWord(tistream& fIn, tstring& word)
{
const locale loc = fIn.getloc();              // Get stream locale.
word = TEXT("");
while(1)
    {
    TINT c = fIn.get();                       // Get character.
    if(!fIn.good()) break;                    // Break on failure.
    if(word.size() == 0)                  // Check if first character.
        {
        if(!isgraph(c, loc)) continue;        // Must be graphic,
                                              // Nonspace
        if(isdigit(c, loc)) continue;         // Cannot be digit
        if(ispunct(c, loc)) continue;         // Cannot be
                                              // punctuation
        }
    else                                  // Check for end of word.
        {
        if(!isgraph(c, loc)) break; // Not graphic, possibly space
```

```
        if(ispunct(c, loc)) break;          // Punctuation
        }
    word += tolower(c, loc); // Save character in lowercase.
    }
return word.size();                         // Return word size.
}
// Add a word, or count it if it is already in the tree, using a
// private recursive function. Beware of stack overflow if the
// words are presented in an order.

void WordTree::AddWord(const tstring& s)
{
pRoot = DoAddWord(pRoot, s);
}

Word* WordTree::DoAddWord(Word* pRoot, const tstring& s)
{
if(pRoot == 0)                              // Adding a new word
    {
    nWords++;
    return new Word(s);
    }
int position = pRoot->Compare(s);
if(position == 0)
    pRoot->Increment();
else if(position < 0)
    pRoot->pLeft = DoAddWord(pRoot->pLeft, s);
else
    pRoot->pRight = DoAddWord(pRoot->pRight, s);
return pRoot;
}

// Print the words in alphabetical order, using a private
// recursive function.

void WordTree::PrintByWord(tostream& fOut)
{
fOut << TEXT("Collated list of ") << nWords
    << TEXT(" unique words...\n");
DoPrintByWord(fOut, pRoot);
fOut << TEXT("\n\n");
}

void WordTree::DoPrintByWord(tostream& fOut, Word* pWord)
{
if(!pWord) return;
```

(continued)

Listing 7-7. *continued*

```
DoPrintByWord(fOut, pWord->pLeft);
fOut << setw(4) << pWord->GetCount() << TEXT(" ")
    << pWord->GetText() << endl;
DoPrintByWord(fOut, pWord->pRight);
}

// Print the words in frequency order, using a sorted array
// of pointers to the Word objects.

static int CompareFrequency(const void* a, const void* b)
{
Word** ppa = (Word**)(a);
Word** ppb = (Word**)(b);
return (*ppb)->GetCount() - (*ppa)->GetCount();
}

void WordTree::PrintByFrequency(tostream& fOut)
{
delete pWordArray;
fOut << TEXT("Frequency list of ") << nWords
    << TEXT(" unique words...\n");
if(!nWords) return;
pWordArray = new Word*[nWords];
int index = 0;
pRoot->InsertYourself(pWordArray, index);
qsort(pWordArray, nWords, sizeof(Word*), CompareFrequency);
for(int i = 0; i < nWords; i++)
    {
    fOut << setw(4) << pWordArray[i]->GetCount() << TEXT(" ");
    fOut << pWordArray[i]->GetText() << endl;
    }
fOut << TEXT("\n\n");
}

// Main program for console environment; uses STDIN and STDOUT

void tMain()
{
WordTree tree;
tree.Scan();
tree.PrintByWord();
tree.PrintByFrequency();
#if _DEBUG
getchar();       // Debugging pause
#endif
}
```

Using TCHAR in C++ templates

The word count program deals with text in the form of characters, strings, and streams. From the earlier versions we know that the *TCHAR* data type is compatible with the SBCS, MBCS, and WCS environments. We also know that tchar.h provides wrappers around the standard library to invoke the proper functions for the specific flavor of *TCHAR* being used.

Now we want to replace the C functions in Listing 7-5 with C++ class operations. The standard C++ library defines the template *basic_string* to encapsulate text strings. Similarly, *basic_istream* and *basic_ostream* encapsulate input and output streams, respectively. For programming convenience, the library also provides the following specializations of these templates:

```
typedef basic_string<char> string;      // Narrow string
typedef basic_string<wchar_t> wstring;  // Wide string
typedef basic_istream<char> istream;    // Narrow input stream
typedef basic_istream<wchar_t> wistream; // Wide input stream
typedef basic_ostream<char> ostream;    // Narrow output stream
typedef basic_ostream<wchar_t> wostream; // Wide output stream
```

We could use these specializations to write bimodal source code by employing conditional compilation, as follows:

```
#ifdef _UNICODE
wstring word;        // Wide string for Unicode
#else
string word;         // Narrow string for SBCS/MBCS
#endif
```

This approach isn't very satisfying because the conditional compilation statements are sprinkled throughout the application, are time-consuming to type, and make the source code difficult to read. As an alternative, we could use wrapper macros as in tchar.h to produce the narrow or wide version, as follows:

```
#ifdef _UNICODE
#define tstring wstring
#else
#define tstring string
#endif
tstring word;
```

Since *wstring* and *string* are data types, we could get better type checking by using *typedef* instead of *#define*, as in this sequence:

```
#ifdef _UNICODE
typedef wstring tstring;
#else
typedef string tstring;
#endif
tstring word;
```

Both of the preceding techniques work, as long as you're happy with *string* and *wstring* as your two options. Furthermore, these are the only convenient solutions if *string* and *wstring* aren't declared as templates, which was the case in earlier versions of the C++ library. The latest version defines strings and streams as templates, and so Listing 7-7 can use a more general approach based on *TCHAR*:

```
typedef basic_string<TCHAR> tstring;
typedef basic_istream<TCHAR> tistream;
typedef basic_ostream<TCHAR> tostream;
```

Since the library contains other text-oriented template classes and functions, it would be nice to have *TCHAR*-based specializations in a header file. Alas, Microsoft didn't do us this favor (at least not in Visual C++ 6), so I've provided them in tcharx.h and its companion file named tcharx. Listing 7-7 doesn't use tcharx because I wanted to show the specializations explicitly.

Changes in the *Word* class

The *Word* class holds one word and its reference counter. The new version carries the word as an embedded *tstring* object rather than as a *TCHAR* pointer. This simplifies the constructor and destructor by eliminating memory management.

The *Compare* function becomes a little more complicated when we use the standard C++ library. The code is

```
int Compare(const tstring& s) const
{
locale loc;
return _USE(loc, collate<TCHAR>).compare
    (
    s.c_str(),
    s.c_str()+ s.size(),
    sText.c_str(),
    sText.c_str()+ sText.size()
    );
}
```

Compare first creates a *locale* object to access the global locale settings. Then it obtains a *collate* facet suitable for *TCHAR* and calls the facet's *compare* method. The four arguments are *TCHAR* pointers to the beginning and end of the two strings being compared.

Listing 7-7 also shows how to use the older C technique for collation if you're more comfortable with that approach. The code is

```
int Compare(const tstring& s) const
{
return tStringCollate(s.c_str(), sText.c_str());
}
```

If you trace the facet-based version into the library, you'll find that it ultimately goes to the same place as the C version. This is a good exercise to perform at least once so that you will gain some understanding of the overhead introduced by C++ locales. It can be significant.

Notice that I used the *c_str* member function to extract a C string from a *tstring* object. Since *tstring* is a specialization of *basic_string* for the *TCHAR* data type, *c_str* returns a *TCHAR* pointer, which is compatible with *tStringCollate*.

Changes in *WordTree* initialization

The *WordTree* object is initialized by its *Scan*, *NextWord*, and *AddWord* functions. Listing 7-7 shows how these functions were changed so that they read from a *tistream* and package each word in a *tstring*.

Scan is essentially unchanged except that it takes a *tistream* reference instead of a *FILE* pointer. Similarly, *AddWord* was changed to work with a *tstring* instead of a *TCHAR* pointer.

NextWord first obtains the locale object associated with the input stream for use in the character tests and conversions. Then it enters a loop, calling *tistream::get* to fetch the next character into an integer. A call to *tistream::good* ensures that the fetch succeeded. Each character is filtered through a series of locale-sensitive tests using template functions such as *isgraph*. These, of course, are different from the C functions of the same name, since the templates take a locale object as the second argument. Each valid character is converted to lowercase by the *tolower* template function, which also takes a locale argument. Then the character is appended to the word by means of the overloaded addition operator.

Changes in *WordTree* printing

The printing functions were all changed so that they use *tostream* and overloaded shift operators to generate the output reports. Notice that quoted strings must be wrapped in *TEXT* or *_T* macros in order to work with *TCHAR* text.

The use of *TCHAR* in conjunction with the overloaded shift operator can cause problems because of some ambiguity in the meaning of *wchar_t*. The C++ standard implies that *wchar_t* should be a distinct data type. In other words, even though it's an unsigned short integer, the compiler should be able to tell the difference. Unfortunately, Visual C++ 6 doesn't see the distinction between *wchar_t* and *unsigned short*, and so the following code produces the wrong output in a Unicode program such as this one:

```
#include <iostream>
void wmain()
{
wchar_t x = L'A';
cout << x << L'B' << L"C" << L"D" << endl;
}
```

Instead of seeing *ABCD* on the output device, you'll see *6566CD*. This happens because the stream's shift operator is overloaded to handle unsigned short integers, and that's exactly what the first two characters appear to be. They are converted into decimal number strings (*65* for letter A and *66* for letter B) instead of the Unicode characters that they actually represent. Notice that the letters C and D appear correctly because they're string literals rather than character literals, and the shift operator doesn't get confused.

MBCS in Microsoft's Standard C++ Library?

As we've seen, Microsoft added many extensions to the standard C library in order to provide better support for MBCS programming. The tchar.h wrappers call these extensions as necessary so that some MBCS algorithms aren't much more complicated than the equivalent SBCS or WCS versions, as I showed in Listing 7-6.

The story is quite different for the C++ library. Even though you can hide character width differences by using *TCHAR* to define bimodal types such as *tstring*, you can't get those classes to use the tchar.h wrappers. For instance, the C++ version of *isprint* (a member of the *ctype* facet template class) won't call Microsoft's *_ismbcprint* function even if you use *TCHAR* as the template parameter.

This isn't really a problem because, surprisingly, the modern C++ version of *isprint* doesn't even call *isprint* or *iswprint* from the standard C library. The latest C++ library contains a complete rewrite of all text processing operations in the form of template classes and functions, and so it has very little interaction with the older text functions in the C library. The new implementation is, for the most part, able to cope with MBCS strings and streams by using *mbstate_t* items. As the program moves forward and backward through strings or streams, the current position isn't just an index, but also includes the MBCS shift status. This helps eliminate errors that occur when a program develops an index or a pointer to an interior byte of a multibyte character.

Despite the improved MBCS support in the C++ library, I believe you should remain wary of pure MBCS programming. The C++ standard was a moving target through most of the 1990s, and commercial compilers inevitably lag behind it in some areas and lead it in others. For instance, Visual C++ 6 includes a circa-1996 implementation of the C++ standard, which you must upgrade with the Dinkum library or its equivalent in order to get the most recent MBCS features.

You'll generally find it safer and more efficient to use "MBCS on the outside and Unicode on the inside." That way, you'll avoid nasty surprises when your code inadvertently overlooks the *mbstate_t* data at an inopportune moment or when you stumble across a bug in a relatively new and unexplored part of the library.

Microsoft's Visual C++ 6 implementation of the C++ library takes care of the MBCS and Unicode conversion automatically for pure text files because it's based on their underlying C library, which supports wide streams, as I mentioned earlier. In other words, streams that are opened in text mode are automatically converted between the external MBCS representation and the internal Unicode representation. You can verify this by building the Unicode version of Listing 7-7 and feeding it an MBCS or SBCS file as we did earlier with Listing 7-6.

What about situations in which MBCS text resides in a file containing binary data? Clearly you must incorporate conversion calls at the appropriate spots to translate between the MBCS and Unicode representations. Let's extend the word count program to illustrate this technique. We'll add object persistence to the *WordTree* and *Word* classes so that we can save the dictionary in a stream file.

Changing the class declarations

The first step is to add *Load* and *Save* functions to both classes, plus a static data member in *WordTree* that serves as a version stamp and a stream-based constructor for the *Word* class. These are declared as follows:

```
void Load(ifstream& fArchive);          // WordTree and Word
void Save(ofstream& fArchive) const;    // WordTree and Word
static unsigned long version;           // WordTree only
Word(ifstream& fArchive)                // Word only
    : pLeft(0), pRight(0), nUsed(0)
    { Load(fArchive); }
```

The idea here is that the owner of the *WordTree* object simply calls *WordTree:: Save* or *WordTree::Load* to save or load the dictionary. The *WordTree* object then calls the *Load* or *Save* function in the root *Word* object, which then propagates the call recursively throughout the tree by following its left and right links. Here's some test code that saves and reloads the tree created in the main program by scanning the standard input file:

```
void tMain()
{
WordTree tree;
tree.Scan();
tree.PrintByWord();

// Save the tree.
ofstream fSave("words.out", ios_base::out | ios_base::binary);
tree.Save(fSave);
fSave.close();
```

(continued)

```
// Load it back.
ifstream fLoad("words.out", ios_base::in | ios_base::binary);
tree.Load(fLoad);
fLoad.close();
tree.PrintByWord();
}
```

If everything works correctly, the test should send two identical reports to the standard output file and should leave the dictionary archived in the *words.out* file. Notice that the archive must be opened in binary mode because it contains mixed text and binary data.

Persistence in the *WordTree* class

For the *WordTree* class, the *Load* and *Save* functions are fairly simple, as shown in Listing 7-8.

```
unsigned long WordTree::version = 0x00010000;      // Version stamp

void WordTree::Save(ofstream& fArchive) const
{
fArchive.write((char*)&version, sizeof(version)); // Save version
                                                  // number.
fArchive.write((char*)&nWords, sizeof(nWords));   // Save word count.
if(nWords) pRoot->Save(fArchive);          // Save words recursively.
}


void WordTree::Load(ifstream& fArchive)
{
Reset();                                    // Make sure tree is empty.
unsigned long fVersion;                     // Load version number.
fArchive.read((char*)&fVersion, sizeof(fVersion));
if(version != fVersion)                     // Compatibility check
    throw "WordTree::Load -- version mismatch";
fArchive.read((char*)&nWords, sizeof(nWords));   // Load word count.
if(nWords) pRoot = new Word(fArchive);      // Load the words.
}
```

Listing 7-8. *Persistence in the* WordTree *class.*

Save begins by writing an unsigned long integer representing the version number followed by another integer representing the number of words in the tree. Both integers must be handled by the archive's *read* and *write* methods rather than by its overloaded shift operators. The shift operators produce and consume text and are therefore inappropriate for binary data. Given a version number of 0x00010000, the left-shift operator would send the decimal number string 65536 to the archive stream.

The version number is a static data member of the *WordTree* class. I always add some kind of version stamp to any persistent class that might evolve. Suppose our customers ask us to change the program so that it remembers which files have already been scanned into the dictionary. This file list logically belongs in the *WordTree* class as a persistent data item, and so the updated *Save* function will include statements that send the list to the archive. But the updated *Load* function must be able to read existing archives created by earlier versions as well as new archives containing the file list. By saving a version number with the object, *Load* can distinguish a new archive from an old one and react accordingly. This example simply throws an exception if *Load* doesn't recognize the version stamp. A more robust implementation would probably make a dummy entry in the file list to indicate that some words were obtained from unidentified files.

After saving the version number and word count, *WordTree::Save* calls the *Save* function in the root *Word* object. Similarly, *WordTree::Load* creates the root *Word* object using the archive stream as a constructor argument. In both cases, the *Word* functions operate recursively to reconstruct the tree, as I'll explain next.

Persistence in the *Word* class

The interesting conversions between MBCS and Unicode occur in the *Load* and *Save* functions of the *Word* class, as shown in Listing 7-9. These versions use C library functions for the conversions when operating in the Unicode mode.

```
void Word::Save(ofstream& fArchive) const
{
fArchive.write((char*)&nUsed, sizeof(nUsed)); // Save usage count.
char flags = (pLeft ? 2 : 0) | (pRight ? 1 : 0);
fArchive.write(&flags, 1);                   // Save recursion flags.
#ifdef _UNICODE                              // Save Unicode as MBCS.
short n = wcstombs(0, sText.c_str(), 0);
if(n <= 0) throw "Word::Save -- MBCS conversion error";
char* p = new char[n+1];
wcstombs(p, sText.c_str(), n+1);
#else                                        // Save SBCS/MBCS as is.
short n = sText.size();
const char* p = sText.c_str();
#endif
```

Listing 7-9. *Persistence in the* Word *class.* *(continued)*

Listing 7-9. *continued*

```
fArchive.write((char*)&n, sizeof(n));
fArchive.write(p, n);
#ifdef _UNICODE
delete p;
#endif
if(pLeft) pLeft->Save(fArchive);              // Save left branch.
if(pRight) pRight->Save(fArchive);            // Save right branch.
}


void Word::Load(ifstream& fArchive)
{
fArchive.read((char*)&nUsed, sizeof(nUsed)); // Load usage count.
char flags;
fArchive.read(&flags, 1);                     // Load recursion flags.
short n;
fArchive.read((char*)&n, sizeof(n));  // Load string length (chars).
char* p = new char[n+1];
fArchive.read(p, n);                          // Load string.
p[n] = 0;
#ifdef _UNICODE                               // Convert MBCS to Unicode.
n = mbstowcs(0, p, 0);
if(n <= 0) throw "Word::Load -- MBCS conversion error";
wchar_t* q = new wchar_t[n+1];
mbstowcs(q, p, n+1);
sText = q;
delete q;
#else
sText = p;
#endif
delete p;
if(flags & 2) pLeft = new Word(fArchive);
if(flags & 1) pRight = new Word(fArchive);
}
```

Save first writes the usage counter as a long integer, followed by a flag byte indicating whether the left and right branches contain pointers. Next comes the word length in bytes, written as a short integer, followed by the text bytes without a null terminator. These last two items are produced differently for the Unicode and non-Unicode cases.

If *_UNICODE* isn't defined, *Save* simply writes the string size, obtained by calling *sText.size*, followed by the string itself, obtained from *sText.c_str*. If *_UNICODE* is defined, *Save* uses *wcstombs* to compute the required number of bytes for the MBCS representation. Then it allocates a character array of that size and calls *wcstombs* again to perform the conversion. After writing the length and the MBCS text, *Save* deletes the MBCS string.

Load operates in a similar manner. After fetching the word count and flag byte, it reads the string length, allocates a buffer, reads the string, and appends a null byte. If _UNICODE isn't defined, the string is copied to *sText*. If _UNICODE is defined, *Load* calls *mbstowcs* to compute the number of Unicode characters in the MBCS string, allocates a buffer of that size, calls *mbstowcs* again to perform the conversion, copies the result to *sText*, and deletes the Unicode buffer. In both cases, *Load* deletes the MBCS buffer after processing the text.

Both *Save* and *Load* are recursive functions. The former calls itself directly for the left and right branches if the corresponding pointer isn't null. The latter calls itself indirectly by constructing left and right nodes corresponding to the archived flags. *Load* uses the constructor that accepts an input stream argument, and that constructor delegates the call back to the *Load* function. Once again, ain't recursion wonderful?

If you're concerned about performance when processing large word trees, you might be tempted to give Listing 7-9 a tune-up. The *Save* function allocates and releases a temporary buffer and calls *wcstombs* twice. *Load* is even worse because it allocates and releases two temporary buffers and calls *mbstowcs* twice. Listing 7-10 shows a version that eliminates one conversion call and all memory allocations in both functions. To accomplish this, the functions assume that no word will require more than 150 bytes in its MBCS representation.[11]

```
void Word::Save(ofstream& fArchive) const
{
fArchive.write((char*)&nUsed, sizeof(nUsed)); // Save usage count.
char flags = (pLeft ? 2 : 0) | (pRight ? 1 : 0);
fArchive.write(&flags, 1);                     // Save recursion flags.
#ifdef _UNICODE                                // Save Unicode as MBCS.
char p[150];                                   // 150-byte word is max!
short n = wcstombs(p, sText.c_str(), sizeof(p));
if(n <= 0) throw "Word::Save -- MBCS conversion error";
#else                                          // Save SBCS/MBCS as is.
short n = sText.size();
const char* p = sText.c_str();
#endif
```

Listing 7-10. *Tuning the* Word *persistence functions.*   *(continued)*

---

11. This implies that even if every MBCS character requires 2 bytes, the program can track words of up to 75 characters. For European languages that use single-byte representations, a word can contain up to 150 (actually 149) characters. I suppose this is a reasonable limitation, although people in Wales might disagree, since I've been told that some of their villages have single-word names containing several hundred letters.

Listing 7-10. *continued*

```
fArchive.write((char*)&n, sizeof(n));
fArchive.write(p, n);
if(pLeft) pLeft->Save(fArchive);              // Save left branch.
if(pRight) pRight->Save(fArchive);            // Save right branch.
}
void Word::Load(ifstream& fArchive)
{
fArchive.read((char*)&nUsed, sizeof(nUsed)); // Load usage count.
char flags;
fArchive.read(&flags, 1);                     // Load recursion flags.
short n;
fArchive.read((char*)&n, sizeof(n));  // Load string length (chars).
char p[150];                          // Load string (150 byte max).
if(n >= sizeof(p)) throw "Word::Load -- invalid length";
fArchive.read(p, n);
p[n] = 0;
#ifdef _UNICODE                               // Convert MBCS to Unicode.
wchar_t q[150];
n = mbstowcs(q, p, n+1);
if(n <= 0) throw "Word::Load -- MBCS conversion error";
sText = q;
#else
sText = p;
#endif
if(flags & 2) pLeft = new Word(fArchive);
if(flags & 1) pRight = new Word(fArchive);
}
```

Be wary of stack overflows when you use techniques such as the one in Listing 7-10. By placing the temporary buffers on the stack, Listing 7-10 increases the *Save* stack frame by 150 bytes and the *Load* frame by 450. Although this approach is faster than allocating the buffers from the heap, it can lead to a stack overflow when you're working with a large tree that goes down many levels. Remember that this example program makes no attempt to balance the tree, so if the *Scan* function sees incoming words in ascending or descending order, the tree will become very deep, leading to many nested calls when loading or saving.

We can avoid stack overflow by defining the buffers as static members of the *Word* class, since *Load* and *Save* don't require that the buffered data be preserved during a recursive call. Of course, static data members can cause problems in a multi-threaded environment, but that's not an issue here because we're not accessing a tree object from multiple threads. To do so would require a significant redesign, which you might want to tackle as an exercise if you decide to turn this example into a class library for use in other programs.

If you want to be a "pure" C++ programmer, you probably find it unsettling to call C functions such as *mbstowcs* and *wcstombs*. I don't have such qualms, so I tend to freely intermix the C and C++ library in my programs. But you can eliminate the C library calls from *Load* and *Save* by employing the locale facet known as *codecvt*. The main purpose of this facet is to handle conversion between narrow and wide character codes, as do *wcstombs* and its fellow C functions. Naturally, the *codecvt* facet does this in a more general (and more verbose) way, as shown in Listing 7-11.

```cpp
#include "tcharx.h"
#include <iomanip>
#include <locale>
using namespace std;

// This class holds one Word and its usage counter.

class Word
{
friend class WordTree;
private:
Word* pLeft;                     // Left branch
Word* pRight;                    // Right branch
tstring sText;                   // Word
long nUsed;                      // Usage count

static char bWork[150];          // MBCS buffer
#ifdef _UNICODE
static wchar_t wWork[150];       // WCS buffer
#endif

public:
Word(const tstring& s) : pLeft(0), pRight(0), nUsed(1), sText(s)
{}
~Word()
    {
    delete pLeft;
    delete pRight;
    }
void Increment()
    { nUsed++; }
long GetCount() const
    { return nUsed; }
const tstring& GetText() const
    { return sText; }
int Compare(const tstring& s) const
    {
    #if 1                        // Use C++ collation method.
    locale loc;
    return _USE(loc, collate<TCHAR>).compare
```

Listing 7-11. *Final word count program using the* codecvt *facet.*   *(continued)*

Listing 7-11. *continued*

```
            (
            s.c_str(),
            s.c_str() + s.size(),
            sText.c_str(),
            sText.c_str() + sText.size()
            );
    #else                          // Use C collation method.
    return tStringCollate(s.c_str(), sText.c_str());
    #endif
    }
void InsertYourself(Word* array[], long& i)
    {
    array[i++] = this;
    if(pLeft) pLeft->InsertYourself(array, i);
    if(pRight) pRight->InsertYourself(array, i);
    }

protected: // Protected members for serialization
Word(ifstream& fArchive) : pLeft(0), pRight(0), nUsed(0)
    { Load(fArchive); }
void Load(ifstream& fArchive);
void Save(ofstream& fArchive) const;
};

// This class holds a collection of words in a tree organized so
// that the leftmost word is the lowest in alphabetical order.

class WordTree
{
private:
static unsigned long version;          // Class version number
Word* pRoot;                           // Root of the tree
long nWords;                           // Word count
Word** pWordArray; // Array of words for frequency report

Word* DoAddWord(Word* pBase, const tstring& s);
void DoPrintByWord(tostream& fOut, Word* pWord);
int NextWord(tistream& fIn, tstring& sWord);

public:
WordTree() : pRoot(0), nWords(0), pWordArray(0) {}
~WordTree() { Reset(); }

void AddWord(const tstring& s);
void PrintByFrequency(tostream& fOut = tStdOut);
void PrintByWord(tostream& fOut = tStdOut);
```

```
void Reset();
int Scan(tistream& fIn = tStdIn, bool bReset=true);
void Load(ifstream& fArchive);
void Save(ofstream& fArchive) const;
};

// Reset the tree, deleting all words and buffers.

void WordTree::Reset()
{
delete pWordArray;
delete pRoot;
pWordArray = 0;
pRoot = 0;
nWords = 0;
}

// Scan the input file, placing all words into the tree.

int WordTree::Scan(tistream& fIn, bool bReset)
{
tstring word;
if(bReset) Reset();
while(NextWord(fIn, word)) AddWord(word);
return nWords;
}

// Get the next word from the input file.

int WordTree::NextWord(tistream& fIn, tstring& word)
{
const locale loc = fIn.getloc();
word = TEXT("");
while(1)
    {
    TINT c = fIn.get();                 // Get character.
    if(!fIn.good()) break;              // Break on failure.
    if(word.size() == 0)                // Check if first character.
        {
        if(!isgraph(c, loc)) continue;// Must be graphic, nonspace
        if(isdigit(c, loc)) continue;  // Cannot be digit
        if(ispunct(c, loc)) continue;  // Cannot be punctuation
        }
    else                                // Check for end of word.
        {
        if(!isgraph(c, loc)) break; // Not graphic, possibly space
        if(ispunct(c, loc)) break;  // Punctuation
```

(continued)

Listing 7-11. *continued*

```
        }
    word += tolower(c, loc);            // Save character in lowercase.
    }
return word.size();                     // Return word size.
}

// Add a word, or count it if it is already in the tree, using a
// private recursive function. Beware of stack overflow if the
// words are presented in order.

void WordTree::AddWord(const tstring& s)
{
pRoot = DoAddWord(pRoot, s);
}

Word* WordTree::DoAddWord(Word* pRoot, const tstring& s)
{
if(pRoot == 0)                          // Adding a new word
    {
    nWords++;
    return new Word(s);
    }
int position = pRoot->Compare(s);
if(position == 0)
    pRoot->Increment();
else if(position < 0)
    pRoot->pLeft = DoAddWord(pRoot->pLeft, s);
else
    pRoot->pRight = DoAddWord(pRoot->pRight, s);
return pRoot;
}

// Print the words in alphabetical order, using a private
// recursive function.

void WordTree::PrintByWord(tostream& fOut)
{
fOut << TEXT("Collated list of ") << nWords
    << TEXT(" unique words...\n");
DoPrintByWord(fOut, pRoot);
fOut << TEXT("\n\n");
}

void WordTree::DoPrintByWord(tostream& fOut, Word* pWord)
{
if(!pWord) return;
```

```
DoPrintByWord(fOut, pWord->pLeft);
fOut << setw(4) << pWord->GetCount() << TEXT(" ")
     << pWord->GetText() << endl;
DoPrintByWord(fOut, pWord->pRight);
}

// Print the words in frequency order, using a sorted array
// of pointers to the Word objects.

static int CompareFrequency(const void* a, const void* b)
{
Word** ppa = (Word**)(a);
Word** ppb = (Word**)(b);
return (*ppb)->GetCount() - (*ppa)->GetCount();
}

void WordTree::PrintByFrequency(tostream& fOut)
{
delete pWordArray;
fOut << TEXT("Frequency list of ") << nWords
     << TEXT(" unique words...\n");
if(!nWords) return;
pWordArray = new Word*[nWords];
long index = 0;
pRoot->InsertYourself(pWordArray, index);
qsort(pWordArray, nWords, sizeof(Word*), CompareFrequency);
for(long i = 0; i < nWords; i++)
    {
    fOut << setw(4) << pWordArray[i]->GetCount() << TEXT(" ");
    fOut << pWordArray[i]->GetText() << endl;
    }
fOut << TEXT("\n\n");
}

// WordTree serialization

unsigned long WordTree::version = 0x00010000;    // Version stamp

void WordTree::Save(ofstream& fArchive) const
{
fArchive.write((char*)&version, sizeof(version));// Save version
                                                 // number.
fArchive.write((char*)&nWords, sizeof(nWords));  // Save word count.
if(nWords) pRoot->Save(fArchive);         // Save words recursively.
}

void WordTree::Load(ifstream& fArchive)
{
```

(continued)

Listing 7-11. *continued*

```
Reset();                                        // Make sure tree is empty.
unsigned long fVersion;                         // Load version number.
fArchive.read((char*)&fVersion, sizeof(fVersion));
if(version != fVersion)                         // Compatibility check
    throw "WordTree::Load -- version mismatch";
fArchive.read((char*)&nWords, sizeof(nWords));    // Load word count.
if(nWords) pRoot = new Word(fArchive);           // Load the words.
}


// Word serialization

// Conversion facet
typedef codecvt<wchar_t, char, mbstate_t> tConvert_t;


// Static buffers
char Word::bWork[150];                                 // MBCS buffer
#ifdef _UNICODE
wchar_t Word::wWork[150];                               // WCS buffer
#endif

void Word::Save(ofstream& fArchive) const
{
fArchive.write((char*)&nUsed, sizeof(nUsed));    // Save usage count.
char flags = (pLeft ? 2 : 0) | (pRight ? 1 : 0);
fArchive.write(&flags, 1);                        // Save recursion flags.
#ifdef _UNICODE                                   // Save Unicode as MBCS.
locale loc = fArchive.getloc();                   // Get stream locale.
const tConvert_t& fac = _USE(loc, tConvert_t);    // Get conversion
                                                  // facet.

wchar_t* pNextIn;
char* pNextOut;
mbstate_t state = {0};
int res = fac.out
    (
    state,
    sText.c_str(), sText.c_str() + sText.size(),
    pNextIn,
    bWork, bWork+sizeof(bWork) - 1,
    pNextOut
    );
short n = pNextOut - bWork;
const char* p = bWork;
#else                                             // Save SBCS/MBCS as is.
short n = sText.size();
const char* p = sText.c_str();
#endif
fArchive.write((char*)&n, sizeof(n));
fArchive.write(p, n);
```

```
    if(pLeft) pLeft->Save(fArchive);        // Save left branch.
    if(pRight) pRight->Save(fArchive);      // Save right branch.
}

void Word::Load(ifstream& fArchive)
{
fArchive.read((char*)&nUsed,sizeof(nUsed));   // Load usage count.
char flags;                             // Load recursion flags.
fArchive.read(&flags, 1);
short n;                                 // Load string length (chars).
fArchive.read((char*)&n, sizeof(n));
if(n >= sizeof(bWork)) throw "Word::Load -- invalid length";
fArchive.read(bWork, n);
bWork[n] = 0;
#ifdef _UNICODE                          // Convert MBCS to Unicode.
n = mbstowcs(wWork, bWork, n + 1);
if(n <= 0) throw "Word::Load -- MBCS conversion error";
sText = wWork;
#else
sText = bWork;
#endif
if(flags & 2) pLeft = new Word(fArchive);
if(flags & 1) pRight = new Word(fArchive);
}

// Main program for console environment; uses STDIN and STDOUT

void tMain()
{
WordTree tree;

// Load the tree and print words in collation order.
tree.Scan();
tree.PrintByWord();
// Save the tree.
ofstream fSave("words.out",ios_base::out | ios_base::binary);
tree.Save(fSave);
fSave.close();

// Load it back and print again. Reports should match.
ifstream fLoad("words.out",ios_base::in | ios_base::binary);
tree.Load(fLoad);
fLoad.close();
tree.PrintByWord();

#if _DEBUG
getchar();          // Debugging pause
#endif
}
```

(continued)

This is the final version of the word count program and includes all the bells and whistles I've demonstrated throughout this chapter. The *Word* class includes static buffers named *bWork* and *wWork* to assist in converting between narrow (byte) strings and wide strings. These items are included only when _UNICODE is defined because no conversion is necessary in an SBCS or MBCS version of the program.

The *Load* and *Save* functions in the *Word* class now use the following specialization of the *codecvt* facet, which I define as the *tConvert_t* type:

```
typedef codecvt<wchar_t, char, mbstate_t> tConvert_t;
```

This facet has member functions called *in* and *out* that perform essentially the same services as *mbstowcs* and *wcstombs*, respectively. Their names suggest the viewpoint of the C++ committee. The *in* function converts MBCS to WCS, as you would normally want when converting an MBCS file for use internally as Unicode. Likewise, the *out* function converts WCS back to MBCS for output to a file. These functions have more arguments than their C counterparts because they're more flexible. They don't have to process entire strings but can work on the characters between two pointers. They also return pointers to the next character in the input and output areas.[12]

Notice that *Load* and *Save* employ the *codecvt* facet associated with the archive stream. This is better than the earlier approach using C functions because it enables the caller to establish a specific conversion locale for the stream. The earlier approach used the global locale setting, which is the only one available in C.

Also notice that the *in* and *out* functions require an initial setting of the multibyte state, in the form of an *mbstate_t* argument. Since *Load* and *Save* always work with complete strings, they use the "reset" state when calling the facet functions.

---

12. Note that some documentation, such as that from Dinkumware, describes these functions incorrectly. The fourth and seventh arguments aren't pointers but references to pointers so that the function can use them as function outputs.

SUMMARY

The Visual C++ development environment faithfully implements the C and C++ standards, and Microsoft has often stated its intent to track these standards as they evolve. Because the C standard lagged behind the needs of commercial programmers developing international software, particularly those using MBCS, Microsoft added numerous extensions to the C library. These are cleverly hidden behind the tchar.h header file, which enables programmers to use a single source code base for SBCS, MBCS, and Unicode.

The C++ standard addresses international programming more thoroughly and elegantly than the C standard does, and so Microsoft hasn't had to make any extensions to serve their customers. Visual C++ 6, however, uses a circa-1996 implementation of the C++ standard, which omits some international features and contains bugs in others. If you plan to use the C++ library extensively, you should obtain a more recent version from Microsoft (probably in the form of Visual C++ 7) or from Dinkumware, the original author.

Chapter 8

Character Sets in Microsoft Win32

As we saw in Chapter 3, character sets and code pages are nothing more than mappings of human-readable symbols (called *characters*) to machine-readable numbers (called *code points*). These mapping techniques have undergone a lengthy evolutionary process of more than 150 years culminating in Unicode, the first character set that can justifiably be called universal.[1]

If we were starting in a pristine world using today's powerful computing and communication hardware, operating systems, and development tools, we would probably work exclusively in Unicode. The world isn't pristine, however, and so international programs must continue to support less universal character sets using SBCS and MBCS encodings.[2]

This chapter explains how Microsoft Windows 2000 handles Unicode as well as the older character mapping techniques. The chapter also describes Windows 95 and Windows 98, which don't use Unicode internally and provide only a subset of Win32 Unicode services.

---

1. Of course, ISO-10646 is a superset of Unicode and is therefore "more universal."

2. I have no doubt that future programmers using 32-bit interstellar character sets will grouse about the need to support "that ancient Unicode standard."

UNICODE IN WINDOWS 2000

Windows 2000, in its original incarnation as Microsoft Windows NT, was that rare event, a brand new operating system designed from the ground up as a best fit for the capabilities of modern computing hardware and the needs of modern computer users. Since it was a fresh start, it was able to offer programmers a modern character set, namely Unicode, which promised to greatly simplify international software.

This decision caused Windows 2000 to be developed as a native Unicode operating system, which means that it employs wide characters in the following ways:

■ For internal text manipulations

■ For text strings passed through the Win32 API

■ For filenames and properties in the NT file system (NTFS), but not in older file systems such as FAT

■ For text strings embedded in system files such as the Registry database

■ For linkage, debugging, and resource information in executable files

■ For network communication with other Windows 2000 systems

In other words, whenever Windows 2000 is in complete control of the generation, storage, and transmission of textual data, it operates in Unicode. When Windows 2000 isn't in complete control, it doesn't force the use of Unicode. For instance, even though filenames are stored as Unicode strings in an NTFS directory, your data files can contain text encoded in ASCII, EBCDIC, or even Morse code. Similarly, although Windows 2000 knows your program and its external linkages by their Unicode names, it has no interest in how those modules represent text within their address spaces.

Recognizing that they couldn't simply abandon the thousands of existing Windows applications that use older character sets, the Windows 2000 designers added MS-DOS and Win16 emulators that enable well-behaved legacy applications to run unchanged. The emulators take care of translating between the older SBCS/MBCS techniques and the new Unicode character set.[3]

---

3. Windows NT's Win16 support was viewed as an interim step until the most important of these applications could be upgraded to use Win32 and Unicode and the least important faded from the market. But since we still see 30-year-old COBOL programs in daily use, I doubt that Win16 applications will ever completely disappear.

Despite this nod to legacy applications, Windows 2000 is clearly focused on the future instead of the past. Since its original inception as Windows NT, its primary goal has always been to provide a robust environment for the development of new 32-bit applications, with few compromises for older 16-bit software and hardware. So here's the short version of the Unicode story for programmers developing new Windows 2000 applications: *Use Unicode. It works, and it works well!*

UNICODE IN WINDOWS 95 AND WINDOWS 98

While Windows NT was designed primarily for the future, Windows 95 was firmly rooted in the past because it evolved directly from Windows 3.1 and was not a complete rewrite like Windows NT. Thus Windows 95 prolonged the lifespan of existing Win16 platforms while enabling a slower migration to Win32.

By discontinuing support for older Intel processors, Windows 95 was able to include Win32 features, such as the flat addressing model and multithreading. On the other hand, it had to provide a suitable execution environment for nearly all Windows 3.x applications, including many that used undocumented features or directly accessed the hardware and were, therefore, not well-behaved. These conflicting goals were achieved by basing Windows 95 on the traditional Win16 and MS-DOS API and adding a Win32 layer to support new applications.

So let's be honest. Windows 95 and Windows 98 are essentially Windows 3.1 with a dollop of fresh paint to impress users and programmers. Users see a spiffy object-oriented desktop instead of the clunky old Program and File Managers. Programmers see the Win32 API with its simple 32-bit linear addressing model instead of the polyglot Win16 plus MS-DOS API that employs complex segmented addressing. Although these are not trivial improvements, these systems still have their roots firmly planted in the SBCS/MBCS world of Win16 and MS-DOS.

But wait a minute! If Windows 95 and Windows 98 expose themselves to programmers via the Win32 API, how can they not use Unicode? Well, as we'll see in the next section, Win32 comes in two flavors: Unicode and ANSI. Windows 2000 offers both, while Windows 95 and Windows 98 offer primarily the ANSI flavor. In other words, Windows 95 and Windows 98 employ a narrow-character version of Win32.

So here's the short version of the Unicode story for Windows 95 and Windows 98 programmers: *Don't use Unicode. It doesn't work!* Of course, you can employ Unicode or any other character set internally. Just make sure you drop SBCS or MBCS text at the system's doorstep because the version of Win32 provided with Windows 95 and Windows 98 generally doesn't recognize Unicode.[4]

THE BIMODAL WIN32 API

From the preceding descriptions of Unicode in Windows 2000, Windows 95, and Windows 98, it should be clear that Microsoft's Win32 designers faced some serious challenges in attempting to make their API work for all three operating systems. To deal with these conflicting goals, Microsoft created bimodal definitions of many Win32 functions. Each API call that accepts or returns text (whether individual characters or strings) is defined with two names, one having a trailing W and the other having a trailing A. The former works with wide characters (Unicode), while the latter works with narrow characters (ANSI or some other ASCII derivative, hence the trailing A). Windows 2000 implements both versions, while Windows 95 and Windows 98 provide only the ANSI functions.[5]

The header files for Win32 programming in C and C++ make it easy to use the bimodal API by disguising it as shown in this example, which I extracted from *winbase.h* and cleaned up for readability:

```
HMODULE LoadLibraryA(LPSTR lpLibFileName);
HMODULE LoadLibraryW(LPWSTR lpLibFileName);
#ifdef UNICODE
#define LoadLibrary LoadLibraryW
#else
#define LoadLibrary LoadLibraryA
#endif
```

LoadLibrary is a Win32 function that fetches a library module (a DLL) by means of its filename. The header file declares both *LoadLibraryW* and *LoadLibraryA* to deal with Unicode and ANSI strings, respectively, and then it equates *LoadLibrary* to one or the other, depending on the state of the *UNICODE*[6] symbol. You can use the simpler name *LoadLibrary* as long as you define the preprocessor symbol *UNICODE* when compiling the program for the wide-character environment.

---

4. Some of the text-oriented functions, such as *TextOut*, now support Unicode in order to simplify multilingual document processings. This topic is discussed in Chapter 10.

5. Recall from Chapter 4 that the term "ANSI character set" refers to any SBCS or MBCS code page derived from ASCII.

6. The Win32 SDK header files use *UNICODE,* while the C/C++/MFC/ATL header files use *_UNICODE*. The latter also test for the presence of *UNICODE* and set *_UNICODE* appropriately. Nonetheless, it's a good practice to define both symbols explicitly when compiling for Unicode.

This technique enables you to produce source code that's compatible with Windows 2000, Windows 95, and Windows 98, at least with regard to the bimodal API function names. To complete the job, we also need bimodal data types that automatically conform to Unicode or ANSI, depending on the state of the *UNICODE* symbol. In the preceding example, the *LoadLibrary* function requires a string identifying the library file. The A and W function declarations use data types *LPSTR* and *LPWSTR* as pointers to narrow and wide strings, respectively.[7] In the *winnt.h* header file, you'll find these symbols defined as follows, together with a bimodal type *LPTSTR* that is synonymous with *LPWSTR* for a Unicode compilation or with *LPSTR* for an ANSI compilation.

```
typedef char* LPSTR;
typedef wchar_t* LPWSTR;
#ifdef UNICODE
#define LPTSTR LPWSTR
#else
#define LPTSTR LPSTR
#endif
```

This code follows an approach identical to that used by the *tchar.h* header file (see Chapter 7) when defining the bimodal *TCHAR* data type. Indeed, you could rewrite the *LPTSTR* definition using this statement:

```
typedef TCHAR* LPTSTR;
```

By consistently employing bimodal data types, you can use simplified API names such as *LoadLibrary* and produce source code that can be readily compiled for Windows 2000, Windows 95, and Windows 98.

The Win32 header files also provide bimodal definitions for text-sensitive window class names, message codes, notification codes, and COM interfaces. For instance, the toolbar control comes in both Unicode and ANSI flavors, and so its class name and many of its messages have definitions such as the following:

```
// Define toolbar window class name.
#define TOOLBARCLASSNAMEW      L"ToolbarWindow32"
#define TOOLBARCLASSNAMEA      "ToolbarWindow32"
#ifdef  UNICODE
#define TOOLBARCLASSNAME       TOOLBARCLASSNAMEW
#else
#define TOOLBARCLASSNAME       TOOLBARCLASSNAMEA
#endif
```

(continued)

---

7. Win32 perpetuates most of the type definition symbols from Win16, even though they make little sense in a 32-bit environment. *LPSTR* and *LPWSTR* are two prime examples. The prefix *LP* means *long pointer* and was used in Win16 to identify a 32-bit pointer as opposed to one that required only 16 bits.

```
// Define bimodal toolbar messages.
#define TB_GETBUTTONINFOW        (WM_USER + 63)
#define TB_SETBUTTONINFOW        (WM_USER + 64)
#define TB_GETBUTTONINFOA        (WM_USER + 65)
#define TB_SETBUTTONINFOA        (WM_USER + 66)
#ifdef UNICODE
#define TB_GETBUTTONINFO         TB_GETBUTTONINFOW
#define TB_SETBUTTONINFO         TB_SETBUTTONINFOW
#else
#define TB_GETBUTTONINFO         TB_GETBUTTONINFOA
#define TB_SETBUTTONINFO         TB_SETBUTTONINFOA
#endif
```

Thus the Win32 header files use conditional compilation techniques to hide the fact that different functions, message numbers, and data types are needed for the Unicode and ANSI character sets. In addition, as we saw in Chapter 7, Visual C++ provides *tchar.h* to disguise the differences between the narrow and wide data types and functions in the standard C and C++ libraries. These two features together offer the programmer several alternatives when designing a Win32 application in C or C++:

1. **Unicode version for Windows 2000, no support for Windows 95 and Windows 98.** If you need to support only Windows 2000, define the *UNICODE* symbol and kiss SBCS and MBCS goodbye! The resulting program will support the broad range of symbol sets included in Unicode, and your text processing algorithms will be simple because every character will have the same size. Furthermore, the program will use the most efficient form of the API because Windows 2000 won't have to constantly convert between narrow and wide characters.[8] If you must work with SBCS or MBCS files and databases, it's fairly easy to translate to and from Unicode in the I/O routines that form the program's boundary with the outside world, especially if you can use the standard C and C++ libraries.

2. **Single SBCS version for Windows 2000, Windows 95, and Windows 98.** The simplest way to support Windows 2000, Windows 95, and Windows 98 with a single executable is to leave *UNICODE* undefined, use SBCS techniques with unsigned characters, and avoid Windows 2000 features (for example, the security API) that aren't available in Windows 95 and Windows 98. The resulting program will run on both platforms and support the symbol sets

---

8. The ANSI functions in Windows 2000's implementation of the Win32 API are often called a *thunking layer* because they don't add any intelligence (*thinking*) to a program but just perform relatively simple conversions (*thunking*, which isn't yet a real word). In general, a program runs more efficiently if it can avoid the use of thunking layers.

needed by many countries in Europe and the Americas. You will probably not sell many copies in the Asian market or any other locale that requires more than 256 symbols.

3. **Unicode version for Windows 2000 and SBCS version for Windows 95 and Windows 98.** If you must provide some support for Windows 95 and Windows 98 but can restrict complete internationalization to the Windows 2000 version, consider shipping two different executables. Compile the Windows 2000 version in Unicode mode for maximum efficiency and international flexibility. Compile the Windows 95 or Windows 98 version in ANSI mode using SBCS techniques as described above, thereby limiting its international scope to Western Europe and the Americas. Since both versions use fixed-length characters, the text algorithms should be simple and identical as long as you avoid confusion about byte lengths vs. character lengths.

4. **Single MBCS version for Windows 2000, Windows 95, and Windows 98.** If you can stand the pain of MBCS programming, you can build a single executable for use throughout the world on Windows 2000, Windows 95, and Windows 98. Actually, the pain isn't too severe if the program does little text work. A text-intensive program, however, such as a word processor, can become extremely complicated and slow when manipulating MBCS characters internally. For that reason, programmers who choose this path often use Unicode internally and convert to and from MBCS when executing file operations or API calls. In other words, they use the first approach but extend the concept of the program boundary to include the non-I/O API calls.

5. **Unicode version for Windows 2000 and MBCS version for Windows 95 and Windows 98.** If you must support the broadest possible range of character sets in Windows 2000, Windows 95, and Windows 98 but have the luxury of shipping separate executables, use the preceding approach but conditionally compile the MBCS conversions associated with the Win32 API calls. Include the conversions in the Windows 95 or Windows 98 version, and omit them from the Windows 2000 version in order to improve performance by avoiding the ANSI thunking layer.

Visual C++ tools such as the MFC Application Wizard usually default to the fourth technique, producing a single MBCS executable for Windows 2000, Windows 95, and Windows 98. If you are not careful when you flesh out this wizard-generated source code, you can easily, and unintentionally, introduce SBCS algorithms. As an American programmer, I've seen many MFC applications degrade into the second category, SBCS only, due to our general ignorance about MBCS techniques.

WIN32 CONSOLE PROGRAMMING

Although most application programs running on Win32 workstations use the Windows graphical interface, the operating system also supports nongraphical programs through its console feature. In previous chapters, I used console programs to illustrate the international features of C and C++. Now let's briefly examine how to write international programs that call the Win32 console API directly.

Operating system designers have traditionally used the word *console* when referring to the combination of a display, a keyboard, and a mouse or other pointing device.[9] MS-DOS and Windows 3.x treat the PC as a single console system in which the active application program has relatively unfettered access to the devices.

When running on an 80386 processor or later, Windows 3.x can simulate the MS-DOS console environment in order to run several MS-DOS boxes at the same time. This feature is implemented in a subsystem known as the Virtual Machine Manager, or VMM386, which evolved into the basis for Windows 95 and Windows 98.

Win32 builds on this technology to support multiple virtual consoles on a single workstation, exposing the console feature through the API functions listed in Table 8-1. In addition, the Windows 2000 implementation of Win32 separates the MS-DOS environment from the console feature and packages it in a module known as the virtual DOS machine, or VDM. This makes it easy for Windows 2000 to support other character-mode environments such as POSIX and OS/2.

---

9. In many multiuser systems such as those employing UNIX, the console has a high-speed connection to the computer and is used by the system administrator, while normal users work at terminals having relatively slow connections. This distinction is unimportant to most application programs.

Table 8-1. **Win32 Console API Functions**

Function Name	Dual	Description
AllocConsole	No	Allocates a new console for the current process
CreateConsoleScreenBuffer	No	Creates a console output buffer
FillConsoleOutputAttribute	No	Fills an output buffer range with an attribute
FillConsoleOutputCharacter	Yes	Fills an output buffer range with a character
FlushConsoleInputBuffer	No	Discards all records from an input buffer
FreeConsole	No	Detaches current process from a console
GenerateConsoleCtrlEvent	No	Sends a control event to processes sharing a console
GetConsoleCP	No	Gets console input code page
GetConsoleCursorInfo	No	Gets cursor data for an output buffer
GetConsoleMode	No	Gets mode flags for an input or output buffer
GetConsoleOutputCP	No	Gets console output code page
GetConsoleScreenBufferInfo	No	Gets console window size, buffer size, and color attributes
GetConsoleTitle	Yes	Gets console window title
GetLargestConsoleWindowSize	No	Gets largest possible size for a console window
GetNumberOfConsoleInputEvents	No	Gets number of unread records in an input buffer
GetNumberOfConsoleMouseButtons	No	Gets number of buttons on console pointing device
GetStdHandle	No	Gets handle of standard input, output, or error device
PeekConsoleInput	Yes	Peeks at one or more records in an input buffer
ReadConsole	Yes	Reads text from an input buffer
ReadConsoleInput	Yes	Reads one or more records from an input buffer
ReadConsoleOutput	Yes	Reads text and attributes from an output buffer

(continued)

Table 8-1. *continued*

Function Name	Dual	Description
ReadConsoleOutputAttribute	No	Reads one or more attributes from an output buffer
ReadConsoleOutputCharacter	Yes	Reads one or more characters from an output buffer
ScrollConsoleScreenBuffer	No	Moves a block within an output buffer
SetConsoleActiveScreenBuffer	No	Attaches output buffer to console
SetConsoleCP	No	Sets console input code page
SetConsoleCtrlHandler	No	Adds or removes a console control event handler
SetConsoleCursorInfo	No	Sets cursor data for an output buffer
SetConsoleCursorPosition	No	Sets cursor position for an output buffer
SetConsoleMode	No	Sets mode flags for an input or output buffer
SetConsoleOutputCP	No	Sets console output code page
SetConsoleScreenBufferSize	No	Defines rows and columns for an output buffer
SetConsoleTextAttribute	No	Sets color attributes of subsequent output characters
SetConsoleTitle	Yes	Sets console window title
SetConsoleWindowInfo	No	Sets console window size and position
SetStdHandle	No	Sets handle of standard input, output, or error device
WriteConsole	Yes	Writes text to an output buffer
WriteConsoleInput	Yes	Appends records to an input buffer
WriteConsoleOutput	Yes	Writes text and attributes to an output buffer
WriteConsoleOutputAttribute	No	Writes one or more attributes to an output buffer
WriteConsoleOutputCharacter	Yes	Writes one or more characters to an output buffer

Because consoles are virtual, a process that allocates a new console can operate as if it has its own text display, keyboard, and mouse. The operating system maps the virtual display device into a window on the real display and provides an output buffer that resembles the video memory grid familiar to MS-DOS programmers. Each cell in the grid contains a character code and a format specifier. The former uses either the console's output code page or Unicode, and the latter specifies the foreground and background colors for the cell. The console also channels the keyboard and mouse input through a queue much like the Windows message queue so that the real keyboard and mouse can be shared with other processes. The virtual keyboard mechanism translates keystrokes into character codes from the console's input code page or Unicode, depending on whether you access the queue with the ANSI or Unicode API.

Although the console feature is Win32's general environment for character-mode programming, we most often encounter it when working with the VDM to host MS-DOS applications that are our legacy from the 1980s.[10] To that end, the console subsystem makes it easy to use traditional SBCS and MBCS code pages for these older programs as well as Unicode for newer character-mode applications.

As I mentioned earlier, each console has two associated code pages, one for input and one for output. These are both initialized to the page that's most compatible with the hardware, which is called the OEM code page. For example, a PC in the United States typically uses CP437 as the OEM page, while many European machines prefer CP850. The Windows 2000 console API allows you to change the input and output code pages independently, although in most cases you'll want them to be the same. Windows 95 and Windows 98 don't allow a console program to switch pages, although the user can do this with the CHCP command.

If you use wide API functions such as *WriteConsoleW*, the console input and output buffers work with Unicode. Code pages come into play when you call narrow versions of the console API functions such as *WriteConsoleA*. Because the VDM layer, in effect, calls the narrow API, 16-bit programs use the traditional SBCS and MBCS techniques of MS-DOS. If your legacy application is well behaved, you don't even have to rebuild it for Windows 2000, Windows 95, or Windows 98. It will retain whatever international features it had under MS-DOS, using SBCS and MBCS techniques with switched code pages. On the other hand, the ANSI console functions make it fairly easy to convert an MS-DOS program into a native Win32 application that avoids the VDM overhead but retains its SBCS and MBCS algorithms.

---

10. Windows 2000 also provides a POSIX environment to run legacy UNIX programs and an environment for OS/2 character-mode programs.

Native Console Applications

A native console application is one written specifically for the virtual console environment using direct Win32 API calls rather than indirect calls through the VDM layer.[11] It can employ wide characters, narrow characters, or remain relatively aloof from character-set issues by using bimodal programming techniques. I recommend the bimodal approach because it's easy and gives you the best chance of remaining compatible with Windows 95 and Windows 98.[12] Let's examine each technique.

The pure Unicode technique

If you're programming exclusively for Windows 2000, you can use a pure Unicode approach. Listing 8-1 shows a simple Hello program written this way. It prompts the user on the standard output device, gets the user's name from the standard input, and then issues a greeting on the standard output.

```
// Define UNICODE and _UNICODE just to be safe.
#define UNICODE
#define _UNICODE

// Easy way to get Win32 console API
#define WIN32_LEAN_AND_MEAN
#include <windows.h>

#include <tchar.h>

// Test for valid handle.
inline bool IsValidHandle(HANDLE h)
    { return h != INVALID_HANDLE_VALUE; }

// Main program
int wmain(int argc, wchar_t* argv[], wchar_t* envp[])
{

// Check for Windows NT or Windows 2000.
if(GetVersion() & 0x80000000)
    {
    MessageBox
```

Listing 8-1. *Native console program (wide characters only).*

---

11. A primary task of the VDM is to handle the software interrupts, especially INT 21H, that form the MS-DOS API.

12. I've observed that once a programmer starts to use the Win32 API directly, rather than through the standard C and C++ libraries, the program can quickly become incompatible with Windows 95 and 98. I think this happens because the full-blown Win32 API is so powerful and so much fun to use that the programmer forgets that Windows 9x provides only a subset.

```
            (
            NULL,
            _T("This program requires Windows NT or Windows 2000."),
            _T("Error"),
            MB_OK
            );
        return(1);
        }


    // Initialize handles.
    HANDLE hStdIn = INVALID_HANDLE_VALUE;
    HANDLE hStdOut = INVALID_HANDLE_VALUE;
    DWORD nChars;

    // Get standard input and output handles; silent abort on failure.
    hStdIn = GetStdHandle(STD_INPUT_HANDLE);
    if(!IsValidHandle(hStdIn)) return -1;
    hStdOut = GetStdHandle(STD_OUTPUT_HANDLE);
    if(!IsValidHandle(hStdOut)) return -1;

    // Ask for user's name.
    wchar_t* pPrompt = L"What is your name?\n";
    WriteConsoleW(hStdOut, pPrompt, lstrlenW(pPrompt), &nChars, 0);

    // Append it to the end of hello message.
    wchar_t message[100] = L"Hello, ";
    int nPrefix = lstrlenW(message);
    ReadConsoleW(hStdIn, &message[nPrefix],
                sizeof(message)/sizeof(wchar_t)-nPrefix, &nChars, 0);

    // Say "hello" to user.
    WriteConsoleW(hStdOut, message, nPrefix+nChars, &nChars, 0);

    return 0;
    }
```

Notice that this version employs the wide-character API functions and that all text is of the ugly *wchar_t* data type as defined in the C and C++ standards. The main entry point is *wmain* so that the command line arguments, if we need them, will be presented as Unicode strings. You should generally define the *UNICODE* and *_UNICODE* symbols before including the Win32 header files, although this example compiles and runs correctly even if you omit these symbols because it explicitly calls the wide-character API functions.

The *wmain* function begins with a version check to ensure that the program is running on a Unicode platform. If you attempt to run it on a Windows 95, Windows 98, or Win32S system, it displays an error in a message box.[13] This error message is triggered by the result of the *GetVersion* API, which indicates these earlier systems by returning a 32-bit version number with its high-order bit set. If this check were omitted, the program would appear to exit immediately when started under Windows 95 and Windows 98. This behavior occurs because the wide console functions such as *ReadConsoleW* are stubbed off and return false to indicate failure, and so the program simply runs to completion without doing any damage. In a more complicated program, these Unicode API failures could cause system problems or confuse the user, so you should always include the version test at the beginning of a pure Unicode program.

The pure ANSI technique

Listing 8-2 shows the same program written for narrow characters. This is close to traditional C programming except for the use of the Win32 API instead of standard C library functions such as *getchar* and *putchar*. The example works correctly with all SBCS or MBCS code pages because it merely copies from console input to output without performing any character-oriented operations on the console text.

```
// Easy way to get Win32 console API
#define WIN32_LEAN_AND_MEAN
#include <windows.h>

// Test for valid handle.
inline bool IsValidHandle(HANDLE h)
    { return h != INVALID_HANDLE_VALUE; }

// Main program
int main(int argc, char* argv[], char* envp[])
{
// Initialize handles.
HANDLE hStdIn = INVALID_HANDLE_VALUE;
HANDLE hStdOut = INVALID_HANDLE_VALUE;
DWORD nChars;

// Get standard input and output handles; silent abort on failure.
hStdIn = GetStdHandle(STD_INPUT_HANDLE)
```

Listing 8-2. *Native console program (narrow characters only).*

---

13. Notice that even though message boxes are graphical display items, you can create them within console programs. In fact, a process can manipulate any combination of console and graphical windows.

```
    if(!IsValidHandle(hStdIn)) return -1;
    hStdOut = GetStdHandle(STD_OUTPUT_HANDLE);
    if(!IsValidHandle(hStdOut)) return -1;

    // Ask for user's name.
    char* pPrompt = "What is your name?\n";
    WriteConsoleA(hStdOut, pPrompt, lstrlenA(pPrompt), &nChars, 0);

    // Append it to the end of hello message.
    char message[100] = "Hello, ";
    int nPrefix = lstrlenA(message);
    ReadConsoleA(hStdIn, &message[nPrefix],
                 sizeof(message)-nPrefix, &nChars, 0);

    // Say "hello" to user.
    WriteConsoleA(hStdOut, message, nPrefix+nChars, &nChars, 0);

    return 0;
    }
```

The bimodal technique

Unlike the first version, the program in Listing 8-2 will run under Windows 95 and Windows 98 as well as Windows 2000. But since the narrow API isn't optimal for Windows 2000, you might want to produce bimodal source code that can be conditionally compiled to use wide or narrow characters. Listing 8-3 shows how to accomplish this by employing the *tchar.h* header file previously described in Chapter 7.

```
// Easy way to get Win32 console API
#define WIN32_LEAN_AND_MEAN
#include <windows.h>

// Need tchar.h for bimodal types and macros.
#include <tchar.h>

// Test for valid handle.
inline bool IsValidHandle(HANDLE h)
    { return h != INVALID_HANDLE_VALUE; }

// Compute character size of a buffer.
// This should be in tchar.h.
#define _tsizeof(buffer) (sizeof(buffer)/sizeof(TCHAR))
```

Listing 8-3. *Native console program (wide or narrow characters).*   *(continued)*

Listing 8-3. *continued*

```
// Main program
int _tmain(int argc, TCHAR* argv[], TCHAR* envp[])
{
// Initialize handles.
HANDLE hStdIn = INVALID_HANDLE_VALUE;
HANDLE hStdOut = INVALID_HANDLE_VALUE;
DWORD nChars;

// Get standard input and output handles; silent abort on failure.
hStdIn = GetStdHandle(STD_INPUT_HANDLE);
if(!IsValidHandle(hStdIn)) return -1;
hStdOut = GetStdHandle(STD_OUTPUT_HANDLE);
if(!IsValidHandle(hStdOut)) return -1;
// Ask for user's name.
TCHAR* pPrompt = _T("What is your name?\n");
WriteConsole(hStdOut, pPrompt, lstrlen(pPrompt), &nChars, 0);

// Append it to the end of hello message.
TCHAR message[100] = _T("Hello, ");
int nPrefix = lstrlen(message);
ReadConsole(hStdIn, &message[nPrefix],
            _tsizeof(message)-nPrefix, &nChars, 0);

// Say "hello" to user.
WriteConsole(hStdOut, message, nPrefix+nChars, &nChars, 0);

return 0;
}
```

The main entry point is *_tmain,* all text is defined using the *TCHAR* data type and related macros, and the program calls the bimodal console API functions having neither the A nor the W suffix. So the same source code can be compiled for SBCS, MBCS, or Unicode by properly defining *_MBCS* and *_UNICODE*, as described in Chapter 7.

The trickiest aspect of this example is the cumbersome compile-time computation needed to determine the number of characters that will fit in a buffer. One of the most common bimodal programming errors is to use a byte length where you need a character length or vice-versa. Therefore, I like to hide this computation behind a macro such as *_tsizeof*, which simply computes buffer sizes in terms of characters instead of bytes. This macro should really be a part of the *tchar.h* header file.[14]

---

14. Chapter 7 describes the *tcharx.h* header file that I devised to extend *tchar.h* with easier names and missing features. Among the latter is the *tSizeOf* macro, which is identical to *_tsizeof* as defined in this example.

Why bother with the console API?

At this point, you're probably wondering why anyone would want to use the console API. After all, you could write the preceding example in standard C as shown in Listing 8-4, which is a lot easier to type than the preceding versions that use the console API. Somewhere under the covers, the C library calls the appropriate Win32 functions, saving you the trouble of learning yet another set of complicated functions.

```
#include <tchar.h>
#include <stdio.h>

int _tmain(int argc, TCHAR* argv[], TCHAR* envp[])
{
putts(_T("What is your name?"));
TCHAR message[100] = _T("Hello, ");
int nPrefix = _tcslen(message);
gets(&message[nPrefix]);
putts(message);
return 0;
}
```

Listing 8-4. *Bimodal console program using the standard C library.*

The real power of the console API appears, however, when you want to provide a better user interface than a "glass teletype," the traditional UNIX paradigm that's enshrined in the standard C and C++ libraries. The standard libraries implement the line-oriented query-response user interface that was popular in the 1960s and 1970s. They don't support the high-performance, forms-oriented, memory-mapped video programs that are popular on MS-DOS workstations.[15]

For instance, Listing 8-5 is a full-screen version of the Hello program. It begins by erasing the entire screen to a blue background and prompting for the user's name in the top line of the console window. Then it erases the top line, displays the name in the center of the window, and waits for a keystroke as a signal to exit.

```
// Easy way to get Win32 console API
#define WIN32_LEAN_AND_MEAN
#include <windows.h>
```

Listing 8-5. *Console program using full-screen mode.*   *(continued)*

---

15. Traditionally, when a UNIX program wanted to work in full-screen mode instead of line mode, it used an inband signalling technique, such as DEC VT-100 escape sequences, to control the screen. The *cursor* library offers a memory-mapped video environment that is device independent, but it isn't part of the C standard.

Listing 8-5. *continued*

```
// Need tchar.h for bimodal types and macros.
#include <tchar.h>

// Test for valid handle.
inline bool IsValidHandle(HANDLE h)
    { return h != INVALID_HANDLE_VALUE; }

// Compute character size of a buffer.
// This should be in tchar.h.
#define _tsizeof(buffer) (sizeof(buffer)/sizeof(TCHAR))

// Main program
int _tmain(int argc, TCHAR* argv[], TCHAR* envp[])
{
DWORD nChars;                               // # of chars processed
CONSOLE_SCREEN_BUFFER_INFO cbInfo;          // Output buffer info
COORD pos = {0, 0};                         // Current position
WORD caDefault =                            // Default char attribute
    BACKGROUND_BLUE | BACKGROUND_INTENSITY |
    FOREGROUND_GREEN | FOREGROUND_RED | FOREGROUND_INTENSITY;

// Initialize handles.
HANDLE hStdIn = INVALID_HANDLE_VALUE;
HANDLE hStdOut = INVALID_HANDLE_VALUE;

// Get standard input and output handles; silent abort on failure.
hStdIn = GetStdHandle(STD_INPUT_HANDLE);
if(!IsValidHandle(hStdIn)) return -1;
hStdOut = GetStdHandle(STD_OUTPUT_HANDLE);
if(!IsValidHandle(hStdOut)) return -1;

// Erase the screen.
SetConsoleTextAttribute(hStdOut, caDefault);
GetConsoleScreenBufferInfo(hStdOut, &cbInfo);
FillConsoleOutputCharacter
    (
    hStdOut,
    _T(' '),
    cbInfo.dwSize.X * cbInfo.dwSize.Y,
    pos,
    &nChars
    );
FillConsoleOutputAttribute
    (
    hStdOut,
    caDefault,
```

```
        cbInfo.dwSize.X * cbInfo.dwSize.Y,
        pos,
        &nChars
        );

// Ask for user's name.
TCHAR* pPrompt = _T("What is your name? ");
pos.Y = cbInfo.srWindow.Top;
pos.X = cbInfo.srWindow.Left;
SetConsoleCursorPosition(hStdOut, pos);
WriteConsole(hStdOut, pPrompt, lstrlen(pPrompt), &nChars, 0);

// Append name to the end of hello message.
TCHAR message[100] = _T("Hello, ");
int nPrefix = lstrlen(message);
ReadConsole(hStdIn, &message[nPrefix],
            _tsizeof(message)-nPrefix, &nChars, 0);

// Erase the input line.
FillConsoleOutputCharacter
    (
    hStdOut,
    _T(' '),
    cbInfo.srWindow.Right - pos.X + 1,
    pos,
    &nChars
    );

// Say "hello" to user in center of screen.
pos.Y = cbInfo.srWindow.Top +
        (cbInfo.srWindow.Bottom - cbInfo.srWindow.Top) / 2;
pos.X = cbInfo.srWindow.Left +
        (cbInfo.srWindow.Right - cbInfo.srWindow.Left) / 2
        - lstrlen(message) / 2;
SetConsoleCursorPosition(hStdOut, pos);
WriteConsole(hStdOut, message, nPrefix+nChars, &nChars, 0);

// Prompt for a keystroke to terminate.
TCHAR* pExit = _T("Press any key to exit.");
pos.Y += 2;
pos.X = cbInfo.srWindow.Left +
        (cbInfo.srWindow.Right - cbInfo.srWindow.Left) / 2
        - lstrlen(pExit) / 2;
SetConsoleCursorPosition(hStdOut, pos);
WriteConsole(hStdOut, pExit, lstrlen(pExit), &nChars, 0);
```

(continued)

Listing 8-5. *continued*

```
// Wait for keystroke.
SetConsoleMode(hStdIn, 0);
ReadConsole(hStdIn, &message, 1, &nChars, 0);

return 0;
}
```

The *CONSOLE_SCREEN_BUFFER_INFO* structure and the *COORD* structures are the keys to full-screen console operations. The former gives the dimensions of the virtual output area as well as the area currently visible in the console window. The window can't be larger than the virtual area, but it can be smaller, in which case the console subsystem displays the necessary scroll bars. The latter specifies the cursor position. To erase the screen, the program computes the virtual screen buffer size by multiplying its dimensions, positions the cursor at the upper left coordinate (0,0), and calls *FillConsoleOutputCharacter* and *FillConsoleOutputAttribute*. In this case, I filled the screen with spaces, set the background color to blue, and set the foreground color to white. The console uses a 16-color palette just like the old CGA video adapter.

The only other tricky aspect of Listing 8-5 is the *SetConsoleMode* function that the program calls just before it begins waiting for the exit signal. The console is initially in the line input mode, which means that *ReadConsole* doesn't return until the user presses the Enter key. In addition, the console defaults to echo mode so that typed characters appear on the screen automatically. Since the example program is simply waiting for any single keystroke as a termination signal, I turned off these two modes so that *ReadConsole* would return immediately after receiving a keystroke.

Switching Code Pages in Console Programs

Console code pages determine how characters are represented in an application program that doesn't use Unicode. The operating system assigns the default OEM code page to each new virtual console, but the application program can change this setting using *SetConsoleCP* and *SetConsoleOutputCP*. The former changes the input code page, while the latter changes the one used for output. Most of the time, you'll want these to be the same, so don't forget to call both functions. Since Microsoft used the misleading name *SetConsoleCP* instead of *SetConsoleInputCP*, it's easy to forget that you must also call *SetConsoleOutputCP*.

The console I/O subsystem undertakes the messy task of translating between the hardware encoding and the code pages specified by the software. For instance, a PC keyboard delivers keystrokes using hardware-dependent scan codes, so the console input handler must determine what type of keyboard is in use and then convert the scan codes to characters in the input code page. The handler must also convert special actions, such as Ctrl+C, to input events instead of characters. The application program can catch these events by using *SetConsoleControlHandler*.

As I said earlier, for most console applications you simply live with the code page settings established by the operating system or the user, but in rare cases you might need to change the input page, the output page, or both. For instance, suppose you have a library of text-oriented functions designed for use in the Windows environment where CP1252 is the default. Now you're working on a console program and want to use the library there but you're concerned that it might contain CP1252 dependencies. In order to avoid problems, you should switch the console to CP1252 instead of the OEM page established by the operating system.

Listing 8-6 is a handy utility program that switches the console output page and then displays the symbols corresponding to the 256 codes in the page. Figure 8-1 shows the console window when the program is displaying CP1252.

```
// Easy way to get Win32 console API
#define WIN32_LEAN_AND_MEAN
#include <windows.h>

// Use standard C formatting functions.
#include <stdio.h>
#include <stdlib.h>

// Need tchar.h for bimodal types and macros.
#include <tchar.h>

// Test for valid handle.
inline bool IsValidHandle(HANDLE h)
    { return h != INVALID_HANDLE_VALUE; }

// Compute character size of a buffer.
// This should be in tchar.h.
#define _tsizeof(buffer) (sizeof(buffer)/sizeof(TCHAR))

// Clear the screen and set cursor to upper left of window.
void ClearScreen
```

Listing 8-6. *Switching the console output control page.* *(continued)*

Listing 8-6. *continued*

```
    (
    HANDLE hConOut,
    TCHAR c = _T(' '),
    WORD attr = BACKGROUND_BLUE | BACKGROUND_GREEN |
                BACKGROUND_RED | BACKGROUND_INTENSITY
    )
{
DWORD nChars;                              // # of chars processed
CONSOLE_SCREEN_BUFFER_INFO cbInfo;        // Output buffer info
COORD pos = {0, 0};                       // Current position
SetConsoleTextAttribute(hConOut, attr);
GetConsoleScreenBufferInfo(hConOut, &cbInfo);
FillConsoleOutputCharacter
    (
    hConOut,
    _T(' '),
    cbInfo.dwSize.X * cbInfo.dwSize.Y,
    pos,
    &nChars
    );
FillConsoleOutputAttribute
    (
    hConOut,
    attr,
    cbInfo.dwSize.X * cbInfo.dwSize.Y,
    pos,
    &nChars
    );
}

// Wait for a keystroke.
TCHAR WaitForKey(HANDLE hConIn)
{
DWORD mode;
TCHAR c;
DWORD nChars;
GetConsoleMode(hConIn, &mode);
SetConsoleMode(hConIn, 0);
ReadConsole(hConIn, &c, 1, &nChars, 0);
SetConsoleMode(hConIn, mode);
return c;
}

// Main program
int _tmain(int argc,TCHAR* argv[], TCHAR* envp[])
```

```
{
DWORD nChars;                                    // # of chars processed

// Initialize handles.
HANDLE hStdIn = INVALID_HANDLE_VALUE;
HANDLE hStdOut = INVALID_HANDLE_VALUE;

// Get standard input and output handles; silent abort on failure.
hStdIn = GetStdHandle(STD_INPUT_HANDLE);
if(!IsValidHandle(hStdIn)) return -1;
hStdOut = GetStdHandle(STD_OUTPUT_HANDLE);
if(!IsValidHandle(hStdOut)) return -1;

// Tell user to switch to TrueType font.
TCHAR* pTrueTypeMsg =
    _T("For proper viewing of code page characters, ")
    _T("use the properties menu\n")
    _T("to switch to a TrueType font. Press any key to continue.\n");
WriteConsole(hStdOut, pTrueTypeMsg,
            lstrlen(pTrueTypeMsg), &nChars, 0);
WaitForKey(hStdIn);

// Loop until user enters null code page.
DWORD ModeOut;                                   // Saves output mode.
GetConsoleMode(hStdOut, &ModeOut);
while(1)
    {
    CONSOLE_SCREEN_BUFFER_INFO cbInfo;           // Output buffer info
    COORD pos;                                   // Current position
    TCHAR buffer[100];                           // Console buffer

    // Initialize.
    ClearScreen(hStdOut);
    GetConsoleScreenBufferInfo(hStdOut, &cbInfo);

    // Display current code page title.
    SetConsoleMode(hStdOut, 0);
    unsigned cp = GetConsoleOutputCP();
    nChars = _stprintf(buffer, _T("CODE PAGE %u"), cp);
    pos.Y = cbInfo.srWindow.Top + 2;
    pos.X = cbInfo.srWindow.Left +
            (cbInfo.srWindow.Right -
             cbInfo.srWindow.Left - (short)nChars) / 2;
    SetConsoleCursorPosition(hStdOut, pos);
    WriteConsole(hStdOut, buffer, nChars, &nChars, 0);
```

(continued)

Listing 8-6. *continued*

```
// Display the code page.
nChars = _stprintf(buffer,
                    _T("  0 1 2 3 4 5 6 7 8 9 A B C D E F"));
pos.Y += 2;
pos.X = cbInfo.srWindow.Left +
        (cbInfo.srWindow.Right -
        cbInfo.srWindow.Left - (short)nChars) / 2;
SetConsoleCursorPosition(hStdOut, pos);
WriteConsole(hStdOut, buffer, nChars, &nChars, 0);
pos.Y += 1;
for(unsigned i = 0; i < 16; i++)
    {
    nChars = _stprintf(buffer,_T("%01X "), i);
    for(unsigned j = 0; j < 16; j++)
        nChars += _stprintf(&buffer[nChars], _T(" %c"),
        (j << 4 | i));
    pos.Y += 1;
    SetConsoleCursorPosition(hStdOut, pos);
    WriteConsole(hStdOut, buffer, nChars, &nChars, 0);
    }
SetConsoleMode(hStdOut, ModeOut);

// Ask for a code page number.
pos.Y += 2;
pos.X = cbInfo.srWindow.Left;
SetConsoleCursorPosition(hStdOut, pos);
TCHAR* pPrompt = _T("Enter a code page number, ")
                 _T("or press ENTER to quit: ");
WriteConsole(hStdOut, pPrompt, lstrlen(pPrompt), &nChars, 0);

// Get code page number.
ReadConsole(hStdIn, buffer, _tsizeof(buffer), &nChars, 0);
cp = _ttoi(buffer);
if(!nChars || (cp == 0)) break;

// Select it for console output.
if(!SetConsoleOutputCP(cp))
    {
    nChars = _stprintf
        (
        buffer,
        _T("Could not select code page %u. ")
        _T("Press any key to try again.\n"),
        cp
        );
    WriteConsole(hStdOut, buffer, nChars, &nChars, 0);
```

```
            WaitForKey(hStdIn);
            }
        }

    return 0;
    }
```

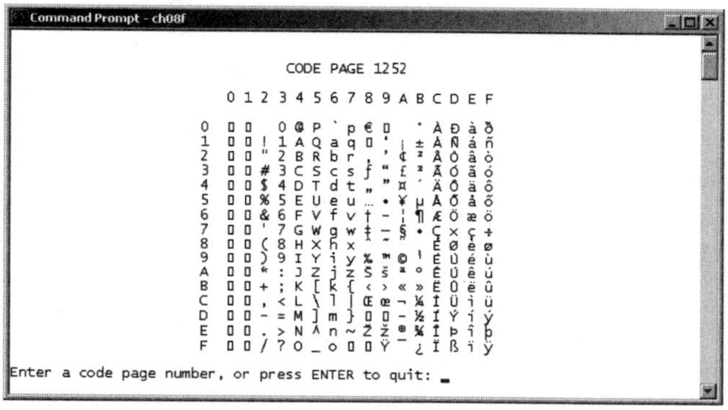

Figure 8-1. *Output of Listing 8-6.*

I developed this utility by modifying the full-screen Hello example in List-ing 8-5. First I repackaged the screen clearing and keyboard wait sequences into the *ClearScreen* and *WaitForKey* functions because the program needs this logic in several places. Then I replaced the user prompt and message display state-ments in the Hello program with a loop that performs the following operations:

1. Clears the screen, and displays a title showing the current output code page obtained by calling *GetConsoleOutputCP*. Notice that the program deactivates all special output operations, such as newline processing, by calling *SetConsoleOutputMode*.

2. Displays the symbols for the output code page as a 16-by-16 grid with hexadecimal legends on the top and left. The program then calls *SetConsoleOutputMode* to restore normal output operations using the mode that was saved before the program entered the loop.

3. Prompts the user for another code page and loops until the user enters a valid page number or terminates by simply pressing the Enter key. The page is valid if *SetConsoleOutputCP* returns a non-zero result, indicating that the page has been switched.

4. After the page switch, the program loops back to step 1.

Although this loop follows the console programming rules, it won't produce the correct display on a typical PC for anything except the OEM code page. This is because the console window usually defaults to an OEM font that can only display the OEM page. In order to display other pages, the window must use a TrueType font containing the proper symbols. Surprisingly, *SetConsoleOutputCP* doesn't activate a compatible font, and the console API doesn't enable the program to do it with a different function. So Listing 8-6 prompts the user to select an appropriate font before entering the main loop. I produced Figure 8-1 by first selecting the Lucida Console font, which is compatible with most of the SBCS code pages. I'll say more about fonts and code pages in Chapters 9 and 10.

WIN32 GUI PROGRAMMING

After this lengthy description of character set issues in console programs, you probably expect (dread?) an even longer treatment of the Win32 GUI environment, namely Microsoft Windows. After all, the console API pales in comparison to the hundreds of functions and messages in the Windows API, so aren't the character set issues in the GUI world much more complicated?

Well, fear not! The Windows story is essentially the same as the console story. That is, the Win32 API supports international Windows programming with a bimodal API, and its header files do an excellent job of disguising the differences between narrow and wide characters. This means that traditional Win16 functions such as *GetWindowText* now come in two flavors, *GetWindowTextA* and *GetWindowTextW*, for narrow and wide characters, respectively. In addition, the many data structures and messages associated with Windows have bimodal definitions. For instance, when you call *RegisterWindowClass* and pass a *WNDCLASS* structure, you're really calling *RegisterWindowClassA* or *RegisterWindowClassW* and passing *WNDCLASSA* or *WNDCLASSW*, depending on the *UNICODE* setting.

As with console programs, Win32 GUI applications can bolster the bimodal API with *tchar.h* and the standard C and C++ libraries to help hide character set differences. The Visual C++ wizards employ these techniques to produce source code that can be compiled for SBCS, MBCS, or Unicode. MBCS is currently the default (at least through Visual C++ 6) because it's compatible with Windows 95, Windows 98, and Windows 2000.

As I mentioned earlier, Windows 95 and Windows 98 don't provide much of the wide-character (Unicode) API, so you must use MBCS techniques, at least at the program boundaries. To facilitate MBCS graphical programming, the operating system activates an ANSI code page[16] based on the user's choice of

---

16. The term *ANSI code page* indicates that the character set is derived from ASCII and generally follows the rules of ISO-2022, as I described in Chapter 4.

locale. GUI applications use ANSI instead of OEM pages because the latter usually sacrifice precious code points for line drawing symbols, which you don't need when operating in graphical mode. By using these line drawing code points for other symbols, an ANSI code page such as CP1252 can serve a broader range of locales with SBCS representations.

An application program can't directly change the current ANSI code page, although the operating system will change it if necessary when the program selects a different locale, as I explain in Chapter 9. In addition, the Win32 API includes functions such as *MultiByteToWideChar* and *WideCharToMultiByte* that enable applications to access any of the ANSI pages that are installed regardless of which page is active. This capability is important when you want to use MBCS on the outside and Unicode on the inside.

Browsing Code Pages in Windows

To illustrate the use of code pages in the Windows environment, I developed a simple code page browser that presents displays like the ones shown in Figure 8-2 and Figure 8-3. This is an MFC document/view application using the single document interface (SDI). Although it calls *TextOutW* to draw Unicode characters, it runs on a Windows 98 system because that portion of the Unicode API is implemented there.

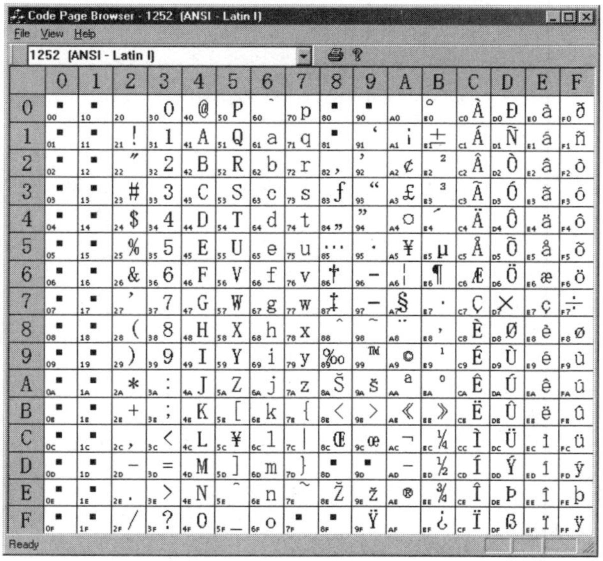

Figure 8-2. *Code page browser showing CP1252 (United States and Europe).*

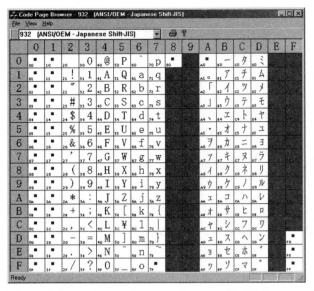

Figure 8-3. *Code page browser showing CP932 (Japanese).*

After constructing the skeleton code with the Application Wizard, I removed the menu, toolbar, and accelerator items related to file and document processing because the browser doesn't require them. Then I derived a class named *CcpToolBar* from *CToolBar* in order to place a combo box on the toolbar. An object of this type replaces the standard toolbar that the Application Wizard embeds in the frame window object. Listing 8-7 shows the class declaration.

```
class CcpToolBar : public CToolBar
{
public:
    BOOL Initialize();                     // Initialize the toolbar.
    void LoadCodePages(UINT cp = GetACP()); // Load the code
                                           // page list.
    BOOL SetCodePage(UINT cp);             // Set the current code page.

    CComboBox m_CodePages;                 // Code page list
    UINT m_CodePage;                       // Current code page
    wchar_t m_UnicodeMapping[256];         // Unicode mapping

    static CcpToolBar* m_pLoading;         // Used by CP enumeration
```

Listing 8-7. CcpToolBar *class declaration.*

```
protected:
    afx_msg void OnSelectCodePage();      // Combo notification

    DECLARE_MESSAGE_MAP()
};
```

Details of the *CcpToolBar* class

CcpToolBar contains a combo box named *m_CodePages* that displays a list of all code pages installed on the system. To position the combo box on the toolbar, I overlaid a dummy button named *ID_CodePages* using the *Initialize* function shown in Listing 8-8. The dummy button is a subterfuge to keep the resource editor happy and allow the combo box to have a tool tip and flyby help message. *Initialize* replaces it with a separator that's wide enough to show the code page names. Microsoft recommends 12 units on each side of the combo box, and I discovered empirically that 300 units is an adequate width for the names, so I use 300 + 12 * 2 = 324 units as the width of the separator.

```
BOOL CcpToolBar::Initialize()
{
// Replace toolbar button with wide separator.
int index = CommandToIndex(ID_CodePages);
SetButtonInfo
    (
    index,                 // Index to combo box
    ID_CodePages,          // Combo box id
    TBBS_SEPARATOR,        // Toolbar style
    324                    // Width + 24 for separators
    );

// Overlay separator with combo box.
CRect r;
GetItemRect(index,&r);
r.left += 12;             // Space on left
r.right -= 12;            // Space on right
r.bottom = r.top + 150;   // Bottom of dropdown list
if(!m_CodePages.Create
    (
    CBS_DROPDOWN | WS_VISIBLE | WS_TABSTOP | WS_VSCROLL,
    r,
    this,
    ID_CodePages
    ))
```

Listing 8-8. *Placing the combo box on the toolbar.*   *(continued)*

Listing 8-8. *continued*

```
        {
        TRACE0("Failed to create combo box\n");
        return FALSE;
        }

    // Load the code page list.
    LoadCodePages();
    return TRUE;
    }
```

Just before returning, *Initialize* calls *LoadCodePages* (see Listing 8-9) in order to fill the combo box with the names of all code pages installed on the system. Loading the combo box requires a call to *EnumSystemCodePages* in the Win32 API, which in turn makes repeated calls to *cbEnumSystemCodePages*. This is the typical way in which Win32 enumerates its collections, but in this case the API doesn't allow for a piece of caller data to be passed to the callback function. Therefore, *CcpToolBar* contains a static pointer named *m_pLoading* so that the callback function can find the toolbar.

LoadCodePages saves its *this* pointer in *m_pLoading*, resets the combo box, and then calls *EnumSystemCodePages*. Each time *cbEnumSystemCodePages* is called, it receives a string that contains the code page number. The callback function converts this string to an integer, checks the result by calling *IsValidCodePage*, and then uses *GetCPInfoEx* to obtain a more descriptive name for the code page. The descriptive name and page number are then added to the combo box. *IsValidCodePage* and *GetCPInfoEx* are Win32 API functions. The latter isn't available in Windows 95, but it was added to Windows 98.

LoadCodePages accepts a code page number as its only argument. Referring to Listing 8-7, notice that this argument defaults to the value provided by *GetACP*, a Win32 function that returns the ANSI code page for the thread. If the code page isn't zero, *LoadCodePages* calls *SetCodePage* as its final act before returning.

```
// Used by cbEnumSystemCodePages to find the toolbar object
CcpToolBar* CcpToolBar::m_pLoading = 0;

// Callback function
static BOOL CALLBACK cbEnumSystemCodePages(LPTSTR pCodePage)
{
// Convert code page string to number.
UINT cp = _ttoi(pCodePage);
if(!IsValidCodePage(cp)) return TRUE;
```

Listing 8-9. *Loading the combo box.*

```
// Get code page name.
CPINFOEX info;
if(!GetCPInfoEx(cp, 0, &info)) return TRUE;

// Add string and page number to combo list.
int i = CcpToolBar::
        m_pLoading->m_CodePages.AddString(info.CodePageName);
CcpToolBar::m_pLoading->m_CodePages.SetItemData(i, cp);

return TRUE;
}

// Load the combo box with all installed code pages.
void CcpToolBar::LoadCodePages(UINT cp)
{
m_pLoading = this;                // Used by callback (not thread safe)
m_CodePages.ResetContent();
EnumSystemCodePages(cbEnumSystemCodePages, CP_INSTALLED);
if(cp) SetCodePage(cp);
}
```

Listing 8-10 shows *SetCodePage*, which creates the Unicode mapping of the specified code page. After calling *IsValidCodePage* to check its argument, the function creates a 256-byte table representing the code points in that page. For an SBCS code page the table simply contains values from 0 to 255. For a DBCS code page, the table contains 0 in the slots corresponding to lead bytes. *IsDBCSLeadByteEx* is the Win32 function that checks whether a value is a lead byte in a specified code page. The standard C function *isleadbyte* and its Win32 equivalent, *IsDBCSLeadByte*, are not useful here because they only check the current code page, that is, the page returned by *GetACP*.

```
BOOL CcpToolBar::SetCodePage(UINT cp)
{
// Validate the new code page.
if(!IsValidCodePage(cp)) return FALSE;

// Build the MBCS code point buffer.
BYTE codes[256];
for(unsigned i = 0; i < 256; i++)
    codes[i] = IsDBCSLeadByteEx(cp, (BYTE)i) ? 0 : (BYTE)i;
```

Listing 8-10. *Setting the code page to display.*   *(continued)*

Listing 8-10. *continued*

```
// Convert to Unicode.
MultiByteToWideChar
    (
    cp,
    MB_PRECOMPOSED,
    (char*)codes,
    256,
    m_UnicodeMapping,
    256
    );

// Replace lead bytes with U+FFFD.
for(i = 1; i < 256; i++)
    if(!codes[i]) m_UnicodeMapping[i] = 0xFFFD;

// Save the code page number, and update the combo box.
m_CodePage = cp;
CString s;
s.Format(_T("%u"), cp);
int index = m_CodePages.SelectString(-1, s);

// Update the document and view (unless in startup mode).
CMainFrame* pFrame = DYNAMIC_DOWNCAST(CMainFrame, GetParentFrame());
if(!pFrame) return TRUE;
CDocument* pDoc = pFrame->GetActiveDocument();
if(!pDoc) return TRUE;
m_CodePages.GetLBText(index, s);
pDoc->SetTitle(s);
pDoc->UpdateAllViews(0);

return TRUE;
}
```

After constructing the byte table, *SetCodePage* converts it to an equivalent Unicode table by calling *MultiByteToWideChar*. This is a Win32 API service that, together with *WideCharToMultiByte,* you'll learn to love if you use Unicode on the inside and MBCS on the outside. They're similar to the standard C functions *mbstowcs* and *wcstombs* and to the standard C++ *codecvt* facet, but the API calls are more direct. That is, they don't require you to call *setlocale* or create *locale* objects.

In this case, I requested *MultiByteToWideChar* to produce its Unicode characters in the *m_UnicodeMapping* member of *CcbToolBar*. The *MB_PRE-COMPOSED* flag tells the function to generate precomposed character codes rather than separate codes for the base character and its diacritical marks. This ensures that the 256 input bytes produce exactly 256 Unicode values.

After *MultiByteToWideChar* returns, *SetCodePage* scans the byte table to find the lead bytes, and it replaces the corresponding entries in the Unicode table with U+FFFD, the Unicode value that denotes an undefined code point. The drawing logic detects and shades these undefined code points in the display grid.

As its final actions, *SetCodePage* ensures that the combo box selection matches the current code page and then it updates the document and view. It sets the document title to the code page name so that information will appear in the window caption. The program updates the view indirectly by calling *UpdateAllViews* in the document object.

CcbToolBar includes a function named *OnSelectCodePage* to handle the selection event from the combo box as shown in Listing 8-11. This function is wired into the message map in the normal way, and it calls *SetCodePage*.

```
void CcpToolBar::OnSelectCodePage()
{
int i = m_CodePages.GetCurSel();
if(i < 0) return;
UINT cp = (UINT)m_CodePages.GetItemData(i);
if(cp == m_CodePage) return;
SetCodePage(cp);
}
```

Listing 8-11. *Combo box event handler.*

Drawing in the *CcpView* class

While walking through the Application Wizard steps to produce this program, I made the view class derive from *CScrollView* instead of *CView*. Then in the *OnInitialUpdate* function, shown in Listing 8-12, I called *SetScaleToFitSize* in order to get a stretchy view without scroll bars. The view window has a logical size of 1700-by-1700 units and contains a cell grid, with each cell occupying a 100-by-100 area. The grid therefore contains 17 rows and 17 columns, and *CScrollView* scales the window so that the entire grid is always visible.

```
void CcpView::OnInitialUpdate()
{
CScrollView::OnInitialUpdate();
SetScaleToFitSize(m_WindowSize);
CMainFrame* pFrame = DYNAMIC_DOWNCAST(CMainFrame, GetParentFrame());
if(pFrame) pFrame->m_wndToolBar.Initialize();
}
```

Listing 8-12. *Initializing the view.*

As with most GUI applications, I had the most fun developing the drawing logic, encapsulated in the *OnDraw* function shown in Listing 8-13. The function first saves the device context (DC) state and initializes for transparent text output, which leaves the cell background undisturbed. *OnDraw* then creates a font suitable for displaying Unicode characters within the grid. I used the MS Mincho font because it's a big Unicode font that covers a large number of symbol sets.

```
CSize CcpView::m_CellSize(100, 100);
CSize CcpView::m_FontCellSize(80, 80);
CSize CcpView::m_WindowSize(1700, 1700);

void CcpView::OnDraw(CDC* pDC)
{
// Save current DC settings and establish ours.
pDC->SaveDC();
pDC->SetBkMode(TRANSPARENT);
COLORREF rgbOldBkColor = pDC->GetBkColor();

// Get a Unicode font in the proper size.
CFont font;
if(font.CreateFont
    (
    m_FontCellSize.cy,               // Height
    0,                               // Width (default)
    0,                               // Escapement (normal)
    0,                               // Orientation (horizontal)
    FW_DONTCARE,                     // Weight
    0,                               // Italic
    0,                               // Underline
    0,                               // Strikeout
    DEFAULT_CHARSET,                 // Character set
    OUT_DEFAULT_PRECIS,              // Mapping precision
    CLIP_DEFAULT_PRECIS,             // Clipping precision
    DEFAULT_QUALITY,                 // Quality
    DEFAULT_PITCH,                   // Pitch and family
    _T("MS Mincho")
    )) pDC->SelectObject(&font);

// Color the title row and column.
CRect rRow(0, 0, m_WindowSize.cx, m_CellSize.cy-1);
CRect rCol(0, 0, m_CellSize.cx-1, m_WindowSize.cy);
pDC->FillSolidRect(&rRow, RGB(192, 192, 192));
pDC->FillSolidRect(&rCol, RGB(192, 192, 192));
```

Listing 8-13. *Drawing the character grid.*

```
// Fill the title row.
CString s;
CRect rCell;
rCell.top = 0;
rCell.bottom = m_CellSize.cy - 1;
rCell.left = m_CellSize.cx;
pDC->SetBkColor(RGB(192, 192, 192));
for(int x = 0; x < 16; x++)
    {
    rCell.right = rCell.left + m_CellSize.cx - 1;
    s.Format(_T("%X"), x);
    pDC->DrawText(s, &rCell, DT_SINGLELINE | DT_VCENTER | DT_CENTER);
    rCell.left += m_CellSize.cx;
    }

// Fill the title col.
rCell.left = 0;
rCell.right = m_CellSize.cx - 1;
rCell.top = m_CellSize.cy;
for(int y = 0; y < 16; y++)
    {
    rCell.bottom = rCell.top + m_CellSize.cy - 1;
    s.Format(_T("%X"), y);
    pDC->DrawText(s, &rCell, DT_SINGLELINE | DT_VCENTER | DT_CENTER);
    rCell.top += m_CellSize.cy;
    }

// Fill the grid.
pDC->SetBkColor(rgbOldBkColor);
UINT OldAlign = pDC-
>SetTextAlign(TA_RIGHT | TA_BOTTOM | TA_NOUPDATECP);
rCell.left = m_CellSize.cx;
CMainFrame* pFrame = DYNAMIC_DOWNCAST(CMainFrame, GetParentFrame());
if(pFrame) for(x = 0; x < 16; x++)
    {
    rCell.top = m_CellSize.cy;
    rCell.right = rCell.left + m_CellSize.cx - 1;
    for(y = 0; y < 16; y++)
        {
        rCell.bottom = rCell.top + m_CellSize.cy - 1;
        wchar_t uc =
            pFrame->m_wndToolBar.m_UnicodeMapping[(x << 4) | y];
        if(uc != 0xFFFD) :: TextOutW
            (
            pDC->m_hDC,
            rCell.right - (m_CellSize.cx - m_FontCellSize.cx),
            rCell.bottom - (m_CellSize.cy - m_FontCellSize.cy) / 2,
```

(continued)

251

Listing 8-13. *continued*

```
            &uc,
            1
            );
        else
            {
            pDC->FillSolidRect(&rCell, RGB(192, 0, 0));
            pDC->SetBkColor(rgbOldBkColor);
            }
        rCell.top += m_CellSize.cy;
        }
    rCell.left += m_CellSize.cx;
    }
pDC->SetTextAlign(OldAlign);

// Insert cell coordinates.
CFont font1;
if(font1.CreateFont
    (
    m_FontCellSize.cy / 3,         // Height
    0,                             // Width (default)
    0,                             // Escapement (normal)
    0,                             // Orientation (horizontal)
    FW_DONTCARE,                   // Weight
    0,                             // Italic
    0,                             // Underline
    0,                             // Strikeout
    ANSI_CHARSET,                  // Character set
    OUT_DEFAULT_PRECIS,            // Mapping precision
    CLIP_DEFAULT_PRECIS,           // Clipping precision
    DEFAULT_QUALITY,               // Quality
    DEFAULT_PITCH,                 // Pitch and family
    _T("Lucida Console")
    ))
    {
    pDC->SelectObject(&font1);
    rCell.left = m_CellSize.cx + 5;
    for(x = 0; x < 16; x++)
        {
        rCell.top = m_CellSize.cy;
        rCell.right = rCell.left + m_CellSize.cx - 1;
        for(y = 0; y < 16; y++)
            {
            TCHAR b[3];
            wsprintf(b, _T("%02X"), (x << 4) | y);
            rCell.bottom = rCell.top + m_CellSize.cy - 1;
            pDC->DrawText
```

```
                    (
                    b,
                    2,
                    &rCell,
                    DT_SINGLELINE | DT_NOPREFIX | DT_BOTTOM
                    );
                rCell.top += m_CellSize.cy;
                }
            rCell.left += m_CellSize.cx;
            }
        }

// Draw the grid lines.
for(x = rCol.right; x <= m_WindowSize.cx; x += m_CellSize.cx)
    {
    pDC->MoveTo(x, 0);
    pDC->LineTo(x, m_WindowSize.cy);
    }
for(y = rRow.bottom; y < m_WindowSize.cy; y += m_CellSize.cy)
    {
    pDC->MoveTo(0, y);
    pDC->LineTo(m_WindowSize.cx, y);
    }

// Restore DC settings.
pDC->RestoreDC(-1);
```

Notice the static members *m_WindowSize*, *m_CellSize*, and *m_FontCellSize*, which specify the grid dimensions. Each character is drawn in an 80-by-80 area centered in a 100-by-100 cell. When working with fonts, I usually get the best results by letting the system's font mapper do most of the work. Therefore, I specified only the cell height and the face name and used default settings for everything else.

OnDraw next shades the top row and left column and fills them with hexadecimal characters to identify the interior cells. Then it fills the character cells by calling *TextOutW* for each displayable entry in *m_UnicodeMapping*. If a table entry contains U+FFFD, *OnDraw* shades the corresponding cell but doesn't draw a character there. See Figure 8-3 for an example of a grid containing these shaded cells. I used *TextOutW* to draw the Unicode characters because that function is available in Windows 95 and Windows 98, whereas *DrawTextW* is not.

After drawing the contents of each cell, *OnDraw* places the hexadecimal code point in the lower left corner of each cell, inserts grid lines, restores the DC, and exits. I drew the grid lines last to avoid partial erasures due to coordinate scaling. If I had drawn the grid lines earlier, some of them would get clobbered by *FillSolidRect* when it shaded the lead byte cells.

Printing in the *CcpView* class

MFC makes it easy for a view to support printing and previewing, and so I decided to include those features in the code page browser. This required that I correct a problem in *CScrollView* by overriding *OnPrepareDC*, as shown in Listing 8-14.

The scaling logic in *CScrollView* assumes that the DC is being prepared for display in the view window, not in the preview window or on the printer itself. This omission usually causes the print or preview output to be too small, especially if the printer has a resolution of 600 dpi or greater. After calling the base class, my *OnPrepareDC* override adjusts the viewport extent to match the physical capabilities of the printer, which causes the character page to fill the page.

```
void CcpView::OnPrepareDC(CDC* pDC, CPrintInfo* pInfo)
{
CSize s(pDC->GetDeviceCaps(HORZRES), pDC->GetDeviceCaps(VERTRES));
CScrollView::OnPrepareDC(pDC, pInfo);
if(!pInfo) return;
CSize size(pDC->GetDeviceCaps(HORZRES), pDC->GetDeviceCaps(VERTRES));
pDC->SetViewportExt(size);
}
```

Listing 8-14. *Adding print and print preview to the code page browser.*

SUMMARY

The Win32 API is bimodal with regard to character widths. In other words, it provides dual versions of each text-oriented function, one for narrow characters and one for wide characters. The Win32 header files disguise this duality by defining each text-oriented function as a macro that calls the appropriate version based on the setting of the *UNICODE* symbol. This approach is similar to *tchar.h*, which disguises the different C library functions that must be used for SBCS, MBCS, and WCS processing.

The Win32 console feature supports character-mode programs that use MBCS or Unicode techniques. Consoles also form the foundation for the virtual DOS machine (VDM) feature that supports traditional MS-DOS programs using MBCS. Other character environments such as POSIX and OS/2 also utilize consoles. To facilitate MBCS programming in any of these situations, the console API provides control over the code pages used for keyboard input and screen output, although it doesn't provide a convenient method for a program to adjust the console display font.

The Win32 graphical user interface (GUI) is based on the traditional Windows API with modifications for Unicode operation. Since the modified API is bimodal, Windows programs can operate in MBCS, Unicode, or a mixture. Keyboard input and screen output in MBCS mode use the current ANSI code page, which is established by the user's regional settings or the program's selected locale, as described in Chapter 9.

Chapter 9

Locales in Win32

International programming is affected not only by the different symbol sets used throughout the world, but also by the way various cultures employ their particular symbols to represent common concepts such as numbers, dates, times, and money. Chapter 8 showed how Win32 copes with symbol set differences by supporting both MBCS and WCS (Unicode) programming techniques. In this chapter, we'll examine the impressive locale features built into Win32 that enable international programmers to deal with multiple-locale formatting issues in a standard way.

Early international programmers wrote custom input and output code to resolve locale related problems. This customization was necessary because the prevalent operating systems provided little or no support for locale differences. Indeed, the C and C++ standards that we examined in Chapters 4, 5, and 6 continue to define the locale feature so that it can be fully implemented even if the operating system has no international features. The standards require only that the operating system provide an unimpeded byte-oriented path to the I/O devices.

As operating systems evolved to more than just simple command-line processors such as Unix and MS-DOS, they could no longer remain aloof from international issues. Users of GUI systems demanded consistent adoption of local idioms throughout the user interface, and this could be achieved only by making the operating system aware of these idioms.

At first OS vendors answered this demand just as early vendors of international applications had done—that is, by shipping a custom version to each important market. These localized versions had prompters, error messages, and other user interface components tailored to a single language used in that locale, such as English, French, German, Japanese, and so on.

As international programming expanded during the 1990s, this single-locale solution quickly revealed its limitations. Workstations are often shared by users who have different preferences—for example, a help desk staffed with an English-speaking user for one shift and a Spanish speaker for another. Users often have to mix several locales—for example, a catalog salesperson who must quickly quote prices in a different currency according to the customers' needs. Application programmers want to establish different locale settings for each process or thread, such as in a server process that spawns worker threads tailored to the corresponding client locales.

These mixed-locale scenarios forced OS vendors to combine several single-locale versions into packages such as Roman (Western Europe and the Americas), Greek-Cyrillic (Eastern Europe), Hebrew-Arabic (Middle East and North Africa), Asian (China, Japan, and Korea), and Indic (Indian subcontinent). Microsoft used this technique when producing the international versions of Microsoft Windows 3.1, Windows 95, and Windows 98.

To reduce the expense of supporting multiple versions and to address an even broader set of multiple-locale scenarios, Microsoft decided to ship a single version of Microsoft Windows 2000 for the entire world. This is possible because Windows 2000 employs Unicode throughout and has a robust locale database containing formatting rules for all locales. Application programmers see these international features in the form of the National Language Support (NLS) API discussed in this chapter and the multilingual (ML) API discussed in Chapter 10.

LOCALE IDENTIFIERS

The locale identifier, or LCID,[1] serves as the key to Win32's support for multiple locales. The administrator assigns a default LCID when installing the system. Each user inherits the system default LCID and can change it by means of the Regional Settings applet in the Control Panel. The user's LCID choice then flows to the threads created on the user's behalf. An application program can change the LCID setting for a thread by calling the appropriate API functions.

---

1. This is usually pronounced "el cid" as in the Spanish warlord, which is why I usually write "an LCID" instead of "a LCID."

LCID Fields

An LCID is a 32-bit unsigned integer in the form shown in Figure 9-1. Bits 0 through 9 and bits 10 through 15 contain the primary and secondary language identifiers. Together, this 16-bit unsigned item is called the language identifier, or LANGID. Bits 16 through 19 contain the sort identifier, or SORTID, and bits 20 through 23 contain the sort version number. Bits 24 through 31 are currently unused and must be set to 0.

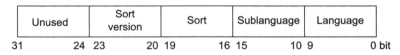

Figure 9-1. *LCID fields.*

The primary and secondary language identifiers are also called the language and sublanguage. They serve essentially the same purpose as the language and country names in standard C and C++. (See Chapters 5 and 6.) For programming convenience, the language and sublanguage numbers have symbolic names defined in the winnt.h header file, as shown in Tables 9-1 and 9-2.

The Win32 header files also provide macros to compose and decompose language identifiers, as shown in the following example, which constructs a LANGID value for English as used in the United Kingdom and then extracts the primary and secondary portions:

```
LANGID x = MAKELANGID(LANG_ENGLISH, SUBLANG_ENGLISH_UK);
LANGID xPrimary = PRIMARYLANGID(x);
LANGID xSecondary = SUBLANGID(x);
```

Several of the primary and secondary identifiers have special meanings. The value 0, defined as *LANG_NEUTRAL* and *SUBLANG_NEUTRAL*, indicates a "language neutral" situation; this value might apply to a program that contains no locale sensitivities. You can also combine *LANG_NEUTRAL* with *SUBLANG_DEFAULT* or *SUBLANG_SYS_DEFAULT* to refer to the default language for the current user or the system. These special language identifiers have the following symbolic definitions:

```
#define LANG_SYSTEM_DEFAULT (MAKELANGID(LANG_NEUTRAL,
                             SUBLANG_SYS_DEFAULT))
#define LANG_USER_DEFAULT (MAKELANGID(LANG_NEUTRAL,
                           SUBLANG_DEFAULT))
```

Table 9-3 lists the SORTID values that can be placed in bits 16 through 19 of an LCID. All locales support the default sorting order, and some also allow other sorting orders. For instance, German text can be sorted in the default order or in the modified order used by German telephone books for easy access to names that sound similar even though they are spelled differently, such as Schultz and Shultz.

The winnt.h header file contains several macros that simplify the use of sort identifiers. The following statements show how you can use these macros to create an LCID suitable for the German language as spoken in Switzerland, with text sorted according to the German telephone book:

```
LANGID lang = MAKELANGID(LANG_GERMAN, SUBLANG_GERMAN_SWISS);
LCID lcid = MAKELCID(langGermanSwiss, SORT_GERMAN_PHONE_BOOK);
SORTID sortid = SORTIDFROMLCID(lcidGerman);
```

Notice that you cannot freely intermix language, sublanguage, and sort symbols because not all combinations are valid. For instance, it makes no sense to use *LANG_ENGLISH* together with *SUBLANG_ARABIC_SYRIA* and *SORT_GERMAN_PHONE_BOOK*. That's why the sublanguage and sort symbols usually include the primary language name.

Table 9-4 lists the LCIDs supported by recent Win32 systems, with all sort identifiers set to the default value 0. I extracted this information from preliminary Windows 2000 documentation, and it will undoubtedly grow in the future as new locales are added. Notice that some LCIDs support only Unicode characters. Since they have no ANSI-derived code page for SBCS or MBCS programming, these Unicode locales are available only in Windows 2000.

Table 9-1. **Primary Language Identifiers**

ID	Symbol	Language
0x00	*LANG_NEUTRAL*	Neutral
0x01	*LANG_ARABIC*	Arabic
0x02	*LANG_BULGARIAN*	Bulgarian
0x03	*LANG_CATALAN*	Catalan
0x04	*LANG_CHINESE*	Chinese
0x05	*LANG_CZECH*	Czech
0x06	*LANG_DANISH*	Danish
0x07	*LANG_GERMAN*	German
0x08	*LANG_GREEK*	Greek
0x09	*LANG_ENGLISH*	English
0x0a	*LANG_SPANISH*	Spanish
0x0b	*LANG_FINNISH*	Finnish
0x0c	*LANG_FRENCH*	French
0x0d	*LANG_HEBREW*	Hebrew

ID	Symbol	Language
0x0e	*LANG_HUNGARIAN*	Hungarian
0x0f	*LANG_ICELANDIC*	Icelandic
0x10	*LANG_ITALIAN*	Italian
0x11	*LANG_JAPANESE*	Japanese
0x12	*LANG_KOREAN*	Korean
0x13	*LANG_DUTCH*	Dutch
0x14	*LANG_NORWEGIAN*	Norwegian
0x15	*LANG_POLISH*	Polish
0x16	*LANG_PORTUGUESE*	Portuguese
0x18	*LANG_ROMANIAN*	Romanian
0x19	*LANG_RUSSIAN*	Russian
0x1a	*LANG_CROATIAN*	Croatian
0x1a	*LANG_SERBIAN*	Serbian
0x1b	*LANG_SLOVAK*	Slovak
0x1c	*LANG_ALBANIAN*	Albanian
0x1d	*LANG_SWEDISH*	Swedish
0x1e	*LANG_THAI*	Thai
0x1f	*LANG_TURKISH*	Turkish
0x20	*LANG_URDU*	Urdu
0x21	*LANG_INDONESIAN*	Indonesian
0x22	*LANG_UKRAINIAN*	Ukrainian
0x23	*LANG_BELARUSIAN*	Belarusian
0x24	*LANG_SLOVENIAN*	Slovenian
0x25	*LANG_ESTONIAN*	Estonian
0x26	*LANG_LATVIAN*	Latvian
0x27	*LANG_LITHUANIAN*	Lithuanian
0x29	*LANG_FARSI*	Farsi
0x2a	*LANG_VIETNAMESE*	Vietnamese
0x2b	*LANG_ARMENIAN*	Armenian
0x2c	*LANG_AZERI*	Azeri
0x2d	*LANG_BASQUE*	Basque
0x2f	*LANG_MACEDONIAN*	Macedonian
0x36	*LANG_AFRIKAANS*	Afrikaans
0x37	*LANG_GEORGIAN*	Georgian
0x38	*LANG_FAEROESE*	Faeroese

(continued)

Table 9-1. *continued*

ID	Symbol	Language
0x39	LANG_HINDI	Hindi
0x3e	LANG_MALAY	Malay
0x3f	LANG_KAZAK	Kazak
0x41	LANG_SWAHILI	Swahili
0x43	LANG_UZBEK	Uzbek
0x44	LANG_TATAR	Tatar
0x45	LANG_BENGALI	Bengali
0x46	LANG_PUNJABI	Punjabi
0x47	LANG_GUJARATI	Gujarati
0x48	LANG_ORIYA	Oriya
0x49	LANG_TAMIL	Tamil
0x4a	LANG_TELUGU	Telugu
0x4b	LANG_KANNADA	Kannada
0x4c	LANG_MALAYALAM	Malayalam
0x4d	LANG_ASSAMESE	Assamese
0x4e	LANG_MARATHI	Marathi
0x4f	LANG_SANSKRIT	Sanskrit
0x57	LANG_KONKANI	Konkani
0x58	LANG_MANIPURI	Manipuri
0x59	LANG_SINDHI	Sindhi
0x60	LANG_KASHMIRI	Kashmiri
0x61	LANG_NEPALI	Nepali

Table 9-2. Secondary Language Identifiers

ID	Symbol	Language
0x00	SUBLANG_NEUTRAL	Neutral
0x01	SUBLANG_DEFAULT	Default
0x02	SUBLANG_SYS_DEFAULT	System default
0x01	SUBLANG_ARABIC_SAUDI_ARABIA	Arabic (Saudi Arabia)
0x02	SUBLANG_ARABIC_IRAQ	Arabic (Iraq)
0x03	SUBLANG_ARABIC_EGYPT	Arabic (Egypt)
0x04	SUBLANG_ARABIC_LIBYA	Arabic (Libya)
0x05	SUBLANG_ARABIC_ALGERIA	Arabic (Algeria)
0x06	SUBLANG_ARABIC_MOROCCO	Arabic (Morocco)

ID	Symbol	Language
0x07	*SUBLANG_ARABIC_TUNISIA*	Arabic (Tunisia)
0x08	*SUBLANG_ARABIC_OMAN*	Arabic (Oman)
0x09	*SUBLANG_ARABIC_YEMEN*	Arabic (Yemen)
0x10	*SUBLANG_ARABIC_SYRIA*	Arabic (Syria)
0x11	*SUBLANG_ARABIC_JORDAN*	Arabic (Jordan)
0x12	*SUBLANG_ARABIC_LEBANON*	Arabic (Lebanon)
0x13	*SUBLANG_ARABIC_KUWAIT*	Arabic (Kuwait)
0x14	*SUBLANG_ARABIC_UAE*	Arabic (U.A.E.)
0x15	*SUBLANG_ARABIC_BAHRAIN*	Arabic (Bahrain)
0x16	*SUBLANG_ARABIC_QATAR*	Arabic (Qatar)
0x01	*SUBLANG_AZERI_CYRILLIC*	Azeri (Cyrillic)
0x02	*SUBLANG_AZERI_LATIN*	Azeri (Latin)
0x01	*SUBLANG_CHINESE_TRADITIONAL*	Chinese (Traditional)
0x02	*SUBLANG_CHINESE_SIMPLIFIED*	Chinese (Simplified)
0x03	*SUBLANG_CHINESE_HONGKONG*	Chinese (Hong Kong SAR, PRC)
0x04	*SUBLANG_CHINESE_SINGAPORE*	Chinese (Singapore)
0x05	*SUBLANG_CHINESE_MACAU*	Chinese (Macau)
0x01	*SUBLANG_DUTCH*	Dutch
0x02	*SUBLANG_DUTCH_BELGIAN*	Dutch (Belgium)
0x01	*SUBLANG_ENGLISH_US*	English (United States)
0x02	*SUBLANG_ENGLISH_UK*	English (United Kingdom)
0x03	*SUBLANG_ENGLISH_AUS*	English (Australia)
0x04	*SUBLANG_ENGLISH_CAN*	English (Canada)
0x05	*SUBLANG_ENGLISH_NZ*	English (New Zealand)
0x06	*SUBLANG_ENGLISH_EIRE*	English (Ireland)
0x07	*SUBLANG_ENGLISH_SOUTH_AFRICA*	English (South Africa)
0x08	*SUBLANG_ENGLISH_JAMAICA*	English (Jamaica)
0x09	*SUBLANG_ENGLISH_CARIBBEAN*	English (Caribbean)
0x0a	*SUBLANG_ENGLISH_BELIZE*	English (Belize)
0x0b	*SUBLANG_ENGLISH_TRINIDAD*	English (Trinidad)
0x0c	*SUBLANG_ENGLISH_ ZIMBABWE*	English (Zimbabwe)
0x0d	*SUBLANG_ENGLISH_ PHILIPPINES*	English (Philippines)
0x01	*SUBLANG_FRENCH*	French
0x02	*SUBLANG_FRENCH_BELGIAN*	French (Belgium)
0x03	*SUBLANG_FRENCH_CANADIAN*	French (Canada)

(continued)

Table 9-2. *continued*

ID	Symbol	Language
0x04	*SUBLANG_FRENCH_SWISS*	French (Switzerland)
0x05	*SUBLANG_FRENCH_LUXEMBOURG*	French (Luxembourg)
0x06	*SUBLANG_FRENCH_MONACO*	French (Monaco)
0x01	*SUBLANG_GERMAN*	German
0x02	*SUBLANG_GERMAN_SWISS*	German (Switzerland)
0x03	*SUBLANG_GERMAN_AUSTRIAN*	German (Austria)
0x04	*SUBLANG_GERMAN_LUXEMBOURG*	German (Luxembourg)
0x05	*SUBLANG_GERMAN_LIECHTENSTEIN*	German (Liechtenstein)
0x01	*SUBLANG_ITALIAN*	Italian
0x02	*SUBLANG_ITALIAN_SWISS*	Italian (Switzerland)
0x02	*SUBLANG_KASHMIRI_INDIA*	Kashmiri (India)
0x01	*SUBLANG_KOREAN*	Korean
0x01	*SUBLANG_LITHUANIAN*	Lithuanian
0x01	*SUBLANG_MALAY_MALAYSIA*	Malay (Malaysia)
0x02	*SUBLANG_MALAY_BRUNEI_DARUSSALAM*	Malay (Brunei Darussalam)
0x02	*SUBLANG_NEPALI_INDIA*	Nepali (India)
0x01	*SUBLANG_NORWEGIAN_BOKMAL*	Norwegian (Bokmal)
0x02	*SUBLANG_NORWEGIAN_NYNORSK*	Norwegian (Nynorsk)
0x01	*SUBLANG_PORTUGUESE*	Portuguese
0x02	*SUBLANG_PORTUGUESE_BRAZILIAN*	Portuguese (Brazil)
0x02	*SUBLANG_SERBIAN_LATIN*	Serbian (Latin)
0x03	*SUBLANG_SERBIAN_CYRILLIC*	Serbian (Cyrillic)
0x01	*SUBLANG_SPANISH*	Spanish (Castilian)
0x02	*SUBLANG_SPANISH_MEXICAN*	Spanish (Mexico)
0x03	*SUBLANG_SPANISH_MODERN*	Spanish (Modern)
0x04	*SUBLANG_SPANISH_GUATEMALA*	Spanish (Guatemala)
0x05	*SUBLANG_SPANISH_COSTA_RICA*	Spanish (Costa Rica)
0x06	*SUBLANG_SPANISH_PANAMA*	Spanish (Panama)
0x07	*SUBLANG_SPANISH_DOMINICAN_REPUBLIC*	Spanish (Dominican Republic)
0x08	*SUBLANG_SPANISH_VENEZUELA*	Spanish (Venezuela)
0x09	*SUBLANG_SPANISH_COLOMBIA*	Spanish (Colombia)
0x0a	*SUBLANG_SPANISH_PERU*	Spanish (Peru)
0x0b	*SUBLANG_SPANISH_ARGENTINA*	Spanish (Argentina)
0x0c	*SUBLANG_SPANISH_ECUADOR*	Spanish (Ecuador)

ID	Symbol	Language
0x0d	*SUBLANG_SPANISH_CHILE*	Spanish (Chile)
0x0e	*SUBLANG_SPANISH_URUGUAY*	Spanish (Uruguay)
0x0f	*SUBLANG_SPANISH_PARAGUAY*	Spanish (Paraguay)
0x10	*SUBLANG_SPANISH_BOLIVIA*	Spanish (Bolivia)
0x11	*SUBLANG_SPANISH_EL_SALVADOR*	Spanish (El Salvador)
0x12	*SUBLANG_SPANISH_HONDURAS*	Spanish (Honduras)
0x13	*SUBLANG_SPANISH_NICARAGUA*	Spanish (Nicaragua)
0x14	*SUBLANG_SPANISH_PUERTO_RICO*	Spanish (Puerto Rico)
0x01	*SUBLANG_SWEDISH*	Swedish
0x02	*SUBLANG_SWEDISH_FINLAND*	Swedish (Finland)
0x01	*SUBLANG_URDU_PAKISTAN*	Urdu (Pakistan)
0x02	*SUBLANG_URDU_INDIA*	Urdu (India)
0x01	*SUBLANG_UZBEK_LATIN*	Uzbek (Latin)
0x02	*SUBLANG_UZBEK_CYRILLIC*	Uzbek (Cyrillic)

Table 9-3. Sort Identifiers

ID	Symbol	Sorting Order
0x0	*SORT_DEFAULT*	Default order
0x0	*SORT_JAPANESE_XJIS*	Japanese XJIS order
0x1	*SORT_JAPANESE_UNICODE*	Japanese Unicode order
0x0	*SORT_CHINESE_BIG5*	Chinese BIG5 order
0x0	*SORT_CHINESE_PRCP*	PRC Chinese phonetic order
0x1	*SORT_CHINESE_UNICODE*	Chinese Unicode order
0x2	*SORT_CHINESE_PRC*	PRC Chinese stroke count order
0x3	*SORT_CHINESE_BOPOMOFO*	Traditional Chinese Bopomofo order
0x0	*SORT_KOREAN_KSC*	Korean KSC order
0x1	*SORT_KOREAN_UNICODE*	Korean Unicode order
0x1	*SORT_GERMAN_PHONE_BOOK*	German phone book order
0x0	*SORT_HUNGARIAN_DEFAULT*	Hungarian default order
0x1	*SORT_HUNGARIAN_TECHNICAL*	Hungarian technical order
0x0	*SORT_GEORGIAN_TRADITIONAL*	Georgian traditional order
0x1	*SORT_GEORGIAN_MODERN*	Georgian modern order

Table 9-4. **Locale Identifiers**

ID	Language
0x0000	Language neutral
0x0400	Process default language
0x0436	Afrikaans
0x041c	Albanian
0x0401	Arabic (Saudi Arabia)
0x0801	Arabic (Iraq)
0x0c01	Arabic (Egypt)
0x1001	Arabic (Libya)
0x1401	Arabic (Algeria)
0x1801	Arabic (Morocco)
0x1c01	Arabic (Tunisia)
0x2001	Arabic (Oman)
0x2401	Arabic (Yemen)
0x2801	Arabic (Syria)
0x2c01	Arabic (Jordan)
0x3001	Arabic (Lebanon)
0x3401	Arabic (Kuwait)
0x3801	Arabic (U.A.E.)
0x3c01	Arabic (Bahrain)
0x4001	Arabic (Qatar)
0x042b	Armenian; Unicode only
0x044d	Assamese; Unicode only
0x042c	Azeri (Latin)
0x082c	Azeri (Cyrillic)
0x042d	Basque
0x0423	Belarusian
0x0445	Bengali; Unicode only
0x0402	Bulgarian
0x0455	Burmese
0x0403	Catalan
0x0404	Chinese (Taiwan Region)
0x0804	Chinese (PRC)
0x0c04	Chinese (Hong Kong SAR, PRC)
0x1004	Chinese (Singapore)
0x1404	Chinese (Macau)

ID	Language
0x041a	Croatian
0x0405	Czech
0x0406	Danish
0x0413	Dutch (Netherlands)
0x0813	Dutch (Belgium)
0x0409	English (United States)
0x0809	English (United Kingdom)
0x0c09	English (Australia)
0x1009	English (Canada)
0x1409	English (New Zealand)
0x1809	English (Ireland)
0x1c09	English (South Africa)
0x2009	English (Jamaica)
0x2409	English (Caribbean)
0x2809	English (Belize)
0x2c09	English (Trinidad)
0x3009	English (Zimbabwe)
0x3409	English (Philippines)
0x0425	Estonian
0x0438	Faeroese
0x0429	Farsi
0x040b	Finnish
0x040c	French (Standard)
0x080c	French (Belgium)
0x0c0c	French (Canada)
0x100c	French (Switzerland)
0x140c	French (Luxembourg)
0x180c	French (Monaco)
0x0437	Georgian; Unicode only
0x0407	German (Standard)
0x0807	German (Switzerland)
0x0c07	German (Austria)
0x1007	German (Luxembourg)
0x1407	German (Liechtenstein)
0x0408	Greek
0x0447	Gujarati; Unicode only

(continued)

Table 9-4. *continued*

ID	Language
0x040d	Hebrew
0x0439	Hindi; Unicode only
0x040e	Hungarian
0x040f	Icelandic
0x0421	Indonesian
0x0410	Italian (Standard)
0x0810	Italian (Switzerland)
0x0411	Japanese
0x044b	Kannada; Unicode only
0x0860	Kashmiri (India)
0x043f	Kazakh
0x0457	Konkani; Unicode only
0x0412	Korean
0x0812	Korean (Johab)
0x0426	Latvian
0x0427	Lithuanian
0x0827	Lithuanian (Classic)
0x042f	Macedonian
0x043e	Malay (Malaysian)
0x083e	Malay (Brunei Darussalam)
0x044c	Malayalam; Unicode only
0x0458	Manipuri
0x044e	Marathi; Unicode only
0x0861	Nepali (India); Unicode only
0x0414	Norwegian (Bokmal)
0x0814	Norwegian (Nynorsk)
0x0448	Oriya; Unicode only
0x0415	Polish
0x0416	Portuguese (Brazil)
0x0816	Portuguese (Standard)
0x0446	Punjabi; Unicode only
0x0418	Romanian
0x0419	Russian
0x044f	Sanskrit; Unicode only
0x0c1a	Serbian (Cyrillic)
0x081a	Serbian (Latin)
0x0459	Sindhi

ID	Language
0x041b	Slovak
0x0424	Slovenian
0x040a	Spanish (Traditional Sort)
0x080a	Spanish (Mexican)
0x0c0a	Spanish (Modern Sort)
0x100a	Spanish (Guatemala)
0x140a	Spanish (Costa Rica)
0x180a	Spanish (Panama)
0x1c0a	Spanish (Dominican Republic)
0x200a	Spanish (Venezuela)
0x240a	Spanish (Colombia)
0x280a	Spanish (Peru)
0x2c0a	Spanish (Argentina)
0x300a	Spanish (Ecuador)
0x340a	Spanish (Chile)
0x380a	Spanish (Uruguay)
0x3c0a	Spanish (Paraguay)
0x400a	Spanish (Bolivia)
0x440a	Spanish (El Salvador)
0x480a	Spanish (Honduras)
0x4c0a	Spanish (Nicaragua)
0x500a	Spanish (Puerto Rico)
0x0430	Sutu
0x0441	Swahili (Kenya)
0x041d	Swedish
0x081d	Swedish (Finland)
0x0449	Tamil; Unicode only
0x0444	Tatar (Tatarstan)
0x044a	Telugu; Unicode only
0x041e	Thai
0x041f	Turkish
0x0422	Ukrainian
0x0420	Urdu (Pakistan)
0x0820	Urdu (India)
0x0443	Uzbek (Latin)
0x0843	Uzbek (Cyrillic)
0x042a	Vietnamese

The Basic LCID API

As mentioned, an LCID is associated with the system, with each user, and with each thread. You can access these settings through the small set of Win32 API functions listed in Table 9-5.

Table 9-5. **Basic LCID API Functions**

Function Name	Description
ConvertDefaultLocale	Converts an LCID with default fields to a real LCID
EnumSystemLocales	Enumerates the locales that are installed or supported
GetSystemDefaultLangID	Gets the LANGID for the system
GetSystemDefaultLCID	Gets the LCID for the system
GetThreadLocale	Gets the LCID for the current thread
GetUserDefaultLangID	Gets the LANGID for the current user
GetUserDefaultLCID	Gets the LCID for the current user
IsValidLocale	Checks whether a locale is installed or supported
SetThreadLocale	Sets the LCID for the current thread

Listing 9-1 shows a console program that illustrates the use of these functions. First the program displays the LANGID and LCID for the system and the current user. Then it shows the LCID for the main thread and changes to the German locale. Last it creates a child thread that displays its initial LCID and changes to the French locale.

```
#include <stdio.h>
#include <tchar.h>

#define WIN32_LEAN_AND_MEAN
#include <windows.h>

// Child thread
DWORD WINAPI ThreadProc(void *p)
{
LCID lcidCreator = (LCID)p;
DWORD idThread = GetCurrentThreadId();
LCID lcidThread = GetThreadLocale();
_tprintf(_T("Thread %u LCID = 0x%08X, Creator LCID = 0x%08X\n"),
        idThread, lcidThread, lcidCreator);
LANGID lang = MAKELANGID(LANG_FRENCH, SUBLANG_FRENCH);
LCID lcid = MAKELCID(lang, SORT_DEFAULT);
```

Listing 9-1. *Accessing LCIDs in Win32.*

```
if(!SetThreadLocale(lcid))
    _tprintf(_T("Could not change thread %u locale to 0x%08X\n"),
            idThread, lcid);
else
    {
    lcidThread = GetThreadLocale();
    if(lcidThread != lcid) _tprintf
        (
        _T("Requested thread %u locale as 0x%08X but got 0x%08X\n"),
        idThread,
        lcid,
        lcidThread
        );
    else _tprintf(_T("Changed thread %u LCID to 0x%08X\n"),
                idThread, lcid);
    }
return 0;
}

// Main program
void _tmain()
{
LANGID langSys = GetSystemDefaultLangID();
_tprintf(_T("System default LANGID = 0x%04X\n"), langSys);

LCID lcidSys = GetSystemDefaultLCID();
_tprintf(_T("System default LCID = 0x%08X\n\n"), lcidSys);

LANGID langUser = GetUserDefaultLangID();
_tprintf(_T("User default LANGID = 0x%04X\n"), langUser);

LCID lcidUser = GetUserDefaultLCID();
_tprintf(_T("User default LCID = 0x%08X\n\n"), lcidUser);

DWORD idThread = GetCurrentThreadId();
LCID lcidThread = GetThreadLocale();
_tprintf(_T("Thread %u LCID = 0x%08X\n\n"), idThread, lcidThread);

LANGID lang = MAKELANGID(LANG_GERMAN, SUBLANG_GERMAN);
LCID lcid = MAKELCID(lang, SORT_DEFAULT);
if(!SetThreadLocale(lcid))
    _tprintf(_T("Could not change thread %u locale to 0x%08X\n"),
            idThread, lcid);
else
```

(continued)

Listing 9-1. *continued*

```
    {
    lcidThread = GetThreadLocale();
    if(lcidThread != lcid) _tprintf
        (
        _T("Requested thread %u locale as 0x%08X but got 0x%08X\n"),
        idThread,
        lcid,
        lcidThread
        );
    else _tprintf(_T("Changed thread %u LCID to 0x%08X\n"),
                idThread, lcid);
    }

DWORD idChild;
HANDLE hChild = CreateThread(0, 0, ThreadProc, (void*)lcid,
                            CREATE_SUSPENDED, &idChild);
if(!hChild) _tprintf(_T("\nCould not create child thread\n"));
else
    {
    _tprintf(_T("\nCreated child thread %u\n"), idChild);
    ResumeThread(hChild);
    WaitForSingleObject(hChild, INFINITE);
    _tprintf(_T("Child thread terminated\n\n"));
    CloseHandle(hChild);
    }

#if _DEBUG
_gettchar();        // Debugging pause
#endif
}
```

Figure 9-2 shows the program's output. Notice that my system uses 0x409 for the system and user LANGID and LCID. This corresponds to *LANG_ENGLISH* and *SUBLANG_ENGLISH_US* with the default sorting option. After *SetThreadLocale* in the *main* function is called, the thread's LCID becomes 0x407—the German language as spoken in Germany.

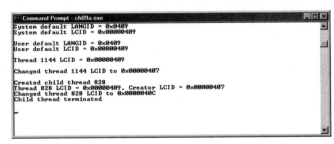

Figure 9-2. *Output of Listing 9-1.*

Next notice what happens in the child thread. Its initial LCID is 0x409 even though the main thread is using 0x407 when it creates the child. This discrepancy indicates that each new thread begins with the user's default LCID (also called the process LCID), not with the LCID of its creator thread. In other words, LCIDs do not propagate automatically from thread to thread. If you want the new thread to use its creator's LCID, you can pass that information by means of the *void* pointer, as Listing 9-1 demonstrates.

This sample console program uses the result of *SetThreadLocale* to determine whether the German and French LCIDs have valid entries in the system's locale database. You can also use *IsValidLocale* to explicitly check a locale, as shown here:

```
LANGID lang = MAKELANGID(LANG_FRENCH, SUBLANG_FRENCH);
LCID lcid = MAKELCID(lang, SORT_DEFAULT);
if(!IsValidLocale(lcid, LCID_INSTALLED))
{
    /* Locale not installed */
}
if(!IsValidLocale(lcid, LCID_SUPPORTED))
{
    /* Locale not supported */
}
```

The *LCID_INSTALLED* flag causes *IsValidLocale* to check whether the specified LCID is installed. If it is, then you can use it in functions such as *SetThreadLocale*. The *LCID_SUPPORTED* flag checks whether the specified LCID is defined, even though it may not be installed on the current system.

Sometimes you need to produce a list of all LCIDs that are installed or supported. The *EnumSystemLocales* function provides the means to do this, as shown in Listing 9-2. The main program invokes this function twice, first requesting the installed locales and then requesting the supported locales. These requests use the *LCID_INSTALLED* and *LCID_SUPPORTED* options as described earlier in conjunction with *IsValidLocale*. The *LCID_ALTERNATE_SORTS* flag is also supplied in each call to obtain LCIDs that have alternative sorting algorithms.

```
#include <stdio.h>
#include <tchar.h>

#define WIN32_LEAN_AND_MEAN
#include <windows.h>

// Callback function
static int nLocales = 0;
static BOOL CALLBACK cbEnumSystemLocales(LPTSTR p)
```

Listing 9-2. *Enumerating LCIDs.* *(continued)*

Listing 9-2. *continued*

```
{
_tprintf(_T(" %s"), p);
if(!(++nLocales & 7)) _tprintf(_T("\n"));
return TRUE;
}

// Main program
void _tmain()
{
_tprintf(_T("Installed locales...\n"));
BOOL ok = EnumSystemLocales
    (
    cbEnumSystemLocales,
    LCID_INSTALLED | LCID_ALTERNATE_SORTS
    );
if(!ok) _tprintf(_T("\nCannot enumerate LCID_INSTALLED |")
                _T(" LCID_ALTERNATE_SORTS\n"));
else _tprintf(_T("\n%d locales are installed\n"), nLocales);

_tprintf(_T("\nSupported locales...\n"));
nLocales = 0;
ok = EnumSystemLocales
    (
    cbEnumSystemLocales,
    LCID_SUPPORTED | LCID_ALTERNATE_SORTS
    );
if(!ok) _tprintf(_T("\nCannot enumerate LCID_SUPPORTED |")
                _T(" LCID_ALTERNATE_SORTS\n"));
else _tprintf(_T("\n%d locales are supported\n"), nLocales);

#if _DEBUG
_gettchar();        // Debugging pause
#endif
}
```

During each of the enumeration calls described above, the system repeatedly invokes the callback function *cbEnumSystemLocales* until all locales have been enumerated or the function returns *FALSE*. The system passes each LCID as a string of 8 hexadecimal digits, which the callback function simply sends to the standard output stream. The static variable *nLocales* counts the number of LCIDs and inserts a line break in the stream so that no more than 8 LCIDs appear on each line.

Figure 9-3 shows the output of the LCID enumerations on a system running Windows 2000 Professional (Build 2195). A total of 132 locales are installed out of the 133 supported by that version.

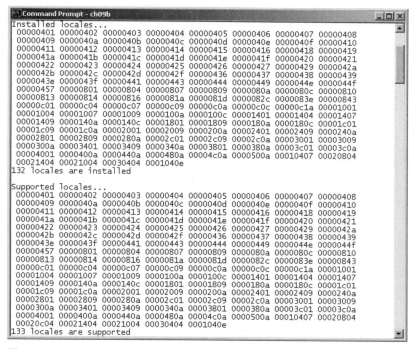

Figure 9-3. *Output of Listing 9-2.*

This program won't run on Windows 95 or Windows 98 unless you remove the *LCID_ALTERNATE_SORTS* options on the two calls to *EnumSystemLocales*.[2] When I made that change and ran the program on a Windows 98 (Second Edition) system, it reported that 77 locales were installed and 99 were supported.

Now you know how to query, enumerate, and change LCIDs in your application programs. But what good is that knowledge? In other words, what effects do these LCIDs have on the program? Lots! Many Win32 API functions use LCIDs either implicitly or explicitly to determine how to handle text and perform other locale-sensitive operations. Win32 usually employs the thread LCID implicitly unless a specific locale is specified as a function argument. Before we examine how LCIDs permeate the API, let's first explore the locale database, which contains the actual rules that these API functions consult when going about their business.

---

2. The Win32 online documentation implies that *LCID_ALTERNATE_SORTS* is supported in Windows 95 and Windows 98. This appears to be an error.

THE LOCALE DATABASE

The locale database provides application programs with a repertoire of rules for performing locale-sensitive operations such as text formatting, conversion, and sorting. Chapters 5 and 6 described these rules from the viewpoint of the C and C++ standards, which were designed to be independent of any particular operating system. This section looks at the locale database from the perspective of Win32.

How Win32 Stores Locale Information

The Win32 locale database contains records corresponding to the installed LCIDs. Each record provides rules for processing data in the language and sublanguage identified by its LCID. The database resides in a set of files referenced by Registry keys, with each LCID having one key in the following Registry path:

```
HKEY_LOCAL_MACHINE\System\CurrentControlSet\Control\NLS\Language
```

The files have .NLS extensions and reside in the System or System32 folder under the main OS directory, which is usually Windows or Winnt. Of course, knowing where the NLS files reside isn't very useful because Microsoft hasn't published the file format and supplies no tools for extending the database with new locales. So, instead of accessing the files directly, you always reach them through Win32 API functions. *GetLocaleInfo* is the primary Win32 API function for reading the rules in a locale record, and *SetLocaleInfo* enables a program to change some (not many) of the rules.

As mentioned earlier, the system and its registered users have default LCIDs. Typically a new user account inherits the system LCID, although the network administrator can assign a different LCID when creating a new account. The user can subsequently employ the Control Panel's Regional Settings applet to adjust some of the rules or to select a different locale. Application programs running on the user's behalf can call *GetLocaleInfo* to query the database for any rule in the system and can call *SetLocaleInfo* to change a subset of the rules. This changeable subset is stored in the following Registry path:

```
HKEY_CURRENT_USER\Control Panel\International
```

The keys in this path generally correspond to the *LCTYPE* symbols in Table 9-6, except that the Registry names do not begin with *LOCALE_* and they use mixed case instead of all uppercase characters. The values corresponding to these keys are null-terminated Unicode strings. Figure 9-4 is a screen shot from the Registry Editor (*regedit*) showing this information on my Windows 2000 system.

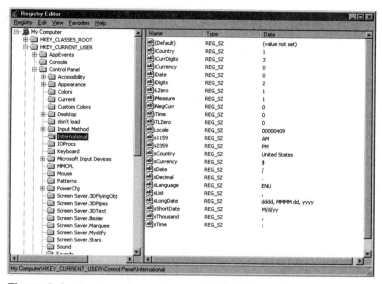

Figure 9-4. *Registry settings for user's default locale.*

Because changes to the locale database are stored in the current user's part of the Registry, each user can have a distinct set of customizations. This feature is handy when several people share the same workstation, such as multiple shifts in a sales or customer support center. For instance, a support person on the day shift might be working with Spanish-speaking customers, but the evening shift person using the same workstation could configure it to support English speakers.

Using *GetLocaleInfo*

GetLocaleInfo is a dual (both ANSI and Unicode) function that has the following generic definition in the winnls.h header file:

```
int GetLocaleInfo
    (
    LCID locale,        // Locale identifier
    LCTYPE LCType,      // Type of information
    LPTSTR lpLCData,    // Address of buffer for information
    int cchData         // Size of buffer
    );
```

This function obtains one item from the locale database record for the specified LCID. The item is returned in the buffer whose address and length are given by *lpLCData* and *cchData*, respectively. The ANSI version, *GetLocaleInfoA*, requires the length in bytes; *GetLocaleInfoW* requires length to be the number of characters.[3]

If the buffer pointer is not null, the function fetches the locale information and returns the number of bytes or characters that it placed into the buffer. However, if you call the function with a null pointer in *lpLCData*, it just returns a value indicating the number of bytes or characters required. This allows you to dynamically allocate the buffer at exactly the right size.

A return value of *0* indicates that the function failed because of insufficient buffer space or an invalid argument. As with most Win32 API functions, you can obtain the specific details of the failure by calling *GetLastError*.

For the *Locale* argument, you can specify an actual LCID or the special symbols *LOCALE_SYSTEM_DEFAULT* or *LOCALE_USER_DEFAULT*. The function fails if the LCID is not installed.

The *LCType* argument identifies the particular locale field to be returned. This argument is an *LCTYPE* item, which is actually an unsigned integer. For programming convenience, winnls.h defines symbols beginning with *LOCALE_* for the valid *LCTYPE* codes, as shown in Table 9-6. Those table entries with asterisks are changeable items which will be covered in the next section. You can adjust the behavior of *GetLocaleInfo* by ORing several optional flags into the *LCTYPE* code, as follows:

- The *LOCALE_NOUSEROVERRIDE* flag asks the function to return the original system setting for the locale item, ignoring any changes that the user made through the Control Panel or that the program made with *SetLocaleInfo*.

- The *LOCALE_USE_CP_ACP* flag asks *GetLocaleInfoA* to use the system ANSI code page for the return string. Normally the function uses the code page associated with the specified LCID. The Unicode version, *GetLocaleInfoW*, ignores this flag because it returns Unicode characters for all locales.

- The *LOCALE_RETURN_NUMBER* flag asks the function to return the locale item as a number instead of a text string. This flag applies only to items whose *LCTYPE* symbols have an *I* after the leading *LOCALE_*, as in *LOCALE_ICOUNTRY*. The return buffer specified by *lcLCData* must be large enough to hold a 4-byte integer. This flag only became available in Windows 2000, so you shouldn't use it if your program must operate in a Windows 95, Windows 98, or Windows NT environment.

---

3. Recall that the *tSizeOf* macro described in Chapter 7 returns the proper value, either bytes or characters, for a TCHAR array, depending on the ANSI or Unicode compilation mode.

Table 9-6. Locale Type Codes

Symbol	Description
LOCALE_FONTSIGNATURE	Font signature
	Bit mask that determines the relationship between a locale and a font; not null-terminated
LOCALE_ICALENDARTYPE*	Calendar type code
	1 Gregorian (localized)
	2 Gregorian (English)
	3 Year of the Emperor (Japan)
	4 Year of the Taiwan Region
	5 Tangun Era (Korea)
	6 Hijri (Arabic lunar calendar)
	7 Thai
	8 Hebrew lunar calendar
	9 Gregorian Middle East French calendar
	10 Gregorian Arabic calendar
	11 Gregorian transliterated English calendar
	12 Gregorian transliterated French calendar
LOCALE_ICENTURY	Century format specifier for short date
	0 2 digits
	2 4 digits
LOCALE_ICOUNTRY	Country code, based on international phone codes; also called the IBM country/region code
LOCALE_ICURRDIGITS*	Number of fractional digits for the local monetary format
LOCALE_ICURRENCY*	Monetary symbol position for positive amounts
	0 Prefix with no separation, such as $1.23
	1 Suffix with no separation, such as 1.23$
	2 Prefix with separator, such as $ 1.23
	3 Suffix with separator, such as 1.23 $

(continued)

Table 9-6. *continued*

Symbol	Description
LOCALE_IDATE	Ordering for short date format
	0 Month-Day-Year
	1 Day-Month-Year
	2 Year-Month-Day
LOCALE_IDAYLZERO	Leading zeros in day field for short date format
	0 No leading zeros
	1 Leading zeros
LOCALE_IDEFAULTANSICODEPAGE	Default ANSI code page
LOCALE_IDEFAULTCODEPAGE	Default OEM code page
LOCALE_IDEFAULTCOUNTRY	Default country code, corresponding to the sublanguage field in the LCID
LOCALE_IDEFAULTEBCDICCODEPAGE	Default EBCDIC code page
LOCALE_IDEFAULTLANGUAGE	Default language identifier, corresponding to the primary language field in the LCID
LOCALE_IDEFAULTMACCODEPAGE	Default Macintosh code page
LOCALE_IDIGITS*	Number of fractional digits
LOCALE_IDIGITSUBSTITUTION	Digit substitution code, which determines the shape of the 10 digits
	0 Context mode, in which the digit shape depends on previous text
	1 None or Arabic mode, using Unicode digits
	2 Native, using digit shapes provided by the *LOCALE_SNATIVEDIGITS* item
LOCALE_IFIRSTDAYOFWEEK*	First day of week
	0 *LOCALE_SDAYNAME1*
	1 *LOCALE_SDAYNAME2*
	2 *LOCALE_SDAYNAME3*
	3 *LOCALE_SDAYNAME4*
	4 *LOCALE_SDAYNAME5*
	5 *LOCALE_SDAYNAME6*
	6 *LOCALE_SDAYNAME7*
LOCALE_IFIRSTWEEKOFYEAR*	First week of year
	0 Week containing first day of year
	1 First full week of year
	2 First week containing at least four days

Symbol	Description
LOCALE_IINTLCURRDIGITS	Number of fractional digits for the international monetary format
LOCALE_ILANGUAGE	Language identifier, corresponding to the low 16 bits of the LCID
LOCALE_ILDATE	Ordering for long date format
	0 Month-Day-Year
	1 Day-Month-Year
	2 Year-Month-Day
*LOCALE_ILZERO**	Leading zeros for decimal number fields
	0 No leading zeros
	1 Leading zeros
*LOCALE_IMEASURE**	Measurement system
	0 Metric
	1 English (United States)
LOCALE_IMONLZERO	Leading zeros in *Month* field for short date format
	0 No leading zeros
	1 Leading zeros
*LOCALE_INEGCURR**	Negative currency format
	0 ($1.23)
	1 −$1.23
	2 $−1.23
	3 $1.23−
	4 (1.23$)
	5 −1.23$
	6 1.23−$
	7 1.23$−
	8 −1.23 $
	9 −$ 1.23
	10 1.23 $−
	11 $ 1.23−
	12 $ −1.23
	13 1.23− $
	14 ($ 1.23)
	15 (1.23 $)

(continued)

Table 9-6. *continued*

Symbol	Description
LOCALE_INEGNUMBER*	Negative number format
	0 (1.23)
	1 −1.23
	2 − 1.23
	3 1.23−
	4 1.23 −
LOCALE_INEGSEPBYSPACE	Separator between monetary symbol and negative amount
	0 No separator
	1 Separator
LOCALE_INEGSIGNPOSN	Negative sign position code for monetary format
	0 Parentheses around symbol and amount
	1 Sign precedes number
	2 Sign follows number
	3 Sign precedes monetary symbol
	4 Sign follows monetary symbol
LOCALE_INEGSYMPRECEDES	Monetary symbol position for negative amounts
	0 Symbol follows amount
	1 Symbol precedes amount
LOCALE_IOPTIONALCALENDAR	Additional calendar types, supplied as a null-separated list of the codes listed for *ICALENDARTYPE*, with code 0 indicating that there are no additional calendars
LOCALE_IPAPERSIZE*	Paper size code
	0 U.S. letter size
	1 U.S. legal size
	2 A3 size
	3 A4 size
LOCALE_IPOSSEPBYSPACE	Separator between monetary symbol and positive amount
	0 No separator
	1 Separator

Symbol	Description
LOCALE_IPOSSIGNPOSN	Positive sign position code for monetary format
	1 Sign precedes number
	2 Sign follows number
	3 Sign precedes monetary symbol
	4 Sign follows monetary symbol
LOCALE_IPOSSYMPRECEDES	Monetary symbol position for positive amounts
	0 Symbol follows amount
	1 Symbol precedes amount
LOCALE_ITIME*	Time format specifier
	0 12-hour format
	1 24-hour format
LOCALE_ITIMEMARKPOSN	Position of AM/PM marker in time format
	0 Marker follows time
	1 Marker precedes time
LOCALE_ITIMEMARKERUSE	Time marker usage code
	0 Use with 12-hour format
	1 Use with 24-hour format
	2 Use with both 12-hour and 24-hour format
	3 Never use
LOCALE_ITLZERO	Leading zeros in time fields
	0 No leading zeros
	1 Leading zeros
LOCALE_S1159*	AM designator
LOCALE_S2359*	PM designator
LOCALE_SABBREVCTRYNAME	Abreviation for country name, based on ISO 3166
LOCALE_SABBREVDAYNAME1	Abbreviation for Monday
LOCALE_SABBREVDAYNAME2	Abbreviation for Tuesday
LOCALE_SABBREVDAYNAME3	Abbreviation for Wednesday
LOCALE_SABBREVDAYNAME4	Abbreviation for Thursday
LOCALE_SABBREVDAYNAME5	Abbreviation for Friday
LOCALE_SABBREVDAYNAME6	Abbreviation for Saturday

(continued)

Table 9-6. *continued*

Symbol	Description
LOCALE_SABBREVDAYNAME7	Abbreviation for Sunday
LOCALE_SABBREVLANGNAME	Abbreviation for language name, using the two-letter ISO 639 symbol followed by a third letter indicating the sublanguage
LOCALE_SABBREVMONTHNAME1	Abbreviation for January
LOCALE_SABBREVMONTHNAME2	Abbreviation for February
LOCALE_SABBREVMONTHNAME3	Abbreviation for March
LOCALE_SABBREVMONTHNAME4	Abbreviation for April
LOCALE_SABBREVMONTHNAME5	Abbreviation for May
LOCALE_SABBREVMONTHNAME6	Abbreviation for June
LOCALE_SABBREVMONTHNAME7	Abbreviation for July
LOCALE_SABBREVMONTHNAME8	Abbreviation for August
LOCALE_SABBREVMONTHNAME9	Abbreviation for September
LOCALE_SABBREVMONTHNAME10	Abbreviation for October
LOCALE_SABBREVMONTHNAME11	Abbreviation for November
LOCALE_SABBREVMONTHNAME12	Abbreviation for December
LOCALE_SABBREVMONTHNAME13	Abbreviation for 13th month, if it is used
LOCALE_SCOUNTRY	Localized country name
LOCALE_SCURRENCY*	Local monetary symbol
LOCALE_SDATE*	Date separator
LOCALE_SDAYNAME1	Long name for Monday
LOCALE_SDAYNAME2	Long name for Tuesday
LOCALE_SDAYNAME3	Long name for Wednesday
LOCALE_SDAYNAME4	Long name for Thursday
LOCALE_SDAYNAME5	Long name for Friday
LOCALE_SDAYNAME6	Long name for Saturday
LOCALE_SDAYNAME7	Long name for Sunday
LOCALE_SDECIMAL*	Decimal (fraction) separator for nonmonetary amounts
LOCALE_SENGCOUNTRY	Country name in English
LOCALE_SENGCURRNAME	Currency name in English
LOCALE_SENGLANGUAGE	Language name in English

Symbol	Description
LOCALE_SGROUPING*	Grouping of digits to the left of the decimal point for nonmonetary amounts, represented as a list of numbers separated by semicolons—for example, the string *3;0* specifies grouping by thousands, as in 123,456,789, and the string *3;2;0* specifies Indic grouping of the first thousand and subsequent hundreds, as in 12,34,56,789
LOCALE_SINTLSYMBOL	International monetary symbol, based on ISO 4217
LOCALE_SISO3166CTRYNAME	Country/region name, based on ISO 3166
LOCALE_SISO639LANGNAME	Language name, based on ISO 639
LOCALE_SLANGUAGE	Localized language name
LOCALE_SLIST*	List item separator, typically a comma
LOCALE_SLONGDATE*	Long date format string
LOCALE_SMONDECIMALSEP*	Decimal (fraction) separator for monetary amounts
LOCALE_SMONGROUPING*	Grouping of digits to the left of the decimal point for monetary amounts (see *SGROUPING* for details)
LOCALE_SMONTHNAME1	Long name for January
LOCALE_SMONTHNAME2	Long name for February
LOCALE_SMONTHNAME3	Long name for March
LOCALE_SMONTHNAME4	Long name for April
LOCALE_SMONTHNAME5	Long name for May
LOCALE_SMONTHNAME6	Long name for June
LOCALE_SMONTHNAME7	Long name for July
LOCALE_SMONTHNAME8	Long name for August
LOCALE_SMONTHNAME9	Long name for September
LOCALE_SMONTHNAME10	Long name for October
LOCALE_SMONTHNAME11	Long name for November
LOCALE_SMONTHNAME12	Long name for December
LOCALE_SMONTHNAME13	Long name for 13th month, if used
LOCALE_SMONTHOUSANDSEP*	Thousands separator for monetary amounts

(continued)

Table 9-6. *continued*

Symbol	Description
LOCALE_SNATIVECTRYNAME	Native country name
LOCALE_SNATIVECURRNAME	Native currency name
LOCALE_SNATIVEDIGITS	Native 0 to 9 digits
LOCALE_SNATIVELANGNAME	Native language name
LOCALE_SNEGATIVESIGN*	Negative sign
LOCALE_SPOSITIVESIGN*	Positive sign
LOCALE_SSHORTDATE*	Short date format string
LOCALE_SSORTNAME	Localized name of sorting method
LOCALE_STHOUSAND*	Thousands separator for nonmonetary amounts
LOCALE_STIME*	Time separator
LOCALE_STIMEFORMAT*	Time format string
LOCALE_SYEARMONTH*	Year-month format string

To demonstrate the use of *GetLocaleInfo*, I developed a locale browser that produces the display shown in Figure 9-5. This is an MFC application with the Windows Explorer interface, consisting of a tree view on the left and a list view on the right. The tree contains a hierarchical display of the installed LCIDs, and the list shows the locale settings for the selected LCID. I'll defer the blow-by-blow description of the source code until later in this chapter, after the discussion of Win32 calendars in the section "Designing a Locale Browser."

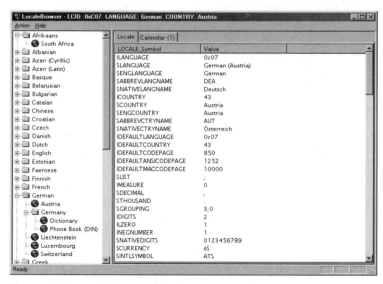

Figure 9-5. *Locale browser display.*

Using *SetLocaleInfo*

Although the system provides correct settings for all *LCTYPE* items in each locale record, the user or a program can change some of the items to adjust for slight differences in a particular locale. For example, you might need to change the number of decimal places in currency amounts or the way in which negative amounts are displayed.

Changeable items are those with asterisks in Table 9-6. The user can adjust these items through the Regional Settings applet in the Control Panel, and an application program can accomplish the same thing using *SetLocaleInfo*. The changes are stored in the user's Registry path, as described in the section "How Win32 Stores Locale" earlier in this chapter.

Listing 9-3 shows a little console program that illustrates how to use *SetLocaleInfo*. The program first reports the current state of the *LOCALE_IDIGITS* setting. (See Table 9-6.) Then it uses *SetLocaleInfo* to change *LOCALE_IDIGITS* to 3 and reports the new setting or displays an error message. Next it reports the default setting by using the *LOCALE_NOUSEROVERRIDE* option on *GetLocaleInfo*. Figure 9-6 shows the program output.

```
void _tmain()
{
TCHAR b[128], bOld[128];
LCID lcid = LOCALE_USER_DEFAULT;

GetLocaleInfo(lcid, LOCALE_IDIGITS, bOld, 128);
_tprintf(_T("\nLOCALE_IDIGITS is \"%s\"\n"), bOld);

if(SetLocaleInfo(lcid, LOCALE_IDIGITS, _T("3")))
    {
    GetLocaleInfo(lcid, LOCALE_IDIGITS, b, 128);
    _tprintf(_T("LOCALE_IDIGITS is \"%s\" after SetLocaleInfo\n"),
            b);
    GetLocaleInfo(lcid, LOCALE_IDIGITS | LOCALE_NOUSEROVERRIDE,
                b, 128);
    _tprintf(_T("LOCALE_IDIGITS is \"%s\" using no override option\n"),
            b);
    // Restore original setting.
    SetLocaleInfo(lcid, LOCALE_IDIGITS, bOld);

    }
else
    {
    LPTSTR pMsg;
    FormatMessage
```

Listing 9-3. *Using* SetLocaleInfo.   *(continued)*

Listing 9-3. *continued*

```
      (
      FORMAT_MESSAGE_ALLOCATE_BUFFER | FORMAT_MESSAGE_FROM_SYSTEM |
      FORMAT_MESSAGE_IGNORE_INSERTS,
      0,
      GetLastError(),
      lcid,
      (LPTSTR)&pMsg,
      0,
      0
      );
  MessageBox (0, pMsg, _T("Error"), MB_OK | MB_ICONINFORMATION);
   LocalFree(pMsg);
   }

#if _DEBUG
_gettchar();        // Debugging pause
#endif
}
```

Figure 9-6. *Output of Listing 9-3.*

Notice that, as a final step, this demonstration program restores the original *LOCALE_IDIGITS* setting obtained by the first call to *GetLocaleInfo*. Failure to do this can cause other programs to behave strangely because the locale change persists after the program terminates.

WORKING WITH DATE FORMATS AND CALENDARS

Unlike the C and C++ standards, which heavily favor the Gregorian calendar, Win32 supports at least a dozen other calendars. These calendar types are identified by the symbols shown in Table 9-7, which are defined in the winnls.h header file using the data type *CALID*, a 32-bit unsigned integer. The values in this table correspond to the possible settings for the *LOCALE_ICALENDARTYPE* and *LOCALE_IOPTIONALCALENDAR* items in Table 9-6.

Table 9-7. Calendar Type Codes

Symbol	Value	Calendar Type
CAL_GREGORIAN	1	Gregorian (localized) calendar
CAL_GREGORIAN_US	2	Gregorian (U.S.) calendar
CAL_JAPAN	3	Japanese Emperor Era calendar
CAL_TAIWAN	4	Taiwan Region Era calendar
CAL_KOREA	5	Korean Tangun Era calendar
CAL_HIJRI	6	Hijri (Arabic lunar) calendar
CAL_THAI	7	Thai calendar
CAL_HEBREW	8	Hebrew lunar calendar
CAL_GREGORIAN_ME_FRENCH	9	Gregorian Middle East French calendar
CAL_GREGORIAN_ARABIC	10	Gregorian Arabic calendar
CAL_GREGORIAN_XLIT_ENGLISH	11	Gregorian transliterated English calendar
CAL_GREGORIAN_XLIT_FRENCH	12	Gregorian transliterated French calendar

LOCALE_ICALENDARTYPE specifies the default, or native, calendar for the locale; *LOCALE_IOPTIONALCALENDAR* specifies an optional secondary calendar, with the value 0 indicating that there is no secondary calendar. The other calendar items in Table 9-6 are associated with the default calendar, and they are only a subset of the information available. You must use Win32 functions other than *GetLocaleInfo* to obtain the remaining information about the default calendar or any information about the alternate calendar.

Table 9-8 lists the Win32 functions that provide access to the extended Win32 calendar information and that support date formatting operations. The *Ex* suffix indicates functions that were extended for Windows 2000, such as *EnumCalendarInfoEx*. The earlier versions remain available for compatibility with older Win32 platforms.

Table 9-8. **Win32 Date Formatting and Calendar Access Functions**

Function Name	*Description*
EnumCalendarInfo(Ex)	Enumerates calendar information for a locale
EnumDateFormats(Ex)	Enumerates the date formats for a locale
GetCalendarInfo	Gets a calendar item
GetDateFormat	Formats a date as a string
SetCalendarInfo	Sets a calendar item for the current user

Using *GetDateFormat*

The *GetDateFormat* function[4] makes it fairly easy to produce a date string if you're willing to accept the default short or long date format for the locale. For example, Listing 9-4 is a simple console program that enables you to enter an LCID and view the current date formatted in the default short, long, and year-month styles as well as in a custom style. Figure 9-7 shows the program output for the default LCID (0x409 on my system) and for the French and German LCIDs, 0x40C and 0x407.

```
#include <stdio.h>
#include <stdlib.h>
#include <tchar.h>

#define WINVER 0x0500              // Includes Windows 2000 stuff
#define WIN32_LEAN_AND_MEAN        // Exclude GUI stuff
#include <windows.h>

// Main program
void _tmain()
{
SYSTEMTIME t;
GetSystemTime(&t);
while(1)
    {
    TCHAR b[100];
    LPTSTR p;
    _tprintf(_T("\nEnter an LCID " ));
    _tprintf(_T("(use 0x in front of hexadecimal) ==> "));
    if(!_getts(b)) break;
```

Listing 9-4. *Default date formatting.*

---

4. *GetNumberFormat*, *GetCurrencyFormat*, *GetDateFormat*, and *GetTimeFormat* have misleading names. They don't really get any formatting information; instead, they apply a specified format to some data in order to produce a formatted string. They should probably have names like *FormatNumber*, *FormatCurrency*, *FormatDate*, and *FormatTime*.

```
    LCID lcid = _tcstoul(b, &p, 0);
    if(lcid == 0) lcid = GetThreadLocale();
    if(!IsValidLocale(lcid, LCID_INSTALLED))
        {
        _tprintf(_T("LCID 0x%08X is not available\n"), lcid);
        continue;
        }
    _tprintf(_T("Formatted dates for LCID 0x%08X...\n"), lcid);
    GetDateFormat
        (
        lcid,                           // Locale identifier
        DATE_SHORTDATE,                 // Flags
        &t,                             // Date and time info
        0,                              // Date format (defaulted)
        b,                              // Output buffer
        100                             // Buffer length
        );
    _tprintf(_T("DATE_SHORTDATE ==> \"%s\"\n"), b);
    GetDateFormat
        (
        lcid,                           // Locale identifier
        DATE_LONGDATE,                  // Flags
        &t,                             // Date and time info
        0,                              // Date format (defaulted)
        b,                              // Output buffer
        100                             // Buffer length
        );
    _tprintf(_T("DATE_LONGDATE ==> \"%s\"\n"), b);
    GetDateFormat
        (
        lcid,                           // Locale identifier
        DATE_YEARMONTH,                 // Flags
        &t,                             // Date and time info
        0,                              // Date format (defaulted)
        b,                              // Output buffer
        100                             // Buffer length
        );
    _tprintf(_T("DATE_YEARMONTH ==> \"%s\"\n"), b);
    GetDateFormat
        (
        lcid,                           // Locale identifier
        0,                              // Flags
        &t,                             // Date and time info
        _T("'M='M, 'D='d"),             // Date format
        b,                              // Output buffer
        100                             // Buffer length
        );
    _tprintf(_T("\"'M='M, 'D='d\" ==> \"%s\"\n"), b);
    }
}
```

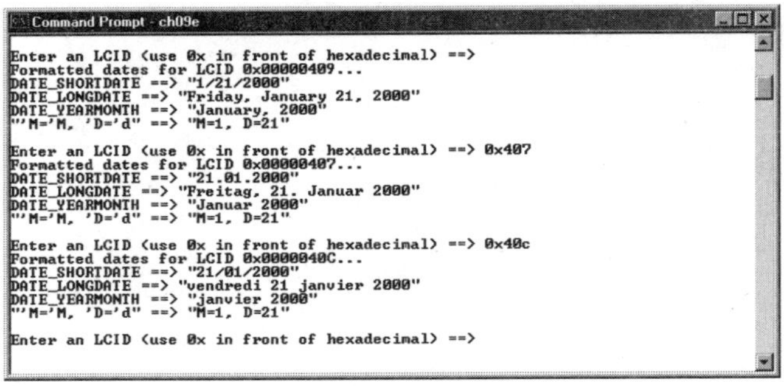

Figure 9-7. *Output of Listing 9-4.*

GetDateFormat accepts date information as a *SYSTEMTIME* structure whose pointer is passed as the third argument. In this example, I could have supplied a null pointer, thereby causing the function to use the current system date.

The second argument specifies the formatting style using symbols defined in the winnls.h header file. Table 9-9 shows the date style codes and the corresponding locale database items that contain the default format strings.

Table 9-9. Default Locale Items for Date Styles

Date Style	*Locale Info for Default Format String*
DATE_SHORTDATE	*LOCALE_SSHORTDATE*
DATE_LONGDATE	*LOCALE_SLONGDATE*
DATE_YEARMONTH	*LOCALE_SYEARMONTH*

The second argument can also include (by using a logical OR operation) the *LOCALE_NOUSEROVERRIDE* and *LOCALE_USE_CP_ACP* flags described earlier for *GetLocaleInfo*. If you want to use the locale's alternative calendar for formatting, include the flag *DATE_USE_ALT_CALENDAR*, which is ignored if the locale has only one calendar.

Sometimes you need to deviate from the default date formats. In those cases, you must either fetch an alternative format string from the locale database or construct a format string and pass it as the fourth argument to *GetDateFormat*. This format string is often called a picture string; it can contain the codes listed in Table 9-10. For example, the picture string *dd MMM yyyy* produces the military date format—, such as *04 NOV 1999* for November 4, 1999, in the U.S. locale (LCID 0x409).

Table 9-10. **Date Format Picture Codes**

Picture Code	Description
d	Day of month as digits, with no leading zero for single-digit days
dd	Day of month as digits, with leading zero for single-digit days
ddd	Day of week as three-letter abbreviation, specified by the *LOCALE_ SABBREVDAYNAME* item
dddd	Day of week as full name, specified by the *LOCALE_SDAYNAME* item
M	Month as digits, with no leading zero for single-digit months
MM	Month as digits, with leading zero for single-digit months
MMM	Month as three-letter abbreviation, specified by the *LOCALE_ SABBREVMONTHNAME* item
MMMM	Month as full name, specified by the *LOCALE_SMONTHNAME* item
y	Year as last two digits, with no leading zero for years less than 10
yy	Year as last two digits, with leading zero for years less than 10
yyyy	Year as four digits
gg	Era or period string, specified by the calendar's *CAL_SERASTRING* item; ignored if the date to be formatted does not have an associated era or period string

Boilerplate characters that conflict with the picture codes in Table 9-10 must be enclosed in single quotes, as in the picture string *'M='M, 'D='d,* which produces *M=11, D=4* as the formatted date. Listing 9-4 and Figure 9-7 illustrate the use of this particular custom date format. Notice that the second argument of *GetDateFormat* should not specify a default format code (see Table 9-9) when the fourth argument points to a picture string. The default format trumps the picture string.

Accessing the Calendar Database

As mentioned, the calendar items in Table 9-6 cover only a subset of the information about the default calendar for the specified locale. The system maintains complete details for the default calendar and any alternatives in a separate calendar database. For example, the *gg* picture code in Table 9-10 refers to a calendar item named *CAL_SERASTRING* that isn't available through *GetLocaleInfo.* You must use *GetCalendarInfo* or *EnumCalendarInfo(Ex)* to access this additional information about the default calendar and to get any information about alternative calendars. These functions use the calendar type information symbols listed in Table 9-11.

Table 9-11. **Calendar Type Information Codes**

Symbol	Description
CAL_ICALINTVALUE	Calendar type code (see Table 9-7)
CAL_ITWODIGITYEARMAX	Integer value indicating upper boundary of the two-digit year range (Windows 98 and Windows 2000)
CAL_IYEAROFFSETRANGE	One or more null-terminated strings that specify the year offsets for each of the era ranges; last string has extra terminating null character—for example, *1989\01926\01912\01868\0* for calendar type 3
CAL_SABBREVDAYNAME1	Abbreviation for Monday
CAL_SABBREVDAYNAME2	Abbreviation for Tuesday
CAL_SABBREVDAYNAME3	Abbreviation for Wednesday
CAL_SABBREVDAYNAME4	Abbreviation for Thursday
CAL_SABBREVDAYNAME5	Abbreviation for Friday
CAL_SABBREVDAYNAME6	Abbreviation for Saturday
CAL_SABBREVDAYNAME7	Abbreviation for Sunday
CAL_SABBREVMONTHNAME1	Abbreviation for January
CAL_SABBREVMONTHNAME2	Abbreviation for February
CAL_SABBREVMONTHNAME3	Abbreviation for March
CAL_SABBREVMONTHNAME4	Abbreviation for April
CAL_SABBREVMONTHNAME5	Abbreviation for May
CAL_SABBREVMONTHNAME6	Abbreviation for June
CAL_SABBREVMONTHNAME7	Abbreviation for July
CAL_SABBREVMONTHNAME8	Abbreviation for August
CAL_SABBREVMONTHNAME9	Abbreviation for September
CAL_SABBREVMONTHNAME10	Abbreviation for October
CAL_SABBREVMONTHNAME11	Abbreviation for November
CAL_SABBREVMONTHNAME12	Abbreviation for December
CAL_SABBREVMONTHNAME13	Abbreviation for 13th month, if used
CAL_SCALNAME	Name of calendar
CAL_SDAYNAME1	Long name for Monday
CAL_SDAYNAME2	Long name for Tuesday
CAL_SDAYNAME3	Long name for Wednesday
CAL_SDAYNAME4	Long name for Thursday
CAL_SDAYNAME5	Long name for Friday
CAL_SDAYNAME6	Long name for Saturday

Symbol	Description
CAL_SDAYNAME7	Long name for Sunday
CAL_SERASTRING	One or more null-terminated strings that specify the Unicode characters (in the form *Uxnnnn*) corresponding to the eras enumerated in *CAL_IYEAROFFSETRANGE*; last string has an extra terminating null character—for example, *Ux337B\0Ux337C\0Ux337D\0Ux337E\0* for calendar type 3
CAL_SLONGDATE	Long date formats
CAL_SMONTHNAME1	Long name for January
CAL_SMONTHNAME2	Long name for February
CAL_SMONTHNAME3	Long name for March
CAL_SMONTHNAME4	Long name for April
CAL_SMONTHNAME5	Long name for May
CAL_SMONTHNAME6	Long name for June
CAL_SMONTHNAME7	Long name for July
CAL_SMONTHNAME8	Long name for August
CAL_SMONTHNAME9	Long name for September
CAL_SMONTHNAME10	Long name for October
CAL_SMONTHNAME11	Long name for November
CAL_SMONTHNAME12	Long name for December
CAL_SMONTHNAME13	Long name for 13th month, if used
CAL_SSHORTDATE	Short date formats for this calendar type
CAL_SYEARMONTH	Year/month formats (Windows 98 and Windows 2000)

For example, suppose you want to find all available long date formats for a locale. If you call *GetLocaleInfo* to obtain *LOCALE_SLONGDATE*, you will get only the default format. Listing 9-5 demonstrates how to obtain the rest of the information using *EnumCalendarInfo(Ex)*. Figure 9-8 shows a sample of the program's output.

```
#include <stdio.h>
#include <stdlib.h>
#include <tchar.h>

#define WINVER 0x0500              // Includes Windows 2000 stuff
#define WIN32_LEAN_AND_MEAN        // Excludes GUI stuff
```

Listing 9-5. *Enumerating long date formats.*   *(continued)*

Listing 9-5. *continued*

```
#include <windows.h>

// Callback function
#if WINVER >= 0x500
static BOOL CALLBACK cbEnumCalendarInfo(LPTSTR p, CALID cal)
{
_tprintf(_T("%3u: %s\n"), cal, p);
return TRUE;
}
#else
static BOOL CALLBACK cbEnumCalendarInfo(LPTSTR p)
{
_tprintf(_T("%s\n"), p);
return TRUE;
}
#endif

// Main program
void _tmain()
{
while(1)
    {
    TCHAR b[32];
    LPTSTR p;
    _tprintf(_T("\nEnter an LCID"));
    _tprintf(_T(" (use 0x in front of hexadecimal) ==> "));
    if(!_getts(b)) break;
    LCID lcid = _tcstoul(b, &p, 0);
    if(lcid == 0) lcid = GetThreadLocale();
    if(!IsValidLocale(lcid, LCID_INSTALLED))
        {
        _tprintf(_T("LCID 0x%08X is not available\n"), lcid);
        continue;
        }
    _tprintf(_T("Calendar info for LCID 0x%08X...\n"), lcid);
    #if WINVER >= 0x500
    BOOL ok = EnumCalendarInfoEx
    #else
    BOOL ok = EnumCalendarInfo
    #endif
        (
        cbEnumCalendarInfo,
        lcid,
        ENUM_ALL_CALENDARS,
        CAL_SLONGDATE
        );
    if(!ok) _tprintf(_T("*** Enumeration error ***\n"));
    }
}
```

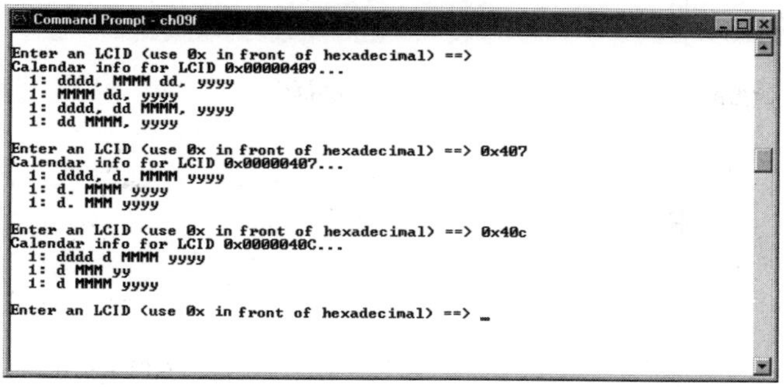

Figure 9-8. *Output of Listing 9-5.*

In this example, I used the *WINVER* preprocessor symbol to determine which enumeration function to call. Because *EnumCalendarInfoEx* is available only in Windows 2000 and later, I check *WINVER* for a value of 0x0500 or greater.[5] The extended enumerator provides the calendar type code to the callback function, which the program displays in front of each format string. Figure 9-8 shows that the United States, French, and German locales use only calendar type 1, which is Gregorian.

For earlier versions, the sample program calls *EnumCalendarInfo*. I could have called *EnumDateFormats* instead because it behaves exactly like *EnumCalendarInfo* when you call the latter with the *ENUM_ALL_CALENDARS* option. You might prefer *EnumDateFormats* because it has a simpler protocol and uses the same symbols as *GetDateFormat*. (See Table 9-9.)

WORKING WITH TIME FORMATS

Win32 provides two functions for working with time formats: *GetTimeFormat* and *EnumTimeFormats*. These functions are similar to the date formatting functions described in the preceding section except that they use different picture codes, as shown in Table 9-12.

---

5. Windows 2000 continues the Windows NT version number sequence, so from a programming perspective *WINVER* of Windows 2000 is 0x0500.

Table 9-12. **Time Format Picture Codes**

Picture Code	Description
h	Hours, with no leading zero for single-digit hours; 12-hour clock
hh	Hours, with leading zero for single-digit hours; 12-hour clock
H	Hours, with no leading zero for single-digit hours; 24-hour clock
HH	Hours, with leading zero for single-digit hours; 24-hour clock
m	Minutes, with no leading zero for single-digit minutes
mm	Minutes, with leading zero for single-digit minutes
s	Seconds, with no leading zero for single-digit seconds
ss	Seconds, with leading zero for single-digit seconds.
t	Single-character time marker string, such as A or P
tt	Multicharacter time marker string, such as AM or PM.

Listing 9-6 is a console program that illustrates the use of these functions. The program enumerates all time formats for a user-specified locale and produces a time string for each picture. Figure 9-9 shows the typical results for several locales.

```
#include <stdio.h>
#include <stdlib.h>
#include <tchar.h>

#define WINVER 0x0500          // Includes Windows 2000 stuff
#define WIN32_LEAN_AND_MEAN    // Excludes GUI stuff
#include <windows.h>

// Global data function
SYSTEMTIME g_SystemTime;
LCID g_LCID;

// Callback function
static BOOL CALLBACK cbEnumTimeFormats(LPTSTR p)
{
TCHAR b[100];
GetTimeFormat
    (
    g_LCID,                                  // Locale
    LOCALE_USE_CP_ACP | TIME_NOSECONDS,      // Use ANSI CP
                                             // for non-Unicode.
    &g_SystemTime,             // Date and time info
    p,                         // Format picture
    b,                         // Output buffer
```

Listing 9-6. *Enumerating and using time formats.*

```
    100                              // Buffer size (TCHAR units)
    );
_tprintf(_T("\"%s\" ==> \"%s\"\n"), p, b);
return TRUE;
}


// Main program
void _tmain()
{
GetSystemTime(&g_SystemTime);
while(1)
    {
    TCHAR b[32];
    LPTSTR p;
    _tprintf(_T("\nEnter an LCID " ));
    _tprintf(_T(" (use 0x in front of hexadecimal) ==> "));
    if(!_getts(b)) break;
    g_LCID = _tcstoul(b, &p, 0);
    if(g_LCID == 0) g_LCID = GetThreadLocale();
    if(!IsValidLocale(g_LCID, LCID_INSTALLED))
        {
        _tprintf(_T("LCID 0x%08X is not available\n"), g_LCID);
        continue;
        }
    _tprintf(_T("Time formats for LCID 0x%X...\n"), g_LCID);
    BOOL ok = EnumTimeFormats
        (
        cbEnumTimeFormats,
        g_LCID,
        LOCALE_USE_CP_ACP
        );
    if(!ok) _tprintf(_T("*** Enumeration error ***\n"));
    }
}
```

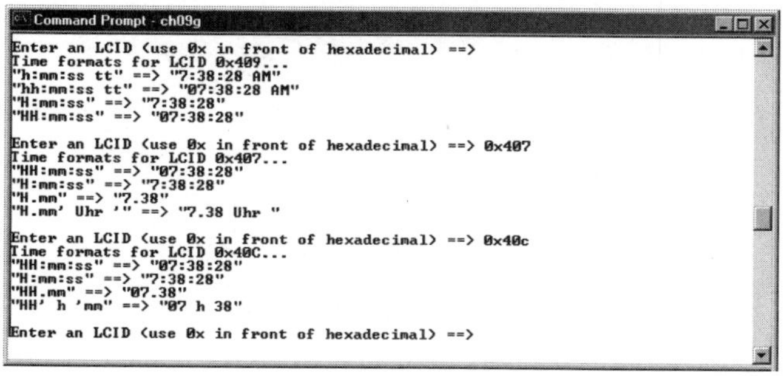

Figure 9-9. *Output of Listing 9-6.*

The fourth argument of *GetTimeFormat* is an optional picture string using the codes shown in Table 9-12. If you supply a null pointer, the function uses the *LOCALE_STIMEFORMAT* item (see Table 9-6) from the specified locale. *GetTimeFormat* also enables you to omit or adjust parts of the formatted output by specifying the appropriate flags in its second argument, as shown in Table 9-13. As with *GetDateFormat,* you can also include the generic flags *LOCALE_NO-USEROVERRIDE* and *LOCALE_USE_CP_ACP.*

Table 9-13. Style Flags for *GetTimeFormat*

Style	Description
TIME_NOMINUTESORSECONDS	No minutes or seconds
TIME_NOSECONDS	No seconds
TIME_NOTIMEMARKER	No AM/PM marker
TIME_FORCE24HOURFORMAT	24-hour time format

WORKING WITH NUMBER FORMATS

The *GetNumberFormat* function punctuates a numeric string according to the rules of a specific locale. Listing 9-7 demonstrates how to use this function, and Figure 9-10 shows the typical output for several locales. The input string should contain digit characters from 0 through 9 with a leading minus sign if the number is negative and a single decimal point if the number has a fractional part. The presence of any other characters causes the function to return 0, in which case you can call *GetLastError* to get more details. If the function succeeds, it returns the number of characters (actually TCHARs) produced in the output buffer.

```
#include <stdio.h>
#include <stdlib.h>
#include <tchar.h>

#define WINVER 0x0500           // Includes Windows 2000 stuff
#define WIN32_LEAN_AND_MEAN     // Excludes GUI stuff
#include <windows.h>

// Function to get the default number information
void GetNumberInfo(LCID lcid, NUMBERFMT& fmt)
{
int n;
TCHAR b[50];
memset(&fmt, 0, sizeof(fmt));
```

Listing 9-7. *Using* GetNumberFormat.

```
GetLocaleInfo(lcid, LOCALE_IDIGITS, b, 50);
fmt.NumDigits = _ttoi(b);
GetLocaleInfo(lcid, LOCALE_ILZERO, b, 50);
fmt.LeadingZero = _ttoi(b);
GetLocaleInfo(lcid, LOCALE_INEGNUMBER, b, 50);
fmt.NegativeOrder = _ttoi(b);
GetLocaleInfo(lcid, LOCALE_SGROUPING, b, 50);
if(_tcschr(b, _T(';'))) fmt.Grouping = 32;
                                    // Hack -- assumes 3;2 format
else fmt.Grouping = _ttoi(b);

n = GetLocaleInfo                   // Get decimal separator.
    (
    lcid,
    LOCALE_SDECIMAL,
    0, 0
    );
if(n > 0)
    {
    fmt.lpDecimalSep = new TCHAR[n];
    GetLocaleInfo
        (
        lcid,
        LOCALE_SDECIMAL,
        fmt.lpDecimalSep,
        n
        );
    }
n = GetLocaleInfo                   // Get group separator.
    (
    lcid,
    LOCALE_STHOUSAND,
    0, 0
    );
if(n > 0)
    {
    fmt.lpThousandSep = new TCHAR[n];
    GetLocaleInfo
        (
        lcid,
        LOCALE_STHOUSAND,
        fmt.lpThousandSep,
        n
        );
    }
}
```

(continued)

Listing 9-7. *continued*

```
// Main program
void _tmain()
{
while(1)
    {
    TCHAR b[100], b1[100];
    LPTSTR p;
    _tprintf(_T("\nEnter an LCID "));
    _tprintf(_T("(use 0x in front of hexadecimal) ==> "));
    if(!_getts(b)) break;
    LCID lcid = _tcstoul(b, &p, 0);
    if(lcid == 0) lcid = GetThreadLocale();
    if(!IsValidLocale(lcid, LCID_INSTALLED))
        {
        _tprintf(_T("LCID 0x%08X is not available\n"), lcid);
        continue;
        }
    _tprintf(_T("\nEnter number such as -123.456 ==> "));
    if(!_getts(b)) break;
    if(GetNumberFormat
        (
        lcid,                       // Locale
        0,                          // Flags
        b,                          // Input string
        0,                          // NUMBERFMT pointer or null
        b1,                         // Output buffer
        100                         // Output buffer size (TCHARs)
        ))
        _tprintf(
            _T("Default number format for LCID 0x%X ==> %s\n"),
            lcid,
            b1);
    else _tprintf(_T("*** Formatting error ***\n"));

    // Produce format with one more decimal place than default.
    NUMBERFMT fmt;
    GetNumberInfo(lcid, fmt);
    fmt.NumDigits++;
    if(GetNumberFormat
        (
        lcid,                       // Locale
        0,                          // Flags
        b,                          // Input string
        &fmt,                       // NUMBERFMT pointer or null
        b1,                         // Output buffer
        100                         // Output buffer size (TCHARs)
        ))
```

```
    _tprintf(
        _T("Customized number format for LCID 0x%X ==> %s\n"),
        lcid,
        b1);
else _tprintf(_T("*** Formatting error ***\n"));
delete fmt.lpDecimalSep;
delete fmt.lpThousandSep;
}
}
```

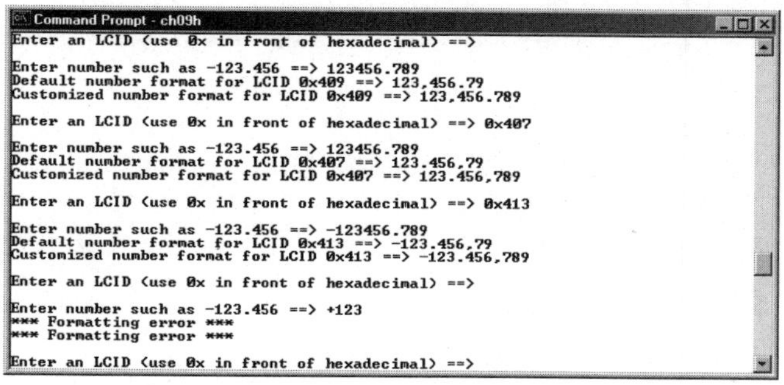

Figure 9-10. *Output of Listing 9-7.*

GetNumberFormat replaces the minus sign and decimal point with characters specified by the locale database. It also rounds the fractional part to the appropriate number of places and inserts grouping characters in the integer part.

If you want to use a format other than the locale's default, you must construct a *NUMBERFMT* structure, which has the following definition:

```
typedef struct _numberfmt
    {
    UINT NumDigits;          // From LOCALE_IDIGITS
    UINT LeadingZero;         // From LOCALE_ILZERO
    UINT Grouping;          // From LOCALE_SGROUPING
    LPTSTR lpDecimalSep;      // From LOCALE_SDECIMAL
    LPTSTR lpThousandSep;      // From LOCALE_STHOUSAND
    UINT NegativeOrder;      // From LOCALE_INEGNUMBER
    } NUMBERFMT;
```

The structure members correspond directly to the locale items mentioned in the comments, except for the *Grouping* member, which should be a value from 0 through 9 if all groups are the same size. Otherwise, *Grouping* can have a value of 32 to indicate that the first group to the left of the fraction point has 3 characters and the remaining groups have 2.

Listing 9-7 includes the function *GetNumberInfo*, which fills a *NUMBERFMT* structure with the default values from a specified locale. This function serves as a starting point for customization. The main program uses this function to build a custom format that has one more decimal place than the default. One problem with *GetNumberInfo* is that you must remember to delete the pointer items to avoid memory leaks. A more sophisticated approach would derive a C++ class from *NUMBERFMT* and clean up the pointers in the destructor.

Notice that the *NUMBERFMT* structure does not contain members defining positive and negative signs. This is probably a Win32 design error, since it limits your ability to completely customize the number format. For instance, to use nondefault sign characters, you must post-process the string produced by *GetNumberFormat*, replacing the default positive or negative indicator with your own choice. Of course, you could use *SetLocaleInfo* to temporarily change *LOCALE_SPOSITIVESIGN* and *LOCALE_SNEGATIVESIGN*, but that seems like a lot of work and could affect other applications running at the same time. A better approach is to derive a C++ class from *NUMBERFMT* as described earlier and then add the missing information as member variables and add member functions to perform the post-processing.

WORKING WITH CURRENCY FORMATS

The procedure for producing currency strings is similar to the number formatting procedure described in the preceding section. You pass a simple numeric string containing digits, an optional decimal point, and an optional leading minus sign to *GetCurrencyFormat*, and you get back a formatted string using either the locale's default rules or your own rules specified in a *CURRENCYFMT* structure, which has the following definition in winnls.h:

```
typedef struct _currencyfmt
    {
    UINT NumDigits;              // From LOCALE_IDIGITS
    UINT LeadingZero;            // From LOCALE_ILZERO
    UINT Grouping;               // From LOCALE_SMONGROUPING
    LPTSTR lpDecimalSep;         // From LOCALE_SMONDECIMALSEP
    LPTSTR lpThousandSep;        // From LOCALE_SMONTHOUSANDSEP
    UINT NegativeOrder;          // From LOCALE_INEGCURR
    UINT PositiveOrder;          // From LOCALE_ICURRENCY
    LPTSTR lpCurrencySymbol;     // From LOCALE_SCURRENCY
} CURRENCYFMT;
```

Listing 9-8 illustrates the use of *GetCurrencyFormat*; typical output is shown in Figure 9-11. As in the number formatting example, I wrote a function named *GetCurrencyInfo* to initialize a *CURRENCYFMT* structure with the default settings for a locale. The function has a third argument, which allows you to select the international or local money format, causing the *lpCurrencySymbol* member to be initialized from *LOCALE_SINTLSYMBOL* or *LOCALE_SCURRENCY*.

```c
#include <stdio.h>
#include <stdlib.h>
#include <tchar.h>

#define WINVER 0x0500          // Includes Windows 2000 stuff
#define WIN32_LEAN_AND_MEAN    // Excludes GUI stuff
#include <windows.h>

// Function to get the default currency information
void GetCurrencyInfo(LCID lcid, CURRENCYFMT& fmt, bool bIntl = false)
{
int n;
TCHAR b[50];
memset(&fmt, 0, sizeof(fmt));

GetLocaleInfo(lcid, LOCALE_ICURRDIGITS, b, 50);
fmt.NumDigits = _ttoi(b);
GetLocaleInfo(lcid, LOCALE_IMONLZERO, b, 50);
fmt.LeadingZero = _ttoi(b);
GetLocaleInfo(lcid, LOCALE_ICURRENCY, b, 50);
fmt.PositiveOrder = _ttoi(b);
GetLocaleInfo(lcid, LOCALE_INEGCURR, b, 50);
fmt.NegativeOrder = _ttoi(b);
GetLocaleInfo(lcid, LOCALE_SMONGROUPING, b, 50);
fmt.Grouping = _ttoi(b);

n = GetLocaleInfo                       // Get currency symbol.
    (
    lcid,
    bIntl ? LOCALE_SINTLSYMBOL : LOCALE_SCURRENCY,
    0, 0
    );
if(n > 0)
    {
    fmt.lpCurrencySymbol = new TCHAR[n];
    GetLocaleInfo
        (
        lcid,
        bIntl ? LOCALE_SINTLSYMBOL : LOCALE_SCURRENCY,
        fmt.lpCurrencySymbol,
        n
        );
    }
```

Listing 9-8. *Using* GetNumberFormat. *(continued)*

Listing 9-8. *continued*

```
n = GetLocaleInfo                        // Get decimal separator.
    (
    lcid,
    LOCALE_SMONDECIMALSEP,
    0, 0
    );
if(n > 0)
    {
    fmt.lpDecimalSep = new TCHAR[n];
    GetLocaleInfo
        (
        lcid,
        LOCALE_SMONDECIMALSEP,
        fmt.lpDecimalSep,
        n
        );
    }
n = GetLocaleInfo                        // Get group separator.
    (
    lcid,
    LOCALE_SMONTHOUSANDSEP,
    0, 0
    );
if(n > 0)
    {
    fmt.lpThousandSep = new TCHAR[n];
    GetLocaleInfo
        (
        lcid,
        LOCALE_SMONTHOUSANDSEP,
        fmt.lpThousandSep,
        n
        );
    }
}

// Main program
void _tmain()
{
while(1)
    {
    TCHAR b[100], b1[100];
    LPTSTR p;
    _tprintf(_T("\nEnter an LCID " ));
    _tprintf(_T("(use 0x in front of hexadecimal) ==> "));
    if(!_getts(b)) break;
    LCID lcid = _tcstoul(b, &p, 0);
```

```
    if(lcid == 0) lcid = GetThreadLocale();
    if(!IsValidLocale(lcid, LCID_INSTALLED))
        {
        _tprintf(_T("LCID 0x%08X is not available\n"), lcid);
        continue;
        }
    _tprintf(_T("\nEnter number such as -123.456 ==> "));
    if(!_getts(b)) break;

    // Produce default currency format.
    if(GetCurrencyFormat
        (
        lcid,                       // Locale
        LOCALE_USE_CP_ACP,          // Flags
        b,                          // Input string
        0,                          // CURRENCYFMT pointer or null
        b1,                         // Output buffer
        100                         // Output buffer size (TCHARs)
        ))
        _tprintf(
            _T("Default local money format for LCID 0x%X ==> %s\n"),
            lcid,
            b1);
    else _tprintf(_T("*** Formatting error ***\n"));

    // Produce international currency format.
    CURRENCYFMT fmt;
    GetCurrencyInfo(lcid, fmt, true);
    if(GetCurrencyFormat
        (
        lcid,                       // Locale
        0,                          // Flags
        b,                          // Input string
        &fmt,                       // CURRENCYFMT pointer or null
        b1,                         // Output buffer
        100                         // Output buffer size (TCHARs)
        ))
        _tprintf(
            _T("Default international money format")
            _T(" for LCID 0x%X ==> %s\n"),
            lcid,
            b1);
    else _tprintf(_T("*** Formatting error ***\n"));
    delete fmt.lpCurrencySymbol;
    delete fmt.lpDecimalSep;
    delete fmt.lpThousandSep;
    }
}
```

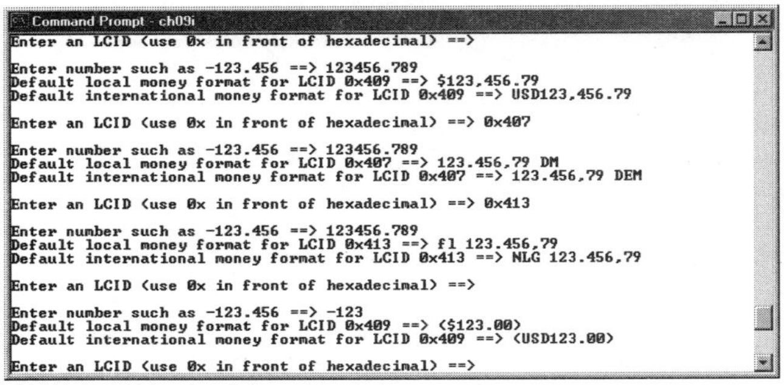

Figure 9-11. *Output of Listing 9-8.*

LOCALE-SENSITIVE TEXT OPERATIONS

The Win32 API includes many text manipulation functions, as shown in Tables 9-14, 9-15, and 9-16. Most of these functions have no locale sensitivity or depend only on code pages, as I described in Chapter 8; others require additional information from the locale database. Comparison of text strings is particularly troublesome because simple numeric ranking of code points seldom produces the correct results. This difficulty often surprises U.S. programmers, who are used to sorting by simply comparing ASCII character values.[6]

The functions in Table 9-14 are traditionally considered the NLS API for text operations, and so they are defined in the winnls.h header file. The other two tables list functions that were originally part of the Microsoft Internet Explorer utility library and have now become a standard feature of Windows 2000. You can find them in the shlwapi.h header file. If you are designing programs that must run on earlier versions of Windows, examine the Win32 documentation carefully because these utility functions might not be present unless you install a specific version of Internet Explorer.

In this section, I'll focus primarily on the comparison and conversion functions in Table 9-14. I won't spend much time on the utility functions in Table 9-15 because they closely mimic the standard C library. Likewise, I won't go into any detail about the functions in Table 9-16 because these functions are fairly simple and don't have a lot of locale sensitivities. The latter two tables are included here so that you can see the complete scope of text support in Windows 2000.

---

6. Mainframe programmers in the United States are probably more aware of sorting issues than PC programmers because the popular mainframe character set EBCDIC is not usually sorted by simply ranking the code point values.

Table 9-14. **Basic Win32 Text Functions**

Function Name	Description
CharLower	Converts a character or null-terminated string to lowercase
CharLowerBuff	Converts a character buffer to lowercase
CharNext	Advances a pointer to the next character using the current code page
CharNextExA	Advances a pointer to the next character using a specified code page
CharPrev	Backs up a pointer to the previous character using the current code page
CharPrevExA	Backs up a pointer to the previous character using a specified code page
CharToOem	Converts a string to the OEM code page
CharToOemBuff	Converts a specified number of characters to the OEM code page
CharUpper	Converts a character or null-terminated string to uppercase
CharUpperBuff	Converts a character buffer to uppercase
CompareString	Compares two character strings
FoldString	Transforms a string
GetStringTypeA	Gets character type information for an ANSI string
GetStringTypeEx	Gets character type information for a string
GetStringTypeW	Gets character type information for a Unicode string
IsCharAlpha	Tests whether a character is alphabetic
IsCharAlphaNumeric	Tests whether a character is alphabetic or numeric
IsCharLower	Tests whether a character is lowercase
IsCharUpper	Tests whether a character is uppercase
LCMapString	Maps a string
lstrcat	Concatenates one string to another
lstrcmp	Compares two strings; the Unicode version (*lstrcmpW*) performs a word comparison, while the ANSI version (*lstrcmpA*) performs a string comparison
lstrcmpi	Compares two strings like *lstrcmp* but without regard to case
lstrcpy	Copies a null-terminated string
lstrcpyn	Copies a null-terminated string with a length limitation
lstrlen	Measures the number of TCHARs in a string
MultiByteToWideChar	Converts a multibyte string to wide characters

(continued)

Table 9-14. *continued*

Function Name	Description
OemToChar	Converts a string from the OEM-defined character set into either an ANSI or wide-character string
OemToCharBuff	Converts the specified number of characters from the OEM code page
WideCharToMultiByte	Converts a wide character string to multibyte characters
wsprintf	Produces a formatted string
wvsprintf	Produces a formatted string using a variable argument list

Table 9-15. **Win32 General String Functions**

Function Name	Description
ChrCmpI	Performs a case-insensitive comparison of two characters
StrCat	Same as *lstrcat*
StrCatN	Same as *StrCat* but with a length limitation
StrChr	Finds first occurrence of a character in a string
StrChrI	Case-insensitive version of *StrChr*
StrCmp	Compares two strings, returning the difference in value of the first nonmatching characters
StrCmpI	Same as *lstrcmpi*
StrCmpN	Compares two strings, returning the difference in value of the first nonmatching characters; stops after comparing *N* characters
StrCmpNI	Case-insensitive version of *StrCmpN*
StrCpy	Same as *lstrcpy*
StrCpyN	Same as *lstrcpyn*
StrCSpn	Searches for the first occurrence of any character from a specified set; returns the index of that character or the null terminator
StrCSpnI	Case-insensitive version of *StrCSpn*
StrDup	Duplicates a string, using *LocalAlloc* to obtain memory
StrFormatByteSize	Formats a size value into a string representing bytes, kilobytes, megabytes, or gigabytes
StrFromTimeInterval	Converts a millisecond value to a string representing hours, minutes, and seconds
StrIntlEqN	Performs a length-limited case-sensitive comparison of two strings using the current thread locale; uses *CompareString* internally

Function Name	Description
StrIntlEqNI	Case-insensitive version of *IntlStrEqN*
StrPBrk	Finds the first occurrence of any character from a specified set; returns a pointer to that character or a null pointer if no matching character was found
StrRChr	Finds last occurrence of a character in a string
StrRChrI	Case-insensitive version of *StrRChr*
StrRStrI	Finds the last occurrence of one string within another, using case-insensitive comparison
StrSpn	Measures the length of the first substring within a string that consists only of characters from a specified set
StrStr	Finds the first occurrence of one string within another
StrStrI	Case-insensitive version of *StrStr*
StrToInt	Converts a decimal string to an integer; *StrToLong* is an alias for this function
StrToIntEx	Converts a decimal or hexadecimal string to an integer
StrTrim	Trims a string to remove all leading and trailing occurrences of characters from a specified set

Table 9-16. **Win32 Path and URL String Functions**

Function Name	Description
PathAddBackslash	Appends a backslash to a path
PathAddExtension	Appends an extension to a path
PathAppend	Appends a string to a path
PathBuildRoot	Builds a root path from a drive number
PathCanonicalize	Creates the canonical form of a path by pruning specified nodes
PathCombine	Combines two paths into one
PathCommonPrefix	Compares two paths to determine whether they share a common prefix
PathCompactPath	Inserts ellipses into a path to make it fit a specified pixel width
PathCompactPathEx	Inserts ellipses into a path to make it fit a specified character width
PathCreateFromUrl	Creates a path from a file URL
PathFileExists	Checks whether a file exists
PathFindExtension	Finds the extension part of a path
PathFindFileName	Finds the filename part of a path
PathFindNextComponent	Finds the next component of a path

(continued)

Table 9-16. *continued*

Function Name	Description
PathFindOnPath	Finds a file by searching the specified absolute path or, if the path is relative, by searching the standard directories, the PATH variable, or a specified list of directories
PathFindSuffixArray	Determines whether a path has a suffix (extension) matching one in the specified array
PathGetArgs	Finds the command-line arguments following a path
PathGetCharType	Determines the type of a path character, such as a wildcard character or one that is only valid in long paths
PathGetDriveNumber	Gets the drive number from a path
PathIsContentType	Checks whether a path is of a specified content type
PathIsDirectory	Checks whether a path is a directory
PathIsDirectoryEmpty	Checks whether a path is an empty directory
PathIsFileSpec	Checks whether a path is a file specification—that is, a string containing no drive or directory punctuation characters
PathIsHTMLFile	Checks whether a path specifies an HTML file
PathIsLFNFileSpec	Checks whether a path is a long filename
PathIsNetworkPath	Checks whether a path begins with a double slash and has the UNC format, specifying a network location
PathIsPrefix	Checks whether a path has a valid prefix of the specified type
PathIsRelative	Checks whether a path is relative
PathIsRoot	Checks whether a path begins at a root directory
PathIsSameRoot	Checks whether two paths have the same root
PathIsSystemFolder	Checks whether a path specifies a system folder
PathIsUNC	Checks for a valid UNC path
PathIsUNCServer	Checks whether a path specifies a UNC server only
PathIsUNCServerShare	Checks whether a path specifies a shared resource on a UNC server
PathIsURL	Checks whether a string is a valid URL
PathMakePretty	Converts a path to all lowercase
PathMakeSystemFolder	Converts an existing folder to a system folder
PathMatchSpec	Searches a string using MS-DOS wildcards
PathParseIconLocation	Parses a path name and icon index into separate parts
PathQuoteSpaces	Encloses a path in quotation marks if the path contains spaces.
PathRelativePathTo	Creates a relative path from one file or folder to another
PathRemoveArgs	Removes the arguments following a path
PathRemoveBackslash	Removes the trailing backslash from a path
PathRemoveBlanks	Removes leading and trailing blanks from a path

Function Name	*Description*
PathRemoveExtension	Removes the extension from a path
PathRemoveFileSpec	Removes the file specification from a path
PathRenameExtension	Changes the extension in a path
PathSearchAndQualify	Checks whether a path is correctly formatted and fully qualified
PathSetDlgItemPath	Sets the text of a control in the dialog box, using *PathCompactPath* to make the path fit
PathSkipRoot	Parses a path, ignoring the drive or UNC server/share parts
PathStripPath	Removes the leading part of a fully qualified path, leaving only the filename and extension
PathStripToRoot	Removes all parts of the path except the root
PathUndecorate	Removes annotations and attributes in square brackets from a path
PathUnExpandEnvStrings	Replaces the leading part of a path with an environment variable reference
PathUnmakeSystemFolder	Converts an existing system folder to a normal folder
PathUnquoteSpaces	Removes quotation marks surrounding a path
UrlApplyScheme	Analyzes a URL and applies the appropriate scheme prefix, such as *http://* or *file://*.
UrlCanonicalize	Converts a URL to canonical form by inserting escape sequences and removing redundancies
UrlCombine	Combines a relative URL and a base
UrlCompare	Checks whether two URLs are logically equal
UrlCreateFromPath	Converts a path to a canonical URL
UrlEscape	Replaces unsafe characters in a URL with the appropriate escape sequences
UrlEscapeSpaces	Replaces space characters in a URL with escape sequences
UrlGetLocation	Gets the location part of a URL, which starts with a ? or # character
UrlGetPart	Gets the specified part of a URL
UrlHash	Hashes a URL for storage in a buffer of specified size
UrlIs	Checks whether a URL is of a specified type
UrlIsFileUrl	Checks whether a URL refers to a file
UrlIsNoHistory	Checks for a "no history" URL
UrlIsOpaque	Checks for an "opaque" URL
UrlUnEscape	Replaces URL escape sequences with normal characters
UrlUnEscapeInPlace	Same as *UrlUnEscape* except that the source string is overwritten

String Comparison

Traditional C and C++ programs rely on the character encoding scheme (that is, on the values that represent the characters) to provide the proper ranking of text strings. Here's a typical implementation of *strcmp* using this technique:

```
int strcmp(char *pa, char *pb)
{
while(*pa && (*pa == *pb)) pa++, pb++;
return *pa - *pb;
}
```

The function returns a negative, zero, or positive result, indicating whether string A ranks below, the same as, or above string B. This return value is simply the difference between the first nonmatching character values in the two strings or zero if both strings are the same length and have all matching characters.

This technique rarely produces correct results in an international programming environment. For instance, the letters A through Z occupy code points 0x41 through 0x5A in the ANSI and Unicode character sets. The accented letters used in European languages are always above that range, even though they should usually be ranked near the unaccented form. For instance, it might be appropriate to rank the letters A, À, and Á as equal even though they have the values 0x41, 0xC0, and 0xC1.

The word counting example in Chapter 7 illustrated how to use the standard C and C++ collation services to compare strings according to the rules of the current locale. The equivalent Win32 service, *CompareString*, has the following protocol:

```
int CompareString
    (
    LCID Locale,       // Locale identifier
    DWORD dwCmpFlags,  // Comparison-style options
    LPCTSTR lpString1, // Pointer to first string
    int cchCount1,     // Size of first string (TCHARs)
    LPCTSTR lpString2, // Pointer to second string
    int cchCount2      // Size of second string (TCHARs)
    );
```

This function compares corresponding characters in the two strings, stopping at the first unequal pair or when one of the strings is exhausted. The two count arguments specify the string lengths in TCHAR units. Either count argument can be −1 to indicate that the corresponding string is null-terminated.

A return value of 0 indicates an error; one of the constants listed in Table 9-17 is returned if the function succeeds. You can map these constants to the traditional *strcmp* return values by subtracting the value 2. Also note that because

CompareString compares lexically, not physically, a *CSTR_EQUAL* return does not mean that the two strings are physically identical. They may, in fact, contain different characters. If you want to test for physical identity, use a memory comparison function such as *memcmp* from the standard C library.

Table 9-17. *CompareString* Return Values

Constant	Value	Description
CSTR_LESS_THAN	1	String 1 ranks below string 2.
CSTR_EQUAL	2	String 1 ranks the same as string 2.
CSTR_GREATER_THAN	3	String 1 ranks above string 2.

Table 9-18 lists the style flags that affect the comparison algorithm. Although the *NORM* flags are self-explanatory, they do have some nuances for specific locales. Consult the Microsoft Visual C++ documentation for *CompareString* if you don't get the expected result.

Table 9-18. Style Flags for *CompareString* Function

Flag	Description
NORM_IGNORECASE	Ignores case
NORM_IGNOREKANATYPE	Does not differentiate between Hiragana and Katakana characters—corresponding Hiragana and Katakana characters compare as equal
NORM_IGNORENONSPACE	Ignores nonspacing characters
NORM_IGNORESYMBOLS	Ignores symbols
NORM_IGNOREWIDTH	Does not differentiate between a single-byte character and the same character as a double-byte character
SORT_STRINGSORT	Treats punctuation the same as symbols

The *SORT_STRINGSORT* flag is useful in locales where the apostrophe and hyphen serve as intraword punctuation symbols. Without this flag, *CompareString* performs *word sort*, in which the apostrophe and hyphen are ignored. With the flag, the function performs a *string sort*, which treats the apostrophe and hyphen like any other punctuation character, ranking them before numbers and letters. Table 9-19 compares how several words are ranked using these two sorting techniques.

Table 9-19. Word and String Sorts

Word Sort	String Sort
billing	bill's
bills	billing
bill's	bills

The Win32 versions of *lstrcmp* and *lstrcmpi* functions in Table 9-14 call *CompareString* internally, using the word sorting technique—there is no way to make them perform a string sort. But be aware that in 16-bit versions of Windows, these functions did perform a string sort. This discrepancy can cause problems when you update an older Windows program to run in the 32-bit environment.

Character Classification

The standard C and C++ libraries contain many functions that classify characters. For instance, *isalpha* tests whether a character belongs to the alphabetic class, and *ispunct* tests for a punctuation character. Win32 combines all of these classification methods into a powerful function named *GetStringTypeEx*. This function is a refinement of the older *GetStringTypeA* and *GetStringTypeW* services, which could not be hidden behind a bimodal macro because of an unfortunate design error that caused them to require different arguments. *GetStringTypeEx* has the following definition:

```
BOOL GetStringTypeEx
    (
    LCID Locale,         // Locale identifier
    DWORD dwInfoType,    // Information type options
    LPCTSTR lpSrcStr,    // Pointer to source string
    int cchSrc,          // Size of source string (TCHARs)
    LPWORD lpCharType    // Pointer to buffer for output
    );
```

This function examines each character in the source string and stores a flag or code word in the output buffer. If *cchSrc* is −1, the scan stops at the null terminator of the source string; otherwise, it stops after processing the specified number of TCHARs.

If the scan is successful, the function returns a nonzero value. Unfortunately, this value is not the number of valid words in the output buffer, which you need in order to process the results. This is not a problem in an SBCS or a WCS situation, because the buffer contains one word for each TCHAR. But for MBCS, a character might require several bytes, and so the output buffer does not necessarily contain one word for each TCHAR. In that case, you need to use *MultiByteToWideChar* to measure the number of Unicode characters produced by converting the multibyte string. This is just another "gotcha" for MBCS programmers!

The LCID argument is used only for *GetStringTypeExA* to convert a multibyte string to Unicode.[7] The actual character tests are not locale-dependent because they use the character classifications defined in the Unicode standard. The tests are identified by the information type flags listed in Table 9-20. Currently you can request three kinds of classification information.

Table 9-20. Character Type Information Codes

Information Type	Description
CT_CTYPE1	Gets character type information
CT_CTYPE2	Gets bidirectional layout information
CT_CTYPE3	Gets text processing information

CT_CTYPE1 requests information corresponding to the traditional C classifications. For each character, the output buffer contains a 16-bit word using the flags shown in Table 9-21. Note that these are bit flags, and so several can be set in the same output word. For instance, *C1_ALPHA* often occurs with either *C1_LOWER* or *C1_UPPER*.

Table 9-21. Character Type 1 Information—Basic Classification Flags

Name	Value	Description
C1_UPPER	0x0001	Uppercase
C1_LOWER	0x0002	Lowercase
C1_DIGIT	0x0004	Decimal digit
C1_SPACE	0x0008	Space character
C1_PUNCT	0x0010	Punctuation
C1_CNTRL	0x0020	Control character
C1_BLANK	0x0040	Blank character
C1_XDIGIT	0x0080	Hexadecimal digit
C1_ALPHA	0x0100	Linguistic character: alphabetic, syllabary, or ideographic

---

7. Since *GetStringTypeExA* in effect calls *MultiByteToWideChar* internally, and since you need to call *MultiByteToWideChar* to determine the output buffer length, you can save time by performing the conversion yourself and then calling *GetStringTypeExW*.

CT_CTYPE2 requests information needed to lay out text in a bidirectional environment, such as one of the Arabic locales. For each character, the output buffer contains a 16-bit word using the codes shown in Table 9-22. These codes are mutually exclusive—that is, they are not bit flags.

Table 9-22. Character Type 2 Information—Bidirectional Classification Codes

Name	Value	Description
Strong		
C2_LEFTTORIGHT	0x0001	Left to right
C2_RIGHTTOLEFT	0x0002	Right to left
Weak		
C2_EUROPENUMBER	0x0003	European number, European digit
C2_EUROPESEPARATOR	0x0004	European numeric separator
C2_EUROPETERMINATOR	0x0005	European numeric terminator
C2_ARABICNUMBER	0x0006	Arabic number
C2_COMMONSEPARATOR	0x0007	Common numeric separator
Neutral		
C2_BLOCKSEPARATOR	0x0008	Block separator
C2_SEGMENTSEPARATOR	0x0009	Segment separator
C2_WHITESPACE	0x000A	White space
C2_OTHERNEUTRAL	0x000B	Other neutral layouts
Not applicable		
C2_NOTAPPLICABLE	0x0000	No implicit directionality (for example, control codes)

CT_CTYPE3 requests extended information corresponding to the character classifications defined by the POSIX programming community. For each character, the output buffer contains a 16-bit word using the flags shown in Table 9-23. As with the type 1 information, these are bit flags.

Table 9-23. Character Type 3 Information—Extended Classification Flags

Name	Value	Description
C3_NONSPACING	0x0001	Nonspacing mark
C3_DIACRITIC	0x0002	Diacritic nonspacing mark
C3_VOWELMARK	0x0004	Vowel nonspacing mark

Name	Value	Description
C3_SYMBOL	0x0008	Symbol
C3_KATAKANA	0x0010	Katakana character
C3_HIRAGANA	0x0020	Hiragana character
C3_HALFWIDTH	0x0040	Half-width character
C3_FULLWIDTH	0x0080	Full-width character
C3_IDEOGRAPH	0x0100	Ideographic character
C3_KASHIDA	0x0200	Arabic Kashida character
C3_LEXICAL	0x0400	Punctuation that is counted as part of the word (Kashida, hyphen, feminine/masculine ordinal indicators, equal sign, and so forth)
C3_ALPHA	0x8000	All linguistic characters (alphabetic, syllabary, and ideographic)
C3_NOTAPPLICABLE	0x0000	Not applicable

String Conversion

Chapter 8 showed how to convert SBCS/MBCS (ANSI) strings to WCS (Unicode) and vice versa by calling *MultiByteToWideChar* and *WideCharToMultiByte*. In addition to those relatively simple conversions, Win32 includes two other string conversion functions, *LCMapString* and *FoldString*.

Using *LCMapString*

LCMapString performs a wide variety of string operations, including case conversion, byte swapping, sort key generation, and display width homogenization. The winnls.h header file defines the *LCMapString* function as follows:

```
int LCMapString
    (
    LCID Locale,         // Locale identifier
    DWORD dwMapFlags,    // Mapping flags
    LPCTSTR lpSrcStr,    // Address of source string
    int cchSrc,          // Number of TCHARs in source string
    LPTSTR lpDestStr,    // Address of destination buffer
    int cchDest          // Size of destination buffer
    );
```

In general, this function scans the characters in the source string and produces either a transformed string or a sort key in the output buffer. If the output is a transformation of the source, both strings use the same character encoding, either ANSI or Unicode, with the ANSI code page determined by the specified LCID. If the output is a sort key, it is always a null-terminated byte string even if the source string is Unicode.

The *LCMapString* function processes the number of TCHARs specified by *cchSrc*. If that value is −1, the function stops at the source string's null terminator. The return value is the number of TCHARs or sort key bytes that were placed in the output buffer. If the buffer is too small, the function fails and returns 0. If *cchDest* is 0, the function ignores the output buffer pointer and returns the required buffer size in TCHARs or sort key bytes. This enables you to dynamically allocate a buffer of exactly the right size.

The *dwMapFlags* argument specifies the type of mapping to be applied to the source string. It can contain ORed combinations of the values listed in Table 9-24. This is a complicated function, so be sure to examine the Win32 documentation before using it, especially if you are combining flags. Many combinations are not allowed. Next I'll explain one of the more common uses— namely, generating sort keys.

Table 9-24. Mapping Flags for *LCMapString*

Flag	*Description*
LCMAP_BYTEREV	Reverses bytes so that, for example, 0x1234 becomes 0x3412; primarily useful for adjusting Unicode strings being interchanged between big endian and little endian systems
LCMAP_FULLWIDTH	Maps narrow display characters to wide display characters
LCMAP_HALFWIDTH	Maps wide display characters to narrow display characters where possible
LCMAP_HIRAGANA	Maps Katakana characters to Hiragana
LCMAP_KATAKANA	Maps Hiragana characters to Katakana where possible
LCMAP_LINGUISTIC_CASING	Uses linguistic case rules rather than file system rules; valid only with LCMAP_LOWERCASE or LCMAP_UPPERCASE
LCMAP_LOWERCASE	Maps uppercase to lowercase
LCMAP_SIMPLIFIED_CHINESE	Maps traditional to simplified Chinese
LCMAP_SORTKEY	Produces a sort key
LCMAP_TRADITIONAL_CHINESE	Maps simplified to traditional Chinese
LCMAP_UPPERCASE	Maps lowercase to uppercase
NORM_IGNORECASE	Ignores case
NORM_IGNOREKANATYPE	Does not distinguish between Hiragana and Katakana characters
NORM_IGNORENONSPACE	Ignores nonspacing accent characters
NORM_IGNORESYMBOLS	Ignores symbol characters

Flag	Description
NORM_IGNOREWIDTH	Does not distinguish between the single-byte and double-byte representation of the same character
SORT_STRINGSORT	Treats intraword punctuation the same as other symbols

When you need to sort a large number of strings, *CompareString* can become a performance bottleneck because it will repeatedly convert the strings to sort keys in order to perform its locale-sensitive comparison. You can save time by performing this conversion once and saving the keys. Then you can use a simple comparison routine such as *strcmp* to compare the keys.

LCMapString generates a sort key by mapping an ANSI or Unicode source string into a null-terminated array of unsigned characters (bytes). The sort key is not really a displayable character string because its bytes do not correspond to any particular code page. Nonetheless, it accurately reflects the sorting weights of the characters in the original string.

You don't really need to know the structure of sort keys in order to use them, but since this is an interesting (and powerful) Win32 feature, I'll delve into some of the details. To assist in this exploration, I wrote a little dialog program that accepts an input string and displays the corresponding sort key in hexadecimal. Figure 9-12 shows the output of this sort key browser after producing a key for the vowels A, E, I, O, and U in the unaccented form followed by the grave and acute accented forms. Listing 9-9 shows the *OnTransform* function that does the mapping when the user clicks the Transform button. This event handler calls *LCMapString* twice, first to get the required length of the output buffer and then again to actually generate the sort key.

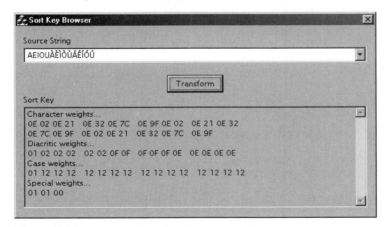

Figure 9-12. *Output of sort key browser.*

```
void CSortKeyDlg::OnTransform()
{
static LPTSTR parts[] =                      // Key part names.
    {
    _T("Character weights...\r\n"),
    _T("\r\nDiacritic weights...\r\n"),
    _T("\r\nCase weights...\r\n"),
    _T("\r\nSpecial weights...\r\n"),
    0
    };
if(!UpdateData(TRUE)) return;                // Update members from dialog.
int i, j, k, n;                             // Miscellaneous

// Allocate key buffer.
BYTE* pKey;
n = LCMapString
    (
    LOCALE_USER_DEFAULT,                     // LCID
    LCMAP_SORTKEY,                           // Mapping flags
    m_sInput, -1,                            // Source string and length
    0, 0                                     // No buffer yet
    );
if(n <= 0)
    {
    LPTSTR pMsg;
    FormatMessage
        (
        FORMAT_MESSAGE_ALLOCATE_BUFFER |
        FORMAT_MESSAGE_FROM_SYSTEM |
        FORMAT_MESSAGE_IGNORE_INSERTS,
        NULL,
        GetLastError(),
        MAKELANGID(LANG_NEUTRAL, SUBLANG_DEFAULT),
        (LPTSTR)&pMsg,
        0,
        0
        );
    AfxMessageBox(pMsg, MB_OK | MB_ICONINFORMATION);
    LocalFree(pMsg);
    return;
    }
pKey = new BYTE[n];

// Map the string.
n = LCMapString
    (
    LOCALE_USER_DEFAULT,                     // LCID
```

Listing 9-9. *Transforming strings to sort keys.*

```
      LCMAP_SORTKEY,                  // Mapping flags
      m_sInput, -1,                   // Source string and length
      (LPTSTR)pKey, n                 // Output buffer and length
      );

// Convert key to displayable string.
m_sOutput.Empty();
for(i = j = k = 0; i < n; i++, j++)
    {
    if((i == 0) || (pKey[i] == 0x01))
        {
        m_sOutput += parts[k++];
        j = 0;
        }
    if(j)
        {
        if(!(j & 15)) m_sOutput += _T("\r\n");
        else if(!(j & 3)) m_sOutput += _T("  ");
        }
    TCHAR b[4];
    wsprintf(b, _T("%02X "), pKey[i]);
    m_sOutput += b;
    }
delete pKey;
UpdateData(FALSE);
}
```

My browser displays the sort key as a sequence of bytes in hexadecimal, with a title before each part. The parts are separated by bytes containing the value 1, and the key is terminated by a zero byte. If you call *LCMapString* with just the *LCMAP_SORTKEY* flag as I did in this example, the function produces a key containing a character part, a diacritics (accents) part, and a case part. Some locales might produce one or two additional parts to meet their own particular needs.

The first part of the key contains 16-bit character collation codes with their bytes swapped to facilitate byte-by-byte comparison. These codes ignore diacritical marks, which is why all three forms of A have the byte sequence 0E 02. The second part of the key covers diacritical, or accent, differences. The unaccented letters all have code 02, while the grave and acute accents produce codes of 0F and 0E, respectively. The third part handles case differences. In this situation, all letters are uppercase, which is denoted by code 12. This example has no extra parts, although the 01 codes are still present before the terminator.

You probably need to pore over Figure 9-12 for a while to understand how this type of key works in string comparisons. In effect, the key breaks the comparison operation into three phases. First it ranks the characters without regard to their accents. If the strings are equal after that ranking, the key then ranks them according to their diacritical marks. If they are still equal at that point, the key finally ranks them by case.

Using *FoldString*

FoldString is a string conversion function for Windows NT and Windows 2000 that is similar to *LCMapString* but has some different options and a simpler calling sequence, as shown here:

```
int FoldString
    (
    DWORD dwMapFlags,    // Mapping options
    LPCTSTR lpSrcStr,    // Source string
    int cchSrc,          // Source string size in TCHARs
    LPTSTR lpDestStr,    // Destination buffer
    int cchDest          // Destination buffer size in TCHARs
    );
```

The source string length in *cchSrc* can be −1, indicating that the string has a null terminator. The function returns the number of TCHARs it placed in the output buffer, or 0 if the buffer is too small or some other problem occurred. If you specify a *cchDest* value of 0, the return value specifies the number of TCHARs required for the output buffer.

Notice that *FoldString* does not accept an LCID argument. If you call the ANSI version, *FoldStringA*, it uses the ANSI code page associated with the current locale. Since this function is available only in Windows NT and Windows 2000, you will most often call it to process Unicode strings.

Table 9-25 describes the mapping flags you can specify in the *dwMapFlags* argument. Except for *MAP_FOLDCZONE*, these flags are for the most part self-explanatory. The Unicode compatibility zone covers the code points U+F900 through U+FFEF. This range contains special forms of characters that are defined in other ranges. For instance, the range U+F900 through U+FAFF encodes CJK ideographs that represent different pronunciations of ideographs in the standard CJK range. This technique facilitates round-trip mapping between Unicode and MBCS encodings that assign different codes to the different pronunciations. When you want to process Unicode characters without regard to pronunciation, *MAP_FOLDCZONE* can be used to ensure that each character has one and only one code point. This is a one-way process, since several compatibility codes might map to the same standard code.

Table 9-25. **Mapping Flags for *FoldString***

Flag	*Description*
MAP_FOLDCZONE	Maps characters from the Unicode compatibility zone to their normal Unicode equivalents
MAP_FOLDDIGITS	Maps localized digits to the Unicode characters 0 through 9
MAP_PRECOMPOSED	Maps each base and accent pair to a single precomposed character; cannot be combined with *MAP_COMPOSITE*
MAP_COMPOSITE	Maps each precomposed character to a separate base and accent character; cannot be combined with *MAP_PRECOMPOSED*
MAP_EXPAND_LIGATURES	Maps each ligature character to separate characters— for example, the ligature æ expands to the two characters *a* and *e*; cannot be combined with *MAP_ PRECOMPOSED* or *MAP_COMPOSITE*

LOCALE-SENSITIVE RESOURCES

Well-designed Windows applications separate their "look and feel" into distinct pieces. The "look" consists of dialog boxes, menus, toolbars, text strings, and other visible artifacts that are stored in a resource database. The "feel" is defined by the program logic that manipulates these resources. Keeping these pieces separate enables programmers to concentrate on what they do best, leaving professional UI artists relatively free to design an attractive product.

A resource database is typically specified by a simple script produced with a visual editor such as the dialog, menu, and toolbar editors built into Microsoft Visual Studio. The resource compiler then processes the script file, which is also called the RC file because of its normal extension, to produce a binary file having a RES extension. The individual resource items are identified by integers.[8]

An application programmer can choose to attach the RES file to the program's executable image (an EXE or DLL file) or to ship it separately. In the latter case, the RES file is converted into a DLL that the application dynamically loads when it needs to access the resources.

Win32 resource databases can be subdivided into language-dependent sections. For instance, an RC file can define a string resource in English, French, and German. When the program requests that string by its number, Win32 returns the appropriate version based on the current locale.

---

8. Although some resource types allow string identifiers instead of numbers, this feature is seldom used.

Although multilingual resources are convenient for the programmer, they can be difficult to manage. For example, if the UI artists are scattered throughout the world, they might have trouble coordinating their work on the same multilingual database. Furthermore, if the UI has many design elements or supports a lot of languages, the program's memory footprint will become too large when it loads the multilingual resource database. You can solve these problems by physically dividing the database into DLLs, with one DLL for each language or language group. The program then loads the appropriate DLL when the locale changes. Let's examine both techniques in more detail.

Multilingual Resources

Listing 9-10 shows a simple multilingual resource script (an RC file) that defines three strings *(English*, *French*, and *German)* using the same resource identifier, *IDS_HelloWorld*, which is defined as the value 100 in the resource.h header file. I can use the same identifier because each string is placed in a different language section of the resource database, using the *LANGUAGE* keyword. The *pragma* statements specify the code pages that the resource compiler should use to convert the string into Unicode. Since I used the Windows default page (CP1252), I could have omitted the *pragma* statements or could have used a single *pragma* statement at the beginning of the resource script.

```
#include <winnt.h>
#include "resource.h"

LANGUAGE LANG_ENGLISH, SUBLANG_ENGLISH_US
#pragma code_page(1252)
STRINGTABLE DISCARDABLE
    BEGIN
    IDS_HelloWorld "English"
    END

LANGUAGE LANG_FRENCH, SUBLANG_FRENCH
#pragma code_page(1252)
STRINGTABLE DISCARDABLE
    BEGIN
    IDS_HelloWorld "French"
    END

LANGUAGE LANG_GERMAN, SUBLANG_GERMAN
#pragma code_page(1252)
STRINGTABLE DISCARDABLE
    BEGIN
    IDS_HelloWorld "German"
    END
```

Listing 9-10. *Multilingual resource script.*

Listing 9-11 shows how to use the multilingual resource. This console program[9] accepts an LCID from the console keyboard, validates it, sets the thread locale, and fetches the string *IDS_HelloWorld* from the resource database. The special LCID codes 0 and −1 represent the default user locale and the default system locale.

```c
#include <stdio.h>
#include <stdlib.h>
#include <tchar.h>

#define WIN32_LEAN_AND_MEAN     // Excludes GUI stuff
#include <windows.h>

#include "resource.h"

void _tmain()
{
HMODULE hModule = GetModuleHandle(0);
LCID lcidDefault = GetThreadLocale();
while(1)
    {
    TCHAR b[100];
    LPTSTR p;
    _tprintf
        (_T("\nEnter an LCID (use 0x in front of hexadecimal) ==> "));
    if(!_getts(b)) break;
    LCID lcid = _tcstol(b, &p, 0);
    if(lcid == 0) lcid = lcidDefault;
    if(lcid == -1) lcid = MAKELCID(LANG_USER_DEFAULT, SORT_DEFAULT);
    else if(lcid == -2)
        lcid = MAKELCID(LANG_SYSTEM_DEFAULT, SORT_DEFAULT);
    else if(!IsValidLocale(lcid, LCID_INSTALLED))
        {
        _tprintf(_T("LCID 0x%08X is not available\n"), lcid);
        continue;
        }
    SetThreadLocale(lcid);
    int ret = LoadString(hModule, IDS_HelloWorld, b,
                    sizeof(b)/sizeof(TCHAR));
    if(ret <= 0)
        _tprintf(_T("LCID 0x%08X: Cannot find resource\n"), lcid);
    else _tprintf(_T("LCID %08X \"%s\"\n"), lcid, b);
    SetThreadLocale(lcidDefault);
    }
}
```

Listing 9-11. *Using a multilingual resource.*

---

9. Some programmers are surprised that you can use resources with console programs, since resources are normally associated with Windows programs.

Figure 9-13 shows the program input and output. Notice that LCIDs 0x409, 0x407, and 0x40C use the English, German, and French resources as expected. Both the user and system locales use English resources because my system defaults to LCID 0x409. For any LCID that isn't explicitly specified as a resource section, the *LoadString* function uses the default system LCID. If the default system LCID doesn't correspond to a resource *LANGUAGE* section, *LoadString* accesses the first section.

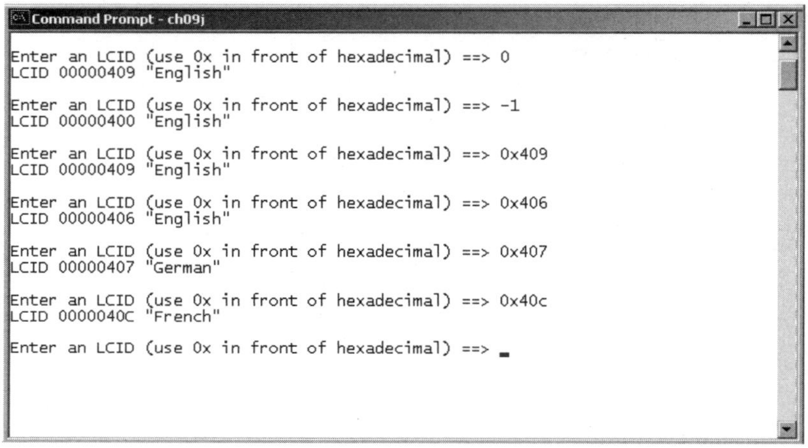

```
Command Prompt - ch09j                                          _ □ X
Enter an LCID (use 0x in front of hexadecimal) ==> 0
LCID 00000409 "English"

Enter an LCID (use 0x in front of hexadecimal) ==> -1
LCID 00000400 "English"

Enter an LCID (use 0x in front of hexadecimal) ==> 0x409
LCID 00000409 "English"

Enter an LCID (use 0x in front of hexadecimal) ==> 0x406
LCID 00000406 "English"

Enter an LCID (use 0x in front of hexadecimal) ==> 0x407
LCID 00000407 "German"

Enter an LCID (use 0x in front of hexadecimal) ==> 0x40c
LCID 0000040C "French"

Enter an LCID (use 0x in front of hexadecimal) ==> _
```

Figure 9-13. *Output of multilingual resource program.*

DLL-Based Resources

Multilingual resources are easy to build and maintain in the Visual C++ environment because the resource editors are fully aware of the *LANGUAGE* statement. Nonetheless, many programmers prefer to place the resources for each language or language group into a separate DLL. This technique can simplify project management when the UI artists and translators are not located in the same office, since each one can then work independently on his or her DLL.

Producing a resource DLL is pretty simple with Visual C++. You create an empty DLL project, add the RC file and related resource files to the project, and adjust the linker settings to include the /NOENTRY option. This adjustment causes the DLL to be built with no entry point and no default startup code.

Listing 9-12 shows how to use resource DLLs instead of multilingual resources. The main program is produced by the Ch09k project on the companion CD, and I created two related DLL projects named Ch09k_0407 and Ch09k_ 040C to contain the German and French resources. In each DLL project, I adjusted the linker settings to include the /NOENTRY option and to place the DLL file in the same directory as the main program.

```
#include <stdio.h>
#include <stdlib.h>
#include <tchar.h>

#define WIN32_LEAN_AND_MEAN      // Excludes GUI stuff
#include <windows.h>

#include "resource.h"

void _tmain()
{
TCHAR fmt[] = _T("ch09k_%04x.dll");
TCHAR name[MAX_PATH];

HMODULE hModule = GetModuleHandle(0);
LCID lcidDefault = GetThreadLocale();
while(1)
    {
    TCHAR b[100];
    LPTSTR p;
    _tprintf
        (_T("\nEnter an LCID (use 0x in front of hexadecimal) ==> "));
    if(!_getts(b)) break;
    LCID lcid = _tcstol(b, &p, 0);
    if(lcid == 0) lcid = lcidDefault;
    if(lcid == -1) lcid = MAKELCID(LANG_USER_DEFAULT, SORT_DEFAULT);
    else if(lcid == -2)
        lcid = MAKELCID(LANG_SYSTEM_DEFAULT, SORT_DEFAULT);
    else if(!IsValidLocale(lcid, LCID_INSTALLED))
        {
        _tprintf(_T("LCID 0x%08X is not available\n"), lcid);
        continue;
        }
    LANGID lang = LANGIDFROMLCID(lcid);
    _stprintf(name, fmt, lang);
    HMODULE hRes = LoadLibraryEx(name, 0, LOAD_LIBRARY_AS_DATAFILE);
    if(!hRes) hRes = hModule;
    SetThreadLocale(lcid);
    int ret = LoadString(hRes, IDS_HelloWorld, b,
                         sizeof(b)/sizeof(TCHAR));
    if(ret <= 0)
        _tprintf(_T("LCID 0x%08X: Cannot find resource\n"), lcid);
    else _tprintf(_T("LCID %08X \"%s\"\n"), lcid, b);
    SetThreadLocale(lcidDefault);
    if(hRes != hModule) FreeLibrary(hRes);
    }
}
```

Listing 9-12. *Using resource DLLs.*

Notice that when you use resource DLLs, you should adopt some file naming convention. Here I just appended the LANGID (in hexadecimal) to the *ch09k_* prefix. Another popular approach is to use three-character ISO language abbreviations such as "deu" and "fra" in place of the "dll" extension.

Also note that the resource DLLs must be in a place where the *LoadLibraryEx* function can find them. The easiest approach is to place these DLLs in the same directory as the executable. It's usually not a good idea to put them in the Windows system directory or to reference them with an absolute path.

I kept the English resources in the main executable to serve as the default. This isn't necessary as long as you make sure that one of the resource DLLs is always loaded. In fact, if the program requires many resource items, you can reduce the memory requirements by not binding a default resource to the executable. In other words, when this sample program runs in France, the English resources are loaded but not used.

This example uses *_stprintf* to build the DLL file name by appending the hexadecimal LANGID to the file name prefix. Then it calls *LoadLibraryEx* to fetch the DLL as a data file. If this calling succeeds, the function returns a module handle, which can then be used with the various resource access functions.[10] When the program is finished with the DLL, the program calls *FreeLibrary* to release it.

Message Resources

Win32 API functions generally report errors by returning 32-bit codes. The *FormatMessage* API function converts error codes into localized messages for display to the user. The Win32 messages are stored in multilingual resources attached to the various system components or in system resource DLLs. You can use the same technique to enhance your program with a repertoire of 32-bit codes and their corresponding localized messages.

First you must understand how Win32 partitions the 32-bit message code spectrum. Table 9-26 shows the fields that comprise a message code. Programmers often test the sign bit to determine success or failure, with a negative value representing failure. If you use signed integer tests on error codes, be sure to define or cast these codes as *LONG* rather than *DWORD*, because the latter is an unsigned integer.

---

10. Windows NT and Windows 2000 can access any resource item using the DLL module handle, but Windows 95 and Windows 98 restrict you to a subset of the resource API. It requires more effort to access some resource types in these systems. See the Win32 SDK documentation for more details about this difference.

Table 9-26. **Message Code Fields**

Bits	Meaning
31 – 30	00 for success 01 for information 10 for warning 11 for failure
29 – 28	Must be 0
27 – 16	Facility code; the values from 0 through 255 (0x000 through 0x0FF) are reserved for the system; values from 256 through 4095 (0x100 through 0xFFF) are for application usage
15 – 0	Message number, relative to the facility

You use the message compiler (MC) to define a repertoire of message codes and their localized strings. This compiler is a Visual Studio utility program that you normally integrate into a project as an early step similar to the resource compiler. MC accepts a message script file and produces several output files: a single header file with an .H extension, a binary file with a .BIN extension for each language, and a single resource script file with an .RC extension. The H file contains *#define* symbols for the message codes. The BIN files contain the tables that correlate message codes to text strings for the various languages. The RC file can be included in your project if you want a multilingual message resource. Otherwise, you can build a resource DLL for each BIN file.

Listing 9-13 shows a simple message script that defines three codes and their messages in English and French. I won't provide a detailed explanation of the MC script syntax. You can obtain that information from the Win32 SDK, which provides the complete MC source code as well as several sample programs. Clearly the script defines each message code in terms of its three components, using the tags *MessageId*, *Severity*, and *Facility*. The *SymbolicName* specifies the *#define* symbol that programmers will use for the code. The remainder of each message definition consists of the *Language* tag followed by a multiline message. A line containing nothing but a period ends the message.

```
MessageIdTypedef=LONG

SeverityNames=(Success=0x0:STATUS_SEVERITY_SUCCESS
              Informational=0x1:STATUS_SEVERITY_INFORMATIONAL
              Warning=0x2:STATUS_SEVERITY_WARNING
              Error=0x3:STATUS_SEVERITY_ERROR
              )
```

Listing 9-13. *Message script file.*

(continued)

Listing 9-13. *continued*

```
FacilityNames=(MyApp=0x100:FACILITY_MYAPP)

LanguageNames=(English=0x409:MSG00409)
LanguageNames=(French=0x40C:MSG0040C)

MessageId=0x1
Severity=Error
Facility=MyApp
SymbolicName=MSG_BAD_COMMAND
Language=English
You have chosen an incorrect command.
.

Language=French
Vous avez choisi un ordre inexact.
.

MessageId=0x2
Severity=Warning
Facility=MyApp
SymbolicName=MSG_BAD_BREATH
Language=English
Please use mouthwash.
.

Language=French
S'il vous plaît utilisez le bain de bouche.
.

MessageId=0x3
Severity=Success
Facility=MyApp
SymbolicName=MSG_NO_BANANAS
Language=English
Yes, we have no bananas.
.

Language=French
Oui, nous n'avons pas de bananes.
.
```

Listing 9-14 shows the header file produced by the message compiler, and Listing 9-15 shows the RC file. Notice that a message resource is item 1 in resource category 11.

```
#define FACILITY_MYAPP                   0x100

#define STATUS_SEVERITY_WARNING          0x2
#define STATUS_SEVERITY_SUCCESS          0x0
#define STATUS_SEVERITY_INFORMATIONAL    0x1
```

Listing 9-14. *Header file from the message compiler.*

```
#define STATUS_SEVERITY_ERROR          0x3
#define MSG_BAD_COMMAND                ((LONG)0xC1000001L)
#define MSG_BAD_BREATH                 ((LONG)0x81000002L)
#define MSG_NO_BANANAS                 ((LONG)0x01000003L)
LANGUAGE 0xc, 0x1
1 11 MSG0040C.bin
LANGUAGE 0x9, 0x1
1 11 MSG00409.bin
```

Listing 9-15. *Resource script file from the message compiler.*

Listing 9-16 is a simple program that displays the message identified as MSG_BAD_COMMAND, and Figure 9-14 shows the program output. Notice that *FormatMessage*, unlike *LoadString*, does not choose a default language if it fails to find a message resource for the specified language. You have to supply that logic. In this example, I generated the string *Cannot find message* in that case, but it's usually better to generate the actual message in a default language.

```c
#include <stdio.h>
#include <stdlib.h>
#include <tchar.h>

#define WIN32_LEAN_AND_MEAN      // Excludes GUI stuff
#include <windows.h>

#include "messages.h"

void _tmain()
{
DWORD code = MSG_BAD_COMMAND;
LCID lcidDefault = GetThreadLocale();
while(1)
    {
    TCHAR b[100];
    LPTSTR p;
    _tprintf(
        _T("\nEnter an LCID (use 0x in front of hexadecimal) ==> "));
    if(!_getts(b)) break;
    LCID lcid = _tcstol(b, &p, 0);
    if(lcid == 0) lcid = lcidDefault;
    if(lcid == -1) lcid = MAKELCID(LANG_USER_DEFAULT, SORT_DEFAULT);
    else if(lcid == -2) lcid = MAKELCID(LANG_SYSTEM_DEFAULT,
                                        SORT_DEFAULT);
    else if(!IsValidLocale(lcid, LCID_INSTALLED))
```

Listing 9-16. *Program that uses custom message resources.*   *(continued)*

Listing 9-16. *continued*

```
        {
        _tprintf(_T("LCID 0x%08X is not available\n"), lcid);
        continue;
        }
    LANGID lang = LANGIDFROMLCID(lcid);
    BOOL bSuccess = FormatMessage
        (
        FORMAT_MESSAGE_FROM_HMODULE |        // Gets message from
                                             // EXE or DLL.
        FORMAT_MESSAGE_ALLOCATE_BUFFER,      // Allocates a buffer.
        0,                                   // Uses this EXE.
        code,                                // Message number
        lang,                                // Language
        (LPTSTR)&p,                          // Message text
        100,                                 // Number of TCHARs
        0                                    // No insertion strings
        );
    if (!bSuccess)
        _tprintf(_T("LCID 0x%08X: Cannot find message\n"), lcid);
    else
        {
        _tprintf(_T("CODE 0x%08X  LCID %08X %s\n"), code, lcid, p);
        LocalFree((HLOCAL)p);
        }
    }
}
```

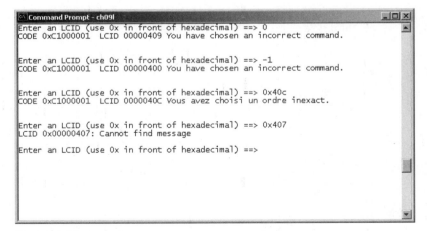

Figure 9-14. *Output of message resource sample program.*

DESIGNING A LOCALE BROWSER

Although you can inspect the Win32 locale database through the Regional Settings applet in the Control Panel, I found that the applet didn't show all of the items in a programmer-friendly form. So I decided this chapter wouldn't be complete unless I designed a locale database browser as a handy programming utility.

Like Windows Explorer, my locale browser has a tree view in the left pane and a list view in the right pane. The MFC Application Wizard produces this two-pane framework when you specify a document/view project with the Windows Explorer style. I then augmented the framework by adding a tab control at the top of the list view, thereby enabling the user to switch between the basic locale item list and one or more additional list views displaying calendar items. Figures 9-15 and 9-16 show the two list views for LCID 0x409, the United States.

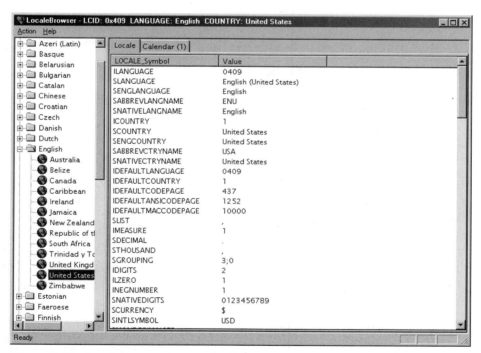

Figure 9-15. *Locale browser showing locale item view.*

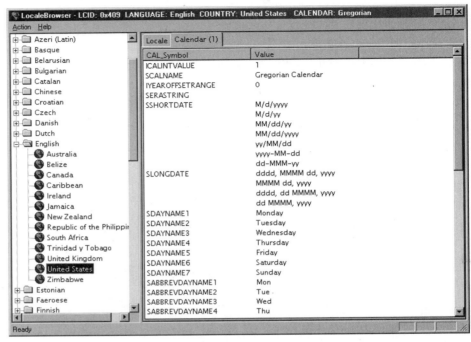

Figure 9-16. *Locale browser showing calendar item view.*

Listings 9-17 and 9-18 show the tree view class declaration and implementation. Much of this code is boilerplate, such as the *PreCreateWindow* function, which initializes the tree to display expansion buttons and to draw lines connecting the nodes. *OnInitialUpdate* completes the initialization by first loading the images that are displayed at the left of the tree nodes and then calling *LoadLocaleTree* to populate the tree.

```
class ClcTreeView : public CTreeView
{
public:
    static ClcTreeView* m_pThis;      // Used by callback functions
    int m_nNodes;                     // Number of nodes
    CImageList m_Images;              // Bitmaps for LCID nodes
    CFont m_Font;                     // Tree font

    int ClcTreeView::LoadLocaleTree(DWORD mode);
    BOOL cbLoadLocaleTree(LPTSTR pLCID);
    void OnChooseTreeFont();

    class ClcDoc* GetDocument();
    virtual ~ClcTreeView();
```

Listing 9-17. *Locale browser—tree view class declaration.*

```
    #ifdef _DEBUG
    virtual void AssertValid() const;
    virtual void Dump(CDumpContext& dc) const;
    #endif

protected:
    ClcTreeView();
    DECLARE_DYNCREATE(ClcTreeView)

    //{{AFX_MSG(ClcTreeView)
    afx_msg void OnTreeItemExpanded(NMHDR* pNMHDR, LRESULT* pResult);
    afx_msg void OnTreeSelChanged(NMHDR* pNMHDR, LRESULT* pResult);
    //}}AFX_MSG
    DECLARE_MESSAGE_MAP()

    //{{AFX_VIRTUAL(ClcTreeView)
    public:
    virtual void OnDraw(CDC* pDC);
    virtual BOOL PreCreateWindow(CREATESTRUCT& cs);
    protected:
    virtual void OnInitialUpdate();
    //}}AFX_VIRTUAL
};

#ifndef _DEBUG  // Debug version in lcTreeView.cpp
inline ClcDoc* ClcTreeView::GetDocument()
    { return (ClcDoc*)m_pDocument; }
#endif
```

```
//============================================================
// The tree view displays the LCIDs in a user friendly way.
//
//============================================================
IMPLEMENT_DYNCREATE(ClcTreeView, CTreeView)

BEGIN_MESSAGE_MAP(ClcTreeView, CTreeView)
    //{{AFX_MSG_MAP(ClcTreeView)
    ON_NOTIFY_REFLECT(TVN_ITEMEXPANDED, OnTreeItemExpanded)
    ON_NOTIFY_REFLECT(TVN_SELCHANGED, OnTreeSelChanged)
    //}}AFX_MSG_MAP
END_MESSAGE_MAP()
//============================================================
//
// Construction, destruction, and dummy draw function
//
//============================================================
```

Listing 9-18. *Locale browser—tree view class implementation.* (continued)

Listing 9-18. *continued*

```
cTreeView::ClcTreeView()
{
}


ClcTreeView::~ClcTreeView()
{
}

BOOL ClcTreeView::PreCreateWindow(CREATESTRUCT& cs)
{
cs.style |= TVS_HASLINES | TVS_HASBUTTONS | TVS_LINESATROOT;
return CTreeView::PreCreateWindow(cs);
}

void ClcTreeView::OnDraw(CDC* pDC)
{
}
//=============================================================
//
// Diagnostics
//
//=============================================================
#ifdef _DEBUG
void ClcTreeView::AssertValid() const
{
CTreeView::AssertValid();
}

void ClcTreeView::Dump(CDumpContext& dc) const
{
CTreeView::Dump(dc);
}

ClcDoc* ClcTreeView::GetDocument() // Non-debug version is inline.
{
ASSERT(m_pDocument->IsKindOf(RUNTIME_CLASS(ClcDoc)));
return (ClcDoc*)m_pDocument;
}
#endif //_DEBUG
//=============================================================
//
// Initialization
//
//=============================================================
void ClcTreeView::OnInitialUpdate()
{
CTreeView::OnInitialUpdate();
#ifdef UNICODE
```

```
TCHAR FontName[] = _T("Lucida Sans Unicode");
#else
TCHAR FontName[] = _T("Lucida Sans");
#endif
ASSERT(m_Font.CreatePointFont(90, FontName));
SetFont(&m_Font);

m_Images.Create(16, 16, ILC_COLOR | ILC_MASK, 0, 8);
m_Images.Add(AfxGetApp()->LoadIcon(IDI_FolderClosed));
m_Images.Add(AfxGetApp()->LoadIcon(IDI_FolderOpen));
m_Images.Add(AfxGetApp()->LoadIcon(IDI_Earth));
GetTreeCtrl().SetImageList(&m_Images, TVSIL_NORMAL);
LoadLocaleTree(LCID_INSTALLED | LCID_ALTERNATE_SORTS);
}
//================================================================
//
// Load the locale tree with LANGID at level 0, SUBLANGID at
// level 1, and SORTID at level 2. Level 2 is present only for
// locales having alternate sorting algorithms.
//
//================================================================

// The callback function delegates to ClcTreeView::cbLoadLocaleTree
// via static pointer. This is necessary because EnumSystemLocales
// does not pass a DWORD of caller data like other enumerators. This
// technique is not thread safe because of the shared pointer,
// but it's not an issue in this program.
ClcTreeView* ClcTreeView::m_pThis = 0;
static BOOL CALLBACK cbEnumSystemLocales(LPTSTR p)
{
return ClcTreeView::m_pThis->cbLoadLocaleTree(p);
}

// Add one LCID to the tree, consisting of nodes
// at levels 0 and 1, plus a node at level 2 if the
// LCID has a non-zero SORTID.
BOOL ClcTreeView::cbLoadLocaleTree(LPTSTR pLCID)
{
LPTSTR pEnd;
LCID lcid = _tcstoul(pLCID, &pEnd, 16);
if(*pEnd) return FALSE;

LANGID lgid = LANGIDFROMLCID(lcid);
WORD Lang = PRIMARYLANGID(lgid);
WORD SubLang = SUBLANGID(lgid);
WORD SortType = SORTIDFROMLCID(lcid);
WORD SortVersion = SORTVERSIONFROMLCID(lcid);
TCHAR b[128];
CString sLang, sSubLang, sSort;
```

(continued)

Listing 9-18. *continued*

```
if(!GetLocaleInfo(lcid, LOCALE_SENGLANGUAGE, b, 128))
    return FALSE;
sLang = b;
if(!GetLocaleInfo(lcid, LOCALE_SENGCOUNTRY, b, 128))
    return FALSE;
sSubLang = b;

if(!GetLocaleInfo(lcid, LOCALE_SSORTNAME, b, 128))
    sSort.Format(_T("Sort #%d"), SortType);
else sSort = b;

CString sNode, sSubNode;
HTREEITEM hNode, hSubNode, hSortNode, hItem;
hNode = GetTreeCtrl().GetRootItem();
while(hNode)
    {
    sNode = GetTreeCtrl().GetItemText(hNode);
    if(!sLang.Compare(sNode))
        {
        HTREEITEM hSubNode = GetTreeCtrl().GetChildItem(hNode);
        while(hSubNode)
            {
            sSubNode = GetTreeCtrl().GetItemText(hSubNode);
            if(!sSubLang.Compare(sSubNode))
                {
                hSortNode = GetTreeCtrl().InsertItem(sSort,
                                                     hSubNode);
                hItem = hSortNode;
                break;
                }
            hSubNode = GetTreeCtrl().GetNextSiblingItem(hSubNode);
            }
        if(!hSubNode)
            {
            hSubNode = GetTreeCtrl().InsertItem(sSubLang,
                                                0, 0, hNode);
            if(SortType)
                {
                hSortNode = GetTreeCtrl().InsertItem(sSort, hSubNode);

                hItem = hSortNode;
                }
            else hItem = hSubNode;
            }
        break;
        }
    hNode = GetTreeCtrl().GetNextSiblingItem(hNode);
    }
```

```
if(!hNode)
    {
    hNode = GetTreeCtrl().InsertItem(sLang, 0, 0);
    hSubNode = GetTreeCtrl().InsertItem(sSubLang, 0, 0, hNode);
    if(SortType)
        {
        hSortNode = GetTreeCtrl().InsertItem(sSort, hSubNode);
        hItem = hSortNode;
        }
    else hItem = hSubNode;
    }
GetTreeCtrl().SetItemData(hItem, lcid);
GetTreeCtrl().SetItemImage(hItem, 2, 2);

m_nNodes++;
return TRUE;
}

// Helper function that loads and organizes the tree
int ClcTreeView::LoadLocaleTree(DWORD mode)
{
m_pThis = this;
m_nNodes = 0;

// Build the tree by enumerating LCIDs.
BOOL ok = EnumSystemLocales
    (
    (LOCALE_ENUMPROC)cbEnumSystemLocales,
    mode
    );

// Sort the tree alphabetically and insert default sort nodes where
// alternate sorts are defined.
GetTreeCtrl().SortChildren(0);
HTREEITEM hNode, hSubNode, hSortNode;
hNode = GetTreeCtrl().GetRootItem();
while(hNode)
    {
    GetTreeCtrl().SortChildren(hNode);
    hSubNode = GetTreeCtrl().GetChildItem(hNode);
    while(hSubNode)
        {
        if(GetTreeCtrl().ItemHasChildren(hSubNode))
            {
            LCID lcid = GetTreeCtrl().GetItemData(hSubNode);
            GetTreeCtrl().SetItemData(hSubNode, 0);
            TCHAR b[128];
            if(!GetLocaleInfo(lcid, LOCALE_SSORTNAME, b, 128))
                _tcscpy(b, _T("Default"));
```

(continued)

Listing 9-18. *continued*

```
            hSortNode = GetTreeCtrl().InsertItem(b, 2, 2, hSubNode,
                                                 TVI_FIRST);
            GetTreeCtrl().SetItemData(hSortNode, lcid);
            GetTreeCtrl().SetItemImage(hSubNode, 0, 0);
            }
        hSubNode = GetTreeCtrl().GetNextSiblingItem(hSubNode);
        }
    hNode = GetTreeCtrl().GetNextSiblingItem(hNode);
    }

return m_nNodes;
}
//================================================================
//
// Adjust the folder icon to indicate whether a node is
// expanded or contracted.
//================================================================
void ClcTreeView::OnTreeItemExpanded(NMHDR* pNMHDR,
                                     LRESULT* pResult)
{
NM_TREEVIEW* p = (NM_TREEVIEW*)pNMHDR;
int nImage = 1;
switch(p->action)
    {
    case TVE_COLLAPSE:
    case TVE_COLLAPSERESET:
    nImage = 0;
    }
GetTreeCtrl().SetItemImage(p->itemNew.hItem, nImage, nImage);
*pResult = 0;
}
//================================================================
//
// Update the list view when the node selection changes.
//
//================================================================
void ClcTreeView::OnTreeSelChanged(NMHDR* pNMHDR, LRESULT* pResult)
{
NM_TREEVIEW* p = (NM_TREEVIEW*)pNMHDR;
LCID lcid = GetTreeCtrl().GetItemData(p->itemNew.hItem);
ClcDoc* pDoc = GetDocument();
ASSERT_VALID(pDoc);
pDoc->UpdateAllViews(this, lcid, 0);
if(!lcid && !(p->itemNew.state & TVIS_EXPANDED))
    GetTreeCtrl().Expand(p->itemNew.hItem, TVE_EXPAND);
*pResult = 0;
}
```

The tree has three levels: language, country, and sort type. *LoadLocaleTree* calls *EnumSystemLocales*, as in the previous example. Win32 passes each LCID to *cbEnumSystemLocales*, which simply delegates the call to *cbLoadLocaleTree* in the tree view class. This callback function uses *GetLocaleInfo* to obtain the text strings identifying the language, country, and sort type.[11] It then enters a fairly complicated set of nested loops to insert these strings into the tree. Each language has a branch at the top level, and each country using that language (that is, each sublanguage) has a branch at the next level with its nondefault sort algorithms as leaf nodes. The LCID is stored in the country node for the default sort type or in the sort node for other types. The node images are set to show a closed folder at the language level and a world globe at the other levels.

When *EnumSystemLocales* returns, *LoadLocaleTree* sorts each tree level into ascending alphabetical order. It also finds country branches that have nondefault sort nodes, adds a default sort node to each, and adjusts the country node so that it will appear as a folder.

OnTreeItemExpanded is wired to the *TVN_ITEMEXPANDED* notification through the MFC message map. It adjusts the image to show an open or closed folder corresponding to the item state. Similarly, *OnTreeSelChanged* catches the *TVN_SELCHANGED* event. If the LCID in the item data of the new selection is 0, that item is a folder and is expanded. Otherwise, the new item is a leaf of the tree at either the country or the sort level. In all cases, the LCID is passed to the list view's *OnUpdate* event by means of the *UpdateAllViews* function in the document object. This enables the list view to hide itself when the LCID is 0 and to refresh the display when the LCID changes.

Listings 9-19 and 9-20 show the list view class declaration and implementation. As in the tree view, much of this class is MFC boilerplate, with the interesting work concentrated in *OnInitialUpdate*, *OnUpdate*, and *LoadList*.

```
class CLocaleView : public CView
{
    DECLARE_DYNCREATE(CLocaleView)
    DECLARE_MESSAGE_MAP()

protected:
    CLocaleView();

    enum
```

Listing 9-19. *Locale browser—list view class declaration.*   *(continued)*

---

11. I used the English version of the language and sublanguage strings because this is a programmer's tool and C++ programmers must have some knowledge of English. If you want to use the localized language and sublanguage strings, change the *GetLocaleInfo* calls to request *LOCALE_SLANGUAGE* and *LOCALE_SCOUNTRY*.

Listing 9-19. *continued*

```
    {
    IDC_Tabs            = 100,
    IDC_ListLocale      = 101,
    IDC_ListCal         = 102,
    };

    CTabCtrl m_Tabs;            // Tab control
    CListCtrl m_ListLocale;     // Locale info list
    CListCtrl m_ListCal;        // Calendar info list

    CListCtrl* m_pList;         // Active list

    CFont m_Font;              // Current font
    LCID m_LCID;               // Current locale ID
    CALID m_CALID;             // Current calendar ID
    CString m_Language;        // Current language name
    CString m_Country;         // Current country name
    CString m_CalName;         // Current calendar name

    //{{AFX_MSG(CLocaleView)
    afx_msg int OnCreate(LPCREATESTRUCT lpCreateStruct);
    afx_msg BOOL OnEraseBkgnd(CDC* pDC);
    afx_msg void OnSize(UINT nType, int cx, int cy);
    //}}AFX_MSG
    afx_msg void OnTabSelChange(NMHDR* pNMHDR, LRESULT* pResult);

public:
    virtual ~CLocaleView();
    CLocaleBrowserDoc* GetDocument();
    void LoadList();
    void LoadCalList();
    void OnChooseListFont();
    void SetTitle();

    #ifdef _DEBUG
    virtual void AssertValid() const;
    virtual void Dump(CDumpContext& dc) const;
    #endif

    // ClassWizard generated virtual function overrides
    //{{AFX_VIRTUAL(CLocaleView)
    public:
    virtual void OnDraw(CDC* pDC);  // Overridden to draw this view
    virtual BOOL PreCreateWindow(CREATESTRUCT& cs);
    protected:
    virtual void OnInitialUpdate(); // Called first time
                                    // after construct
    //virtual BOOL OnPreparePrinting(CPrintInfo* pInfo);
```

```
    //virtual void OnBeginPrinting(CDC* pDC, CPrintInfo* pInfo);
    //virtual void OnEndPrinting(CDC* pDC, CPrintInfo* pInfo);
    virtual void OnUpdate(CView* pSender, LPARAM lHint, CObject* pHint);
    //}}AFX_VIRTUAL
};

#ifndef _DEBUG  // Debug version in LocaleView.cpp
inline CLocaleBrowserDoc* CLocaleView::GetDocument()
    { return (CLocaleBrowserDoc*)m_pDocument; }
#endif
```

```
//===============================================================
//
// The list view displays the settings for a single locale.
//
//===============================================================
IMPLEMENT_DYNCREATE(CLocaleView, CView)

BEGIN_MESSAGE_MAP(CLocaleView, CView)
    //{{AFX_MSG_MAP(CLocaleView)
    ON_WM_CREATE()
    ON_WM_ERASEBKGND()
    ON_WM_SIZE()
    //}}AFX_MSG_MAP
    ON_NOTIFY(TCN_SELCHANGE, IDC_Tabs, OnTabSelChange)
END_MESSAGE_MAP()
//===============================================================
//
// Locale information table, used to populate the list view.
// Note that the strings are not localized because they represent
// programming symbols that are the same in all locales.
//
//===============================================================
typedef struct
    {
    LCTYPE type;
    LPTSTR name;
    } LCTYPEINFO;

static LCTYPEINFO lcTypes[] =
    {
    LOCALE_ILANGUAGE                    ,_T("ILANGUAGE"),
    LOCALE_SLANGUAGE                    ,_T("SLANGUAGE"),
```

Listing 9-20. *Locale browser—list view class implementation.*   *(continued)*

345

Listing 9-20. *continued*

```
      LOCALE_SENGLANGUAGE              ,_T("SENGLANGUAGE"),
      LOCALE_SABBREVLANGNAME           ,_T("SABBREVLANGNAME"),
      LOCALE_SNATIVELANGNAME           ,_T("SNATIVELANGNAME"),
      LOCALE_ICOUNTRY                  ,_T("ICOUNTRY"),
      LOCALE_SCOUNTRY                  ,_T("SCOUNTRY"),
      LOCALE_SENGCOUNTRY               ,_T("SENGCOUNTRY"),
      LOCALE_SABBREVCTRYNAME           ,_T("SABBREVCTRYNAME"),
      LOCALE_SNATIVECTRYNAME           ,_T("SNATIVECTRYNAME"),
      LOCALE_IDEFAULTLANGUAGE          ,_T("IDEFAULTLANGUAGE"),
      LOCALE_IDEFAULTCOUNTRY           ,_T("IDEFAULTCOUNTRY"),
      LOCALE_IDEFAULTCODEPAGE          ,_T("IDEFAULTCODEPAGE"),
      LOCALE_IDEFAULTANSICODEPAGE      ,_T("IDEFAULTANSICODEPAGE"),
      LOCALE_IDEFAULTMACCODEPAGE       ,_T("IDEFAULTMACCODEPAGE"),
      LOCALE_SLIST                     ,_T("SLIST"),
      LOCALE_IMEASURE                  ,_T("IMEASURE"),
      LOCALE_SDECIMAL                  ,_T("SDECIMAL"),
      LOCALE_STHOUSAND                 ,_T("STHOUSAND"),
      LOCALE_SGROUPING                 ,_T("SGROUPING"),
      LOCALE_IDIGITS                   ,_T("IDIGITS"),
      LOCALE_ILZERO                    ,_T("ILZERO"),
      LOCALE_INEGNUMBER                ,_T("INEGNUMBER"),
      LOCALE_SNATIVEDIGITS             ,_T("SNATIVEDIGITS"),
      LOCALE_SCURRENCY                 ,_T("SCURRENCY"),
      LOCALE_SINTLSYMBOL               ,_T("SINTLSYMBOL"),
      LOCALE_SMONDECIMALSEP            ,_T("SMONDECIMALSEP"),
      LOCALE_SMONTHOUSANDSEP           ,_T("SMONTHOUSANDSEP"),
      LOCALE_SMONGROUPING              ,_T("SMONGROUPING"),
      LOCALE_ICURRDIGITS               ,_T("ICURRDIGITS"),
      LOCALE_IINTLCURRDIGITS           ,_T("IINTLCURRDIGITS"),
      LOCALE_ICURRENCY                 ,_T("ICURRENCY"),
      LOCALE_INEGCURR                  ,_T("INEGCURR"),
      LOCALE_SDATE                     ,_T("SDATE"),
      LOCALE_STIME                     ,_T("STIME"),
      LOCALE_SSHORTDATE                ,_T("SSHORTDATE"),
      LOCALE_SLONGDATE                 ,_T("SLONGDATE"),
      LOCALE_STIMEFORMAT               ,_T("STIMEFORMAT"),
      LOCALE_IDATE                     ,_T("IDATE"),
      LOCALE_ILDATE                    ,_T("ILDATE"),
      LOCALE_ITIME                     ,_T("ITIME"),
      LOCALE_ITIMEMARKPOSN             ,_T("ITIMEMARKPOSN"),
      LOCALE_ICENTURY                  ,_T("ICENTURY"),
      LOCALE_ITLZERO                   ,_T("ITLZERO"),
      LOCALE_IDAYLZERO                 ,_T("IDAYLZERO"),
      LOCALE_IMONLZERO                 ,_T("IMONLZERO"),
      LOCALE_S1159                     ,_T("S1159"),
      LOCALE_S2359                     ,_T("S2359"),
```

```
LOCALE_ICALENDARTYPE              ,_T("ICALENDARTYPE"),
LOCALE_IOPTIONALCALENDAR          ,_T("IOPTIONALCALENDAR"),
LOCALE_IFIRSTDAYOFWEEK            ,_T("IFIRSTDAYOFWEEK"),
LOCALE_IFIRSTWEEKOFYEAR           ,_T("IFIRSTWEEKOFYEAR"),
LOCALE_SDAYNAME1                  ,_T("SDAYNAME1"),
LOCALE_SDAYNAME2                  ,_T("SDAYNAME2"),
LOCALE_SDAYNAME3                  ,_T("SDAYNAME3"),
LOCALE_SDAYNAME4                  ,_T("SDAYNAME4"),
LOCALE_SDAYNAME5                  ,_T("SDAYNAME5"),
LOCALE_SDAYNAME6                  ,_T("SDAYNAME6"),
LOCALE_SDAYNAME7                  ,_T("SDAYNAME7"),
LOCALE_SABBREVDAYNAME1            ,_T("SABBREVDAYNAME1"),
LOCALE_SABBREVDAYNAME2            ,_T("SABBREVDAYNAME2"),
LOCALE_SABBREVDAYNAME3            ,_T("SABBREVDAYNAME3"),
LOCALE_SABBREVDAYNAME4            ,_T("SABBREVDAYNAME4"),
LOCALE_SABBREVDAYNAME5            ,_T("SABBREVDAYNAME5"),
LOCALE_SABBREVDAYNAME6            ,_T("SABBREVDAYNAME6"),
LOCALE_SABBREVDAYNAME7            ,_T("SABBREVDAYNAME7"),
LOCALE_SMONTHNAME1                ,_T("SMONTHNAME1"),
LOCALE_SMONTHNAME2                ,_T("SMONTHNAME2"),
LOCALE_SMONTHNAME3                ,_T("SMONTHNAME3"),
LOCALE_SMONTHNAME4                ,_T("SMONTHNAME4"),
LOCALE_SMONTHNAME5                ,_T("SMONTHNAME5"),
LOCALE_SMONTHNAME6                ,_T("SMONTHNAME6"),
LOCALE_SMONTHNAME7                ,_T("SMONTHNAME7"),
LOCALE_SMONTHNAME8                ,_T("SMONTHNAME8"),
LOCALE_SMONTHNAME9                ,_T("SMONTHNAME9"),
LOCALE_SMONTHNAME10               ,_T("SMONTHNAME10"),
LOCALE_SMONTHNAME11               ,_T("SMONTHNAME11"),
LOCALE_SMONTHNAME12               ,_T("SMONTHNAME12"),
LOCALE_SMONTHNAME13               ,_T("SMONTHNAME13"),
LOCALE_SABBREVMONTHNAME1          ,_T("SABBREVMONTHNAME1"),
LOCALE_SABBREVMONTHNAME2          ,_T("SABBREVMONTHNAME2"),
LOCALE_SABBREVMONTHNAME3          ,_T("SABBREVMONTHNAME3"),
LOCALE_SABBREVMONTHNAME4          ,_T("SABBREVMONTHNAME4"),
LOCALE_SABBREVMONTHNAME5          ,_T("SABBREVMONTHNAME5"),
LOCALE_SABBREVMONTHNAME6          ,_T("SABBREVMONTHNAME6"),
LOCALE_SABBREVMONTHNAME7          ,_T("SABBREVMONTHNAME7"),
LOCALE_SABBREVMONTHNAME8          ,_T("SABBREVMONTHNAME8"),
LOCALE_SABBREVMONTHNAME9          ,_T("SABBREVMONTHNAME9"),
LOCALE_SABBREVMONTHNAME10         ,_T("SABBREVMONTHNAME10"),
LOCALE_SABBREVMONTHNAME11         ,_T("SABBREVMONTHNAME11"),
LOCALE_SABBREVMONTHNAME12         ,_T("SABBREVMONTHNAME12"),
LOCALE_SABBREVMONTHNAME13         ,_T("SABBREVMONTHNAME13"),
LOCALE_SPOSITIVESIGN              ,_T("SPOSITIVESIGN"),
LOCALE_SNEGATIVESIGN              ,_T("SNEGATIVESIGN"),
LOCALE_IPOSSIGNPOSN              ,_T("IPOSSIGNPOSN"),
```

(continued)

Listing 9-20. *continued*

```
    LOCALE_INEGSIGNPOSN              ,_T("INEGSIGNPOSN"),
    LOCALE_IPOSSYMPRECEDES           ,_T("IPOSSYMPRECEDES"),
    LOCALE_IPOSSEPBYSPACE            ,_T("IPOSSEPBYSPACE"),
    LOCALE_INEGSYMPRECEDES           ,_T("INEGSYMPRECEDES"),
    LOCALE_INEGSEPBYSPACE            ,_T("INEGSEPBYSPACE"),

    #if(WINVER >= 0x0400)
    LOCALE_FONTSIGNATURE             ,_T("FONTSIGNATURE"),
    LOCALE_SISO639LANGNAME           ,_T("SISO639LANGNAME"),
    LOCALE_SISO3166CTRYNAME          ,_T("SISO3166CTRYNAME"),
    #endif

    #if(WINVER >= 0x0500)
    LOCALE_IDEFAULTEBCDICCODEPAGE ,_T("IDEFAULTEBCDICCODEPAGE"),
    LOCALE_IPAPERSIZE                ,_T("IPAPERSIZE"),
    LOCALE_SENGCURRNAME              ,_T("SENGCURRNAME"),
    LOCALE_SNATIVECURRNAME           ,_T("SNATIVECURRNAME"),
    LOCALE_SYEARMONTH                ,_T("SYEARMONTH"),
    LOCALE_SSORTNAME                 ,_T("SSORTNAME"),
    LOCALE_IDIGITSUBSTITUTION        ,_T("IDIGITSUBSTITUTION"),
    #endif
    };

typedef struct
    {
    CALID id;
    LPTSTR name;
    } CALIDINFO;

static CALIDINFO CalIDs[] =
    {
    CAL_GREGORIAN                    ,_T("Gregorian"),
    CAL_GREGORIAN_US                 ,_T("Gregorian (US)"),
    CAL_JAPAN                        ,_T("Japanese Emperor Era"),
    CAL_TAIWAN                       ,_T("Taiwan Era"),
    CAL_KOREA                        ,_T("Korean Tangun Era"),
    CAL_HIJRI                        ,_T("Hijri (Arabic Lunar)"),
    CAL_THAI                         ,_T("Thai"),
    CAL_HEBREW                       ,_T("Hebrew (Lunar)"),
    CAL_GREGORIAN_ME_FRENCH
        ,_T("Gregorian Middle East French"),
    CAL_GREGORIAN_ARABIC
        ,_T("Gregorian (Arabic)"),
    CAL_GREGORIAN_XLIT_ENGLISH
        ,_T("Gregorian (Transliterated English)"),
    CAL_GREGORIAN_XLIT_FRENCH
        ,_T("Gregorian (Transliterated French)"),
    };
```

```
typedef struct
    {
    CALTYPE type;
    LPTSTR name;
    } CALTYPEINFO;

static CALTYPEINFO CalTypes[] =
    {
    CAL_ICALINTVALUE           ,_T("ICALINTVALUE"),
    CAL_SCALNAME               ,_T("SCALNAME"),
    CAL_IYEAROFFSETRANGE       ,_T("IYEAROFFSETRANGE"),
    CAL_SERASTRING             ,_T("SERASTRING"),
    CAL_SSHORTDATE             ,_T("SSHORTDATE"),
    CAL_SLONGDATE              ,_T("SLONGDATE"),
    CAL_SDAYNAME1              ,_T("SDAYNAME1"),
    CAL_SDAYNAME2              ,_T("SDAYNAME2"),
    CAL_SDAYNAME3              ,_T("SDAYNAME3"),
    CAL_SDAYNAME4              ,_T("SDAYNAME4"),
    CAL_SDAYNAME5              ,_T("SDAYNAME5"),
    CAL_SDAYNAME6              ,_T("SDAYNAME6"),
    CAL_SDAYNAME7              ,_T("SDAYNAME7"),
    CAL_SABBREVDAYNAME1        ,_T("SABBREVDAYNAME1"),
    CAL_SABBREVDAYNAME2        ,_T("SABBREVDAYNAME2"),
    CAL_SABBREVDAYNAME3        ,_T("SABBREVDAYNAME3"),
    CAL_SABBREVDAYNAME4        ,_T("SABBREVDAYNAME4"),
    CAL_SABBREVDAYNAME5        ,_T("SABBREVDAYNAME5"),
    CAL_SABBREVDAYNAME6        ,_T("SABBREVDAYNAME6"),
    CAL_SABBREVDAYNAME7        ,_T("SABBREVDAYNAME7"),
    CAL_SMONTHNAME1            ,_T("SMONTHNAME1"),
    CAL_SMONTHNAME2            ,_T("SMONTHNAME2"),
    CAL_SMONTHNAME3            ,_T("SMONTHNAME3"),
    CAL_SMONTHNAME4            ,_T("SMONTHNAME4"),
    CAL_SMONTHNAME5            ,_T("SMONTHNAME5"),
    CAL_SMONTHNAME6            ,_T("SMONTHNAME6"),
    CAL_SMONTHNAME7            ,_T("SMONTHNAME7"),
    CAL_SMONTHNAME8            ,_T("SMONTHNAME8"),
    CAL_SMONTHNAME9            ,_T("SMONTHNAME9"),
    CAL_SMONTHNAME10           ,_T("SMONTHNAME10"),
    CAL_SMONTHNAME11           ,_T("SMONTHNAME11"),
    CAL_SMONTHNAME12           ,_T("SMONTHNAME12"),
    CAL_SMONTHNAME13           ,_T("SMONTHNAME13"),
    CAL_SABBREVMONTHNAME1      ,_T("SABBREVMONTHNAME1"),
    CAL_SABBREVMONTHNAME2      ,_T("SABBREVMONTHNAME2"),
    CAL_SABBREVMONTHNAME3      ,_T("SABBREVMONTHNAME3"),
    CAL_SABBREVMONTHNAME4      ,_T("SABBREVMONTHNAME4"),
```

(continued)

Listing 9-20. *continued*

```
    CAL_SABBREVMONTHNAME5      ,_T("SABBREVMONTHNAME5"),
    CAL_SABBREVMONTHNAME6      ,_T("SABBREVMONTHNAME6"),
    CAL_SABBREVMONTHNAME7      ,_T("SABBREVMONTHNAME7"),
    CAL_SABBREVMONTHNAME8      ,_T("SABBREVMONTHNAME8"),
    CAL_SABBREVMONTHNAME9      ,_T("SABBREVMONTHNAME9"),
    CAL_SABBREVMONTHNAME10     ,_T("SABBREVMONTHNAME10"),
    CAL_SABBREVMONTHNAME11     ,_T("SABBREVMONTHNAME11"),
    CAL_SABBREVMONTHNAME12     ,_T("SABBREVMONTHNAME12"),
    CAL_SABBREVMONTHNAME13     ,_T("SABBREVMONTHNAME13"),

    #if(WINVER >= 0x0500)
    CAL_SYEARMONTH             ,_T("SYEARMONTH"),
    CAL_ITWODIGITYEARMAX       ,_T("ITWODIGITYEARMAX")
    #endif
    };
//================================================================
//
// Construction, destruction, and drawing
//
//================================================================
CLocaleView::CLocaleView()
{
m_LCID = 0;
m_CALID = 0;
m_pList = 0;
}


CLocaleView::~CLocaleView()
{
}


BOOL CLocaleView::PreCreateWindow(CREATESTRUCT& cs)
{
return CView::PreCreateWindow(cs);
}


int CLocaleView::OnCreate(LPCREATESTRUCT lpCreateStruct)
{
if(CView::OnCreate(lpCreateStruct) == -1)
    return -1;
CRect r(0, 0, 0, 0);
if(!m_Tabs.Create
    (
    WS_CHILD | WS_VISIBLE | WS_CLIPSIBLINGS,
    r,
```

```
        this,
        IDC_Tabs
        )) return -1;
    if(!m_ListLocale.Create
        (
        WS_CHILD | WS_BORDER | LVS_ALIGNLEFT | LVS_REPORT,
        r,
        this,
        IDC_ListLocale
        )) return -1;
    if(!m_ListCal.Create
        (
        WS_CHILD | WS_BORDER | LVS_ALIGNLEFT | LVS_REPORT,
        r,
        this,
        IDC_ListCal
        )) return -1;
    m_pList = &m_ListLocale;
    return 0;
    }


void CLocaleView::OnSize(UINT nType, int cx, int cy)
{
CView::OnSize(nType, cx, cy);
switch(nType)
    {
    case SIZE_MAXIMIZED:
    case SIZE_RESTORED:
    if(!::IsWindow(m_Tabs.m_hWnd)) break;
    if(!::IsWindow(m_ListLocale.m_hWnd)) break;
    if(!::IsWindow(m_ListCal.m_hWnd)) break;
    CRect r, ri;
    GetClientRect(&r);
    m_Tabs.MoveWindow(&r, TRUE);
    m_Tabs.GetItemRect(0, &ri);
    r.left = ri.left;
    r.top = ri.bottom + 4;
    r.right -= ri.left;
    r.bottom -= 4;
    m_ListLocale.MoveWindow(&r, TRUE);
    m_ListCal.MoveWindow(&r, TRUE);
    }
}


BOOL CLocaleView::OnEraseBkgnd(CDC* pDC)
{
pDC->SaveDC();
```

(continued)

Listing 9-20. *continued*

```
CRect rc;
GetClientRect(&rc);
pDC->FillSolidRect(&rc, RGB(192, 192, 192));
pDC->RestoreDC(-1);
return TRUE;
}


void CLocaleView::OnDraw(CDC* pDC)
{
}
//===============================================================
//
// Initialize the list.
// The column headings and symbols in column 0 are not
// localized because they are used by programmers who must
// understand some English in order to use C++ effectively.
//
//===============================================================
void CLocaleView::OnInitialUpdate()
{
CView::OnInitialUpdate();

#ifdef UNICODE
TCHAR FontName[] = _T("Lucida Sans Unicode");
#else
TCHAR FontName[] = _T("Lucida Sans");
#endif
ASSERT(m_Font.CreatePointFont(90, FontName));
m_ListLocale.SetFont(&m_Font);
m_ListCal.SetFont(&m_Font);
m_Tabs.SetFont(&m_Font);

// Set tabs.
m_Tabs.InsertItem(0, _T("Locale"));

// Set locale list column headings.
m_ListLocale.InsertColumn(0, _T("LOCALE_Symbol"), LVCFMT_LEFT, 180);
m_ListLocale.InsertColumn(1, _T("Value"), LVCFMT_LEFT, 180);

// Set calendar list column headings.
m_ListCal.InsertColumn(0, _T("CAL_Symbol"), LVCFMT_LEFT, 180);
m_ListCal.InsertColumn(1, _T("Value"), LVCFMT_LEFT, 180);
}
//===============================================================
//
// Callback function that loads an enumerated item into a list.
```

```
//
//=============================================================
static CListCtrl* g_pList;
static int g_nEnums;
static BOOL CALLBACK cbEnumCalendarInfo(LPTSTR p)
{
if(g_nEnums++)
    {
    int i = g_pList->GetItemCount();
    g_pList->InsertItem(i, _T(""));
    g_pList->SetItemText(i, 1, p);
    }
return TRUE;
}
//=============================================================
//
// Load the list with information for the current locale.
//
//=============================================================
void CLocaleView::LoadList()
{
int i, j, k, x, y;
TCHAR b[128], b1[128];
CString s;
TCITEM tcItem;
tcItem.mask = TCIF_PARAM;

m_ListLocale.DeleteAllItems();            // Clears the list
int iTabSel = m_Tabs.GetCurSel();         // Clears the calendar tabs
for(i = 1; i < m_Tabs.GetItemCount(); i++)
    m_Tabs.DeleteItem(i);
if(!m_LCID) return;                       // Exits if no LCID

g_pList = &m_ListLocale;
int nInfo = sizeof(lcTypes) / sizeof(LCTYPEINFO);
for(i = 0; i < nInfo; i++)
    {
    j = m_ListLocale.GetItemCount();
    m_ListLocale.InsertItem(j, lcTypes[i].name);
    k = GetLocaleInfo(m_LCID, lcTypes[i].type, b, 128);
    if(k >= 0) switch(lcTypes[i].type)
        {
        case LOCALE_SENGLANGUAGE:
        m_Language = b;
        goto _default;

        case LOCALE_SENGCOUNTRY:
```

(continued)

Listing 9-20. *continued*

```
            m_Country = b;
            goto _default;

            case LOCALE_ICALENDARTYPE:
            tcItem.lParam = _ttoi(b);
            if(tcItem.lParam)
                {
                s.Format(_T("Calendar (%s)"), b);
                m_Tabs.InsertItem(1, s);
                m_Tabs.SetItem(1, &tcItem);
                }
            goto _default;

            case LOCALE_IOPTIONALCALENDAR:
            tcItem.lParam = _ttoi(b);
            if(tcItem.lParam)
                {
                s.Format(_T("Calendar (%s)"), b);
                m_Tabs.InsertItem(2, s);
                m_Tabs.SetItem(2, &tcItem);
                }
            goto _default;

            case LOCALE_FONTSIGNATURE:
            k *= sizeof(TCHAR);
            s.Format(_T("%d bytes"), k);
            m_ListLocale.SetItemText(j++, 1, s);
            for(x = y = 0; y < k; y++)
                {
                if(y && !(y & 7))
                    {
                    m_ListLocale.InsertItem(j, _T(""));
                    m_ListLocale.SetItemText(j++, 1, b1);
                    x = 0;
                    }
                x += _stprintf(&b1[x], _T(" %02X"), (unsigned char)b[y]);
                }
            if(x)
                {
                m_ListLocale.InsertItem(j, _T(""));
                m_ListLocale.SetItemText(j++, 1, b1);
                }
            continue;

            case LOCALE_STIMEFORMAT:
            m_ListLocale.SetItemText(j, 1, b);
```

```
            g_nEnums = 0;
            EnumTimeFormats(cbEnumCalendarInfo, m_LCID, 0);
            continue;

            case LOCALE_SLONGDATE:
            m_ListLocale.SetItemText(j, 1, b);
            g_nEnums = 0;
            EnumDateFormats(cbEnumCalendarInfo, m_LCID, DATE_LONGDATE);
            continue;


            case LOCALE_SSHORTDATE:
            m_ListLocale.SetItemText(j, 1, b);
            g_nEnums = 0;
            EnumDateFormats(cbEnumCalendarInfo, m_LCID, DATE_SHORTDATE);
            continue;

            case LOCALE_SYEARMONTH:
            m_ListLocale.SetItemText(j, 1, b);
            g_nEnums = 0;
            EnumDateFormats(cbEnumCalendarInfo, m_LCID, DATE_YEARMONTH);
            continue;

            default:
            _default:
            m_ListLocale.SetItemText(j, 1, b);
            }
        }
    i = m_Tabs.GetItemCount();
    if(iTabSel >= i) iTabSel = i - 1;
    m_Tabs.GetItem(iTabSel, &tcItem);
    m_CALID = tcItem.lParam;
    LoadCalList();
}
//============================================================
//
// Load the calendar list with information for a specified
// calendar in the current locale.
//
//============================================================
void CLocaleView::LoadCalList()
{
TCHAR b[1024];
LPTSTR p;
int i, j, k;
int nCalIDs = sizeof(CalIDs) / sizeof(CALIDINFO);
int nCalInfo = sizeof(CalTypes) / sizeof(CALTYPEINFO);
```

(continued)

Listing 9-20. *continued*

```
m_ListCal.DeleteAllItems();        // Clears the list
if(!m_LCID) return;                // Must have an LCID

if(!m_CALID)                       // Uses default CALID if none set
    {
    GetLocaleInfo(m_LCID, LOCALE_ICALENDARTYPE, b, 1024);
    m_CALID = _ttoi(b);
    }

for(i = 0; i < nCalIDs; i++) if(CalIDs[i].id == m_CALID)
    {
    m_CalName = CalIDs[i].name;
    break;
    }
if(i >= nCalIDs) return;           // Exits if invalid calendar ID

g_pList = &m_ListCal;              // For enumerated items
for(i = j = 0; i < nCalInfo; i++)
    {
    j = m_ListCal.GetItemCount();
    m_ListCal.InsertItem(j, CalTypes[i].name);
    k = GetCalendarInfo(m_LCID, m_CALID, CalTypes[i].type,
                    b, 128, 0);
    if(k > 0) switch(CalTypes[i].type)
        {
        // Handle compound strings with embedded nulls.
        case CAL_IYEAROFFSETRANGE:
        case CAL_SERASTRING:
        for(p = b; *p && ((p - b) < k); j++, p += lstrlen(p))
            {
            if(p != b) m_ListCal.InsertItem(j, _T(""));
            m_ListCal.SetItemText(j, 1, p);
            }
        continue;

        // Handle date and time items that are not presented
        // as compound strings.
        case CAL_SLONGDATE:
        m_ListCal.SetItemText(j++, 1, b);
        g_nEnums = 0;
        EnumCalendarInfo(cbEnumCalendarInfo, m_LCID, m_CALID,
                    CAL_SLONGDATE);
        continue;

        case CAL_SSHORTDATE:
        m_ListCal.SetItemText(j++, 1, b);
```

```
            g_nEnums = 0;
            EnumCalendarInfo(cbEnumCalendarInfo, m_LCID, m_CALID,
                            CAL_SSHORTDATE);
            continue;

            case CAL_SYEARMONTH:
            m_ListCal.SetItemText(j++, 1, b);
            g_nEnums = 0;
            EnumCalendarInfo(cbEnumCalendarInfo, m_LCID, m_CALID,
                            CAL_SYEARMONTH);
            continue;

            default:
            m_ListCal.SetItemText(j++, 1, b);
            }
        }
}
//================================================================
//
// Update the list when the LCID changes.
//
//================================================================
void CLocaleView::OnUpdate(CView* pSender, LPARAM lHint,
                            CObject* pHint)
{
m_LCID = (LCID)lHint;
if(m_LCID == 0)
    {
    m_ListLocale.ShowWindow(SW_HIDE);
    m_ListCal.ShowWindow(SW_HIDE);
    m_ListCal.DeleteAllItems();
    m_Tabs.ShowWindow(SW_HIDE);
    }
else
    {
    LoadList();
    m_Tabs.ShowWindow(SW_SHOW);
    int i = m_Tabs.GetCurSel();
    if(i < 0) m_Tabs.SetCurSel(0);
    if(i <= 0) m_pList = &m_ListLocale;
    else m_pList = &m_ListCal;
    m_pList->ShowWindow(SW_SHOW);
    }
SetTitle();
}
//================================================================
//
```

(continued)

Listing 9-20. *continued*

```
// Diagnostics
//
//=============================================================
#ifdef _DEBUG
void CLocaleView::AssertValid() const
{
    CView::AssertValid();
}

void CLocaleView::Dump(CDumpContext& dc) const
{
    CView::Dump(dc);
}

CLocaleBrowserDoc* CLocaleView::GetDocument() // Non-debug version
                                              // is inline.
{
    ASSERT(m_pDocument->IsKindOf(RUNTIME_CLASS(CLocaleBrowserDoc)));
    return (CLocaleBrowserDoc*)m_pDocument;
}
#endif //_DEBUG
//=============================================================
//
// Change the font (relayed from main frame).
//
//=============================================================
void CLocaleView::OnChooseListFont()
{
CFontDialog dlg;
LOGFONT lf;
m_Font.GetLogFont(&lf);
dlg.m_cf.lpLogFont = &lf;
dlg.m_cf.Flags |= 0
    | CF_BOTH
    | CF_FORCEFONTEXIST
    | CF_INITTOLOGFONTSTRUCT
    | CF_NOVERTFONTS
    | CF_SCALABLEONLY
    | CF_SCRIPTSONLY
    ;
if(dlg.DoModal() != IDOK) return;
m_Font.DeleteObject();
ASSERT(m_Font.CreateFontIndirect(&lf));
SetFont(&m_Font);
}
//=============================================================
```

```
//
// Change the visible list based on the selected tab.
//
//================================================================
void CLocaleView::OnTabSelChange(NMHDR* pNMHDR, LRESULT* pResult)
{
*pResult = 0;
int i = m_Tabs.GetCurSel();
if(i < 0) return;
m_pList->ShowWindow(SW_HIDE);
if(i == 0)
    {
    m_pList = &m_ListLocale;
    m_CALID = 0;
    m_CalName.Empty();
    }
else
    {
    TCITEM tcItem;
    tcItem.mask = TCIF_PARAM;
    m_Tabs.GetItem(i, &tcItem);
    m_CALID = tcItem.lParam;
    LoadCalList();
    m_pList = &m_ListCal;
    }
m_pList->ShowWindow(SW_SHOW);
SetTitle();
}
//================================================================
//
// Adjust the caption bar based on the current selections.
//
//================================================================
void CLocaleView::SetTitle()
{
CString sTitle;
if(m_LCID == 0) sTitle = _T("No Selection");
else
    {
    sTitle.Format
        (
        _T("LCID: 0x%X  LANGUAGE: %s  COUNTRY: %s "),
        m_LCID,
        (LPCTSTR)m_Language,
        (LPCTSTR)m_Country
        );
    if(m_CALID && m_Tabs.GetCurSel())
```

(continued)

Listing 9-20. *continued*

```
        {
        CString sCalTitle;
        sCalTitle.Format(_T("  CALENDAR: %s"), (LPCTSTR)m_CalName);
        sTitle += sCalTitle;
        }
    }
GetDocument()->SetTitle(sTitle);
}
```

To add a tab control to *CLocaleView*, I had to change the base class from *CListView* to *CView*. Then I added three controls for the tab control, the basic locale list, and the calendar list. The *OnCreate* event handler creates the windows for these three embedded controls, and *OnSize* ensures that they cover the view window properly.

OnInitialUpdate creates a default font for the tab and list controls. Then it creates two columns in each list. The MFC framework next calls *OnUpdate* with the *lHint* parameter set to 0. This makes the list view invisible, and so *OnEraseBkgnd* fills it with a gray color.

When the user selects a locale in the tree view, *OnUpdate* is called with the new LCID in *lHint*. After storing the LCID in *m_LCID*, *OnUpdate* calls *LoadList* to populate the two lists, queries the tab control to determine which list should be visible, and then makes it so.

LoadList loops through the *lcTypes* table to fill the locale item list. This table contains one entry for each locale item, consisting of the *LCTYPE* code and the name of the corresponding symbol without the *LOCALE_* prefix. *LoadList* puts the name into column 0 of the list and calls *GetLocaleInfo* to obtain the information for column 1. Notice that some locale items, such as the font signature, must be specially formatted to fit in a single column. Also, formatting strings for dates and times requires further enumeration so that all combinations will appear in the list.

Before returning, *LoadList* determines which calendar should be displayed and then calls *LoadCalList*, which extracts the appropriate calendar information by repetitively calling *GetCalendarInfo*. If the user subsequently chooses a different calendar tab, the *OnTabSelChange* function calls *LoadCalList* again.

SUMMARY

Win32 includes an extensive locale database with features such as multiple calendars that are not available in standard C and C++. These features are exposed primarily through the NLS API. Most of the API calls are available throughout the Win32 spectrum, including Windows 95, Windows 98, Windows CE, Windows NT, and Windows 2000. They also generally support the ANSI and Unicode character sets.

In Chapters 4 through 9, I've described four ways to write international programs. You can use the standard C library, the standard C++ library, the Microsoft extensions to the standards, or the Win32 NLS API. Which is best, or is there some optimal mixture? Well, that depends on your goals and on what limitations you are willing to accept. I'll provide some practical guidelines in Chapter 11. Before I get to that, however, I must cover some important topics that primarily affect GUI programs that work with multiple languages.

Chapter 10

Multilingual Programming with Win32

The preceding chapters have shown you how to use the features of C, C++, Microsoft Visual C++, and Microsoft Win32 to support different languages. Many international programmers employ these features sparingly to build what I call static locale (SL) applications. This might seem like a contradiction in terms, but SL refers to the way a typical international program works with a single locale for an extended period and then switches to a different locale only at a significant boundary, such as when a new document is opened. But what about more dynamic situations, such as when you must process a document that uses several languages? Microsoft calls this multilingual (ML) programming and has enhanced Win32 to support it. The primary features of ML programming are the multilingual API (ML API), OpenType, and Uniscribe, all of which I'll examine in this chapter.

Although Win32's ML support first appeared in Microsoft Windows 95, it did not reach its full potential until the Microsoft Windows 2000 Multilingual Edition. ML programming can be difficult in a Windows 95 or Windows 98 environment because the system's weak Unicode support leads to complicated code page issues, as I described in Chapters 7 and 8. These character-set problems disappear on a native Unicode system such as Windows 2000, allowing full implementation of the features needed for ML programming.

To highlight the essentials of ML programming, this chapter assumes that you are developing pure Unicode applications for Windows 2000. Nonetheless, many of these techniques are compatible with earlier Windows 95, Windows 98, and Microsoft Windows NT platforms, although in those earlier environments you should preferably employ Unicode on the inside and multibyte character sets on the outside, as discussed in Chapters 7 and 8.

LIMITATIONS OF STANDARD C AND C++

In addition to preferring pure Unicode techniques, ML programs tend to contain many Win32 application programming interface (API) calls even if they also utilize the international features of standard C and C++. The sad fact is that the standards don't enable you to write a robust ML program, although they do offer some ML support.

Chapters 5 and 6 demonstrated this limitation in two sample programs (see Listings 5-2 and 6-5) that create mixed locales with German rules for formatting monetary values, French rules for dates, and U.S. rules for everything else. But these examples produce incorrect displays in the multibyte character set (MBCS) mode, requiring some nonstandard code to select an output code page containing the symbols needed for all three languages. Likewise, if a standard C or C++ ML program needs to accept user input (these examples don't), it must use some nonstandard means to select an input code page covering the mixed locale.

Now, you can avoid the nonstandard code page manipulation by working purely in Unicode, but what about the display font? You need to ensure that the user sees the correct symbols by selecting a font that covers all three languages or by switching fonts as needed. In addition, the user needs some way to enter the ML text from a keyboard suitable for the three languages but arranged in a preferred layout, which might be associated with a fourth language. Is this concept far-fetched? Not if you are a Japanese translator fluent in English, French, and German.

The C and C++ standards say nothing about how to select code pages, fonts, and keyboards; indeed, they are silent on nearly all system-dependent issues that arise in ML programming. This isn't a criticism, because the standards are purposely written to remain relatively aloof from the OS environment. It does mean, however, that Win32 ML applications can't use completely portable C or C++ programming techniques. They will always contain at least a few calls to the Win32 API or to some nonstandard function or class layer over the API.

This restriction might unsettle some programmers who believe that portability is or should be a major goal of all software development, but it's not a problem in the real world. Most of today's ML applications have a GUI and are inherently nonportable because not only do the C and C++ standards ignore basic OS issues as described above, but they also ignore the GUI world. This means that much of your Windows application development, whether SL or ML, will naturally fall outside the scope of the standards.

WHAT IS MULTILINGUAL PROGRAMMING?

Today's workstation users want to enjoy a seamless, "no boundaries" experience, with few distinctions between the operating system and its applications. They want these various parts to work as a unified whole, just as the parts of an automobile work together to get us to our destinations. This is a far cry from the old days, when applications had wildly different user interfaces (UIs) and the system's UI was unique unto itself.

To meet these expectations, you must design your application programs to smoothly and dynamically adapt to the language needs of their users, whether the users express these needs indirectly to the system or directly to the application. The best way to understand this requirement is to examine some typical scenarios.[1]

Scenario 1: Same Machine, Multiple Users

Today you begin your new job at a multinational bank in New York City. Although you speak English fluently, your native language is German, and so you are assigned to cover the German desk. You will be arranging business with banks and investment houses in Germany and producing confirmations and other correspondence in that language. Because of the time zone difference, you will be working from 5 A.M. until noon (but at least you'll avoid most of the New York commuting traffic).

Your manager assigns you to a workstation that serves as the Russian desk from 10 P.M. until 5 A.M. When you arrive at the desk, your Russian counterpart is finishing her tasks, and you notice that the workstation is running with a Russian UI—that is, messages, forms, and dialog boxes produced by both the

---

1. These scenarios were derived from the MSDN article titled "International Support in Microsoft Windows 2000."

system and the applications use Cyrillic characters, and she can type Cyrillic directly on the keyboard. She logs off before leaving, and you see that the system reverts to an English UI.

You log on to the machine with your newly assigned user name and password, and the system interface remains in English. You launch the confirmation application, and it too presents a U.S. interface—for instance, the keyboard doesn't allow you to directly enter accented German characters and monetary values are displayed as dollars instead of deutsche marks. You call the system administrator and tell him you need a German workstation. He suggests that you open the Regional Options applet in the Control Panel and select the German UI, as shown in Figure 10-1. You do so and a message box informs you that the system settings will change the next time you log on.

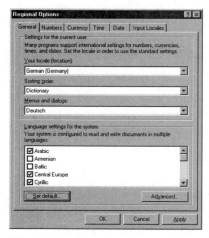

Figure 10-1. *Selecting the user interface language using the Regional Options applet.*

You log off, and then log on again. Now both the system and the confirmation application have a German UI. When you type a confirmation, the keyboard uses the German layout, which allows you to enter accented characters directly. Also monetary amounts, dates, times, and numbers use German formatting rules.

How it works

When the system administrator set up this Windows 2000 workstation, he installed a feature called multilingual user interface.[2] This tool enabled him to specify American English as the system's default UI and to install French, German,

---

2. This feature is available only in the Multilingual Edition of Windows 2000, although the associated API functions are implemented in all versions.

Russian, and Spanish as alternatives. The necessary resource files were copied to the workstation, and the Registry was updated to reflect which languages are present on the system.

Each user controls this feature through the Regional Options applet, which displays a list of UI languages available on the machine, as shown in Figure 10-1. The selection from the Menus And Dialogs list is a user property, and so each user can have a different setting. In this scenario, your coworker chose Russian, while you chose German. The English-speaking network administrator performs remote maintenance of many machines in different countries, and so he uses English for the administrator account on every system.

What it requires

This scenario requires that the system be designed with a dynamically configurable UI. Traditionally, the system UI is static and depends on which localized version you purchase. For instance, you can buy the English, German, or Russian version of Microsoft Windows, and the system's messages, dialog boxes, menus, and so on appear in that language regardless of which locale an application selects for its own UI.

Windows 2000 is available in 24 localized versions: Arabic, Chinese (Simplified), Chinese (Traditional), Czech, Danish, Dutch, English, Finnish, French, German, Greek, Hebrew, Hungarian, Italian, Japanese, Korean, Norwegian, Polish, Portuguese (Brazilian), Portuguese (Iberian), Russian, Spanish, Swedish, and Turkish. Each of these versions has a static system UI. In addition, Microsoft offers a Multilingual Edition that allows each user to choose his or her own system UI, as is required in this scenario. The Multilingual Edition is particularly attractive to large multinational enterprises that have usage scenarios such as this one or that don't want to support a myriad of localized versions.

Scenario 2: Same Application, Multiple Users

You're a graduate student doing research in the university library for your thesis on Italian art. You walk up to a kiosk containing a workstation running a turn-key application that lets you search other libraries throughout the world. The kiosk was previously used by a student looking for certain Czech publications, and he left the workstation in the Czech search mode. You are looking for an Italian treatise on the artists of Florence, and so you click on a globe icon displayed in the application toolbar and select Italian from the language list that appears. The search application is now operating in Italian.

How it works

In this scenario, the application provides a list of the locales it supports. When the user selects a locale, the application calls *SetThreadLocale* so that UI elements such as menus and dialog boxes will be fetched from the appropriate section of the resource database. The keyboard continues to use the normal U.S. layout, and so the user must use an Alt+key combination to enter accented Italian characters.

Notice that the user doesn't need to employ the Regional Options applet to change the UI or locale settings. In fact, because this is a turnkey application, the administrator has secured the workstation so that only the search application is available; the user can't even get to the Control Panel. This is similar to the operation of automated teller machines (ATMs), ticketing systems, gift registration kiosks, and so on.

What it requires

This is the classical multilingual scenario in which the application program allows the user to select the working language, which Microsoft also calls the *user locale*. In this case, the application provides a means for the user to make the selection, but in other cases the application relies on a system tool such as the Regional Options applet. Neither technique changes the system UI, and therefore you don't need to install the Windows 2000 Multilingual Edition. In fact, this scenario is compatible with Windows 95, Windows 98, and Windows NT.

Scenario 3: Handling Multilingual Data

You work for a United Nations agency in Zurich. Your native language is French, but you're fluent in several other languages. Starting with your French notes from a recent meeting, you want to create a single document that contains a meeting summary in French, English, German, Dutch, and Greek.

First you use a multilingual word processor to edit your French notes into a summary document. Then you click on the taskbar to select English as the input language (see Figure 10-2), and you begin translating the French summary into English. The keyboard continues to use the French layout, and the display font is unchanged. After you complete the English translation, you click the taskbar to select German as the input language. The keyboard layout and the display font remain the same, and you proceed with the German translation. Next you perform a Dutch translation in the same way. Last you select Greek as the input language. The keyboard switches to the Greek layout, and the text appears in a Greek font.

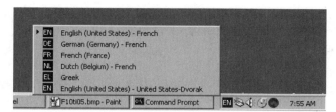

Figure 10-2. *Selecting the input language from the taskbar.*

When you have finished all the translations, you run the spelling checker on the entire document. You correct two minor errors in the English section and one in the Greek section. As you move the cursor from one section to another, the keyboard layout automatically changes so that you can enter the corrections conveniently. You then print the document and send it up the management chain for approval and distribution.

How it works

Clearly the word processor and the operating system are cooperating closely to provide the most convenient work environment for this multilingual user. The operating system offers a taskbar icon that enables the user to select a language and a keyboard layout. Microsoft calls this combination an *input locale*. In addition to the keyboard association, an input locale can also include other input mechanisms, such as an Input Method Editor (IME) or a speech recognizer.[3]

In this scenario, the operating system informs the word processor when the user changes the input locale. In response to this event, the program might have to change the font in order to display the characters of the new input language. Also, it tags each section of the document with the appropriate language identifier (LANGID) so that it can reestablish the input locale when the user moves the cursor in the document. These tags also enable the program to apply the proper spell-checking algorithm to each section.

What it requires

This scenario is an example of dynamic locale switching within an application session at a more microscopic level than in scenario 2. In addition, it is an example of the sometimes intimate relationship between an application and the

---

3. The term *IME* usually refers to the sophisticated keyboard handler used with the Chinese, Japanese, and Korean (CJK) languages, which use thousands of ideograph symbols. In a more general sense, any software that translates keyboard scan codes into character codes is an IME. See Kano, Appendix Q, for illustrations and explanations of the many keyboard layouts supported by Win32 systems. This information is also available on Microsoft's globalization Web site, at *http://www.microsoft.com/globaldev*.

user's input hardware, especially the keyboard. Not only must the application be designed to display symbols from different locales, but also it must offer the user a convenient means to enter those symbols.

In this example, the user selects the input locale by means of a taskbar icon. This feature is available in Windows 2000 and in recent versions of Windows 95, Windows 98, and Windows NT. As an alternative, the application could provide its own selection technique, such as the toolbar list used in scenario 2. Regardless of how the user selects the input locale, the application must somehow store this information in the document if it needs to automatically switch back to that locale later, as was necessary for editing and checking spelling in this word processing scenario.

THE MULTILINGUAL INPUT API

The National Language Support (NLS) API described in Chapter 9 is concerned primarily with internal text processing. For example, it enables a program to construct text strings representing dates, times, money, and other numbers using the rules of a particular locale. Also, the NLS API facilitates comparing, sorting, and converting text using locale-sensitive techniques. In contrast, the ML API is concerned with the external interface—that is, with the relationship between the application program and the UI devices, especially the keyboard and display. Specifically, the ML API enables a program to easily detect and control the keyboard layout and to find fonts that are compatible with the languages being used within the application.

This section describes those aspects of the ML API that are concerned with keyboard input. After that, I'll delve into multilingual output issues, especially those involving font selection.

Keyboard Layouts and Input Locales

Different countries often use their own keyboard layouts to accommodate local symbols and customs. The typical U.S. keyboard (see Figure 10-3) supports USASCII and requires that you use an awkward Alt+key combination to enter other symbols, such as accented characters for European languages.[4] For example, to enter the character Â (capital A with a circumflex) from the normal U.S.

---

4. The keyboard illustrations in this chapter are screen snapshots of the Windows On-Screen Keyboard utility, which is part of the optional Accessibility Package. Although this utility is intended to assist users who have problems accessing their workstations through the normal I/O devices, I've found it quite helpful when testing and documenting ML programs.

keyboard layout, you must hold down the Alt key and press 0194 on the numeric keypad. On the other hand, the French keyboard layout (see Figure 10-4) allows you to enter the same character by pressing ∧ and A in sequence.

Figure 10-3. *U.S. keyboard.*

Figure 10-4. *French keyboard.*

If you switch the input locale to the French language on a system that has a U.S. keyboard, you will notice that the A and Q keys are interchanged and that the circumflex (∧) key moves from Shift+6 to the left square bracket. This is the typical situation when you associate a language with an "unnatural" keyboard. To enter Â on a U.S. keyboard operating with the French layout, you must press [followed by Shift+Q. Pardon the pun, but the key to using an unnatural keyboard layout is to ignore what is printed on the keycaps. Of course, if you're a touch typist, you seldom look at the keys.

Multilingual users are often familiar with several keyboard layouts, but they usually have a preference—most often the keyboard that corresponds to the person's native language or the one on which he or she first learned to touch-type. When dealing with similar languages, such as those derived from Latin, the typist usually accepts minor inconveniences such as Alt+key combinations in order to continue using the preferred keyboard. But when working in a language that requires a significantly different character set (such as Greek, as in scenario 3), most typists find it easier to change the keyboard layout. Otherwise, nearly every character would require an Alt+key sequence. A robust multilingual operating system allows the user to change the layout without rebooting or logging off and on. A robust ML application supports these changes with a minimum of fuss. The word processor in scenario 3 doesn't even require that you close and reopen the document or the application.[5]

In a typical Win32 workstation, the keyboard hardware simply reports the physical location (also called the scan code) of the key being pressed or released. The keyboard software then translates these scan codes into character codes by consulting keyboard layout tables. The system associates a default keyboard translation table with each language, thereby defining the default input locales. Users can adjust these relationships through the Regional Options applet. Application programs can dynamically select the input locale using Win32 API calls. This is how the word processor in scenario 3 automatically establishes the most convenient typing environment when the user moves the cursor around the document while correcting spelling errors.

To establish a multilingual work environment, as in scenario 3, you must set up the system to use the French keyboard when the input locale is French, English, German, or Dutch. For the Greek input locale, you let the system switch to the default Greek layout, which is more convenient for typing that symbol set. This is all done through the Regional Options applet, as shown in Figures 10-5 and 10-6. Figure 10-5 shows the Input Locales tab of the Regional Options applet, where you add or remove input locales that can subsequently be selected using the taskbar or hot keys. Figure 10-6 shows the Input Locale Properties dialog box for the German input locale, with the associated keyboard being changed to the French layout.

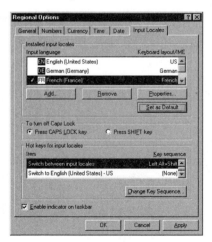

Figure 10-5. *Adjusting input locales using the Regional Options applet.*

---

5. Does such a multilingual word processor exist? Sure. Microsoft Word 2000 is a good example; it operates exactly as described in scenario 3.

Figure 10-6. *Associating a keyboard with an input locale.*

Multilingual Keyboard Functions

Table 10-1 lists the multilingual functions related to the user's input locale.[6] In situations such as scenario 3, you'll use these functions to dynamically control the keyboard translation, typically calling them from the thread that controls your UI. Rarely, if ever, will you call these functions from a worker thread.

Table 10-1. Multiple Keyboard Functions

Function Name	Description
ActivateKeyboardLayout	Sets the input locale for the current thread
GetKeyboardLayout	Gets the input locale for the specified thread
GetKeyboardLayoutList	Gets a list of available input locales
GetKeyboardLayoutName	Gets the name of the current input locale
LoadKeyboardLayout	Adds an input locale to the available list
MapVirtualKey(Ex)	Performs mappings of scan codes, virtual key codes, and characters using the current input locale or a specified one
ToASCII(Ex)	Converts a virtual key code and keyboard state to a multibyte character using the current or specified input locale and its related code page
ToUnicode(Ex)	Converts a virtual key code and keyboard state to Unicode using the current or specified input locale
UnloadKeyboardLayout	Removes an input locale identifier from the list of available locale identifiers
VkKeyScan(Ex)	Converts a character to a virtual key code and keyboard state using the current or specified input locale

Essentially, the keyboard functions manipulate a list of input locales that are available to your program. Win32 represents an input locale as a handle of the type HKL, where *KL* originally stood for "keyboard layout." An HKL is a 32-bit

---

6. Many of these functions have the word *keyboard* in their names because originally they managed only the keyboard input device. When Microsoft generalized to the broader concept of input locales, it continued to use the older function names for compatibility with existing programs.

value similar to, but not the same as, an LCID. The two values are similar in the sense that the lower 16 bits of an HKL and an LCID contain a LANGID.

Recall that each input locale is an association between a language and its user input facility, which typically includes a keyboard device and a scan code translator. As mentioned, the association can also specify an IME and more exotic input mechanisms such as a speech recognizer. Each installed language has a default association with a keyboard layout having the same name as the language. For instance, the French locale generally uses a French keyboard, the United States locale uses the U.S. keyboard, and so on.

To experiment with scenario 3, I used the Regional Options applet to make six input locales available on my system. Figure 10-2 shows how the locales appear in the taskbar's pop-up list.[7] The French and Greek locales use their default keyboards, which are of course French and Greek. Since the user in scenario 3 prefers the French keyboard, I associated it with the U.S. English, Dutch, and German languages. Then I added another association for U.S. English in order to use a Dvorak keyboard.[8]

Listing 10-1 is a simple program that displays the available input locales, and Figure 10-7 shows the program's output for the scenario 3 configuration.

```
#include <stdio.h>
#include <tchar.h>

#define WIN32_LEAN_AND_MEAN
#include <windows.h>

void _tmain()
{
// Could dynamically allocate the array by calling GetKeyboardList
// first with both arguments zero. The return value is the number
// of HKL slots required to hold the entire list.
HKL kbList[20];
int n = GetKeyboardLayoutList(sizeof(kbList)/sizeof(HKL), kbList);
// Save current input locale and report it.
HKL kbSave = GetKeyboardLayout(0);
```

Listing 10-1. *Displaying the available input locales.*

---

7. When you define input locales using the Regional Options applet, you have the option of placing a button on the taskbar that shows the standard two-letter abbreviation for the current input language. When you click this button, a selection list appears showing the available input locales as language-keyboard combinations. You can also define hot-key combinations to switch input locales.

8. The Dvorak keyboard is an alternative to the QWERTY layout used by most U.S. typists. It is arguably more efficient than QWERTY because key placement was carefully calculated to minimize hand motion when typing in English.

```
TCHAR kbName[KL_NAMELENGTH];
GetKeyboardLayoutName(kbName);
_tprintf(_T("Active input locale: 0x%08X \"%s\"\n"), kbSave, kbName);

// Report all available input locales.
_tprintf(_T("Available input locales...\n"));
for(int i = 0; i < n; i++)
    {
    ActivateKeyboardLayout(kbList[i], 0);
    GetKeyboardLayoutName(kbName);
    _tprintf(_T("0x%08X \"%s\"\n"), kbList[i], kbName);
    }
_tprintf(_T("\n"));

// Restore original input locale.
ActivateKeyboardLayout(kbSave, 0);

#if _DEBUG
_gettchar();        // Debugging pause
#endif
}
```

This program obtains the current input locale and its name by calling *GetKeyboardLayout* and *GetKeyboardLayoutName*. After displaying this information, it calls *GetKeyboardLayoutList* to load an array with all available input locale handles. I used a simple fixed-length array, but you can also allocate the array dynamically, as noted in the program comments. Next the program loops through the list and displays each HKL in hexadecimal together with its name string. To obtain the name strings, I had to activate each input locale in turn because *GetKeyboardLayoutName* only retrieves the name of the active input locale. It would be nice if Win32 had a *GetKeyboardLayoutNameEx* function that accepted an HKL argument, but it doesn't.

Figure 10-7. *Output of Listing 10-1.*

The output shown in Figure 10-7 unveils some of the HKL mysteries. Notice that the lower half of each HKL is the LANGID of the input locale. Since the LANGID is also the low 16 bits of an LCID, you can easily correlate Figure 10-7 with the LCIDs listed in Table 9-4. One common ML programming operation is to extract the low 16 bits from an HKL and combine it with the appropriate sorting codes to create an LCID suitable for locale-sensitive operations, as described in Chapter 9.

The upper half of an HKL identifies the keyboard layout or, more generally, the input device and driver requirements. Microsoft's Win32 documentation doesn't completely describe the codes that can appear in this area. Referring again to Figure 10-7, notice that the first four handles contain *0x040C* in this area and *0000040C* for the keyboard layout names. Since 0x040C is the LANGID for French, the system obviously uses a LANGID to indicate the default keyboard for that language. The fifth HKL further confirms this because it has *0x0408* and *00000408* as its keyboard code and name, indicating that the Greek input locale uses the Greek keyboard.

The sixth HKL uses a different scheme in its high-order bits to associate U.S. English with a Dvorak keyboard, which isn't the default for that language. The upper half of the HKL contains *0xF002* as the keyboard code, and *00010409* is the keyboard name string. The Win32 documentation doesn't explain the 0xF002 code, which is presumably an internal value of no significance to an application program. The name string, however, is documented as a LANGID consisting of four hexadecimal digit characters, preceded by four hexadecimal characters that identify one of the keyboards compatible with that language. A prefix of 0000 specifies the default; the alternatives have numbers beginning at 0001. In this example, the Dvorak keyboard is the first alternative for the U.S. locale.

Enumerating the available keyboards

Although the Regional Options applet presents a list of the available keyboards, I was surprised to discover that Win32 offers no function to enumerate them. This omission probably indicates that Microsoft doesn't believe this information is of much use to the typical application programmer. Nonetheless, it is available in the Registry under the following key:

```
HKEY_LOCAL_MACHINE\System\CurrentControlSet\Control\Keyboard Layouts
```

Each keyboard has a subkey, which is an eight-character string of hexadecimal digits, as described earlier. Under each subkey are string values identified as Layout Text and Layout File that contain the keyboard name and driver filename.

Listing 10-2 is my version of an enumeration function that extracts this information from the Registry. I'll happily license this code to Microsoft in return for 1000 shares of Microsoft stock. Just kidding! Actually *EnumKeyboardLayouts* is so simple that Microsoft can have it at no charge. It's a typical Registry access loop that follows the usual conventions for Win32 enumeration functions. It passes each item to a callback function, together with a 32-bit parameter supplied by its caller. The callback function also receives the subkey handle and strings representing the keyboard code, name, and driver. I decided to send the subkey handle in case the callback function needs to extract additional information from the keyboard folder.

```
// Callback function type definition
typedef BOOL (CALLBACK* KBLENUMPROC)(HKEY, LPCTSTR, LPCTSTR,
                                     LPCTSTR, LPARAM);

// Enumerate the keyboard layouts.
long WINAPI EnumKeyboardLayouts(KBLENUMPROC pProc, LPARAM pData)
{
long ret;
HKEY hSystem=0, hCurrentControlSet=0, hControl=0, hKeyboards=0;
try
    {
    ret = RegOpenKeyEx                      // Open HKLM.
        (
        HKEY_LOCAL_MACHINE,
        _T("SYSTEM"),
        0,
        KEY_READ,
        &hSystem
        );
    if(ret != ERROR_SUCCESS) throw ret;
    ret = RegOpenKeyEx                      // Open "CurrentControlSet".
        (
        hSystem,
        _T("CurrentControlSet"),
        0,
        KEY_READ,
        &hCurrentControlSet
        );
    if(ret != ERROR_SUCCESS) throw ret;
    ret = RegOpenKeyEx                      // Open "Control".
        (
        hCurrentControlSet,
        _T("Control"),
        0,
        KEY_READ,
        &hControl
        );
    if(ret != ERROR_SUCCESS) throw ret;
    ret = RegOpenKeyEx                      // Open "Keyboard Layouts".
        (
        hControl,
```

Listing 10-2. *Function to enumerate keyboards.* *(continued)*

Listing 10-2. *continued*

```
            _T("Keyboard Layouts"),
            0,
            KEY_READ,
            &hKeyboards
            );
    if(ret != ERROR_SUCCESS) throw ret;

    BOOL bContinue = TRUE;
    for(DWORD i = 0; bContinue; i++)
        {
        TCHAR kbCode[16];           // Keyboard folder code
        HKEY hKeyboard;             // Keyboard folder handle
        ret = RegEnumKey(hKeyboards, i, kbCode,
                        sizeof(kbCode)/sizeof(TCHAR));
        if(ret != ERROR_SUCCESS) break;
        ret = RegOpenKeyEx
            (
            hKeyboards,
            kbCode,
            0,
            KEY_READ,
            &hKeyboard
            );
        if(ret != ERROR_SUCCESS) break;
        TCHAR kbName[128];              // Keyboard name
        TCHAR kbFile[MAX_PATH];        // Keyboard driver file
        DWORD size = sizeof(kbName);  // Buffer size in bytes
        ret = RegQueryValueEx(hKeyboard, _T("Layout Text"),
                            0, 0, (LPBYTE)kbName, &size);
        if(ret != ERROR_SUCCESS) break;
        size = sizeof(kbFile);
        ret = RegQueryValueEx(hKeyboard, _T("Layout File"),
                            0, 0, (LPBYTE)kbFile, &size);
        if(ret != ERROR_SUCCESS) break;
        RegCloseKey(hKeyboard);
        bContinue = (*pProc)(hKeyboard, kbCode, kbName,
                            kbFile, pData);
        }
    }
catch(...)
    {
    }
if(hKeyboards) RegCloseKey(hKeyboards);
if(hControl) RegCloseKey(hControl);
if(hCurrentControlSet) RegCloseKey(hCurrentControlSet);
if(hSystem) RegCloseKey(hSystem);
return ret;
}
```

To test the keyboard enumerator, I wrote a little browser as a Microsoft Foundation Classes (MFC) dialog application. Figure 10-8 shows its output on my system, scrolled down so that you can see some of the alternative keyboards. The dialog box is filled with a list control, and the *OnInitDialog* function does all of the work to load the list, as shown in Listing 10-3. Notice that I employ the user data pointer to pass the *CListCtrl* object to the callback function.

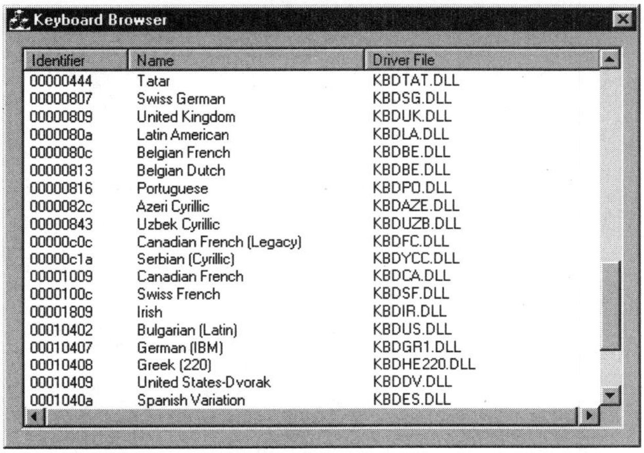

Figure 10-8. *Output of Keyboard Browser program.*

```
// Dialog initialization
BOOL CKeyboardBrowserDlg::OnInitDialog()
{
// MFC boilerplate code removed for brevity

// Set locale list column headings.
m_Keyboards.InsertColumn(0, _T("Identifier"), LVCFMT_LEFT, 80);
m_Keyboards.InsertColumn(1, _T("Name"), LVCFMT_LEFT, 180);
m_Keyboards.InsertColumn(2, _T("Driver File"), LVCFMT_LEFT, 180);

// Load the keyboard list.
EnumKeyboardLayouts(cbEnumKeyboardLayouts, (LPARAM)&m_Keyboards);

return TRUE;
}

// Callback function for EnumKeyboardLayouts
BOOL CALLBACK cbEnumKeyboardLayouts
    (HKEY hKey, LPCTSTR code, LPCTSTR name, LPCTSTR file,
    LPARAM pData)
```

Listing 10-3. *Loading the Keyboard Browser list.* *(continued)*

Listing 10-3. *continued*

```
{
CListCtrl* pList = (CListCtrl*)pData;
int i = pList->GetItemCount();
pList->InsertItem(i, code);
pList->SetItemText(i, 1, name);
pList->SetItemText(i, 2, file);
return TRUE;
}
```

Responding to input locale changes

If your program simply receives input text in Unicode and stores it someplace for later display or transmission, it might not need to know about input locale changes. The system will automatically respond to locale changes by hooking up the proper drivers and input method editors to convert keyboard scan codes to the proper Unicode characters. You get the finished product—namely, Unicode characters.

What if the program needs to process the input text in a locale-sensitive way, such as sorting, comparing, or parsing date, time, number, or monetary strings into numbers? In those cases, you will want to know about input locale changes so that you can make the corresponding adjustments in your text processing algorithms. The system uses the Windows message queue to report these changes because ML applications are almost always graphical.

When the user requests an input locale change, the system sends a *WM_INPUTLANGCHANGEREQUEST* message to the window currently holding the input focus.[9] The message's LPARAM field contains the HKL of the requested input locale, and WPARAM contains some rarely used flags. The application should examine these parameters to determine whether the new input locale is acceptable and, if so, pass the message on to *DefWindowProc*. If the application simply returns 0 from this event, the system refuses the user's request.

DefWindowProc responds to the change request message by switching the input locale for the active process and then sending *WM_INPUTLANGCHANGE* to the top-level window in that process. This message specifies the character set (that is, the ANSI code page) and input locale in WPARAM and LPARAM, respectively. If a window procedure passes the message on to *DefWindowProc*, the system repeats the notification to all child windows at the next level. Using this technique, you can ensure that the change ripples to all of your windows, which is usually desirable.

---

9. Don't you detest those long uppercase symbols that permeate the Win32 API? I think it's a lot easier to read *WM_InputLangChangeRequest*. Sigh…

An ML program usually handles an input locale change by calling *SetThread-Locale* and also adjusting its font repertoire to support the new language, using techniques that I'll discuss in the section "The Multilingual Output API" later in this chapter. In addition, the program often needs to tag its stored text data with the input locale so that the proper conditions can be reestablished when the user moves the cursor into that area later. The exact means of tagging your data is, of course, your choice, but a standard method is available for a program to change the input locale.

Changing the input locale programmatically

Recall that in scenario 3 the word processor switches the input locale when the user moves the cursor from one section of the document to another. The most obvious way to accomplish this is to store the new HKL with the text each time you receive a *WM_INPUTLANGCHANGE* message. In effect, the document is then organized into text blocks delimited by input locales. Then when the cursor moves into a different block, you simply pass that block's HKL to *ActivateKeyboardLayout*.

While this seems logical, it's generally incorrect. Why? Well, an HKL represents a specific association between a language and a keyboard, and generally you can't guarantee that the association is appropriate on a different system. For example, suppose Joe types a document in English on his U.S. keyboard and e-mails it to René, who tries to open the document on her system, where she uses a French keyboard even when working in English. Because Joe's keyboard-language association (that is, his HKL of 0x04090409) isn't defined on René's system, *ActivateKeyboardLayout* can fail or, even worse, force her system to use the U.S. layout for English input.

This implies that the tags in a multilingual document should be language or locale identifiers, not input locale handles. In other words, the program needs to know that Joe entered American English text but not how he did it. Similarly, the word processor doesn't really care that René is editing English text using a French keyboard. Nonetheless, as scenario 3 demonstrates, you do want to honor the user's keyboard preference when moving from one language section to another in the document. Fortunately, *LoadKeyboardLayout* can handle this requirement. Here's a simple function that activates the proper input locale for a given language:

```
HKL SetInputLocale(LCID id)
{
TCHAR s[9];
_stprintf(s, _T("%08X"), LANGIDFROMLCID(id));
return LoadKeyboardLayout    // Return NULL on failure.
  (
  s,                         // Input locale name.
```

(continued)

```
    KLF_ACTIVATE              // Activate locale immediately.
    | KLF_REPLACELANG         // Replace for this language.
    | KLF_SUBSTITUTE_OK       // Honor user preference.
    | KLF_SETFORPROCESS       // Set for entire process.
    );
}
```

This function accepts an LCID, extracts the LANGID, and converts it to a string of eight hexadecimal characters with leading zeros. *LoadKeyboardLayout* uses the string to find a suitable input locale; loads its related driver, translator, and IME modules; and returns the HKL. The function returns a null handle (0) to indicate failure, and you can call *GetLastError* for the details.

The *KLF_ACTIVATE* flag causes the new input locale to be activated immediately, and *KLF_SETFORPROCESS* causes this to occur at the process level, in which case a *WM_INPUTLANGCHANGE* message is generated, as described earlier. This design is convenient because you can use the same message handler to process an input locale change whether it originates externally from the user or internally from some other part of the program.

KLF_REPLACE_LANG causes the new input locale modules to replace any that were previously loaded for the specified language. *KLF_SUBSTITUTE_OK* allows the user or administrator to supply a substitute for the default keyboard. Microsoft recommends that in most cases you should supply 0000 as the device code in the name string and allow substitution so that the current user's preferences are honored.

LoadKeyboardLayout searches the Registry's keyboard layout list (described earlier) to find and load the DLL that handles input operations. In addition, the function consults two lists stored in HKEY_CURRENT_USER under the Keyboard Layout subkey. The Substitutes list (see Figure 10-9) contains a value for each LANGID that uses a nondefault keyboard. The Preload list (see Figure 10-10) identifies the keyboard layouts that should be preloaded for this user. The Regional Options applet maintains these lists, and Figures 10-9 and 10-10 show the arrangement I established for scenario 3.

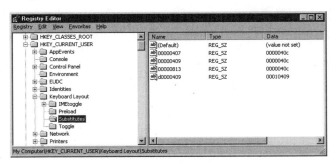

Figure 10-9. *The Substitutes list in the Registry.*

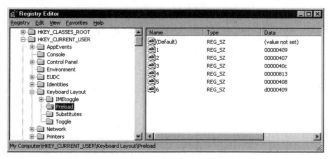

Figure 10-10. *The Preload list in the Registry.*

Working with scan codes

The ML API includes several functions that enable you to access the keyboard translators for the available input locales. These are handy in two situations: handling shortcut keys and simulating keyboard input.

Handling shortcut keys

Shortcut keys, also called accelerators, provide keyboard alternatives for menu and toolbar actions. For instance, Ctrl+A and Ctrl+Z are the conventional shortcuts for the Select All and Undo commands, respectively. Multilingual programs face a dilemma in this area: Should the shortcuts change when the keyboard layout changes, or should they always conform to some "standard" keyboard?

Microsoft has conducted usability studies that suggest that shortcuts should conform to the user's default keyboard regardless of which input locale is active.[10] For instance, if you compare the U.S. and French keyboards in Figures 10-3 and 10-4, you will see that the A and Z keys switch places with Q and W. According to Microsoft's studies, a French user typing on a U.S. keyboard wants to press Ctrl+Q and Ctrl+W (as printed on the keycaps) for the shortcuts that the U.S. user would type as Ctrl+A and Ctrl+Z on the same keyboard. Looking at it from another viewpoint, when a user types in French on a U.S. keyboard, he or she wants to continue using the U.S. keycap lettering for the shortcuts.

The typical Windows program calls *TranslateAccelerator* in its main message loop to look up shortcut keys in an accelerator table that is stored in the resources. The loop is typically very simple, as follows:

```
HACCEL hAccelTable = LoadAccelerators(hInstance, IDR_MAIN);
MSG msg;
while(GetMessage(&msg, 0, 0, 0))
    {
    if(!TranslateAccelerator(msg.hwnd, hAccelTable, &msg))
```

(continued)

---

10. See Kano, pages 179–80.

```
        {
        TranslateMessage(&msg);
        DispatchMessage(&msg);
        }
    }
```

TranslateAccelerator examines keyboard messages to determine whether they match entries in the specified accelerator table, which is usually part of the program's resource database. If a match occurs, the function sends an appropriate command message to the window procedure and returns FALSE.

Listing 10-4 shows how to change a standard message loop so that shortcuts use the default UI keyboard layout.

```
int APIENTRY WinMain(HINSTANCE hInstance,
                     HINSTANCE hPrevInstance,
                     LPSTR     lpCmdLine,
                     int       nCmdShow)
{
// Initialize global variables.
LoadString(hInstance, IDS_APP_TITLE, szTitle, MAX_LOADSTRING);
LoadString(hInstance, IDC_CH10D, szWindowClass, MAX_LOADSTRING);
MyRegisterClass(hInstance);

// Initialize the application.
if (!InitInstance (hInstance, nCmdShow)) return FALSE;

// Get accelerator table.
HACCEL hAccelTable = LoadAccelerators(hInstance, (LPCTSTR)IDC_CH10D);

// Get UI default settings.
LANGID langDefault = GetUserDefaultUILanguage();  // UI language
TCHAR name[9];                                    // Input locale name
_stprintf(name, _T("%08X"), langDefault);
HKL hklDefault = LoadKeyboardLayout               // Input locale handle
    (
    name,
    KLF_NOTELLSHELL | KLF_SUBSTITUTE_OK
    );

// Message loop with accelerators mapped to default UI keyboard
MSG msg;
while(GetMessage(&msg, 0, 0, 0))
    {
    WPARAM vkNew, vkOld;
    vkNew = vkOld = msg.wParam;
    if(hklDefault && (msg.message >= WM_KEYFIRST) &&
        (msg.message <= WM_KEYLAST))
```

Listing 10-4. *Mapping accelerator keys in the main message loop.*

```
        {
        LANGID langCurrent = LOWORD(GetKeyboardLayout(0));
        if(langDefault != langCurrent)
            {
            vkNew = MapVirtualKeyEx(HIWORD(msg.lParam), 3,
                                    hklDefault);
            if(vkNew) msg.wParam = vkNew;
            }
        }
    if(!TranslateAccelerator(msg.hwnd, hAccelTable, &msg))
        {
        msg.wParam = vkOld;
        TranslateMessage(&msg);
        DispatchMessage(&msg);
        }
#ifdef _DEBUG
    else if(vkNew != vkOld) _RPT2        // Trace message.
        (
        _CRT_WARN,
        _T("Accelerator key mapped from %08X to %08X\n"),
        vkOld,
        vkNew
        );
#endif
    }

return msg.wParam;
}
```

To create this application, use the Application Wizard to build a generic Windows program, and then introduce the following changes:

1. During initialization, call *GetUserDefaultUILanguage* to obtain the default UI language for the current user. This function is available only in Windows 2000 and corresponds to the UI language setting shown in Figure 10-1. Notice that this isn't necessarily the same LANGID as returned by *GetUserDefaultLanguage*, which retrieves the user locale setting shown in Figure 10-1.

2. Still during initialization, call *LoadKeyboardLayout* to get the HKL for the default input locale.

3. Within the message loop, check whether the current message is from the keyboard. If so, get the current input locale. If the input locale is using a different language than the default UI, call *MapVirtualKeyEx* to map the virtual key code back to the default input locale.

4. Call *TranslateAccelerator* in the normal way. If it returns FALSE, restore the original virtual key code in the message so that normal keys are processed in the current language.

MFC and similar Windows programming environments usually bury the main message loop deep within the library, but they also provide "hooks" so that you can perform special operations such as UI-sensitive shortcut mapping. MFC offers two virtual functions named *PreCreateWindow* and *PreTranslateMessage* for this purpose. Usually you override these functions in the main window class, as shown in Listing 10-5. In this case, I first changed the existing *PreCreateWindow* function (which was created by the Application Wizard) to save the default LANGID and HKL as member variables in the mainframe object. Then I used the Class Wizard to override *PreTranslateMessage* and added the statements to perform the mapping as described earlier. Notice that the base class version of *PreTranslateMessage* must be called if no shortcut mapping occurred. Failure to do this will cause problems in MFC.

```
// MFC calls this hook before the window is created.
BOOL CMainFrame::PreCreateWindow(CREATESTRUCT& cs)
{
if(!CFrameWnd::PreCreateWindow(cs)) return FALSE;
cs.dwExStyle &= ~WS_EX_CLIENTEDGE;
cs.lpszClass = AfxRegisterWndClass(0);
m_langDefault = GetUserDefaultUILanguage();
TCHAR name[9];
_stprintf(name, _T("%08X"), m_langDefault);
m_hklDefault = LoadKeyboardLayout
    (
    name,
    KLF_NOTELLSHELL | KLF_SUBSTITUTE_OK
    );
return TRUE;
}


// MFC calls this hook before processing a message from the queue.
BOOL CMainFrame::PreTranslateMessage(MSG* pMsg)
{
HACCEL hAccel = GetDefaultAccelerator();
if(hAccel && m_hklDefault &&
    (pMsg->message >= WM_KEYFIRST) && (pMsg->message <= WM_KEYLAST))
    {
    LANGID langCurrent = LOWORD(GetKeyboardLayout(0));
    if(m_langDefault != langCurrent)
        {
        WPARAM vkNew, vkOld;
```

Listing 10-5. *Mapping shortcuts in MFC.*

```
            vkOld = pMsg->wParam;
            vkNew = MapVirtualKeyEx(HIWORD(pMsg->lParam), 3,
                              m_hklDefault);
            if(vkNew)
                {
                pMsg->wParam = vkNew;
                if(::TranslateAccelerator(m_hWnd, hAccel, pMsg))
                    {
                    TRACE(_T("Accelerator key mapped ")
                          _T("from %08X to %08X\n"),
                          vkOld, vkNew);
                    return TRUE;
                    }
                }
            pMsg->wParam = vkOld;
            }
        }
    return CFrameWnd::PreTranslateMessage(pMsg);
    }
```

Although the techniques shown in Listings 10-4 and 10-5 work most of the time, you have to be careful in situations in which messages are not processed by the main loop. This happens most often when you display a dialog box or enter some other restricted mode, such as during a drag-and-drop operation. In those cases, messages are dequeued in a different loop that doesn't perform the UI-sensitive shortcut mapping.

This situation isn't a problem if the application's UI is disabled during the secondary message loop, which is certainly the case for modal dialog boxes, drag-and-drop operations, and other "application modal" states managed by the system. If you write your own secondary message loops, you can add the shortcut mapping logic where appropriate. Alternatively, you can selectively enable and disable accelerators with these three Windows 2000 messages:

- ■ ***WM_CHANGEUISTATE***   Send this message to your main window when you want to enable or disable keyboard shortcuts. Simply allow *DefWindowProc* to handle the message.

- ■ ***WM_QUERYUISTATE***   Send this message to your main window when you need to know whether keyboard shortcuts are enabled or disabled.

- ■ ***WM_UPDATEUISTATE***   *DefWindowProc* sends this message to children of the window that received the *WM_CHANGEUISTATE* message. If you pass this message to *DefWindowProc*, it ripples through the window tree.

As mentioned, these messages are available only in Windows 2000, and they don't seem to be fully implemented on my test platform, which is Windows 2000 RC3 (build 2183). Carefully check the Windows 2000 documentation before using them.

Simulating keyboard input

Sometimes you need to simulate keyboard input by sending *WM_KEYUP* and *WM_KEYDOWN* messages from within your program. In those cases, it's important to use the keyboard mapping that corresponds to the input locale. To do this, you generally need to call some combination of *MapVirtualKeyEx*, *ToAsciiEx*, *ToUnicodeEx*, and *VkKeyScanEx*. Listing 10-6 shows an example.

```
void PostKey(HWND hwnd, HKL hkl, UINT vkey, BOOL bDown)
{
vkey &= 0xFF;
UINT scan = MapVirtualKeyEx(vkey, 0, hkl);
if(bDown) ::PostMessage(hwnd, WM_KEYDOWN, vkey, MAKELONG(1, scan));
else ::PostMessage(hwnd, WM_KEYUP, vkey, MAKELONG(1, scan | 0xC000));
}


void PostKeys(HWND hwnd, HKL hkl, LPCTSTR s)
{
UINT vkNext;             // Next key
UINT vkPrev = 0;         // Previous key
UINT vkDiff = 0;         // Difference flags
while(*s)
    {
    vkNext = VkKeyScanEx(*s++, hkl);
    vkDiff = vkPrev ^ vkNext;
    if(vkDiff & 0x0100)            // Adjust SHIFT state.
        PostKey(hwnd, hkl, VK_SHIFT,
                (vkNext & 0x0100) ? TRUE : FALSE);
    if(vkDiff & 0x0200)            // Adjust CONTROL state.
        PostKey(hwnd, hkl, VK_CONTROL,
                (vkNext & 0x0100) ? TRUE : FALSE);
    if(vkDiff & 0x0400)            // Adjust ALT state.
        PostKey(hwnd, hkl, VK_MENU, (vkNext & 0x0100) ? TRUE : FALSE);
    PostKey(hwnd, hkl, vkNext, TRUE);
    PostKey(hwnd, hkl, vkNext, FALSE);
    vkPrev = vkNext;
    }
if(vkPrev & 0x0100)            // Release SHIFT key.
    PostKey(hwnd, hkl, VK_SHIFT, FALSE);
if(vkPrev & 0x0200)            // Release CONTROL key.
    PostKey(hwnd, hkl, VK_CONTROL, FALSE);
if(vkPrev & 0x0400)            // Release ALT state.
    PostKey(hwnd, hkl, VK_MENU, FALSE);
}
```

Listing 10-6. *Feeding keystroke messages to the queue.*

PostKeys is a function that accepts a window handle, an input locale handle, and a text string. It performs the following operations for each character:

1. Calls *VkKeyScanEx* to convert the character to a virtual key code and a set of state flags for the keyboard layout used by the input locale.

2. Compares the *SHIFT*, *CONTROL*, and *ALT* flags to their previous states. If any have changed, calls *PostKey* to simulate pressing or releasing the corresponding key.

3. Calls *PostKey* twice for the text character to simulate the press and release of the key.

PostKey converts the virtual key code to a scan code by calling *MapVirtualKeyEx*, and then it posts the *WM_KEYDOWN* or *WM_KEYUP* message. After processing all characters, *PostKeys* generates messages to restore the keyboard to its original state.

Although simple, this technique isn't foolproof. It doesn't prevent the user from typing, and so unwanted keystroke messages could get intermingled with those generated by *PostKeys*. Also, it assumes that the keyboard is initially unshifted and that the Ctrl and Alt keys are not pressed. Examine Win32's *SendInput* function for more robust keyboard simulation, such as you might need in a computer-based training (CBT) scenario. *SendInput* places input events directly into the keyboard queue. This technique is considerably more complicated, but it gives you much more control over the keyboard sequencing.

THE MULTILINGUAL OUTPUT API

Proper font selection is the major output issue in international programs that don't have complex script requirements such as right-to-left ordering. As we saw in the console examples in Chapter 5, you often need to use a different font when the locale changes because many fonts contain symbols that cover the needs of just a few languages. In simple situations, you can put this problem in the hands of the user. For instance, in the earlier console examples I assume that the user will open the console property sheet to choose an appropriate font and the programs simply honor that selection. If the user fails to choose a font that contains the necessary symbols and the proper character-set mapping, the program still works correctly on the inside, but it produces garbage on the output device.

More complicated multilingual applications like scenario 3 need to display several languages at the same time. In those cases, the program must be more involved in font management because it can be difficult or impossible for the user to pick the appropriate font or font set. Fortunately, the ML API provides extensive support for these situations in the form of several new functions as well as improved versions of traditional text display functions such as *ExtTextOut*. Before examining these services, let's take a brief look at fonts in general.

Font Terminology

A font is essentially a database of symbols, also called *glyphs,* that can be rendered (drawn) on a compatible output device such as a display screen, printer, or plotter. Although application programs don't generally care how this rendering is done, it's useful to understand the four types of fonts available on most Win32 systems:

- **Raster fonts (also called bitmap fonts)**   Each glyph is represented by a bitmap, and because each bitmap is handcrafted, the glyphs are usually quite attractive. Raster fonts typically include several discrete sizes, and when an application program requests a different size, the system stretches the nearest bitmap to fit. This stretching can produce ugly results, especially in the larger sizes. Raster fonts are often built into hardware such as printers and monitors, and so they are also often called *device fonts.*

- **Vector fonts (also called stroke fonts)**   Each glyph is represented as a set of straight line segments. Although vector fonts are scalable, they are not as attractive as the other font types when the glyphs contain lots of curves. Vector fonts are often used with plotters, which are optimized for vector drawing of engineering documents that require only simple fonts.

- **TrueType fonts (also called outline fonts)**   Each glyph is represented as a set of shapes (typically line segments and Bézier curves) together with hints for adjusting the shapes when the font is resized.[11] TrueType is fairly fast and produces attractive results on all devices. This technology was developed by Apple and Microsoft during the 16-bit era and is fully supported on all Microsoft Windows and Apple Macintosh platforms. Because of its scalability and hardware independence, Windows programmers have long preferred TrueType over bitmap and vector fonts.[12]

---

11. These shaping and hinting rules form a typographic programming language, which is fully described in the TrueType specification available on the Microsoft typography Web site at *http://www.microsoft.com/typography*. This site also contains other specifications, such as OpenType, plus numerous font utility programs.

12. To achieve a consistent look, you can force application programs to use only TrueType fonts. To do this, start the Fonts applet in the Control Panel. From the Tools menu, choose Folder Options to display the Folder Options Properties window. Select the TrueType Fonts tab, and then select the Show Only TrueType Fonts In The Programs On My Computer option.

■ **OpenType fonts (also called TrueType Open fonts)** OpenType is an upward-compatible extension of TrueType that was developed jointly by Microsoft and Adobe in 1997. Each glyph is represented as a set of TrueType or PostScript shapes and hints.[13] In addition, OpenType fonts contain extensive information to facilitate ML programming with Unicode, such as character maps, substitution rules, and rules for forming ligatures and other positional variations. In effect, OpenType implements the shaping rules specified in the Unicode standard.

Since TrueType and OpenType are flexible, scalable, and well suited for international applications that employ the Unicode character set, I will focus on them for the rest of this discussion. Note that application programmers are rarely concerned about the differences between these two font technologies because the Win32 API hides the differences. In general, newer Unicode fonts use OpenType, whereas older ANSI fonts use TrueType. Some font selection dialog boxes use different icons to distinguish between these two types. Figure 10-11 shows the Font dialog box in Microsoft WordPad.

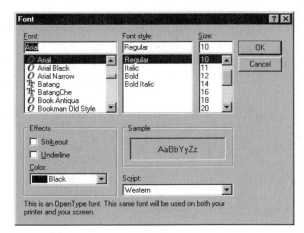

Figure 10-11. *Dialog box showing TrueType and OpenType fonts.*

Font identification

We usually identify a font by its typeface, style, and size, as in "Baskerville Old Face 8-point italic." The typeface—in this case, Baskerville Old Face—is a name that describes the overall appearance of the glyphs and may also identify the

---

13. PostScript is an outline font technology developed by Adobe Systems prior to TrueType. It is supported on many non-Microsoft systems and can also coexist with TrueType on Windows platforms.

origin of the font—usually the typographer who designed the font or the publisher that first used it. For instance, *Baskerville* in Baskerville Old Face refers to typographer John Baskerville, while "Old Face" indicates that the font resembles the lead type used in old newspapers.

The most commonly used typefaces come in two categories: *serif* and *sans serif,* meaning with or without serif marks. Serif fonts tend to be more decorative because the strokes of the letters end in extensions (serifs) that make the letters look as if they were written using an ink pen or a quill. Sans serif fonts have a more mechanical appearance, with no curlicues or other flourishes. Two additional categories are *cursive fonts* and *symbol fonts*. Cursive fonts resemble handwritten script. Symbol fonts assign code points to special symbols instead of letters. Here are some popular typeface names printed in the corresponding font[14]:

Comic Sans (a proportional sans serif font)

MS Mincho (a proportional serif font)

Lucida Handwriting (a handwriting font)

Lucida Sans (a proportional sans serif font)

✋☺☹⊗🖐☀♀ ("IJKLMN" in Wingdings, a symbol font)

A font's style specifies the weight (that is, darkness and thickness) and the slant of the glyphs. The weight is usually described as one of the following: thin, extra light, light, normal, medium, semibold, bold, extra bold, or heavy. The slant is *roman* if the glyphs have an upright appearance or *oblique* if they are slanted. The most popular slant is *italic,* and so many fonts include specific bitmaps or drawing rules for this forward slant style. Other oblique styles such as reverse slants are seldom used, and so most fonts don't offer them. Instead, the rendering program performs a shear transformation on the roman glyphs to produce the desired slant.

The size of a font is the maximum vertical distance needed to draw its glyphs, usually expressed in *points,* where a point is approximately 1/72 inch (more precisely, 0.013837 inch). Since font size depends on the typeface and

---

14. The typical Windows PC has dozens or even hundreds of TrueType fonts installed. Some come with Windows, but most are installed with products such as Microsoft Word. You can find numerous typography Web sites that offer bizarre fonts—for example, *http://www.killerfonts.com* sells fonts based on the handwriting of famous killers like John Dillinger and Jack the Ripper.

style, the font designer usually specifies it. In fonts that include the English alphabet, as do all Win32 fonts, the size is generally the distance from the top of an uppercase M to the bottom of a lowercase g, as shown in Figure 10-12.

 — Font size

Figure 10-12. *Measuring font size.*

If all glyphs in a font are drawn in cells having the same width, the font is said to be *monospaced.* On the other hand, if the cell width varies according to the actual requirements of each glyph, the font is said to be *proportional,* or *proportionally spaced.*

Fonts and character sets

As a glyph database, a font must provide some means of identifying its members. The obvious approach is to assign each glyph a number corresponding to a particular character encoding, such as CP1252. Indeed, many programmers think of fonts and code pages as interchangeable concepts, even though they really have no intrinsic relationship. A font doesn't necessarily contain all of the symbols from any particular character set and could contain symbols from several sets. Furthermore, a font's glyph identification scheme doesn't have to match any particular code page.

So the challenge when working with fonts in a multilingual environment is to find the fonts that contain the symbols you need and then map your character codes into the glyph identifiers. A font of the raster and vector variety usually assigns glyph identifiers to a specific 8-bit code page such as CP437, or else it uses a vendor-specific glyph identification scheme. Either technique places a heavy burden on the international programmer to perform the necessary code page switching or mapping.

TrueType ANSI fonts are more flexible because they identify glyphs according to one or more Windows character sets such as CP1252 or CP1253, which makes them multilingual over a broader range than fonts that support only a single code page. Figure 10-13 shows the code page mapping for the popular Century Schoolbook font. The lower list box on the CharSet/Unicode tab indicates that the font supports CP1250 through CP1254 plus CP1257. If you scroll farther down in the list, you will find that this font also supports many of the older code pages such as CP437 and CP850.

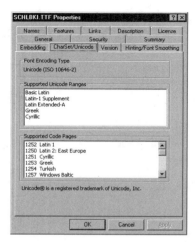

Figure 10-13. *Code page mapping for a TrueType ANSI font.*

To view a font's property sheet, as shown in Figure 10-13, you must install the Font Properties Extensions. This free utility program is available from the Microsoft Typography Web site at *http://www.microsoft.com/typography*. After installing the extensions, simply right-click on a TrueType font (TTF) file, a TrueType collection (TTC) file, or other font file to view the font properties. If you really get into TrueType technology, you will also want to download the Font Dump utility, a console program that shows all the gory internals of a font file.

As I've mentioned, ML programming is easiest with Unicode because you need not be concerned about code pages and variable character lengths. It should be no surprise then that Unicode fonts, whether TrueType or OpenType, are the most flexible for ML programming. A Unicode font typically contains glyphs from several Unicode ranges, and so you can often find a single font that supports the languages you need, thereby eliminating the need to switch fonts dynamically within a text string. Furthermore, OpenType fonts contain information that helps implement the special glyph shaping rules defined in the Unicode standard for languages such as Arabic and Indic.

Does this mean that a Unicode application can use only fonts that are explicitly identified as Unicode? No, because all TrueType fonts support Unicode mapping, although many of them save space by including a limited subset of the glyphs defined in the Unicode standard. A font advertises these subsets through the Supported Unicode Ranges property, which is the upper list box on the CharSet/Unicode tab in the Font Properties window shown in Figure 10-13. The ranges correspond to the Unicode standard. For instance, Basic Latin ranges from U+0000 to U+007F, and Cyrillic ranges from U+0400 to U+04FF.

The only significant difference between a TrueType ANSI font and a TrueType Unicode font is that the former supports a single ANSI code page, whereas the latter supports several.[15] Under the covers, all TrueType fonts use Unicode to identify the glyphs.

Font Programming Fundamentals

To achieve a degree of device independence, Win32 application programs work with *logical fonts,* which are system objects traditionally constructed by the *CreateFont* or *CreateFontIndirect* API functions. With either function, the application describes the logical font by supplying some or all of the information associated with the *LOGFONT* structure, shown in Listing 10-7, and the function returns an object handle of the *HFONT* type. Before drawing text on a display device, the application asks the operating system's font mapper to choose a *physical font* that is compatible with the display device and is the closest match to the desired logical font. This logical-to-physical association occurs when the application calls *SelectObject* to attach a logical font to a device context.[16]

```
#define LF_FACESIZE 32

typedef struct
{
LONG     lfHeight;               // Font height
LONG     lfWidth;                // Average character width
LONG     lfEscapement;           // Escapement angle
LONG     lfOrientation;          // Baseline orientation angle
LONG     lfWeight;               // Font weight
BYTE     lfItalic;               // TRUE if italic
BYTE     lfUnderline;            // TRUE if underlined
BYTE     lfStrikeOut;            // TRUE if strikeout
BYTE     lfCharSet;              // Character set
BYTE     lfOutPrecision;         // Output precision
BYTE     lfClipPrecision;        // Clipping precision
BYTE     lfQuality;              // Output quality
BYTE     lfPitchAndFamily;       // Font pitch and family
TCHAR    lfFaceName[LF_FACESIZE]; // Typeface name
} LOGFONT;
```

Listing 10-7. *Logical font structure.*

---

15. Because of the relative sizes of their TTF files, TrueType ANSI and Unicode fonts are often called "little" and "big" fonts, respectively.

16. The font mapper works its magic without much prompting from the application program. It offers only one control parameter through the *SetMapperFlags* function, which enables you to force the selection of physical fonts that match the aspect ratio (character width vs. height) of the device.

LOGFONT structure members

To use fonts successfully, you must become adept at constructing proper font descriptions. It would be nice if you could simply use a text string such as *"Times Roman Bold Italic 12 Point for English, French, and German"* and have the system search for the matching font. Alas, a text description lacks the necessary precision, and so you must learn to work with the *LOGFONT* structure in detail.[17] In this section, we'll look at the *LOGFONT* structure members.

lfHeight

The *lfHeight* member specifies the height in logical units of the font's character cell or character. This signed value is also known as the *em height* and is the character cell height minus the internal-leading height. The font mapper interprets the sign as follows:

Value	Meaning
> 0	The font mapper transforms this value into device units and matches it against the cell height of the available fonts.
0	The font mapper uses a default height value when it searches for a match.
< 0	The font mapper transforms this value into device units and matches its absolute value against the character height of the available fonts.

For all height comparisons, the font mapper looks for the largest font that doesn't exceed the requested size. This mapping occurs when the font is used for the first time. For the MM_TEXT mapping mode, you can use the following formula to specify a height for a font with a specified point size:

```
lfHeight = -MulDiv(PointSize, GetDeviceCaps(hDC, LOGPIXELSY), 72);
```

lfWidth

The *lfWidth* member specifies the average width, in logical units, of characters in the font. If this value is 0, the aspect ratio of the device is matched against the digitization aspect ratio of the available fonts to find the closest match, as determined by the absolute value of the difference.

lfEscapement

The *lfEscapement* member specifies the angle, in tenths of degrees, between the escapement vector and the x-axis of the device. The escapement vector is parallel to the baseline of a row of text.

---

17. *CreateFontIndirect* accepts a *LOGFONT* structure, whereas *CreateFont* accepts the same information as a lengthy list of arguments. Most of the programmers I know prefer to use *CreateFontIndirect*.

In Windows NT and Windows 2000, the *SetGraphicsMode* API determines how the escapement and orientation angles interact. If the graphics mode is set to GM_ADVANCED, you can specify the escapement angle of the string independently of the orientation angle of the string's characters. If the graphics mode is set to GM_COMPATIBLE, *lfEscapement* specifies both the escapement and orientation, and you should set *lfOrientation* to the same value.

In Windows 95, the *lfEscapement* member specifies both the escapement and the orientation angle, and you should set *lfOrientation* to the same value.

lfOrientation

The *lfOrientation* member specifies the angle, in tenths of degrees, between each character's baseline and the x-axis of the device.

lfWeight

The *lfWeight* member specifies the weight of the font in the range 0 through 1000—for example, 400 is normal and 700 is bold. If this value is 0, a default weight is used. The values listed in the following table are defined for programming convenience:

Value	*Weight*
FW_DONTCARE	0
FW_THIN	100
FW_EXTRALIGHT	200
FW_ULTRALIGHT	200
FW_LIGHT	300
FW_NORMAL	400
FW_REGULAR	400
FW_MEDIUM	500
FW_SEMIBOLD	600
FW_DEMIBOLD	600
FW_BOLD	700
FW_EXTRABOLD	800
FW_ULTRABOLD	800
FW_HEAVY	900
FW_BLACK	900

lfItalic

The *lfItalic* member specifies an italic font if set to TRUE.

lfUnderline

The *lfUnderline* member specifies an underlined font if set to TRUE.

lfStrikeOut

The *lfStrikeOut* member specifies a strikeout font if set to TRUE.

lfCharSet

The *lfCharSet* member specifies the glyphs that the application requires in the font, as described in the following table. Most of these values relate directly to code pages; additional values may be defined in future versions of Windows.

Character Set	Code Page	Comments
ANSI_CHARSET	1252	The Windows character set used in the United States and Western Europe. Note that this setting has a value of 0, so you will get this character set if you simply clear the *LOGFONT* structure. To invoke the actual font mapper default behavior, you must explicitly set this item to DEFAULT_CHARSET.
ARABIC_CHARSET	1256	Available in Windows 2000 or in the Middle Eastern edition of other versions of Windows.
BALTIC_CHARSET	1257	
CHINESEBIG5_CHARSET	950	
DEFAULT_CHARSET		In Windows 95 and Windows 98, the font mapper will substitute a font from any typeface if the specified typeface isn't available. In Windows 2000, the font mapper will use the ANSI character set corresponding to the current locale.
EASTEUROPE_CHARSET	1250	
GB2312_CHARSET	936	
GREEK_CHARSET	1253	
HANGEUL_CHARSET	949	Same as HANGUL_CHARSET.
HANGUL_CHARSET	949	
HEBREW_CHARSET	1255	Available in Windows 2000 or in the Middle Eastern edition of other versions of Windows.
JOHAB_CHARSET	1361	
MAC_CHARSET		Used for compatibility with Apple Macintosh systems.
OEM_CHARSET		Used for compatibility with MS-DOS.
RUSSIAN_CHARSET	1251	
SHIFTJIS_CHARSET	932	
SYMBOL_CHARSET		
THAI_CHARSET	874	Available in Windows 2000 or in the Thai edition of other versions of Windows.
TURKISH_CHARSET	1254	
VIETNAMESE_CHARSET		

lfOutPrecision

The *lfOutPrecision* member specifies the output precision, which defines how closely the output must match the requested font's height, width, character orientation, escapement, pitch, and font type. It can have one of the following values:

Value	*Meaning*
OUT_CHARACTER_PRECIS	Chooses the font with a size that closely matches the requested size. This value isn't used in Windows NT and Windows 2000.
OUT_DEFAULT_PRECIS	Specifies default font mapping.
OUT_DEVICE_PRECIS	Instructs the font mapper to choose a device font when the system contains multiple fonts with the same name.
OUT_OUTLINE_PRECIS	In Windows NT and Windows 2000, this value instructs the font mapper to choose from TrueType and other outline-based fonts.
OUT_RASTER_PRECIS	Instructs the font mapper to choose a raster font when the system contains multiple fonts with the same name.
OUT_STRING_PRECIS	This value isn't used by the font mapper but is returned when a raster font is enumerated.
OUT_STROKE_PRECIS	In Windows NT and Windows 2000, this value isn't used by the font mapper but is returned when an outline or a vector font is enumerated. In Windows 95 and Windows 98, this value instructs the font mapper to choose a vector font when the system contains multiple fonts with the same name. Also returned when a TrueType or vector font is enumerated.
OUT_TT_ONLY_PRECIS	Instructs the font mapper to choose only TrueType fonts. If no TrueType fonts are installed on the system, the font mapper returns to default behavior.
OUT_TT_PRECIS	Instructs the font mapper to choose a TrueType font when the system contains multiple fonts with the same name.

Applications can use OUT_DEVICE_PRECIS, OUT_RASTER_PRECIS, OUT_TT_PRECIS, and OUT_TT_ONLY_PRECIS to control how the font mapper makes a selection when the operating system contains more than one font with a specified name. For example, if an operating system contains a font named Symbol in raster and TrueType form, OUT_TT_PRECIS causes the font mapper to choose the TrueType version. Furthermore, OUT_TT_ONLY_PRECIS forces the font mapper to always choose a TrueType font even if it must substitute a TrueType font of another name.

lfClipPrecision

The *lfClipPrecision* member specifies the clipping precision, which defines how to clip characters that are partially outside the clipping region. It can have one or more of the following values:

Value	Meaning
CLIP_CHARACTER_PRECIS	Chooses a font that allows character clipping.
CLIP_DEFAULT_PRECIS	Specifies default clipping behavior.
CLIP_EMBEDDED	Applications must specify this value to use an embedded read-only font.
CLIP_LH_ANGLES	Indicates that the rotation for all fonts depends on whether the orientation of the coordinate system is left-handed or right-handed. If this value isn't set, device fonts always rotate counterclockwise, and the rotation of other fonts depends on the orientation of the coordinate system. See the *nOrientation* parameter used in the *CreateFont* function for more details.
CLIP_MASK	Not used.
CLIP_STROKE_PRECIS	Not used by the font mapper, but returned when a raster, vector, or TrueType font is enumerated.
	In Windows NT and Windows 2000, for compatibility, this value is always returned when applications enumerate fonts.
CLIP_TT_ALWAYS	Not used.

lfQuality

The *lfQuality* member specifies the output quality, which defines how carefully the graphics device interface (GDI) must attempt to match the logical font attributes to those of an actual physical font. It can have one of the following values:

Value	Meaning
ANTIALIASED_QUALITY	Font is always antialiased (smoothed) if the font supports it and the size isn't too small or too large.
DEFAULT_QUALITY	Appearance of the font doesn't matter.
DRAFT_QUALITY	Appearance of the font is less important than when PROOF_QUALITY is used. Scaling is enabled for raster fonts, which means that more font sizes are available but the quality may be lower. Bold, italic, underline, and strikeout fonts are synthesized if necessary.
NONANTIALIASED_QUALITY	Font is never antialiased (smoothed).
PROOF_QUALITY	Quality of the font is more important than exact matching of the logical font attributes. Scaling is disabled for raster fonts, and the font closest in size is chosen. Although the chosen font size may not be mapped exactly when PROOF_QUALITY is used, the quality of the font is high and there is no distortion of appearance. Bold, italic, underline, and strikeout fonts are synthesized if necessary.

If neither ANTIALIASED_QUALITY nor NONANTIALIASED_QUALITY is selected, the font is smoothed only if the user chooses smooth screen fonts in the Control Panel.

lfPitchAndFamily

The *lfPitchAndFamily* member specifies the pitch and family of the font in bits 0 through 3 and 4 through 7, respectively. The pitch can have one of the following values: DEFAULT_PITCH, FIXED_PITCH, or VARIABLE_PITCH. Fixed and variable pitch fonts are also called monospace and proportional fonts, respectively. The font family describes the look of a font in a general way and is used when the exact typeface isn't known or isn't available. It can have one of the values listed at the top of the next page, which can be ORed with the appropriate pitch constant.

Value	Description
FF_DECORATIVE	Novelty fonts such as Old English.
FF_DONTCARE	Used when information about a font doesn't matter or doesn't exist.
FF_MODERN	Fonts with a constant stroke width, with or without serifs. Monospace fonts are usually modern, such as Pica, Elite, and CourierNew.
FF_ROMAN	Serif fonts with a variable stroke width, such as Times New Roman.
FF_SCRIPT	Fonts designed to look like handwriting, such as Freestyle Script and Lucida Handwriting.
FF_SWISS	Sans serif fonts with a variable stroke width, such as Lucida Sans.

lfFaceName

The *lfFaceName* member is a null-terminated string specifying the typeface name of the font. The string length can't exceed 32 characters, including the null terminator. If the string is empty, the font mapper uses the first font that matches the other specified attributes.

Populating a *LOGFONT* structure

Programmers use three common techniques for populating a *LOGFONT* structure with enough information to correctly describe a font: do it yourself, ask the user to do it, or ask the system to do it. Let's examine each technique.

Method 1: Creating your own font description

This technique is essentially guesswork. You start with an empty *LOGFONT* structure (initialized to all zero), fill in the items that are important to you, and let the font mapper find the closest physical font. The selection may vary from one machine to another, depending on which fonts are installed.

The font mapper usually does a pretty good job of honoring your request, especially if the system has a large number of fonts available. Of course, the more information you provide in the *LOGFONT* description, the more likely you are to wind up with a font that meets your needs. For the most consistent results, you should specify at least the typeface (*lfFaceName*), height (*lfHeight*), pitch and family (*lfPitchAndFamily*), and character set (*lfCharSet*). For special effects such as bold, italic, or rotated text, you will need to initialize additional items in the structure.

To help eliminate some of the guesswork, I developed a utility program that I call the LOGFONT Explorer. It's an MFC application that lets you fill in a *LOGFONT* structure and then view the corresponding physical font. The source code is included on the companion CD. Figure 10-14 shows an example of its output. In this case, I initialized the *LOGFONT* structure for the Monotype Corsiva typeface with a height of 50 logical units (here, screen pixels), an escapement angle of 35 degrees, and a weight of 100.

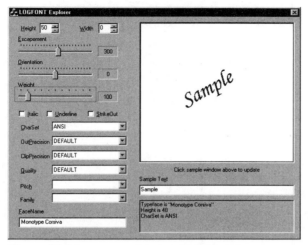

Figure 10-14. *Output of the LOGFONT Explorer program.*

Because of its unpredictable behavior, many programmers avoided this technique in earlier versions of Windows. Most TrueType fonts were installed as separately purchased font packs or in conjunction with word processors and other purchased products. To ensure that a desired font was available to your application, you had to license it and include it with your product. Windows now contains a much richer set of fonts, including Arial and Times New Roman, and if you stick to the built-in TrueType repertoire, this technique is effective and simple. At the very least, you can expect to find the following TrueType fonts in Windows 95, Windows 98, Windows NT, and Windows 2000:

- **MS Shell Dlg**   This is a placeholder for the locale-dependent system typeface. The mapping between this name and an actual typeface name is established during system installation or when a user changes the system locale.

- **Arial**   A proportional sans-serif font with a modern look, often used for dialog boxes, fax documents, and other situations in which serifs might appear too cluttered. Also available in several styles, such as **Arial Black** and Arial Narrow.

- **Courier New**   A monospace font similar to Pica on a typewriter. Typically used by source code editors such as Microsoft Visual Studio and other document processors in which each character must be the same size.

- **Times New Roman**   A proportional serif font often used for letters, reports, and books.

The MS Shell Dlg font can save some effort when you're internationalizing a legacy application that's unaware of the enhanced role now played by *lfCharSet*. MS Shell Dlg represents the typeface that should be used for screen elements such as menus and dialog boxes that will contain non-ANSI glyphs related to the system locale. The font mapper consults the Registry to find the actual typeface that should be used with the current system locale.[18] Simply by changing from the traditional Helv or MS Sans Serif to this special typeface, you can ensure that your dialog boxes use a font that is compatible with the system locale.

Because the physical font associated with MS Shell Dlg can vary greatly from one system to another, Microsoft recommends that you avoid this technique when developing new programs. Instead, use *lfCharSet* to select a font that is compatible with the locale.

Method 2: Getting font information from the user

In many applications, you can simply open the Font dialog box, shown in Figure 10-15, and pass the resulting LOGFONT to the font mapper with full assurance that the user will see the desired font.

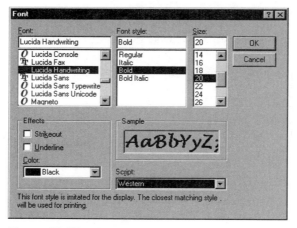

Figure 10-15. *The Font dialog box.*

The Font dialog box is managed by the *ChooseFont* API function and its related *CHOOSEFONT* structure. These are well documented in the Visual C++ help system and in just about every Windows programming book, so I won't repeat that lengthy description here. I will, however, show you how to fix a deficiency in MFC's wrapper class for *ChooseFont*, which is called *CFontDialog*.

---

18. You can find MS Shell Dlg and other font substitutes in the following registry path: HKEY_LOCAL_MACHINE\SOFTWARE\MICROSOFT\Windows NT\Current Version\FontSubstitutes.

I often want to provide an Apply button so that the user can view the font in action without closing the dialog box. *ChooseFont* supports this button through a callback function (also known as a hook function) whose address is passed in the *CHOOSEFONT* structure. MFC's wrapper class doesn't offer any C++ support for the Apply button, so I derived a *CFontDialogWithApply* class to add that feature. Listing 10-8 shows the new class and an example of a menu command handler that uses it. Complete source code is included on the companion CD.

```cpp
// Font dialog that supports the Apply button
class CFontDialogWithApply : public CFontDialog
{
public:
CFontDialogWithApply
    (
    LPLOGFONT lplfInitial = NULL,
    DWORD dwFlags = CF_EFFECTS | CF_SCREENFONTS,
    CDC* pdcPrinter = NULL,
    CWnd* pParentWnd = NULL
    ) : CFontDialog(lplfInitial, dwFlags, pdcPrinter, pParentWnd)
{
s_pHook = m_cf.lpfnHook;            // Save old hook.
s_pNotify = pParentWnd ? pParentWnd : GetOwner();
m_cf.lpfnHook = ChooseFontHook;     // Insert our hook.
m_cf.Flags |= CF_APPLY;             // Show the Apply button.
};

private:

// Although this class contains the following shared variables,
// it should be thread-safe because the variables are used only
// within a modal dialog state.
static LPCFHOOKPROC s_pHook;        // Saves old hook function pointer
static CWnd* s_pNotify;             // Notification window

// Hook function acquires LOGFONT from dialog, creates font handle,
// and sends WM_SETFONT to the owner window.
static UINT CALLBACK ChooseFontHook(HWND hWnd, UINT msg,
                                    WPARAM p1, LPARAM p2)
{
if((msg == WM_COMMAND) && (LOWORD(p1) == psh3)
   && (HIWORD(p1) == BN_CLICKED))
    {
    LOGFONT lf;
    ::SendMessage(hWnd, WM_CHOOSEFONT_GETLOGFONT, 0, (LPARAM)&lf);
```

Listing 10-8. *Supporting the Apply button in MFC's* CFontDialog *class.*   *(continued)*

Listing 10-8. *continued*

```
    HFONT hFont = CreateFontIndirect(&lf);
    if(hFont) s_pNotify->SendMessage(WM_SETFONT, (WPARAM)hFont, TRUE);
    }
if(s_pHook) return (*s_pHook)(hWnd, msg, p1, p2);
return 0;
}
};


// Static members of CFileDialogWithApply
LPCFHOOKPROC CFontDialogWithApply::s_pHook = 0;
CWnd* CFontDialogWithApply::s_pNotify = 0;


// Command handler for "Choose Font..." menu item
void CCh10eView::OnChooseFont()
{
LOGFONT lf;
m_Font.GetLogFont(&lf);
CFontDialogWithApply dlg
    (
    &lf,                // LOGFONT for initialization
    // Flags
    CF_EFFECTS | CF_FORCEFONTEXIST | CF_SCREENFONTS,
    0,                  // Printer DC
    this                // Parent window
    );
if(dlg.DoModal() == IDOK)
    {
    dlg.GetCurrentFont(&lf);
    HFONT hFont = CreateFontIndirect(&lf);
    SendMessage(WM_SETFONT, (WPARAM)hFont, TRUE);
    }
}


// WM_SETFONT handler, which is not supported
// by one of the ON_WM macros
LRESULT CCh10eView::OnSetFont(WPARAM p1, LPARAM p2)
{
m_Font.DeleteObject();
m_Font.Attach((HFONT)p1);
if(p2)
    {
    Invalidate();
    UpdateWindow();
    }
return 0;
}
```

The improved class is fairly easy to use. You typically instantiate it in a command handler and adjust the options to fit your needs. The constructor automatically sets the *CF_APPLY* option and inserts the necessary hook function. If you want to insert your own hook after the constructor returns, be sure to pass unprocessed callbacks to my hook. In turn, I process only the Apply button and pass all other callbacks to MFC's hook.

Next you have to catch the *WM_SETFONT* message in the owner window class, which is usually a *CView* derivative. You may have to insert the handler manually, because some versions of the Class Wizard don't support this message. Remember to declare the handler function in the view class, add an *ON_MESSAGE* macro to the message map, and (of course) implement the function.

Method 3: Enumerating logical fonts

Sometimes it's inconvenient to use the Font dialog box. For instance, you might want to offer the popular UI paradigm in which a font selection combo box appears on a toolbar. Surprisingly, this facility isn't yet built into Windows, but it's fairly easy to implement using the font enumeration API functions. In general, you invoke *EnumFontFamiliesEx* and receive a callback with a *LOGFONT* for each physical font. By retaining one or more of these *LOGFONT* structures for subsequent use with *CreateFontIndirect*, you can ensure that the font mapper will find an exact match when it performs the logical-to-physical conversion.

As mentioned, many applications use this technique to offer the user a drop-down list of typefaces and sizes. Unfortunately, the system doesn't support this feature with an API function similar to *ChooseFont* or a combo box style like *CB_DIR*. Listing 10-9 shows a simple C++ class that I use for this purpose.

```
class CFontCombo
{
HWND m_hWnd;                            // Combo or list box

static int WINAPI CALLBACK cbEnumFontFamiliesEx
    (
    const ENUMLOGFONTEX *plf,           // Logical font data
    const NEWTEXTMETRICEX *ppf,         // Physical font data
    DWORD FontType,                     // Font type
    LPARAM lParam                       // CFontList pointer
    )
{
CFontCombo* pFontList = (CFontCombo*)lParam;
TCHAR b[4 + sizeof(plf->elfFullName) + sizeof(plf->elfScript)];
LRESULT x;
if(plf->elfFullName[0])
```

Listing 10-9. *Enumerating fonts into combo and list boxes.*   *(continued)*

Listing 10-9. *continued*

```
        {
        wsprintf(b, _T("%s (%s)"), plf->elfFullName, plf->elfScript);
        x = SendMessage
            (pFontList->m_hWnd, CB_ADDSTRING, 0, (LPARAM)b);
        }
    else x = SendMessage
        (pFontList->m_hWnd, CB_ADDSTRING, 0,
         (LPARAM)plf->elfLogFont.lfFaceName);
    if(x < 0) return FALSE;
    LOGFONT* p = new LOGFONT;
    memcpy(p, &plf->elfLogFont, sizeof(p));
    SendMessage(pFontList->m_hWnd, CB_SETITEMDATA, x, (LPARAM)p);
    return TRUE;
    }

public:
CFontCombo() : m_hWnd(0) {}
virtual ~CFontCombo() { Detach(TRUE); }

void Attach(HWND hWnd)
    {
    Detach(TRUE);
    m_hWnd = hWnd;
    }

HWND Detach(BOOL bEmpty = FALSE)
    {
    HWND h = m_hWnd;
    if(h && bEmpty)
        {
        LRESULT i = SendMessage(h, CB_GETCOUNT, 0, 0);
        while(i-- > 0)
            {
            LOGFONT* p = (LOGFONT*)SendMessage(h, CB_GETITEMDATA,
                                                i, 0);
            delete p;
            }
        m_hWnd = 0;
        }
    return h;
    }

BOOL Load(LPCTSTR lfFaceName = 0, BYTE lfCharSet = DEFAULT_CHARSET,
          HDC hDC=0)
    {
    if(!m_hWnd) return FALSE;
```

```
    LOGFONT lf;
    memset(&lf, 0, sizeof(lf));
    if(lfFaceName) _tcsncpy(lf.lfFaceName, lfFaceName,
                            sizeof(lf.lfFaceName));
    lf.lfCharSet = lfCharSet;
    SendMessage(m_hWnd, CB_RESETCONTENT, 0, 0);
    HDC dc = hDC;
    if(!dc) dc = GetDC(m_hWnd);
    EnumFontFamiliesEx(dc, &lf, (FONTENUMPROC)cbEnumFontFamiliesEx,
                       (LPARAM)this, 0);
    if(!hDC) ReleaseDC(m_hWnd, dc);
    return TRUE;
    }
};
```

CFontCombo accepts a handle to a combo box through its *Attach* function. Once a handle is attached, you can call the *Load* function to populate the list with enumerated font names.

Load accepts arguments corresponding to the *LOGFONT* members *lfFace-Name* and *lfCharSet*, together with a device context handle. The function can also supply appropriate default settings for these arguments. It then initializes a *LOGFONT* structure and calls *EnumFontFamiliesEx*. This API function should now be used instead of the obsolete *EnumFonts* and *EnumFontFamilies*, because the older functions don't accept a character-set specifier.

The callback function *cbEnumFontFamiliesEx* is called for each physical font that's compatible with the device context and matches the typeface name and character set. This function combines the full typeface name with the script name to produce a string that it inserts into the list box or combo box. The script name is a people-friendly representation of *lfCharSet*. Next the function duplicates the *LOGFONT* information on the heap and saves the corresponding pointer in the list. The application program can call the *Detach* function to release the *LOGFONT* blocks, or the destructor will release the blocks if a combo box is still attached when the *CFontCombo* object is destroyed.

Figure 10-16 shows some typical output from this font enumerator when *Load* is invoked with no typeface name and the default character set. In that case, *EnumFontFamiliesEx* enumerates the styles and character sets of all fonts, producing a very long list on most systems. An international program would typically specify a character set corresponding to the current locale, thereby ensuring that the user sees only fonts that contain the necessary glyphs. In fact, you should generally avoid *DEFAULT_CHARSET* because it can confuse the user.

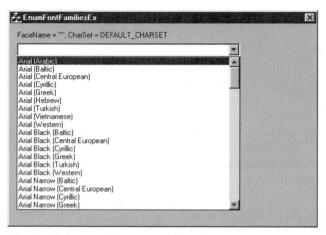

Figure 10-16. *Output of* CFontList *class.*

Font Programming in International Applications

An international application that works with just one locale at a time, such as scenarios 1 and 2 described earlier in this chapter, usually has just one simple font requirement: You must design the program so that it always uses fonts containing the glyphs required by the active locale. You accomplish this by ensuring that the *lfCharSet* member of the *LOGFONT* structure specifies the required glyph set.

ML applications have more difficult requirements because it can be a challenge to find a font or a set of fonts in the proper style containing the glyphs needed for the multiple locales. Windows 2000, with its improvements to the text rendering API functions and the text-oriented controls, provides a great deal of help in this area. Furthermore, Windows 2000 includes a major extension to the ML API called Uniscribe, which is also available as an add-on for Windows 95 and Windows 98. Uniscribe is particularly adept at handling the complex script rules typical of Arabic, Indic, and other non-European languages. Let's examine the improvements to the traditional API and text controls in detail before concluding this chapter with an introduction to Uniscribe.

Improved text rendering functions

Many traditional nonglobal applications use *plain text* techniques, meaning that each window displays its text using a single font. Other applications use multiple fonts in a window, but they employ plain text techniques. In general, a plain text application divides the window into rectangles called *text blocks*. The size of each block is independent of the text it contains, and the program uses a single font per block. For instance, a line-oriented editor such as Notepad or the editor in Visual Studio divides the window into text lines. A report program would typically divide the window into columns, with each column using a single font, even though the font could differ from one column to another. A spreadsheet grid is a more extreme example in which each cell uses a single font that isn't necessarily the same as that used for other cells.

Microsoft made it fairly easy to internationalize existing plain text programs by improving the traditional text measuring and rendering API functions *TextOut*, *ExtTextOut*, *TabbedTextOut*, *DrawText*, and *GetTextExtentPoint32*. We've seen one of these improvements already—namely, the ability of these functions to handle Unicode even in Windows 95 and Windows 98. Indeed, some plain text programs can be internationalized just by converting them from ANSI to Unicode and selecting big fonts that cover the desired locales. This serendipitous situation occurs when the text windows are used only for output and the program produces each text block with a single API call.

Problems can arise, however, when the program writes a text block incrementally, perhaps as the user types characters on the keyboard or when the program allows the user to edit the text within a block. Both cases require the program to become involved with the individual glyphs. When appending input characters to a text block, the program must know precisely where to draw the next character. When allowing the user to edit or select text, the program must manage the precise positioning of a text cursor (typically a vertical stroke).

Traditional programs use *GetTextExtentPoint32*, *GetCharWidth32*, and *GetCharABCWidths* for these positioning operations. Listing 10-10 shows a portion of an MFC program that displays a line of characters as they are typed on the keyboard. The *OnChar* function is called for each incoming character.

```
class CCh10gView : public CView
{
CPoint m_FirstPos, m_NextPos;    // First and next character position
CString m_Text;                  // Text line
CFont m_Font;                    // Current font
// Other view stuff...
};


// Handle WM_CHAR event.
void CCh10gView::OnChar(UINT nChar, UINT nRepCnt, UINT nFlags)
{
if(_istprint(nChar))             // Check if displayable character.
    {
    #ifdef WRONG_WAY             // NOT GOOD FOR COMPLEX SCRIPTS
    HideCaret();                 // Hide the caret.
    CClientDC dc(this);          // Get a device context.
    CFont* pOldFont = dc.SelectObject(&m_Font);
    dc.TextOut                   // Draw the character.
```

Listing 10-10. *Proper handling of* WM_CHAR *for complex scripts.*   *(continued)*

Listing 10-10. *continued*

```
        (
        m_NextPos.x,                // Horizontal position of next char
        m_NextPos.y,                // Vertical position of next char
        (LPTSTR)&nChar,             // Next character
        1                           // Number of chars
        );
    int width;                      // Update the line width.
    dc.GetCharWidth(nChar, nChar, &width);
    m_NextPos.x += width;
    SetCaretPos(m_NextPos);         // Adjust the caret position.
    ShowCaret();
    m_Text += (TCHAR)nChar;         // Save the character.
    dc.SelectObject(pOldFont);      // Clean up the DC.
    #else                           // GOOD FOR COMPLEX SCRIPTS
    m_Text += (TCHAR)nChar;         // Save the character.
    Invalidate();                   // Invalidate the entire text block.
    UpdateWindow();                 // Draw it now!
    #endif
    }
else switch(nChar)
    {
    case VK_RETURN:                 // ENTER key resets the line.
    m_Text.Empty();
    m_NextPos = m_FirstPos;
    Invalidate();
    UpdateWindow();
    }
CView::OnChar(nChar, nRepCnt, nFlags);
}


// Handle WM_PAINT event.
void CCh10gView::OnDraw(CDC* pDC)
{
if(m_Text.IsEmpty()) return;
if(GetFocus() == this) HideCaret();
CFont* pOldFont = pDC->SelectObject(&m_Font);
pDC->TextOut(m_FirstPos.x, m_FirstPos.y, m_Text);
CSize size = pDC->GetTextExtent(m_Text);
m_NextPos.x = m_FirstPos.x + size.cx;
pDC->SelectObject(pOldFont);
if(GetFocus() == this)
    {
    SetCaretPos(m_NextPos);
    ShowCaret();
    }
}
```

Many programmers like to code for maximum efficiency by drawing the new character at the end of the text already being displayed. I show this technique as the conditional compilation tagged *WRONG_WAY* because it fails in some locales. The program maintains a point named *m_NextPos* to determine where the next character should be drawn. It uses *CDC::GetCharWidth* to measure the width of each new character and update this point.

The problem is, in some languages the width of a character depends on the surrounding characters. For instance, some locales combine the sequence ae into a single ligature character æ, which is usually not as wide as its two components. Now examine the *OnDraw* function in Listing 10-10. Here I call *CDC::GetTextExtent*, the MFC wrapper function for *GetTextExtentPoint32*, to measure the width of the entire text string. Because Microsoft has internationalized the font shaping algorithms in Windows, this function properly accounts for situations such as ligatures.

This leads to two simple rules for updating existing programs that have this problem: Measure or draw a complete text block in one API call, and don't accumulate text widths incrementally. I've found that the easiest way to do this is to concentrate the text rendering operations in the paint event handler. Then in other parts of the program that change the text, I invalidate the entire text block so that it will be completely redrawn. If this redrawing is occurring in a situation where the user needs immediate feedback, such as the *OnChar* function, I call *UpdateWindow* to force an immediate paint event.

The good news is that this technique usually results in a shorter program. The bad news is that the frequent repaint operations can result in screen flicker while the user is typing. If this flicker is too annoying, you can often tune up the invalidation algorithm so that it works with smaller text blocks.

Improved edit controls

Listing 10-10 shows how to properly position the text cursor at the end of the block. But what if you need to position the cursor within the block, perhaps as part of an editing operation? It's difficult to internationalize a traditional plain text program having this requirement because you can't easily determine individual character spacing using the traditional API functions.[19] Instead, you have to use the Uniscribe API, as described in the next section.

Alternatively, when the user initiates an editing operation, you can overlay the text block with an edit control, which will then properly manage the text cursor and keystrokes. This technique works because Microsoft has improved the edit and rich edit controls for use with locales that have complex script

---

19. Some programmers refer to this as *inline editing,* meaning that the editing operation occurs directly within the application window rather than in a dialog box.

requirements. Many plain text programs, such as spreadsheet grids, already use overlaid edit windows, and so they get this part of internationalization for free.

Listing 10-11 illustrates this technique. When the user clicks the left mouse button, the *OnLButtonDown* handler creates a borderless edit control positioned over the text line. The control is initialized with the current text and font, and its cursor is positioned at the end of the text. As a result, the user can't even tell that the edit control is there. To provide a visual cue that the program is in its editing mode, I derived a simple class from *CEdit* that changes the text color to red. The complete source code is included on the companion CD.

```
//
class CCh10gView : public CView
{
BOOL m_bEditing;          // TRUE if editing
int m_cyLine;             // Line height
CMyEdit m_Edit;           // Edit control that draws in red
// Other view stuff...
};

// Handle WM_LBUTTONDOWN event.
void CCh10gView::OnLButtonDown(UINT nFlags, CPoint point)
{
if(m_bEditing)
    {
    m_Edit.GetWindowText(m_Text);
    m_Edit.ShowWindow(SW_HIDE);
    m_Edit.DestroyWindow();
    m_bEditing = FALSE;
    Invalidate();
    UpdateWindow();
    }
else if(!m_Text.IsEmpty())
    {
    m_bEditing = TRUE;
    CRect r;
    GetClientRect(&r);
    r.left = m_FirstPos.x;
    r.top = m_FirstPos.y;
    r.bottom = r.top + m_cyLine;
    m_Edit.Create
        (
        WS_CHILD | ES_LEFT,
        r,
```

Listing 10-11. *Overlaying text with an edit window.*

```
        this,
        100
        );
    m_Edit.SetFont(&m_Font);
    m_Edit.SetWindowText(m_Text);
    m_Edit.SetSel(m_Text.GetLength(), m_Text.GetLength());
    m_Edit.ShowWindow(SW_SHOW);
    m_Edit.SetFocus();
    }
CView::OnLButtonDown(nFlags, point);
}
```

While the edit overlay technique works fine for simple text blocks, you should seriously consider using the Rich Edit Control for more ambitious situations. Microsoft has greatly enhanced this control to deal with all of the difficult text editing issues that arise in locales having complex script requirements. These new features are in version 3.0 of the control, which is included with Windows 2000 and can be retrofitted to Windows 95, Windows 98, and Windows NT.

Uniscribe, the Unicode Script Processor

Uniscribe is a new Windows 2000 API used by the improved edit controls for complicated text layout situations such as those associated with Arabic and Indic languages. Architecturally, this API fits between client applications and Win32 GDI services such as *ExtTextOut*. Its primary purpose is to standardize the processing of the complex scripts used by Arabic, Indic, and other non-Western languages. Of course, it also handles simple scripts like English and is particularly adept at ML processing in which complex and simple scripts are combined.

Complex scripts

A language is said to use a complex script if text layout algorithms must deal with any of the following issues:

- **Bidirectional rendering** Glyphs read in both left-to-right (LTR) and right-to-left (RTL) order. For instance, Arabic script is usually RTL, but embedded numbers and European words run in the other direction. In a bidirectional (BIDI) environment, the sequence of glyphs on the screen (the physical order) isn't necessarily the same as the keystroke sequence (the logical order). Application programs prefer to process characters in logical order, and so Uniscribe performs the necessary logical-to-physical conversion.

- **Contextual shaping**　The shape of a character changes depending on the surrounding characters. English cursive writing (that is, script handwriting) exhibits this behavior in the following graphic. The lowercase T has a different shape depending on the preceding character.[20] Arabic scripts have many instances of contextual shaping.

  at court

- **Combined characters (ligatures)**　Adjacent characters are combined into a single glyph, as when the vowels ae are combined into a single ligature character æ in some European languages. Arabic has many ligatures.

- **Specialized word break and justification rules**　Some languages have complex rules for dividing words between lines or for justifying (left, right, or center) a line of text. Thai is an example of this type of language.

- **Illegal character combinations**　Some languages don't allow some character combinations. Again, Thai is an example of this situation.

If your application can't handle these situations with edit controls, you will have to learn how to use Uniscribe instead of traditional API calls such as *ExtTextOut*.

Uniscribe architecture

Uniscribe is currently packaged as a DLL named USP10.DLL, which is a standard part of Windows 2000 and can be added to Windows 95, Windows 98, and Windows NT.[21] The Win32 SDK provides the related header file and import library, named USP10.H and USP10.LIB, respectively. The Uniscribe API consists of the functions listed in Table 10-2.

---

20. The current TrueType and OpenType Western handwriting fonts do not use Uniscribe contextual shaping because they were carefully designed to produce a pleasing effect before Uniscribe existed. However, new Western fonts could employ Uniscribe to achieve an even better appearance. And, of course, the contextual shaping rules for Arabic and other non-Western fonts are so complex that no amount of clever font design can achieve the results of OpenType and Uniscribe together.

21. An earlier version was named USP.DLL, but it is now obsolete. If you install USP10 on a Windows 95, Windows 98, or Windows NT system, be wary of conflicts with the earlier library.

Table 10-2. **Uniscribe Functions**

Function	Description
ScriptApplyDigitSubstitution	Applies digit substitution settings
ScriptApplyLogicalWidth	Takes an array of advance widths for a run and generates an array of glyph widths
ScriptBreak	Returns information for determining line breaks
ScriptCacheGetHeight	Returns information about the currently cached font
ScriptCPtoX	Returns the x-offset of a run to either the leading or the trailing edge of a logical character cluster
ScriptFreeCache	Frees a *SCRIPT_CACHE* structure
ScriptGetCMap	Returns the glyph indexes of the characters of a string according to the OpenType *cmap* table
ScriptGetFontProperties	Returns information from the font cache
ScriptGetGlyphABCWidth	Returns the ABC width of a glyph
ScriptGetLogicalWidths	Converts the glyph advance widths to logical widths
ScriptGetProperties	Returns information about the current scripts
ScriptIsComplex	Determines whether a string requires complex script processing
ScriptItemize	Breaks a string into individually shapable items
ScriptJustify	Creates an advance widths table to allow text justification
ScriptLayout	Converts an array of run-embedding levels to a map of visual-to-logical position or logical-to-visual position
ScriptRecordDigitSubstitution	Reads the locale's native digit and digit-substitution settings and then records them in the *SCRIPT_DIGITSUBSTITUTE* structure
ScriptPlace	Uses the glyphs and visual attributes of a run to generate glyph-advance width and two-dimensional offset information
ScriptShape	Takes a Unicode run and generates its glyphs and visual attributes
ScriptStringAnalyse	Analyzes a plain text string
ScriptStringCPtoX	Returns the x-coordinate for the leading or trailing edge of a character position
ScriptStringFree	Frees a *SCRIPT_STRING_ANALYSIS* structure.
ScriptStringGetLogicalWidths	Converts visual widths to logical widths
ScriptStringGetOrder	Creates an array that maps an original character position to a glyph position
ScriptStringOut	Displays a string generated by a prior call to *ScriptStringAnalyse* and optionally adds highlighting

(continued)

Table 10-2. *continued*

Function	Description
ScriptString_pcOutChars	Returns a pointer to the length of a string after clipping
ScriptString_pLogAttr	Returns a pointer to a logical attributes buffer for an analyzed string
ScriptString_pSize	Returns a pointer to a *SIZE* structure for an analyzed string
ScriptStringValidate	Checks the *SCRIPT_STRING_ANALYSIS* structure for invalid sequences
ScriptStringXtoCP	Converts an x-coordinate to a character position
ScriptTextOut	Takes the output of both the *ScriptShape* and *ScriptPlace* calls and then calls the operating system *ExtTextOut* function appropriately
ScriptXtoCP	Converts the x-offset of a run to a logical character position and a flag to indicate whether the x-position fell in the leading or trailing half of the character

This API provides access to the Uniscribe architecture shown in Figure 10-17, which implements many of the Unicode text layout and semantic algorithms specified in the Unicode standard. These algorithms reside in a bidirectional analyzer and in modules called *shaping engines*. The initial version contains shaping engines for Arabic, Hebrew, Thai, Hindi, Tamil, and Vietnamese, although this repertoire will undoubtedly expand.

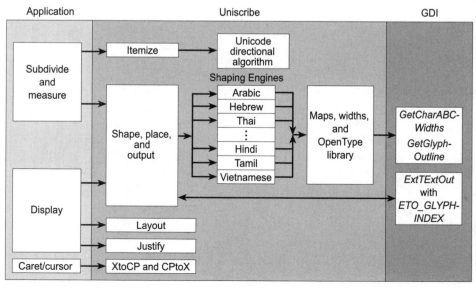

Figure 10-17. *Uniscribe architecture.*

A shaping engine comes into play when the application wants to render characters that fall within the Unicode range handled by the engine. For instance, the Arabic shaping engine handles the range from U+0600 through U+06FF. When an OpenType font is used with Uniscribe, the font doesn't have to duplicate these algorithms, although it can override them. Similarly, an application program can override the Uniscribe shaping engines if it has detailed information enabling it to do a better job. Without any overrides, Uniscribe follows the guidelines in the Unicode standard.

Uniscribe text processing concepts

As you can see in Table 10-2, because it is considerably more complicated than the traditional Win32 text-oriented functions, this API presents a steep learning curve. So let's first review the general approach to text processing using Uniscribe.

Application programmers want to manage simple text strings, preferably represented as arrays of characters positioned in the order in which they were received from the keyboard—that is, in logical order. Uniscribe caters to this preference by managing the subsidiary information needed to lay out a complex text string. This is somewhat different from the traditional Windows API, which retains no information about rendered text.

Uniscribe supports two text rendering scenarios: plain text and formatted text. The plain text scenario, as described earlier, deals with monolithic text strings in which each character is rendered with the same font, color, code page, and so on. In the formatted text scenario, the strings consist of plain text runs, in which each run has different rendering requirements. Obviously, plain text processing is the simpler of the two scenarios, and so you should strive to use this technique whenever possible.

Notice that a multilingual Unicode string can be plain text because it uses the same code page throughout—namely, Unicode. A multilingual ANSI string, however, can't be treated as plain text if it requires several code pages for proper rendering. The application must divide the string into runs that are tagged with the necessary code pages. This extra step is one reason why ML programmers prefer to work in Unicode.

Using Uniscribe with plain text

As you've seen, recent improvements enable you to display complex multilingual plain text strings using traditional functions such as *ExtTextOut*. So why would you want to use Uniscribe? Typically, you'll use Uniscribe when you want to support selection and editing operations directly in a text window without using overlaid edit controls. In other words, the plain text Uniscribe functions enable you to write your own ad hoc editor. These functions begin with *ScriptString* and are described in Table 10-2.

To display plain text using Uniscribe, first call *ScriptStringAnalyse* to build data structures that will subsequently guide the drawing procedure. Then call *ScriptStringOut* to actually draw the text, and last call *ScriptStringFree* to release the rendering data. Listing 10-12 demonstrates how to rewrite the *OnDraw* function from the example described in Listing 10-10 to use Uniscribe instead of the traditional API.

```cpp
// View class
class CMyView : public CView
{
    CString m_Text;                    // Text accumulator
    int m_xText;                       // Current character index

    BOOL m_bClicked;                   // TRUE if repaint after click
    CPoint m_ClickPos;                 // Click position

    CPoint m_FirstPos;                 // First character position
    CPoint m_NextPos;                  // Next character position
    CFont m_Font;                      // Current font
    int m_cyLine;                      // Line height

// Other view stuff...
};

// Handle WM_PAINT event.
void CCh10gView::OnDraw(CDC* pDC)
{
if(m_Text.IsEmpty()) return;           // Do nothing if no text.

if(GetFocus() == this) HideCaret();    // Hide caret and initialize DC.
CFont* pOldFont = pDC->SelectObject(&m_Font);

TEXTMETRIC t;                          // Get font info.
pDC->GetTextMetrics(&t);

CRect r;                               // Get text rectangle.
GetClientRect(&r);
r.left = m_FirstPos.x;
r.top = m_FirstPos.y;
r.bottom = r.top + m_cyLine;


SCRIPT_STRING_ANALYSIS ssa;            // Analyze the string.
HRESULT hr = ScriptStringAnalyse
    (
    pDC->GetSafeHdc(),                 // 1. Device context handle
    (LPCTSTR)m_Text,                   // 2. String pointer
```

Listing 10-12. *Plain text output using Uniscribe.*

```
    m_Text.GetLength(),          // 3. Number of characters
    0,                           // 4. Glyph buffer size (use default)
    #ifdef _UNICODE              // 5. Character set
    -1,                          //    Use -1 if Unicode.
    #else
    t.tmCharSet,                 //    Use font charset if ANSI.
    #endif
    SSA_GLYPHS,                  // 6. Analysis flags
    r.Width(),                   // 7. Clip/justification width
    0,                           // 8. Script control
    0,                           // 9. Script state
    0,                           // 10. Width array
    0,                           // 11. Script tabstops
    0,                           // 12. Character placement array
    &ssa                         // 13. Analysis results handle
    );
ASSERT(SUCCEEDED(hr));


hr = ScriptStringOut            // Draw the string.
    (
    ssa,                         // Analysis handle
    m_FirstPos.x, m_FirstPos.y,  // Reference point
    ETO_OPAQUE | ETO_CLIPPED,    // Opaque painting
    &r,                          // Clipping rectangle
    m_Text.GetLength(),          // Start of selected text
    m_Text.GetLength(),          // End of selected text
    FALSE                        // Normal text
    );
ASSERT(SUCCEEDED(hr));


CSize size = *ScriptString_pSize(ssa);  // Get string display size.
m_NextPos.x = m_FirstPos.x + size.cx;   // Update next char position.

if(GetFocus() == this)                  // Position the caret.
    {
    int bTrail = TRUE;                   // Assume trailing edge for caret.
    if(m_bClicked)                       // Check for a click in the string.
        {
        m_bClicked = FALSE;
        hr = ScriptStringXtoCP           // Get character index.
            (
            ssa,                         // Analysis handle
            m_ClickPos.x,                // X coordinate
            &m_xText,                    // String index
```

(continued)

Listing 10-12. *continued*

```
                &bTrail                       // TRUE if trailing edge
            );
        ASSERT(SUCCEEDED(hr));
        }
    else m_xText = m_Text.GetLength();// If no click, set caret to end.
    CPoint pt(m_NextPos);
    if(m_xText < m_Text.GetLength())  // Not at end of string
        {
        hr = ScriptStringCPtoX        // Convert char index to x position.
            (
            ssa,                      // Analysis handle
            m_xText,                  // String index
            TRUE,                     // Want trailing edge
                                      // Use bTrail for precise clicking
            (int*)&pt.x               // X coordinate (returned)
            );
        ASSERT(SUCCEEDED(hr));
        }
    SetCaretPos(pt);
    ShowCaret();
    }

hr = ScriptStringFree(&ssa);          // Release the analysis handle.
ASSERT(SUCCEEDED(hr));

pDC->SelectObject(pOldFont);          // Clean up the DC.
}

// Handle left button down event.
void CCh10gView::OnLButtonDown(UINT nFlags, CPoint point)
{
CView::OnLButtonDown(nFlags, point);
CRect r;
GetClientRect(&r);
r.left = m_FirstPos.x;
r.top = m_FirstPos.y;
r.right = m_NextPos.x;
r.bottom = r.top + m_cyLine;
if(r.PtInRect(point))
    {
    m_ClickPos = point;
    m_bClicked = TRUE;
    Invalidate();
    UpdateWindow();
    }
}
```

ScriptStringAnalyse is the most complicated function used in Listing 10-12, since it performs the following sequence of Uniscribe calls: *ScriptItemize*, *Script-Shape*, *ScriptPlace*, *ScriptBreak*, *ScriptGetCMap*, *ScriptJustify*, and *ScriptLayout*. *ScriptStringAnalyse* caches the results of these internal operations and returns a handle to that information as a SCRIPT_STRING_ANALYSIS type, which is a void pointer similar to other system handles.

I called *ScriptStringAnalyse* with the arguments typically needed for plain text output. The first three arguments are the device context, string pointer, and number of characters. The fourth argument specifies the number of glyphs that will be needed to render the string, which could be more than the number of characters. By using 0, I requested the default glyph buffer size, which is 150 percent of the string length. The fifth argument identifies the font character set if the string contains ANSI characters. It must be −1 for a Unicode string. The sixth argument is a set of flags that govern the analysis. You must use at least *SSA_GLYPHS* if you will subsequently call *ScriptStringOut*. The seventh argument is the logical width of the clipping or justification area. The eighth through the twelfth arguments are optional pointers to structures and arrays that contain additional input and output information. None of these are needed in this example. Finally, the thirteenth argument points to the handle where the function returns the results of the analysis. Whew! That's a lot of arguments.

Calling *ScriptStringOut* is comparatively simple. The first five arguments resemble those for *ExtTextOut*, except that the analysis handle replaces the device context handle. The final three arguments enable you to apply selection highlighting to a substring.

After drawing the string, I get the display length by calling *ScriptString_pSize*, which is similar to *GetTextExtentPoint32*. Then I set the caret position in one of two ways. If *m_bClicked* is FALSE, the user has not clicked in the string, and so the caret is positioned at the end of the string by setting *m_xText* to the string length. Otherwise, the *OnLButtonDown* event handler (also shown in Listing 10-12) has saved the mouse position in *m_ClickPos*, and so I use *ScriptStringXtoCP* to convert the x-coordinate to a string index that is saved in *m_xText*. In both cases, I call *ScriptStringCPtoX* to convert *m_xText* to a horizontal coordinate, which is used to position the caret.

As part of the cleanup work, *ScriptStringFree* releases all resources associated with the analysis handle. As with device context handles, it's generally not a good idea to hold on to string analysis handles. They can tie up a lot of memory and other resources, and some of the *ScriptString* calls might not work properly when the device context is released while associated with the analysis handle. If you need to save some of the analysis results, use functions such as *ScriptStringGetOrder* and *ScriptStringGetLogicalWidths*. That approach is often necessary when you need more complicated mouse operations than those shown in this example.

Using Uniscribe with formatted text

Formatted text consists of a number of plain text runs, with each run distinguished by a different typeface, weight, slant, character set, color, or other attribute that affects the appearance. Each run is said to have a distinctive style, and the entire string is called a paragraph. This is consistent with word processors, which typically handle text on a paragraph-by-paragraph basis and allow users to select and apply styles to substrings within paragraphs, thereby forming runs.

In fact, the entire concept of formatted text in Uniscribe relates closely to the arcane demands of ML word processing with complex scripts. I suspect that most programmers, when faced with these demands, will elect to use Microsoft's standard word processor component, the Rich Edit Control. Nonetheless, it's worthwhile to have a basic understanding of the low-level Uniscribe functions that you must call when working with formatted text.

A word processor typically maintains each paragraph as a single string with the characters in logical order—that is, in the order in which they were typed. The program also associates a style object with each run in the paragraph. For instance, the following English paragraph has three runs: the leading nonitalicized part, the italicized part, and the trailing nonitalicized part.

The quick *brown fox* jumped over

the lazy dog and fell into the pond. Then

the ugly dog woke up.

To draw this paragraph, a traditional word processor makes three calls to *ExtText-Out*, adjusting the device context before each call so that the run is properly displayed. This procedure is relatively easy to implement with simple scripts such as English and most European languages.

When dealing with complex scripts, each run may need to be further subdivided according to different shaping and positioning rules. For example, here's a paragraph that contains English and Thai Unicode characters, all in the Arial 12-point font.

Here is an example of
Thai script:
ความพยายามอยู่ที่ไหนความสำเร็จอยู่ที่นั่น

Even though from a stylistic viewpoint the paragraph contains only one run, it actually must be rendered in two steps because of the Thai shaping rules. Figure 10-18 is a screen snapshot from Microsoft's Complex Script Sample program showing these shaping rules in action.[22] The Logical Characters area displays the individual Unicode characters that were typed to produce the Formatted Text area directly below. As you can see, some Thai character sequences are combined into single glyphs.

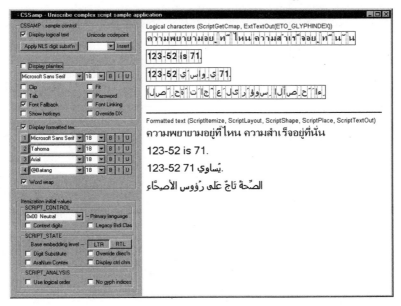

Figure 10-18. *Uniscribe Complex Script Sample program.*

When you present Uniscribe with a complex script like this, it divides the string into items, each of which has similar layout requirements. You must then reexamine the runs and split those that contain item boundaries. Figure 10-19 illustrates this procedure. The original string has three runs with different styles, as represented in the top tier. Uniscribe's analysis then determines that the text requires two layout algorithms, as shown in the middle tier. Because the original run 2 straddles the layout items, the application must split it, producing the final four runs shown in the bottom tier. Each of the final runs is rendered separately using the appropriate device context and layout settings.

---

22. This program was described in the November 1998 issue of *Microsoft Systems Journal* and is included on the companion CD.

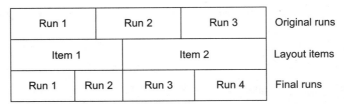

Figure 10-19. *Style runs and layout items.*

Here is a summary of the procedure for laying out a paragraph using Uniscribe:

1. Call *ScriptApplyDigitSubstitution* to initialize *SCRIPT_CONTROL* and *SCRIPT_STATE* structures for digit substitution. Typically, this causes Uniscribe to subsequently replace the standard digit codes (U+0030 through U+0039) with codes appropriate to the language, based on the adjacent characters.

2. Call *ScriptItemize* to divide the string into items distinguished by their shaping and positioning requirements. Uniscribe can detect directional changes within the string by applying the standard Unicode algorithms. Alternatively, you can suppress this feature when using a nonstandard directional scheme. In that case, your run parser should implement the appropriate directional algorithm.

3. Call *ScriptBreak* for each item to identify word boundaries, white space, and other character attributes.

4. Process the run and item information to produce a new set of runs that don't span items, as shown in Figure 10-19.

5. For each run, intialize the device context according to the run style, and then call *ScriptGetCMap*, *ScriptShape*, and *ScriptPlace*. *ScriptCMap* assigns a physical font and gets the glyph indexes. If some characters don't map to valid glyphs, you can either fall back to a different font or allow Uniscribe to use the default glyph in the selected font. *ScriptShape* identifies glyph clusters that merge into a single glyph when rendered. *ScriptPlace* identifies the run's starting point on the display device and generates an array of glyph widths.

6. Sum the widths of the runs in logical order until the line overflows. Then call *ScriptBreak* to break the line on a word boundary, which has the effect of splitting the current run into two parts. This assumes that you want to implement word wrapping within the display window.

At this point, you can save the layout information to improve the performance of the line-by-line drawing procedure. Of course, the layout must be discarded whenever the user makes a significant change, such as adjusting a style within the paragraph, inserting or removing characters, or resizing the display window. Assuming that you have valid layout information when it's time to draw the paragraph, here's the drawing procedure for each line:

1. Call *ScriptLayout* to perform the final layout step in which the runs are physically positioned on the line. This positioning is called the visual order, and you can further refine it by calling *ScriptJustify* to adjust the relative positions of the runs within the line.

2. Call *ScriptTextOut* for each run, in visual order. Finally, something appears on the output device!

These layout and drawing procedures can have many variations, depending on the needs of the application. For instance, a programmer developing a native Arabic application that also supports other locales would naturally add refinements to the Uniscribe bidirectional algorithms. Fortunately, the designers of Uniscribe made it flexible enough to accommodate these variations.

SUMMARY

The apex of international programming is the ML application that handles complex scripts. Before Windows 2000, this was a difficult goal to achieve, for several reasons. First, the typical operating system presented a UI that was restricted to a few, or often just one, language. The Windows 2000 Multilingual Edition has a flexible UI that can change with each user session. Second, application programs could not easily change keyboard layouts without restarting the system. Windows 2000 allows the input locale to change dynamically within a session. Third, application programs could not easily deal with multiple languages within a single document and with complex scripts. Windows 2000 offers advanced international features such as Unicode, OpenType, and Uniscribe to handle these situations.

It's still a challenge to write a completely global application, but the barriers to success are much lower than they were just a few years ago.

Chapter 11

Guidelines for International Programming

Well, it's time to finish this magnum opus so that it gets to the printer before Microsoft Windows 2000 becomes yesterday's news. The trouble is, I keep finding additional interesting topics to include, so I could probably push on for another year or so. That's the nature of international programming. Just when you think you've got it covered, you learn about another language or locale with new requirements.

Nonetheless, I've discussed the major topics that form the foundation for international programming using Microsoft Visual C++ in a Microsoft Win32 environment. These topics include the fundamentals of character sets and locales, the international features in standard C and C++, and the extensions provided by Visual C++. I have also described at length the Win32 National Language Support (NLS) and multilingual (ML) features, especially those in Windows 2000 that handle complex language situations not easily handled by standard C or C++ alone.

In this chapter, I'll summarize this material as a list of guidelines for international programming. But first I want to look at three topics that this book has not yet touched on: developing global Component Object Model (COM) objects, producing localized Web pages, and developing speech-sensitive applications.

INTERNATIONAL COM PROGRAMMING

When it comes to core programming technology, COM is now the "big kahuna" at Microsoft. Nearly all major extensions to Microsoft operating systems are defined as COM interfaces. Examples include the Internet Explorer components, the database components (OLE DB and ADO), the Telephony API (TAPI), Microsoft Agent, and a plethora of Microsoft ActiveX controls.[1] Furthermore, most Microsoft applications, such as the Office and Visual Studio suites, provide COM interfaces for interaction with other non-Microsoft applications.

So if this component technology is really important, why did I ignore it up to now? The answer is that I didn't ignore COM, because the international programming techniques described in earlier chapters can and should be used when you implement COM interfaces. To understand this, you must understand that COM is essentially just a way to define and organize collections of C functions.[2] Sure, COM has evolved to include sophisticated services such as distributed objects, transactions, and automatic context management. But these services are mostly transparent to international programmers, who need to focus only on calling and implementing the C functions defined by COM interfaces.

COM and Character Sets

Because a COM interface is just a set of C functions, it could work with single-byte character set (SBCS), multibyte character set (MBCS), or wide character set (WCS) text using any encoding scheme. Fortunately, Microsoft has consistently recommended that interface functions use Unicode characters for input and output text. In particular, they should use the OLECHAR data type, which is equivalent to *wchar_t*, for single characters or null-terminated strings.[3] If the interface will be used by scripted clients, such as HTML pages, the interface functions must use the BSTR data type, which is an OLECHAR array with a length prefix.

---

1. Uniscribe is a notable exception, and I'm not sure why it was not originally designed as a set of COM interfaces. Clearly there was some COM thinking here, because Uniscribe functions return HRESULT data, just like COM interface functions do. Perhaps the Uniscribe library will be "COM-ified" in a future version, as occurred with TAPI.

2. COM is based on C functions because that's the protocol used for the Win32 API, which can be called directly or indirectly by all programming languages.

3. COM interfaces can't use TCHAR because it is either a narrow or a wide character, depending on the UNICODE preprocessor symbol. COM methods want Unicode characters even from an SBCS or an MBCS client.

Since COM interface functions are required to use Unicode text in their arguments, they usually gain the advantages of wide-character processing, such as the elimination of complicated MBCS processing and the need to switch code pages. True, a COM server that must run on Windows 95 or Windows 98 might have to perform some internal conversions from OLECHAR to ANSI in order to use the non-Unicode API, but this problem is not unique to COM. It's just another variation of "MBCS on the outside and Unicode on the inside," which I've mentioned many times.

COM and Locales

Many COM servers, such as ActiveX controls, are packaged as dynamic-link libraries (DLLs) that run in the client process. If this type of "in process," or *inproc*, component runs in the same thread as its client, it will probably encounter no significant international problems that I have not already discussed because it will use the ambient locale settings of the client's thread.[4] Locale problems can arise, however, in COM servers that run in different threads or processes. Let's look at the three most common situations.

Locales and COM threads

If a component runs on a different thread than its client, the two threads might have different locale settings, which can cause the component to apply incorrect formatting and conversion rules. The typical way to avoid this problem is to define interface methods that explicitly accept a locale identifier (LCID) argument specifying which locale to use. This is a good general rule for any locale-sensitive COM method: to avoid ambiguities and errors, always pass the desired locale as an explicit argument.

When working with legacy components, you might not be able to modify or extend the interface to accept LCID arguments, and you might not even have access to the original source code. You can sometimes deal with this situation by changing the client architecture to force the client and object into the same thread. This generally requires that the object be created by the same thread that will be using it, which is the sensible way to do things anyway.

What if you can't force the object into the client thread? For instance, multithreaded *worker objects* are designed to run on non-user interface threads so that they can perform blocking operations without disturbing the UI. It would be a serious mistake to move one of these worker objects into your UI thread.

---

4. Windows 2000 now supports the thread-neutral apartment (TNA) for components that have no thread affinity and can always run in the caller's thread. This is the ideal configuration for service components that don't need a UI or the ability to block the thread. A locale-sensitive algorithm in a TNA component will use the caller's thread locale.

Instead, you might have to design a multithreaded *shim object* that receives an LCID as an argument, establishes that as the shim's thread locale, and then calls the appropriate method in the real object. The thread switch occurs when the client calls the shim object.

Locales in EXE-based COM servers

When the client and server reside in different processes, the COM interfaces must use explicit LCID arguments because the server has no easy way to discover the client's thread locale. This situation usually arises when a client is driving an EXE-based server through automation interfaces, such as when a Microsoft Word document is hosting a Microsoft Excel spreadsheet. Indeed, Microsoft Office products such as Word and Excel offer many examples of the "right way" to design an automation object model. In particular, many Office objects support the *LanguageID* property, which enables an automation client to specify its locale requirements. Complete details are available in the online help for these products, usually under the topics that describe how to use the object model with Microsoft Visual Basic for Applications (VBA).

Locales in COM surrogates

Some DLL-based components can be configured to reside in a different address space than their clients, running as a separate process under a *surrogate host*. Such a component combines the simplicity of the DLL programming model with the security of the EXE model. This situation arises most often with components that are configured as Microsoft Transaction Server (MTS) packages or as COM+ applications, but nontransactional components can also use the surrogate technique.

At present, you must handle surrogate components with locale sensitivities just like EXE-based components—that is, the interfaces must enable the client to specify locale requirements explicitly as function arguments. I say "at present" because it is technically possible that COM+ might someday provide client locale information as part of the call context block that is passed to each COM method, but I've seen no evidence that this is on the COM team's agenda.

Locale-Sensitive Interfaces

Programmers use the Interface Definition Language (IDL) to define COM interfaces and classes. IDL source files can be generated directly by the programmer using a text editor or indirectly with a higher level tool such as a Visual Studio wizard. The Microsoft IDL compiler (MIDL) then processes these source files to produce type libraries that can be used by clients to call interface methods by name instead of by number.

Like resources, IDL source files can be localized so that method and parameter names as well as other IDL symbols are available in several languages. For example, an English programmer developing a Visual Basic program could use English names for the interface methods and parameters, while a Japanese programmer would write these names in Japanese. This feature is particularly attractive in conjunction with scripting languages because the scripts are often written and maintained by nonprogrammers who might not be comfortable working in a foreign language.

To create localized IDL source files, use the */lcid* option on the MIDL compiler command together with the *lcid* attribute on the type library block. Usually you'll write a base IDL file in a common language such as English, and then each translator will clone the base file, insert the appropriate *lcid* attributes, convert the names to the desired language, and pass the translated source file to MIDL. Consult the MIDL Reference Manual in the MSDN library for full details.

Although this is a powerful feature of COM, I have not seen it used very often. In my experience, COM programmers tend to produce single-language type libraries, which are not subsequently localized along with resources, messages, help files, and other visible parts of the program. This is undoubtedly due to the fact that COM method calls have traditionally been made by compiled client programs using languages rooted in English such as C++, Java, or Basic. This situation is changing as scripting languages such as HTML and VBScript become more popular with casual programmers. I suspect that many script writers would prefer localized COM interfaces, and so you will most likely need to respond by producing multilingual type libraries.

Standard International COM Interfaces

With Microsoft's strong emphasis on COM, you would expect to find some standard interfaces devoted to international programming.[5] Surprisingly, this has not yet occurred to any great degree. For instance, Microsoft offers no COM equivalent to the C++ *locale* and *facet* classes, and although Uniscribe uses a few COM data types like HRESULT, it is not currently a COM server.

If you search the Microsoft Developer Network (MSDN) database for COM interfaces related to international programming, you will discover the Mlang API, which includes *IMultiLanguage* and about a dozen related interfaces. This little-known suite was introduced with Microsoft Internet Explorer 4 to bridge the gap between the NLS features of Win32 and HTTP/HTML, as described next.

---

5. "Standard" in the sense that they are defined by Microsoft.

International Web Programming

It would be strange if the World Wide Web could not handle a multitude of languages. For example, a Swedish user accessing a British company's Web site probably prefers to see pages localized to Swedish. An Italian user simultaneously accessing the same site wants to see Italian pages. Clearly, the Web server has lots of work to do!

Fortunately, Internet standards and protocols such as HTTP and HTML have pretty good (and still evolving) support for the delivery of localized Web pages. The Internet standards having particular importance in international programming are RFC1766, which lists the language identifiers, and RFC2045–RFC2049, which describe the multilingual extensions to the message headers.

HTTP is a simple request/response protocol, and the multilingual extensions don't change that basic approach. Each time a browser requests a page, the request header can specify the user's preferred language in the HTTP_ACCEPT_LANGUAGE item. When the server responds with an HTML page, it can include a CHARSET tag to identify the code page that should be used to display the HTML page.

Internet Explorer employs Mlang objects to convert HTML text to the character set used by the browser window. These components are particularly adept at dealing with the HTML headers, translating from Internet standard character set names into those used by Windows. If you write your own Windows-based browser or need to process HTML pages in other situations, you can employ Mlang in a similar manner. The interfaces are fully described in the MSDN documentation, and the header files reside in the Win32 SDK. The component DLL is installed with Internet Explorer.

Passive Web Sites

Many Web sites contain only passive information, such as product specifications, photographs, news articles, and other reference material. In these situations, site designers have traditionally supported multiple languages by simply cloning the entire site in the desired languages. For example, if a site contains 100 pages in English, you would need another 100 pages to support French. You would then insert a new home page offering the user the choice of English or French. Some international sites display an initial page containing a world map that you click on to indicate your preferred locale.

Although the pages in a passive site don't change because of user input, they typically are updated on a regular basis. For example, a news site wouldn't be very interesting if the headlines stayed the same day after day. This need to update pages can become a maintenance headache if the site has been cloned for several languages. The key to retaining your sanity when you administer this type of site is to minimize the number of pages that you have to touch after they have been cloned and translated.

A completely passive site requires no international programming on the server. The only quasi-technical chore is that the translator must supply the *CHARSET* property so that the browser will display the correct glyphs.

Active Web Sites

Although the Web was originally designed for passive content, it has evolved into an interactive network suitable for product sales, travel reservations, banking, expense reporting, and other applications not envisioned by its original designers. An active Web site interacts with the user to supply dynamically changing content. Search engines are a common example—the server dynamically constructs pages containing links to the sites that match the user's request.

Microsoft is firmly committed to active Web sites and offers lots of technology to facilitate their development. Internet Information Server (IIS) is the controlling element, and it provides several programming environments: DLL extensions through the Internet Server API (ISAPI), Active Server Pages (ASP) sessions, and Common Gateway Interface (CGI) processes.

Unless you are writing a customized browser or ActiveX controls to run on client machines, your multilingual Web work will most likely occur on the server using ASP, Visual Basic or Java Script, ActiveX controls, and custom COM objects to construct and deliver "active pages" whose content changes from one access to another. The typical steps to deliver a page in the proper language are as follows:

1. Obtain the user's language preference from the *ServerVariables* collection in the ASP *Request* object.

2. Access the dynamic data requested by the user. This step may or may not be language sensitive, depending on the nature of the request. For instance, a dictionary access request would need to know the language of the word whose definition is requested, whereas a request for an inventory record by part number would probably use a language-neutral key.

3. Fetch or construct an HTML skeleton page that is appropriate for the user's language. There are a zillion ways to do this, which is why multilingual Web programmers get paid so much.

4. Replace the dynamic fields in the skeleton to form the final response page. Locale-sensitive formatting might be required here for items such as dates, times, money, and other values.

5. Send the complete page via the ASP *Response* object.

The Visual C++ internationalization techniques discussed in this book come into play when you develop ActiveX controls and other COM objects to support this procedure. The work is relatively easy compared to developing a full-fledged Windows application because you don't have to support a UI. The goal of an ASP page is to produce a "real" HTML page, which is nothing but a text stream. This aim implies that your international ASP components will be primarily concerned with text formatting.

INTERNATIONAL SPEECH PROCESSING

Few Windows applications today support speech I/O as part of the user interface, but that will undoubtedly change now that faster processors are available to execute sophisticated speech analysis and synthesis algorithms. With that evolution in mind, Microsoft introduced the Win32 Speech API (SAPI) several years ago with Microsoft Windows NT and Windows 95. You can find the SAPI documentation, header files, and sample programs in the Win32 SDK.

Using the Speech API

SAPI is a COM-based subsystem that supports pluggable engines for text-to-speech (TTS) output and speech recognition (SR) input. Through the COM interfaces, the application can select the engines that most closely match the desired language. If appropriate engines are not installed, the application should deactivate its speech I/O features and fall back to the traditional keyboard-mouse-screen interface. In other words, a speech-enabled application must continue to provide a traditional UI because some users prefer it and others might not have the necessary SAPI engines installed.

SAPI provides a set of ActiveX controls for easy access to its low-level features. Direct speech recognition control and direct speech synthesis control are the two most general controls for speech input and output. Other controls have more specific purposes, including voice command, voice dictation, voice text, and voice telephony.

A typical SAPI application creates a voice text object to convert annotated text to audible speech in the user's language and dialect. A voice command object then receives the user's "utterances" and converts them to events similar to menu or toolbar commands. When the application needs to record the text spoken by the user, it creates a voice dictation object. The voice telephony control facilitates the development of multiline interactive voice response (IVR) systems.

Notice that none of these operations involve any international programming techniques that I have not already discussed. The application manipulates Unicode text strings, even though SAPI is converting the text to speech and vice versa.

Using Microsoft Agent

Microsoft Agent enables you to add animated help characters to your application, similar to those found in Microsoft Office applications. A local COM automation server and a related ActiveX control employ SAPI for speech commands and audible help. Microsoft Agent is included with Windows 2000 and Office 2000, and it can be added to earlier systems as a free download. In fact, if you refer to the ActiveX control on a Web page, the browser will automatically install the control, the server, and the necessary animation files. You can use the stock characters provided by Microsoft (see Figure 11-1), or you can design your own. In addition, you can integrate your help system into the repertoire of the Office 2000 characters when you are developing an Office extension product.

Figure 11-1. *Stock figures for Microsoft Agent.*

Microsoft Agent is essentially a layer built on SAPI that integrates character animation with the TTS and voice command services. In addition, the Microsoft Agent server coordinates shared use of characters by multiple applications. Each application can attach to the server directly, using the server's dual COM interfaces, or through an ActiveX control. In either case, the client specifies a character's language by adjusting the *LanguageID* property, as with the SAPI.

INTERNATIONAL PROGRAMMING GUIDELINES

Throughout this book, I've described international programming techniques you should use and some practices you should avoid. Here I'll summarize these techniques as a set of dos and don'ts:

■ **Do make your life easier when you're developing a new application by using Unicode whenever possible.** If you must support non-Unicode environments such as Windows 95 and Windows 98, use Unicode internally and convert between MBCS and Unicode at the program boundaries. In a pure Unicode program, consider using UTF-8 (compressed Unicode) if you need to overcome limitations of file storage space or data transmission bandwidth.

■ **Do use bimodal character data types such as TCHAR so that your source code will compile correctly for both ANSI and Unicode.** This is particularly important if the initial version of your code must use ANSI for compatibility with Windows 95 and 98. You will probably want to release a Unicode version later, and consistent use of bimodal character types will minimize that effort. Also, it will be easier to share some of the source code with other projects.

■ **Do learn to intermix the best international features from standard C/C++, Visual C++, and Win32.** For instance, the standard C++ collection and stream templates work well with Unicode, whereas the *locale/facet* architecture doesn't support either complex scripts or Uniscribe.

■ **Don't overemphasize the importance of portability by insisting on *only* standard C and C++ techniques.** At present, it's difficult to write completely portable international programs because the standards are quite weak with regard to non-European languages, especially those requiring bidirectional I/O or special shaping. If you want to retain the spirit of standard C++, consider using *facet* derivatives to hide the Win32 API.

■ **Don't make your program difficult to translate.** All visible aspects should be physically separate from the program logic. This restriction applies to nearly all text strings, including those used for creating filenames and those used for *sprintf* formatting. Storage possibilities include message files, resource libraries, and databases. Standard C++ provides a *facet* for message files, and Win32 supports resource libraries. Depending on the technique you choose, you might have to develop or acquire editing tools for use by the translator. If you are working with a professional translation team, they probably have a preferred set of tools and techniques. It's a good idea to research this before getting too far along in the program development. Take every opportunity to speak with translation experts so that you will gradually develop a "feel" for designing UI elements that are easy to translate.

SUMMARY

You might recall a series of television commercials from the early 1970s sponsored by a computer training firm. The scenes showed men and women in white lab coats working around a large mainframe computer in a glass-enclosed room, much like high priests around an altar. The spokesperson encouraged young people to join the select few who were privileged to approach the mighty data processing system.

How times have changed! Personal computers are now ubiquitous in our homes, schools, and offices. A few weeks ago, a member of my church even used his laptop computer with Microsoft PowerPoint to make a fund-raising pitch after the Sunday service. Other computing devices lurk within our telephones, kitchen appliances, audio and video entertainment systems, automobiles, tools, toys, and so on. In one way or another, everyone is now a computer operator, and we don't even have to wear those cheesy lab coats or carry our pens in pocket protectors.

Pundits like to say we now live in the Information Age. That's true, but it's just as true to say we live in the Digital Age or the Software Age. Indeed, software-based systems that process digital information are empowering people to communicate and interact across vast distances in ways that our ancestors could not even imagine.

In this wired world, software developers can no longer assume that computer users have the skills (or the interest) to work with a difficult or an idiosyncratic interface. That's a primary reason for Windows' great success. Windows defines a standard framework so that its application programs can easily adopt the same general look and feel. Unlike those lab-coated acolytes in the commercial, today's user sees the computer as a means to an end, as a tool just like a typewriter or a television set. The best tools are intuitive and unobtrusive, and so the best computer software communicates naturally with the user, employing that person's language.

International programming used to be the purview of a few programmers working for multinational corporations or large computing companies like IBM and Microsoft. For the rest of us, the occasional requirement to display some "weird foreign characters" was a necessary evil. Today, global software is absolutely necessary, and the powerful international features available to the Visual C++ programmer make international programming a much easier proposition.

Bibliography

Books

Apple Computer, Inc. *Guide to Macintosh Software Localization.* Reading, MA: Addison-Wesley, 1992. A useful reference manual containing concise descriptions of many writing and formatting systems used throughout the world.

Carter, Daniel R. *Writing Localizable Software for the Macintosh.* Reading, MA: Addison-Wesley, 1992. Heavy on Mac user-level details and light on programming information, this book is useful only if you want a broad overview of I18N as practiced on the Apple platform.

del Galdo, Elisa, and Jakob Nielson (editors). *International User Interfaces.* New York, NY: John Wiley & Sons, 1996. A collection of reports discussing internationalization from a high-level perspective. No programming details, but some useful case studies that focus on human factors.

Fernandes, Tony. *Global Interface Design.* Chestnut Hill, MA: Academic Press, 1995. Some useful thoughts on visual interface design, bolstered by lots of pictures showing acceptable and unacceptable images in various locales. No programming details.

IBM Corporation. *National Language Information and Design Guide.* North York, Ontario, Canada: IBM Canada (National Language Technical Center), 1988. I received this multivolume guide at an international programming course conducted by IBM in 1989. Although the material predates Unicode and favors IBM mainframes and EBCDIC, it contains many valuable tips gleaned from IBM's 50 years of worldwide computing experience.

Kano, Nadine. *Developing International Software for Windows 95 and Windows NT.* Redmond, WA: Microsoft Press, 1995. Contains extensive details about code pages, Unicode, Input Method Editors, and other international aspects of Win32. Has not been updated for Windows 98, Windows NT 4.0, and Windows 2000, but most of the material is still valid. An online version is available in the MSDN library.

Langer, Angelika, and Klaus Kreft. *Standard C++ IOStreams and Locales: Advanced Programmer's Guide and Reference.* Reading, MA: Addison-Wesley, 2000. This book provides detailed coverage of the international features in standard C++, which I summarized in Chapters 4, 5, and 6.

Although some of these features are more appropriate in the UNIX environment, the book's treatment of standard locales, facets, and streams should be quite useful to Win32 programmers who are interested in portable software.

Luong, Tuoc V., James H. Lok, David J. Taylor, and Kevin Driscoll. *Internationalization: Developing Software for Global Markets*. New York, NY: John Wiley & Sons, 1995. Discusses internationalization from a project management perspective. Offers few programming details, but worthwhile because of the authors' extensive experience directing Borland's I18N efforts.

Musser, David R., and Atul Saini. *STL Tutorial and Reference Guide*. Reading, MA: Addison-Wesley, 1996. A well-written description of the Standard Template Library, which served as the basis for the templates now included in the standard C++ library. Although it doesn't discuss locales and facets, the book describes iterators, containers, and other features that are important in international programming.

O'Donnell, Sandra Martin. *Programming for the World: A Guide to Internationalization*. Englewood Cliffs, NJ: Prentice Hall, 1994. Well-written description of internationalization from the perspective of the C programmer working with UNIX and X/Open. Win32 programmers will be interested in the discussion of I18N issues such as character sets and fonts.

Plauger, P. J. *The Standard C Library*. Englewood Cliffs, NJ: Prentice Hall, 1992. A thorough description of the standard C library, including the locale feature. It's still relatively useful, although it doesn't include the amendments added to support the C++ standard. Best used as a companion to the Visual C++ on-line documentation.

Plauger, P. J. *The Standard C++ Library*. Englewood Cliffs, NJ: Prentice Hall, 1995. A thorough description of the standard C++ library prior to the addition of the locale feature and the standard template library. Although these changes have made the book obsolete, it's sometimes useful when you want to understand why the C++ committee made certain choices.

Tuthill, Bill, and David Smallberg. *Creating Worldwide Software*. Mountain View, CA: Sun Microsystems Press, 1997. Discusses I18N in the UNIX/C environment. Similar to O'Donnell, but with slightly more programming detail and a specific orientation toward the Sun Solaris platform.

Unicode Consortium, The. *The Unicode Standard, Version 2.0*. Reading, MA: Addison-Wesley, 1997. The standard reference for Unicode, containing complete character set tables and detailed explanations of the various sections of the Unicode spectrum. Also presents algorithms for the display of complex scripts.

Uren, Emmanuel, Robert Howard, and Tiziana Perinotti. *Software Internationalization and Localization: An Introduction.* New York, NY: Van Nostrand Reinhold, 1993. Good general discussion of I18N issues bolstered by C programming examples based on Windows 3.1 and UNIX. Although the examples are not very useful for C++ and Win32 programmers, the general concepts presented here are still relevant.

Internet Resources

http://www.ariadne.ac.uk/issue9/trenches An article by Jon Knight, entitled "Internationalisation and the Web," containing a good overview of character sets and other I18N issues as they pertain to the Internet. Hosted by *Ariadne*, a publication of the UK Office for Library and Information Networking at the University of Bath, England.

http://www.hut.fi/u/jkorpela/chars.html An excellent online document by Jukka Korpela entitled "A Tutorial on Character Code Issues." Contains many links to other sites concerned with character set issues and the Internet. Korpela works at the Helsinki University of Technology Computing Centre as an HTML specialist.

http://www.iso.ch Official site of ISO, the International Organization for Standardization. Here you can order ISO documents and learn what the various committees are up to. This is also an example of a multilingual Web site, offering both French and English pages.

http://www.microsoft.com/globaldev Microsoft calls this "The Professional Developer's Site for Software Globalization Information," and it is exactly that. It contains numerous articles, presentations, and reference material related to the I18N efforts of Microsoft and its partners, and also has an extensive set of links to other I18N sites. You'll definitely want this site on your favorites list.

http://www.microsoft.com/typography Hosted by Microsoft's Typography group, this site is for anyone who needs to understand the details of TrueType, OpenType, and other font technologies. It offers many utility programs for download and has lots of links to other typography sites.

http://msdn.microsoft.com/ MSDN is Microsoft's well-known source for technical details, development kits, and other programming information. Many professional software developers subscribe to one of the MSDN services in order to automatically receive updated versions of Microsoft's operating systems and tools. The Web site bolsters these subscriptions with late-breaking information, but much of its content is available to nonsubscribers.

http://www.qsl.net/k7on/rtty/tty.htm An article entitled "The History of Teletype Development" describing how the teletype and ASCII evolved from the telegraph and Morse Code. Originally published by Teletype Corporation in 1963, authored by R.A. Nelson and K.M. Lovitt.

http://www.w3.org Official site of the World Wide Web Consortium, the Internet standardization group. Lots of goodies here.

http://webopedia.internet.com A neat reference site where you can look up computer technology terms such as "baud."

Index

DAVID A. SCHMITT

Dave's computer career began during his high school years in the 1950s when he had the opportunity to work on an early wood-burning system. By improving the stack algorithm, he was able to boost the power and reduce the risk of deadly emissions, which were a serious threat to early programmers.

Soon after electricity was discovered, Bell Labs designed a computer that used semiconductor chips instead of wood chips. Intrigued by this breakthrough, Dave joined that renowned R&D organization, where he was involved with fault-tolerant versions of C and UNIX. After several years, he invented the No Fault System (NFS), which allows a main computer to divorce itself from an I/O channel without a lengthy court proceeding.

During one lab experiment, Dave was injured when a network cable accidentally detached and sprayed him with high-speed bits. While recuperating, he realized that his injuries would have been much more serious if the cable had contained a larger percentage of 1s than 0s. This led to an interest in compression algorithms, and he quickly devised a technique for squeezing all of the 0s out of a bit stream, leaving only the 1s to carry the essential information. This formed the foundation of modern audio and video compressors, which have the goal of reducing all content to a single bit. Always socially conscious, Dave has made several public service commercials warning users that cables must be securely fastened to prevent injuries when handling this dense information.

He has also worked with the music, television, and motion picture industries to ensure that they produce insipid melodies, inane lyrics, and idiotic plots that can be easily compressed to one or two bits.

During the 1980s, Dave and two friends formed Lattice, the pioneering C compiler company. Their compiler was praised because of its strong support for recursive programming, undoubtedly the result of the frequent cursing during its development. They actually had intended to design an RPG compiler, but somehow it morphed into a C development system that was the market leader until it stopped being the market leader. By that time, Lattice had been acquired, the founders had split the money, and yadayadayada.

Today Dave teaches COM programming for DevelopMentor, writes books and articles, and operates a consulting firm called Pivot Corporation. Although well versed in modern computer technology, he is often nostalgic for the good old days and recently upgraded an ancient gas-fired server to run Windows 2000.

About the Companion CD

What's on This CD?

The CD included with this book contains all the sample programs discussed in the book as well as an electronic version of the book. You can find the samples in the Samples folder.

The Sample Programs

An HTML manual is included in the Samples folder to describe each sample program. To view the manual, you need a browser that supports frames.

The sample programs on the CD were built with Microsoft Visual C++ 6.0 Service Pack 3. They will run on Microsoft Windows 2000. Some of the programs were tested on the Windows 98 Second Edition platform to verify compatibility.

Several projects in Chapter 6 require that you use the latest implementation of the standard C++ library in place of the Visual C++ 6.0 version. This library is available from Dinkumware at *http://www.dinkumware.com* as a Visual C++ 6.0 upgrade. Later versions of Visual C++ shouldn't require the Dinkumware library.

Some of the projects in Chapters 9 and 10 require the Windows 2000 versions of the Win32 header and library files. These are in the latest release of the Win32 Platform SDK, available from MSDN at *http://msdn.microsoft.com.*

Installing the Sample Files

You can view the samples from the CD, or you can install them onto your hard disk and use them to create your own applications.

Installing the sample files requires approximately 18.8 MB of disk space. To install the sample files, insert the CD into your CD-ROM drive and run Setup.exe in the Setup folder. If you have trouble running any of the sample files, refer to the Readme.txt file in the root directory of the CD or to the text in the book that describes the sample program.

You can uninstall the files by selecting Add/Remove Programs from the Microsoft Windows Control Panel, selecting International Programming Samples, and clicking the Add/Remove button.

Electronic Version of the Book

The complete text of the printed book, *International Programming for Microsoft Windows*, has been included on the CD as a fully searchable electronic book. To view the electronic book, you must have a system running Windows 95, Windows 98, Windows NT Service Pack 3 (or later), or Windows 2000. You must also have Microsoft Internet Explorer 4.01 or later installed on your system. If you don't have Internet Explorer 4.01 or later, the setup wizard will offer to install Internet Explorer 5. The Internet Explorer setup has been configured to install the minimum files necessary and won't change your current settings or associations.

Microsoft Press Support Information

Every effort has been made to ensure the accuracy of this book and the contents of the companion disc. Microsoft Press provides corrections for books through the World Wide Web at the following address:

http://mspress.microsoft.com/support/

If you have comments, questions, or ideas regarding this book or the companion disc, please send them to Microsoft Press using either of the following methods:

Postal Mail:

Microsoft Press
Attn: International Programming for Microsoft Windows Editor
One Microsoft Way
Redmond, WA 98052-6399

E-mail:

MSPINPUT@MICROSOFT.COM

Please note that product support isn't offered through the preceding mail addresses. For support information regarding Microsoft Visual C++, you can call Standard Support at (425) 635-7011 weekdays between 6 a.m. and 6 p.m. Pacific time. You can also search Microsoft's Support Online at

http://support.microsoft.com/support/

MICROSOFT LICENSE AGREEMENT
Book Companion CD

IMPORTANT—READ CAREFULLY: This Microsoft End-User License Agreement ("EULA") is a legal agreement between you (either an individual or an entity) and Microsoft Corporation for the Microsoft product identified above, which includes computer software and may include associated media, printed materials, and "online" or electronic documentation ("SOFTWARE PRODUCT"). Any component included within the SOFTWARE PRODUCT that is accompanied by a separate End-User License Agreement shall be governed by such agreement and not the terms set forth below. By installing, copying, or otherwise using the SOFTWARE PRODUCT, you agree to be bound by the terms of this EULA. If you do not agree to the terms of this EULA, you are not authorized to install, copy, or otherwise use the SOFTWARE PRODUCT; you may, however, return the SOFTWARE PRODUCT, along with all printed materials and other items that form a part of the Microsoft product that includes the SOFTWARE PRODUCT, to the place you obtained them for a full refund.

SOFTWARE PRODUCT LICENSE

The SOFTWARE PRODUCT is protected by United States copyright laws and international copyright treaties, as well as other intellectual property laws and treaties. The SOFTWARE PRODUCT is licensed, not sold.

1. **GRANT OF LICENSE.** This EULA grants you the following rights:

   a. **Software Product.** You may install and use one copy of the SOFTWARE PRODUCT on a single computer. The primary user of the computer on which the SOFTWARE PRODUCT is installed may make a second copy for his or her exclusive use on a portable computer.

   b. **Storage/Network Use.** You may also store or install a copy of the SOFTWARE PRODUCT on a storage device, such as a network server, used only to install or run the SOFTWARE PRODUCT on your other computers over an internal network; however, you must acquire and dedicate a license for each separate computer on which the SOFTWARE PRODUCT is installed or run from the storage device. A license for the SOFTWARE PRODUCT may not be shared or used concurrently on different computers.

   c. **License Pak.** If you have acquired this EULA in a Microsoft License Pak, you may make the number of additional copies of the computer software portion of the SOFTWARE PRODUCT authorized on the printed copy of this EULA, and you may use each copy in the manner specified above. You are also entitled to make a corresponding number of secondary copies for portable computer use as specified above.

   d. **Sample Code.** Solely with respect to portions, if any, of the SOFTWARE PRODUCT that are identified within the SOFTWARE PRODUCT as sample code (the "SAMPLE CODE"):

      i. **Use and Modification.** Microsoft grants you the right to use and modify the source code version of the SAMPLE CODE, *provided* you comply with subsection (d)(iii) below. You may not distribute the SAMPLE CODE, or any modified version of the SAMPLE CODE, in source code form.

      ii. **Redistributable Files.** Provided you comply with subsection (d)(iii) below, Microsoft grants you a nonexclusive, royalty-free right to reproduce and distribute the object code version of the SAMPLE CODE and of any modified SAMPLE CODE, other than SAMPLE CODE, or any modified version thereof, designated as not redistributable in the Readme file that forms a part of the SOFTWARE PRODUCT (the "Non-Redistributable Sample Code"). All SAMPLE CODE other than the Non-Redistributable Sample Code is collectively referred to as the "REDISTRIBUTABLES."

      iii. **Redistribution Requirements.** If you redistribute the REDISTRIBUTABLES, you agree to: (i) distribute the REDISTRIBUTABLES in object code form only in conjunction with and as a part of your software application product; (ii) not use Microsoft's name, logo, or trademarks to market your software application product; (iii) include a valid copyright notice on your software application product; (iv) indemnify, hold harmless, and defend Microsoft from and against any claims or lawsuits, including attorney's fees, that arise or result from the use or distribution of your software application product; and (v) not permit further distribution of the REDISTRIBUTABLES by your end user. Contact Microsoft for the applicable royalties due and other licensing terms for all other uses and/or distribution of the REDISTRIBUTABLES.

2. **DESCRIPTION OF OTHER RIGHTS AND LIMITATIONS.**

   - **Limitations on Reverse Engineering, Decompilation, and Disassembly.** You may not reverse engineer, decompile, or disassemble the SOFTWARE PRODUCT, except and only to the extent that such activity is expressly permitted by applicable law notwithstanding this limitation.

   - **Separation of Components.** The SOFTWARE PRODUCT is licensed as a single product. Its component parts may not be separated for use on more than one computer.

   - **Rental.** You may not rent, lease, or lend the SOFTWARE PRODUCT.

   - **Support Services.** Microsoft may, but is not obligated to, provide you with support services related to the SOFTWARE PRODUCT ("Support Services"). Use of Support Services is governed by the Microsoft policies and programs described in the user manual, in "online" documentation, and/or in other Microsoft-provided materials. Any supplemental software code provided to you as part of the Support Services shall be considered part of the SOFTWARE PRODUCT and subject to the terms and conditions of this EULA. With respect to technical information you provide to Microsoft as part of the Support Services, Microsoft may use such information for its business purposes, including for product support and development. Microsoft will not utilize such technical information in a form that personally identifies you.

- **Software Transfer.** You may permanently transfer all of your rights under this EULA, provided you retain no copies, you transfer all of the SOFTWARE PRODUCT (including all component parts, the media and printed materials, any upgrades, this EULA, and, if applicable, the Certificate of Authenticity), **and** the recipient agrees to the terms of this EULA.

- **Termination.** Without prejudice to any other rights, Microsoft may terminate this EULA if you fail to comply with the terms and conditions of this EULA. In such event, you must destroy all copies of the SOFTWARE PRODUCT and all of its component parts.

3. **COPYRIGHT.** All title and copyrights in and to the SOFTWARE PRODUCT (including but not limited to any images, photographs, animations, video, audio, music, text, SAMPLE CODE, REDISTRIBUTABLES, and "applets" incorporated into the SOFTWARE PRODUCT) and any copies of the SOFTWARE PRODUCT are owned by Microsoft or its suppliers. The SOFTWARE PRODUCT is protected by copyright laws and international treaty provisions. Therefore, you must treat the SOFTWARE PRODUCT like any other copyrighted material **except** that you may install the SOFTWARE PRODUCT on a single computer provided you keep the original solely for backup or archival purposes. You may not copy the printed materials accompanying the SOFTWARE PRODUCT.

4. **U.S. GOVERNMENT RESTRICTED RIGHTS.** The SOFTWARE PRODUCT and documentation are provided with RESTRICTED RIGHTS. Use, duplication, or disclosure by the Government is subject to restrictions as set forth in subparagraph (c)(1)(ii) of the Rights in Technical Data and Computer Software clause at DFARS 252.227-7013 or subparagraphs (c)(1) and (2) of the Commercial Computer Software—Restricted Rights at 48 CFR 52.227-19, as applicable. Manufacturer is Microsoft Corporation/One Microsoft Way/Redmond, WA 98052-6399.

5. **EXPORT RESTRICTIONS.** You agree that you will not export or re-export the SOFTWARE PRODUCT, any part thereof, or any process or service that is the direct product of the SOFTWARE PRODUCT (the foregoing collectively referred to as the "Restricted Components"), to any country, person, entity, or end user subject to U.S. export restrictions. You specifically agree not to export or re-export any of the Restricted Components (i) to any country to which the U.S. has embargoed or restricted the export of goods or services, which currently include, but are not necessarily limited to, Cuba, Iran, Iraq, Libya, North Korea, Sudan, and Syria, or to any national of any such country, wherever located, who intends to transmit or transport the Restricted Components back to such country; (ii) to any end user who you know or have reason to know will utilize the Restricted Components in the design, development, or production of nuclear, chemical, or biological weapons; or (iii) to any end user who has been prohibited from participating in U.S. export transactions by any federal agency of the U.S. government. You warrant and represent that neither the BXA nor any other U.S. federal agency has suspended, revoked, or denied your export privileges.

DISCLAIMER OF WARRANTY

NO WARRANTIES OR CONDITIONS. MICROSOFT EXPRESSLY DISCLAIMS ANY WARRANTY OR CONDITION FOR THE SOFTWARE PRODUCT. THE SOFTWARE PRODUCT AND ANY RELATED DOCUMENTATION ARE PROVIDED "AS IS" WITHOUT WARRANTY OR CONDITION OF ANY KIND, EITHER EXPRESS OR IMPLIED, INCLUDING, WITHOUT LIMITATION, THE IMPLIED WARRANTIES OF MERCHANTABILITY, FITNESS FOR A PARTICULAR PURPOSE, OR NONINFRINGEMENT. THE ENTIRE RISK ARISING OUT OF USE OR PERFORMANCE OF THE SOFTWARE PRODUCT REMAINS WITH YOU.

LIMITATION OF LIABILITY. TO THE MAXIMUM EXTENT PERMITTED BY APPLICABLE LAW, IN NO EVENT SHALL MICROSOFT OR ITS SUPPLIERS BE LIABLE FOR ANY SPECIAL, INCIDENTAL, INDIRECT, OR CONSEQUENTIAL DAMAGES WHATSOEVER (INCLUDING, WITHOUT LIMITATION, DAMAGES FOR LOSS OF BUSINESS PROFITS, BUSINESS INTERRUPTION, LOSS OF BUSINESS INFORMATION, OR ANY OTHER PECUNIARY LOSS) ARISING OUT OF THE USE OF OR INABILITY TO USE THE SOFTWARE PRODUCT OR THE PROVISION OF OR FAILURE TO PROVIDE SUPPORT SERVICES, EVEN IF MICROSOFT HAS BEEN ADVISED OF THE POSSIBILITY OF SUCH DAMAGES. IN ANY CASE, MICROSOFT'S ENTIRE LIABILITY UNDER ANY PROVISION OF THIS EULA SHALL BE LIMITED TO THE GREATER OF THE AMOUNT ACTUALLY PAID BY YOU FOR THE SOFTWARE PRODUCT OR US$5.00; PROVIDED, HOWEVER, IF YOU HAVE ENTERED INTO A MICROSOFT SUPPORT SERVICES AGREEMENT, MICROSOFT'S ENTIRE LIABILITY REGARDING SUPPORT SERVICES SHALL BE GOVERNED BY THE TERMS OF THAT AGREEMENT. BECAUSE SOME STATES AND JURISDICTIONS DO NOT ALLOW THE EXCLUSION OR LIMITATION OF LIABILITY, THE ABOVE LIMITATION MAY NOT APPLY TO YOU.

MISCELLANEOUS

This EULA is governed by the laws of the State of Washington USA, except and only to the extent that applicable law mandates governing law of a different jurisdiction.

Should you have any questions concerning this EULA, or if you desire to contact Microsoft for any reason, please contact the Microsoft subsidiary serving your country, or write: Microsoft Sales Information Center/One Microsoft Way/Redmond, WA 98052-6399.

Proof of Purchase

1-57231-956-9

Do not send this card with your registration.
Use this card as proof of purchase if participating in a promotion or
rebate offer on *International Programming for Microsoft® Windows®*. Card must be used in conjunction
with other proof(s) of payment such as your dated sales receipt—see offer details.

International Programming for Microsoft® Windows®

WHERE DID YOU PURCHASE THIS PRODUCT?

CUSTOMER NAME

mspress.microsoft.com

Microsoft Press, PO Box 97017, Redmond, WA 98073-9830

OWNER REGISTRATION CARD

Register Today!

1-57231-956-9

Return the bottom portion of this card to register today.

International Programming for Microsoft® Windows®

FIRST NAME | MIDDLE INITIAL | LAST NAME

INSTITUTION OR COMPANY NAME

ADDRESS

CITY | STATE | ZIP

(   )

E-MAIL ADDRESS | PHONE NUMBER

U.S. and Canada addresses only. Fill in information above and mail postage-free.
Please mail only the bottom half of this page.

start faster

go

farther

*For information about Microsoft Press®
products, visit our Web site at*
mspress.microsoft.com

Microsoft®